Disabled children

a legal handbook

Steve Broach is a barrister at Doughty Street Chambers, London, specialising in cases involving children, disabled adults and other vulnerable people. Prior to becoming a barrister, Steve held senior voluntary sector roles at the National Autistic Society, TreeHouse (the national charity for autism education) and most recently as campaign manager of the Every Disabled Child Matters campaign (www.edcm.org.uk). Steve is Chair of AbleChild Africa, a charity supporting organisations working with disabled children across Africa (www.ablechildafrica.org.uk).

Luke Clements is a Professor at Cardiff Law School where he is Director of the Centre for Health and Social Care Law and a consultant solicitor with Scott-Moncrieff, Harbour & Sinclair, London. He has written widely and his recent publications include *Disabled people and the right to life* (Routledge, 2008, jointly with Janet Read), *Community Care and the Law* (4th edition, LAG, 2007, jointly with Pauline Thompson) and *Carers and their Rights* (4th edition, Carers UK, 2010).

Janet Read is an Associate Professor (Reader) Emeritus in the Institute of Health, University of Warwick and an Honorary Professor at Cardiff Law School. Her research and publications focus on the circumstances and rights of disabled children and adults and the development of effective services for them. Her publications include *Disabled People and the Right to Life* (Routledge, 2008), *Disabled Children and the Law* (Jessica Kingsley Publishers, 2006), *Disabled People and European Human Rights* (Policy Press, 2003) (all with Luke Clements) and *Disability, The Family and Society* (Open University Press, 2000). Janet has held a number of practice and management posts in the public and voluntary sectors. She is an editor of the journal *Disability and Society*.

The purpose of the Legal Action Group is to promote equal access to justice for all members of society who are socially, economically or otherwise disadvantaged. To this end, it seeks to improve law and practice, the administration of justice and legal services.

Disabled children

A legal handbook

Steve Broach, Luke Clements and
Janet Read

LAG Legal Action Group
2010

This edition published in Great Britain 2010
by LAG Education and Services Trust Limited
242 Pentonville Road, London N1 9UN
www.lag.org.uk

While every effort has been made to ensure that the details in this text
are correct, readers must be aware that the law changes and that the
accuracy of the material cannot be guaranteed and the author and the
publisher accept no responsibility for any losses or damage sustained.

The rights of the authors to be identified as authors of this work have
been asserted by them in accordance with the Copyright, Designs and
Patents Act 1988.

British Library Cataloguing in Publication Data
a CIP catalogue record for this book is available from the British Library.

Crown copyright material is produced with the permission of the
Controller of HMSO and the Queen's Printer for Scotland.

 This book has been produced using Forest Stewardship
Council (FSC) certified paper. The wood used to produce FSC
certified products with a 'Mixed Sources' label comes from
FSC certified well-managed forests, controlled sources and/or
recycled material.

ISBN 978 1 903307 76 2

Typeset by Regent Typesetting, London
Printed in Great Britain by Hobbs the Printers, Totton, Hampshire

Introduction

This handbook is about the legal rights of disabled children and their families in England and Wales. The law in relation to this important group is complex and frequently misunderstood by those who have duties and responsibilities towards them. Many families also lack essential information about legal matters which substantially affect their lives and about the ways the law might be used to assist them.

Our aim in writing this book is to provide an up-to-date legal guide which can make a contribution towards safeguarding the rights and furthering the interests of disabled children and those close to them. To this end, we have focused on issues which research, as well as our direct contact with children and their families, indicates are particularly important to them. Throughout the book, we try to suggest how the law may be used as a tool to solve problems that disabled children and their families frequently encounter and to help them achieve a quality of life enjoyed by those who do not live with disability.

The handbook seeks to be an authoritative guide to the law and of value to all those working in this field – be they in the charitable, independent or statutory sectors: advisers, advocates, lawyers, social and health care professionals as well as for those in academia – students and educationalists.

Above all, however, we want this text to be available to families with disabled children so that they may use it directly themselves or jointly with an advocate, lawyer or chosen representative. It has been our experience that many disabled young people and their parents access and make very effective use of books and articles about relevant law. This being so, we are delighted that the contents of this book should shortly be available to them free of charge on the internet enabled by the Council for Disabled Children.

The book begins with a chapter which lays down the principles that underpin the approach we take and outlines some basic information about the characteristics and circumstances of disabled children and their families in the UK. It identifies problems that they commonly encounter, the barriers that get in the way of living an ordinary life and some of the interventions and arrangements that are seen to bring about change for the better. Chapter 2 provides an introduction to what we have termed the 'legal fundamentals': the sources of law and the legal framework that apply to this group of children and their families. The subsequent chapters give detailed consideration of the law in specific areas that have been shown to be crucial: children's services, education, health, housing, welfare benefits, carers services, equality and non-discrimination and the transition to adulthood. None of these are, however, discrete topics capable of being considered in isolation from one another. In the lives of children and families as well as in legal and organisational terms, there are substantial overlaps and connections between them. In an effort to make at least some of those connections clear, we have relied heavily on cross-referencing throughout the book.

It is, of course, impossible in one text to do justice to the complexity of the lives, needs and aspirations of disabled children and their families. Similarly, a book of this length cannot cover all aspects of the law relating to every dimension of their lives or everything that might happen to them. Inevitably, choices have had to be made about what to limit and what to leave out altogether. For example, while this book is concerned throughout with the well-being and safety of disabled children, we do not deal specifically with procedures in relation to child protection. Also, this edition does not cover disabled young people in the criminal justice system. It is our intention, however, that material on this important topic will be included in the online version of the book and in any future editions.

In the writing and editing of this handbook we have benefitted greatly from those who have read and provided constructive feedback on the drafts. We are particularly grateful to the following colleagues: Clare Blackburn, Mary Busk, Jeanne Carlin, Keith Clements, Janis Firminger, Louise Franklin, Jo Honigmann, Christine Lenehan, Liz Martin, Camilla Parker, Frank Redmond, Ben Silverstone, Doug Simkiss, Nick Spencer, Philippa Stobbs, Janet Sunman, Pauline Thompson, Zoe Thompson, Peter Woods, Helen Wheatley, Lucia Winters, Ian Wise QC and Victoria Wright.

The chapter on welfare benefits was written by Ben Silverstone, to whom the authors are most grateful for concisely summarising this complex area of law.

Steve Broach would like to thank the following law students at BPP
Law School in London who provided valuable research assistance:

Edward Martin, May Poon, Adam Porte, Natasha Silverman and Colin-Miles Witcher.

We are grateful to the Council for Disabled Children for funding and creating a website to make the contents of this book freely available online. We also thank the Legal Action Group and in particular Esther Pilger for granting the inevitable deadline extension request.

We would welcome all comments, corrections and feedback on this book – particularly suggestions of additional materials – which can be emailed to Steve Broach at s.broach@doughtystreet.co.uk. Despite the extensive assistance we have had in compiling this book, all the mistakes remain our own.

We have endeavoured to state the law as at 23 July 2010.

Steve Broach
Luke Clements
Janet Read

July 2010

Legal entitlements

As set out in chapter 2, the law in relation to disabled children is found in many sources – international conventions, Acts of Parliament, regulations, statutory guidance and so on. Many of these sources of law overlap and there remains significant confusion about what public bodies *must* do to support disabled children (duties) and what they *may* do (powers), an issue again explored in chapter 2 at see paras 2.28–2.31.

To help clarify this confusing picture, we provide below a list of *some* of the key 'entitlements' to which disabled children, young people and their families have the benefit. An entitlement arises where one or more public body has a relevant duty – whether this duty is owed to all disabled children or only to some, for example those with a certain level of need or those in a certain age group.

This summary is only a very general guide, and readers should consult the relevant chapter for necessary background information in relation to each entitlement. It should also be borne in mind that even if a public body only has a power, not a duty, to confer a particular benefit on a disabled child or their family so that no entitlement to the benefit arises, that power still has to be exercised rationally, reasonably and fairly: see para 2.31.

In general terms, disabled children are entitled to have their needs assessed and a person-centred plan put in place to ensure these needs are met, if found to be sufficiently substantial by the assessment. Local areas may seek to address needs using less formal arrangements than those prescribed by the law, for instance by applying the Common Assessment Framework (which has no statutory basis) rather than carrying out an initial or core assessment (see para 3.15). To the extent that disabled children and families are satisfied with the outcomes of these arrangements, this may be acceptable. However, if (as is too frequently the case) disputes emerge between families and public bodies as to the level of services and support to be provided, it is essential to be able to identify with precision exactly what the law requires – in other words, for families to know their rights and to be able to enforce them.

Disabled children are entitled to ...

Children's services

- An *initial assessment* to determine what additional needs for services and support they may have: see para 3.15.
- A *core assessment*, if they may need support from a number of different agencies: see para 3.15.
- A *care plan* following an assessment, which should be a 'realistic plan of action (including services to be provided)': see para 3.33.
- *Services to meet their assessed needs*, where intervention is required to secure their well-being: see paras 3.45–3.47.
- *Suitable accommodation*, if their parent or parents are prevented (for whatever reason) from providing them with suitable accommodation or care: see para 3.78.
- A *personal adviser and pathway plan* after the age of 16 if they are 'leaving care': see paras 10.70–10.72.

Education

- A *statutory assessment* in relation to their special educational needs (SEN), if it *may be* necessary for their special educational provision to be determined by the local education authority (LEA): see para 4.29.
- A *Statement of SEN*, where their statutory assessment shows that it *is* necessary for their special educational provision to be determined by the LEA: see para 4.45.
- All the *special educational provision* quantified and specified in their statement: see paras 4.46–4.47.
- A *transition plan* following the annual review of their statement at age 14: see para 10.22.
- A *learning difficulty assessment* in their last year of school: see paras 10.30–10.31.
- Not be excluded from school, other than as a 'last resort': see para 4.114.
- Suitable education otherwise than in school if they are out of school for whatever reason, regardless of any resource constraints: see paras 4.124–4.125.

Health

- An assessment of their healthcare needs: see paras 5.25–5.26.
- Services to meet their assessed healthcare needs: see paras 5.7 and 5.16–5.18.
- NHS continuing care, if their health needs are complex: see paras 5.54–5.62.
- Age-appropriate child and adolescent mental health services, if they have mental health needs: see paras 5.66–5.83.
- Palliative care, if they have a life-limiting condition: see paras 5.92–5.97.

Housing

- A Disabled Facilities Grant to adapt their home, if such a grant is necessary to facilitate access or make the home safe: see para 6.31.

Benefits

- A wide range of financial benefits, in particular Disability Living Allowance, if the relevant eligibility criteria are met: see chapter 7.

Equality and non-discrimination

- Access to almost every aspect of public life without discrimination, whether direct, indirect or for a reason relating to their disability: see para 9.14, and generally chapter 9.
- Reasonable adjustments to help support their access on an equal footing to their non-disabled peers: paras 9.32–9.33.

Parents, family and friends caring for disabled children are entitled to ...

- Be free from discrimination arising 'by association' with the disabled child: see para 9.18.
- A carer's assessment to help them sustain their caring role and to remain in (or return to) work and to participate in education, training and leisure activities: see para 8.5.
- Services to meet their needs as carers if the assessment shows a critical or substantial risk in a relevant area of their life: see para 8.21.
- Have their caring role taken away, if they are a young carer (see paras 8.38–8.40) or if they are an adult carer who no longer feels able to continue caring (see para 8.17).

Contents

Table of cases

References in the right-hand column are to paragraph numbers.

Table of statutes

References in the right-hand column are to paragraph numbers. Entries in bold denote section reproduced in full.

Table of statutory instruments

References in the right-hand column are to paragraph numbers.

Table of international conventions and European legislation

References in the right-hand column are to paragraph numbers. Entries in bold denote article reproduced in full.

Understanding disabled children's lives

continued

Key points

- Disabled children and their families have the same human rights as others, including the right to the same quality of life as those who do not live with disability.
- The social model of disability assumes that some of the most oppressive and limiting aspects of disabled people's lives are caused by social, environmental and political factors which can be changed.
- The state has core responsibilities to promote the human rights of disabled children and their families and to counter the discrimination they experience.
- 7.3 per cent of children in the UK are disabled, using the Equality Act 2010 definition. The majority live at home with their families.
- Disabled children and their families are worse off financially and have markedly poorer standards of living than those families who do not live with disability. Expenditure is higher but opportunities for earning through paid employment are reduced, particularly for mothers. Many families are in debt and live in unsuitable housing.
- Families provide high levels of care for their disabled children.
- Disabled children and their families face substantial barriers in everyday living and experience high levels of social exclusion.
- Many children and their families have difficulty in accessing services to meet their needs. Provision is complex and information about entitlements frequently unavailable.
- The combination of high levels of need, poor circumstances and lack of support services can have an impact on the health, well-being and opportunities of all family members.
- The early times when disability is identified are stressful for many families.
- While many parents report that they are satisfied with their disabled children's schools, many also experience serious problems in accessing suitable education provision.
- A minority of disabled children live away from their families for some or all of the year: in residential schools, healthcare settings or 'looked after' by local authorities.
- Many disabled young people face considerable difficulties in transition from childhood to adulthood and from children's to adult service provision.

Introduction

1.1   This handbook provides a comprehensive review of the law, in particular social care, education and healthcare law, as it impacts upon disabled children and their families. It is intended to be accessible and valuable for everyone interested in the lives of disabled children, both lawyers and non-lawyers and including disabled children and their families.

1.2   The nature of the difficulties faced by disabled children and their families means that a handbook devoted solely to the law would be a very inadequate tool. Accordingly this handbook also seeks to draw on the expertise of disabled children and their families and on research that highlights their experiences – particularly as to common problems they encounter and services that they value. The most important principles and 'facts of life' for disabled children and their families are set out in this chapter.

Underpinning principles

An ordinary life

1.3   An underpinning principle of this handbook and of the rights-based approach it adopts is that disabled children and those close to them are entitled to enjoy the same human rights as others. This can be summarised as the right to live an ordinary life, a principle that has been expressed in the following terms:

> It should not be regarded as an exotic idea for disabled children and those close to them to aspire to a quality of life comparable to that enjoyed by others who do not live with disability ... it should be seen as unacceptable in the twenty-first century for the lives and experiences of disabled children and their families to be bereft of those features that many others take for granted, features that make an essential contribution to an ordinary and reasonable quality of life.[1]

1.4   The fact that disabled children and their families may have different priorities and need different supports and arrangements to achieve them does not mean that they should be precluded from participating in ordinary experiences enjoyed by others. Living an 'ordinary life' also brings with it the presumption that a disabled child should

---

1   J Read, L Clements and D Ruebain, *Disabled children and the law: research and good practice*, 2nd edn, Jessica Kingsley Publishers, 2006, p17.

generally be brought up in a family setting – one of the principles embedded in the Children Act 1989 (see para 3.5).

The social model of disability

1.5 In the past 25 years, disabled writers and activists have developed the 'social model of disability'.[2] While there are of course differences in emphasis and understanding between some of those developing these ideas,[3] there are a number of common areas of agreement. The social model of disability has contributed to re-shaping the way that disability is understood and has been influential in relation to government policy,[4] international treaties[5] and international classification systems of health, illness and disability.[6]

1.6 The social model makes a distinction between impairment and disability. 'Impairment' is used to refer to physical, sensory and intellectual characteristics or limitations. 'Disability' on the other hand, means the social, economic and political factors that restrict children and adults who have impairments. The social model was born of the experience of disabled people and those close to them. They challenged the understanding of disability at that time and argued that some of the most restricting and 'disabling' experiences in their lives were not, as was often assumed, an inevitable result of living with impairments. On the contrary, it was argued that some of the most oppressive and limiting factors were socially created and as such, needed to be changed by social and political means. This handbook adopts this approach and pays particular regard to features in the broader social contexts that act as barriers to disabled children and their families living ordinary lives and having the opportunities that others may take for granted.

1.7 Such an approach, while focusing on arrangements and provision that can help create conditions in which disabled children and those close to them may flourish, does not, however, underestimate the importance of a child's individual characteristics, including

---

2 For example M Oliver, *Understanding disability*, Macmillan, 1996; J Morris, *Pride against prejudice*, Women's Press, 1991.

3 T Shakespeare, *Disability rights and wrongs*, Routledge, 2006; J Bickenbach, 'Disability rights, law and policy', in G Albrecht, K Seelman and M Bury (eds), *The handbook of disability studies*, Sage, 2001.

4 Prime Minister's Strategy Unit, *Improving the life chances of disabled people*, The Stationery Office, 2005.

5 For example the UN Convention on the Rights of Persons with Disabilities (2006).

6 World Health Organisation, *The international classification of functioning, disability and health: children and youth version*, 2007.

impairments. Like all children, disabled children may benefit from interventions designed to help their individual cognitive, sensory and physical development and well-being. In other words, addressing restrictive social conditions does not mean neglecting the possibility of change and development at an individual level. In any case, the two are often closely linked.

The relevance of human rights

1.8   In addition to the influence of the social model of disability, there has also been growing recognition of the importance of a human rights approach to enhance understanding of the experience of disabled children and to bring about improvements in their lives.[7] The value of such an approach has been summarised as follows:

> At its most basic, it affirms without qualification that disabled people are not 'other': they are unquestionably included within the category and meaning of what it is to be human, and may, therefore, expect all the rights derived from that status. By employing such a normative and unifying approach, the things that happen to disabled children and adults, the lives they lead and the goals they aspire to, may be evaluated against norms or benchmarks established by consensus and sometimes by law, as universal *human* rights.[8]

1.9   In chapter 2 we consider, in outline, the international human rights treaties of greatest relevance to the issues considered in this handbook – the European Convention on Human Rights (ECHR), the UN Convention on the Rights of the Child and the UN Convention on Rights of Persons with Disabilities (see paras 2.3–2.21 below). Reference is also made to the rights safeguarded by these conventions at key points in this text, where they are of particular relevance. It is important, however, to specify key human rights principles that underpin many of these specific rights – and these include the:

- core responsibilities of the state;
- principle of non-discrimination;
- principle of dignity;
- principle of independent living;
- principle of choice;
- principle of cost effectiveness.

7   J Bickenbach, 'Disability rights, law and policy', in G Albrecht, K Seelman and M Bury (eds), *The handbook of disability studies*, Sage, 2001.

8   L Clements and J Read, 'Life, disability and the pursuit of human rights', in L Clements and J Read, *Disabled people and the right to life*, Routledge, 2008, p6.

The core responsibilities of the state

1.10   Given that many of the most oppressive and limiting factors that restrict disabled people are socially created, it follows that addressing these and the consequent exclusion and disadvantage they experience is a core responsibility of the state. As the UN has observed, in a binding (2003) statement:[9]

> The obligation of States parties to the Covenant to promote progressive realization of the relevant rights to the maximum of their available resources clearly requires Governments to do much more than merely abstain from taking measures which might have a negative impact on persons with disabilities. The obligation in the case of such a vulnerable and disadvantaged group is to take positive action to reduce structural disadvantages and to give appropriate preferential treatment to people with disabilities in order to achieve the objectives of full participation and equality within society for all persons with disabilities. This almost invariably means that additional resources will need to be made available for this purpose and that a wide range of specially tailored measures will be required.

1.11   This core obligation, which is given further emphasis in General Comments to the UN Convention on the Rights of the Child,[10] is on the state, not on families or charities. Families are already 'disabled by association'[11] and many carers experience similar levels of social exclusion to those for whom they provide care.[12] This has been recognised by English and Welsh guidance concerning the rights of carers,[13] which states that social workers should not 'assume a willingness by the carer to continue caring, or continue to provide the same level of support'. The law reflects this approach, placing duties on the state to provide a level of support to all disabled people (children and adults) that respects their human rights.

9   General Comment 5 concerning persons with disabilities and the International Covenant on Economic, Social and Cultural Rights, para 9, available at www1.umn.edu/humanrts/gencomm/epcomm5e.htm.

10   General Comment 9 at para 20 at www1.umn.edu/humanrts/crc/comment9.html.

11   *Coleman v Attridge Law* C-303/06 (2008) All ER (EC) 1105, ECJ, considered at paras 9.4 and 9.18.

12   Office of the Deputy Prime Minister, *Breaking the cycle: taking stock of progress and priorities for the future – a report by the Social Exclusion Unit*, 2004, para 6.17.

13   Department of Health, *Practice guidance to the Carers (Recognition and Services) Act 1995*, LAC (96)7, para 9.8 and, in Wales, WOC 16/96 and WHC (96)21.

The principle of non-discrimination

1.12   The principle of non-discrimination runs wider than the obligations under the Equality Act 2010 (see chapter 9) and is essentially the core obligation in the UN Convention on Rights of Persons with Disabilities (see, for example, articles 3, 4, 5 and 6) to provide for true equality of disabled people before the law, to effective legal protection and the right to 'reasonable accommodation'. It brings with it the requirement (for example) that the arrangements for disabled children should not be inferior to those for non-disabled children; that disabled children should not be inappropriately excluded from mainstream schooling for non-disabled children;[14] and that all categories of disabled children be treated equally, ie that the support provided to one category of disabled child should not be materially worse than that provided to others – for example, those with a mental illness should not receive lesser supports than those with a physical impairment.

The principle of dignity

1.13   The concept of 'dignity' is central to many human rights treaties and bodies[15] and is often expressed in terms of respect for 'personal autonomy'/'physical integrity' and of a right to a level of support that does not lead to 'indignity' and that compensates for the disabilities faced by disabled people.[16] In England and Wales, the binding legal basis for the duty on the state to ensure that disabled children are treated 'with dignity' derives from articles 3 and 8 of the ECHR: the basic obligation is to ensure that no one is subjected to degrading treatment (article 3) and that 'respect' is shown for a person's private life (article 8). In this context 'private life' has a broad ranging meaning encompassing a 'person's physical and psychological integrity' and their 'relations with other human beings' and their immediate environment.[17]

1.14   The European Court of Human Rights has expressed the obligation this imposes in the following terms:

---

14   See paras 4.114–4.123 in relation to school exclusions.

15   See, for example, the comments of the European Court of Human Rights in *Pretty v United Kingdom* (2002) 35 EHRR 1 at [65].

16   Judge Greve in her concurring opinion in *Price v UK* (2002) 34 EHRR 1285 at 1296 and see *R (A, B, X and Y) v East Sussex CC and the Disability Rights Commission (No 2)* [2003] EWHC 167 (Admin); (2003) 6 CCLR 194 at [86].

17   *Botta v Italy* (1998) 26 EHRR 241.

> In a civilised country like the United Kingdom, society considers it not only appropriate but a basic humane concern to try to improve and compensate for the disabilities faced by a person in the applicant's situation. In my opinion, these compensatory measures come to form part of the disabled person's physical integrity.[18]

1.15 Much has also been said of the obligation to protect dignity in domestic court judgments, including:

> The recognition and protection of human dignity is one of the core values – in truth the core value – of our society and, indeed, of all the societies which are part of the European family of nations and which have embraced the principles of the Convention. It is a core value of the common law, long pre-dating the Convention.[19]

1.16 The principle of dignity therefore requires action to promote the integration of disabled children and their families in all aspects of social, economic and political life. It requires that the state treats disabled children as individuals in their own right – and not as objects. It means that (where necessary) urgent action be taken to ensure that they do not experience indignity due, for example, to inadequate bathing[20] or toileting[21] facilities or an inability to access their home or communities (see para 3.56 and paras 6.16–6.44 below in relation to the duty to adapt disabled children's homes to meet their needs).

The principle of independent living

1.17 The right to independent living – at its most basic – means that disabled people should not be excluded from mainstream society, for example by being placed unnecessarily in a care home or hospital.

---

18 The concurring opinion of Judge Greve in *Price v United Kingdom* (2002) 34 EHRR 1285 at 1296.

19 Munby J (as he then was) in *R (A, B, X and Y) v East Sussex CC and the Disability Rights Commission (No 2)* [2003] EWHC 167 (Admin); (2003) 6 CCLR 194 at [86].

20 See Complaint nos 02/C/8679, 8681 and 10389 against Bolsover DC, 30 September 2003, where the local government ombudsman held that the ability to manage 'bathing with dignity' was the entitlement of everybody, and see also Complaint no 07C03887 against Bury MBC, 14 October 2009, where the local government ombudsman referred to the 'breathtaking insensitivity' of the council in failing to secure immediate arrangements to enable a mother to bathe her disabled sons.

21 See, for example, *R (Bernard) v Enfield LBC* [2002] EWHC 2282 (Admin); (2002) 5 CCLR 577, where Sullivan J found a violation of article 8 following delayed provision of proper toileting for the applicant – holding (at [33]) that such facilities 'would have restored her dignity as a human being'.

The concept of independent living is, however, much more expansive and is expressed in article 19 of the UN Convention on Rights of Persons with Disabilities (a convention the UK has ratified – see para 2.12 below) in the following terms:

a) persons with disabilities have the opportunity to choose their place of residence and where and with whom they live on an equal basis with others and are not obliged to live in a particular living arrangement;

b) persons with disabilities have access to a range of in-home, residential and other community support services, including personal assistance necessary to support living and inclusion in the community, and to prevent isolation or segregation from the community;

c) community services and facilities for the general population are available on an equal basis to persons with disabilities and are responsive to their needs.

1.18   The courts have held that preserving independence should be a fundamental aim of all social care interventions,[22] that inappropriate institutionalisation is a form of discrimination against disabled people[23] and that while cost may be a factor in deciding whether a care home placement is to be preferred to a community living alternatives, it is unlikely ever to be permissible for it to be the determinative factor.[24]

The principle of choice

1.19   Respect for a person's identity and physical integrity (as protected by article 8 of the ECHR[25]) brings with it a requirement to respect their choices and preferences. Where the state provides support or otherwise intervenes in a disabled person's life, it should, so far as is consistent with its other obligations, ensure that its action promotes the disabled person's and their family's aspirations. A key aspect of this obligation is the duty to take full account of the wishes of the disabled child and the family – in every aspect of the support provided – be it from health, social care, education and so on. This means that

22   *R v Southwark LBC ex p Khana and Karim* [2001] EWCA Civ 999; (2001) 4 CCLR 267 and see also *R (B) v Cornwall CC* [2009] EWHC 491 (Admin) at [10].

23   *Olmstead v LC* 527 US 581(1999), in which the US Supreme Court held that the Americans with Disabilities Act 1990 gave disabled people a qualified right to live in the community rather than in institutions.

24   See, for example, *Gunter v South West Staffordshire PCT* [2005] EWHC 1894 (Admin); (2006) 9 CCLR 121 at [20].

25   See, for example, *Botta v Italy* [1998] 26 EHRR 241, considered at paras 1.13, 2.5 and 2.7.

the family and disabled child's preferences should not be sacrificed merely because they are in conflict with what a council considers to be 'best'[26] and that planning should be 'person centred' and where possible should yield to the personal preferences of the family and disabled child.

The principle of cost effectiveness

1.20 While respect for individual and family preferences is an important principle in relation to meeting the needs of disabled children, it is subject to the principle of 'cost effectiveness'; as a general rule, choice does not trump 'cost'. Where the state has an obligation to meet a disabled child's needs (eg special educational or social care needs), if it is able to meet these fully in one way, it is permitted to refuse to meet them in an alternative, more expensive, way. The principle of cost effectiveness is in reality an essential component of the state's core obligation to 'promote progressive realisation' of the rights of disabled people 'to the maximum of [the state's] available resources': such an obligation requires it to devise cost effective procedures that ensure as many people as possible benefit from its limited resources. However, 'cost effectiveness' should not lead to a minimalist approach to meeting disabled children's needs. Critically, although cost may trump choice, it must not trump dignity or other fundamental human rights.

Consulting disabled children and young people and their families

1.21 A fundamental requirement under the obligation (in ECHR article 8) to show 'respect' for a person's private and family life is to involve them in decisions which concern them – no matter how severe their impairments. This duty is reflected in the policy guidance concerning the assessment of children's social care and special educational needs (see respectively paras 3.14–3.24 and paras 4.28–4.44 below). The absolute importance of communicating with a disabled person to ascertain his wishes, feelings and preferences was emphasised by the court in *R (A and B) v East Sussex CC (No 2)*.[27] This obligation

---

26 For a graphic example of this, see *R (CD) v Anglesey CC* [2004] EWHC 1635 (Admin) considered at paras 3.82 and 10.9.

27 [2003] EWHC 167 (Admin); (2003) 6 CCLR 194.

is likely to extend to proper consultation with family members; in *Re S*,[28] Mr Justice Munby observed that in many situations:

> the devoted parent who … has spent years caring for a disabled child is likely to be much better able than any social worker, however skilled, or any judge, however compassionate, to 'read' his child, to understand his personality and to interpret the wishes and feelings which he lacks the ability to express.

1.22   Disabled children and members of their families should therefore be listened to about both the barriers that get in the way of living an ordinary life and the things that would remove these barriers and otherwise help them. They should also have a right to participate so that their ideas are central to any decision-making. This applies to the planning and operation of services as well as to assessment and service-delivery at an individual level.[29] Whatever the nature of the issues that they are facing and whatever the type of service they are dealing with, children and their parents have the right to expect that professionals and service-providers recognise their knowledge and treat them with respect.

1.23   Individuals within families may have different priorities and different wishes, but all have a right to be heard. While parents may understandably have to prioritise such things as care, finance, housing, health and education, it should come as no surprise that children may put a premium on play, leisure, friendships and school.[30] In recent years there has been greater recognition of the importance of seeking the views of disabled children themselves and understanding their perspectives. In the past, these were neglected, particularly if children did not use standard forms of communication. There are now many tried and tested ways of finding out what disabled children want, using forms of consultation and communication appropriate to their needs.[31]

---

28 [2002] EWHC 2278; [2003] 1 FLR 292 at [49].

29 A Franklin and P Sloper, *Participation of disabled children and young people in decision-making relating to social care*, Social Policy Research Unit, University of York, 2007; HM Treasury and Department for Education and Skills, *Aiming high for disabled children: better support for families*, 2007.

30 B Beresford, R Parveneh and P Sloper, *Priorities and perceptions of disabled children and young people and their parents regarding outcomes from support services*, Social Policy Research Unit, University of York, 2007.

31 Joseph Rowntree Foundation, *Consulting with disabled children and young people*, 2001; Council for Disabled Children and Participation Works, *How to involve children and young people with communication impairments in decision-making*, available from www.participationworks.org.uk; A Knight, A Clark, P Petrie and J Statham, *The views of children and young people with learning disabilities about*

1.24   An obligation to consult with children inevitably invites a discussion about their capacity to understand and to make decisions about certain matters as well as the weight that should be given to their views. The way that the law approaches issues of capacity and consulting children and young people is covered in paras 5.83–5.90 and 10.88–10.92 below.

Disabled children and their families: numbers, characteristics and circumstances

1.25   Good quality data concerning the nature and extent of the population of disabled children has, at least until recently, been limited. Such information is of course important, not least for strategic planning purposes. A detailed analysis of the methodology (and its limitations) of assessing the numbers, characteristics and circumstances of disabled children[32] is to be found in the 2010 study which uses data from the *Family Resources Survey* (FRS).[33]

The population of disabled children

1.26   Data from the FRS estimates there to be 952,741 disabled children in the UK, being 7.3 per cent of the child population.[34] 8.8 per cent of boys and 5.8 per cent of girls are disabled.[35] Disabled children's most commonly-reported difficulties are with memory, concentration,

the support they receive from social services: a review of consultations and methods, Thomas Coram Research Unit, University of London, 2006; The Children's Society online *Disability Toolkit*, accessible at http://sites.childrenssociety.org. uk/disabilitytoolkit/toolkit.

32 The FRS adopts a definition of disability that is compatible with that in the Disability Discrimination Act 1995 and the Equality Act 2010 (see chapter 9).

33 C Blackburn, N Spencer and J Read, 'Prevalence of childhood disability and the characteristics and circumstances of disabled children in the UK: secondary analysis of the Family Resources Survey', (2010) *BMC Pediatrics* 10, p21. Available at www.biomedcentral.com/1471-2431/10/21.

34 C Blackburn, N Spencer and J Read, 'Prevalence of childhood disability and the characteristics and circumstances of disabled children in the UK: secondary analysis of the Family Resources Survey', (2010) *BMC Pediatrics* 10, p21. Because this study used the most recent definition of disability, the prevalence estimates reported show an increase of two percentage points over those often cited previously.

35 C Blackburn, N Spencer and J Read, 'Prevalence of childhood disability and the characteristics and circumstances of disabled children in the UK: secondary analysis of the Family Resources Survey', (2010) *BMC Pediatrics* 10, p21. Available at www.biomedcentral.com/1471-2431/10/21.

learning and communication. Many children have problems in more than one area of daily living; the FRS indicates around a third of disabled children experience between two and four difficulties and more than 10 per cent experience five or more difficulties.[36]

1.27   Since the 1980s there have been changes in the population of disabled children as greater numbers of low birthweight babies (as well as those with multiple and complex impairments) have survived and been cared for at home.[37] This has significant implications for the children and their families as well as for services attempting to meet their needs – for example, increasing the need for techno-logical equipment or procedures, usually managed by parents at home. In addition to administering medication, parents may have to be responsible for tube feeding, assisted ventilation and resuscita-tion procedures, among other interventions. Although national data on this issue is limited, some estimates suggest that there may be about 6,000 technology-dependent children in the UK.[38] In addition, recent years have seen a marked reported increase in numbers of children identified as having autistic spectrum disorders[39] and atten-tion deficit hyperactivity disorder (ADHD).[40]

Family composition

1.28   The majority of disabled children are brought up at home in their families of origin and almost two-thirds of them live in two-parent families. According to a recent study, the proportion who live in lone-parent households (34 per cent) is significantly greater, however, than that for non-disabled children (26 per cent).[41] The majority of these

36 C Blackburn, N Spencer and J Read, 'Prevalence of childhood disability and the characteristics and circumstances of disabled children in the UK: secondary analysis of the Family Resources Survey', (2010) *BMC Pediatrics* 10, p21. Available at www.biomedcentral.com/1471-2431/10/21.

37 A T Gibson, 'Outcome following preterm birth', (2007) *Best practice and research clinical obstetrics and gynaecology*, 21, 5, pp869–882.

38 C Glendinning, C Kirk, S Guiffrida and D Lawton, 'Technology-dependent children in the community: definitions, numbers and costs', (2001) 27 *Child: care, health and development* 321, pp321–334.

39 S Levy, D Mandell and R Schultz, 'Autism', (2009) 374 *The Lancet* 1627, pp1627–1638.

40 E Taylor, 'Developing ADHD', (2009) 50 *Journal of Child Psychiatry and Psychology*, pp126–132.

41 C Blackburn, N Spencer and J Read, 'Prevalence of childhood disability and the characteristics and circumstances of disabled children in the UK: secondary analysis of the Family Resources Survey', (2010) *BMC Pediatrics* 10, p21. Available at www.biomedcentral.com/1471-2431/10/21.

lone-parent households are headed by mothers.[42] While a number of studies have highlighted disabled children's increased chances of being brought up by a lone parent[43] the reasons for this are unclear. Some (but not all) research has found higher separation and divorce rates among parents of disabled children. It is suggested that any increased risk of separation or divorce is most likely to be seen during the early years of a disabled child's life; there is a sharply rising incidence of lone parenthood among disabled children aged 0–2 years after which the rates are fairly constant.[44] It has also been argued that lower re-partnering rates among parents of disabled children whose adult relationships have broken down may contribute to higher numbers of lone-parent households.[45]

1.29   However lone parenthood comes about, it is crucial to recognise that it has considerable implications for children and families. As noted below, it is associated with increased levels of poverty together with restricted access to important material goods and services. This, combined with high parental workloads linked with caring for some disabled children, means that some lone parents and their disabled children are very hard-pressed indeed.

1.30   Recent research has drawn attention to the clustering of childhood and adult disability within households.[46] A 2010 study reported that almost half of disabled children, compared with about a fifth of non-disabled children, live with a parent who also is disabled. In addition, around a quarter of disabled children live with one or

---

42 H Clarke and S McKay, *Exploring disability, family formation and break-up: reviewing the evidence*, Research Report No 514, Department for Work and Pensions, 2008.

43 E Emerson and C Hatton, 'The socio-economic circumstances of children at risk of disability in Britain', (2007) 22 *Disability and society*, pp563–580: see also H Clarke and S McKay, *Exploring disability, family formation and break-up: reviewing the evidence*, Research Report No 514, Department for Work and Pensions, 2008.

44 H Clarke and S McKay, *Exploring disability, family formation and break-up: reviewing the evidence*, Research Report No 514, Department for Work and Pensions, 2008.

45 S Baldwin and J Carlisle, *Social support for disabled children and their families: a review of literature*, HMSO, 1994.

46 H Clarke and S McKay, *Exploring disability, family formation and break-up: reviewing the evidence*, Research Report No 514, Department for Work and Pensions, 2008, and C Blackburn, N Spencer and J Read, 'Prevalence of childhood disability and the characteristics and circumstances of disabled children in the UK: secondary analysis of the Family Resources Survey', (2010) *BMC Pediatrics* 10, p21. Available at www.biomedcentral.com/1471-2431/10/21.

more siblings who are also disabled.[47] While further information and research is needed to help understand how this comes about, it is crucial to recognise the level of need and additional difficulties that may arise when parents and children in the same household are disabled. Studies have also described the hardship among those families with more than one disabled child – for example, the scale of childcare involved, the increased vulnerability to lone parenthood, parental unemployment and reliance on income support.[48]

Low income, material deprivation and debt

1.31   Analysis of the OPCS (Office of Population Censuses and Surveys) disability surveys of the 1980s highlighted the poverty and poor living standards of disabled children in Britain, making them arguably 'the poorest of the poor'.[49] More recent evidence suggests that little has changed.[50] Prevalence rates of disability are higher among children whose parents are manual workers[51] and as a group, disabled children are in substantially more disadvantaged financial and material circumstances than non-disabled children. While the reasons for this are not fully known,[52] it will partly be explained by the significant

47   C Blackburn, N Spencer and J Read, 'Prevalence of childhood disability and the characteristics and circumstances of disabled children in the UK: secondary analysis of the Family Resources Survey' (2010) *BMC Pediatrics* 10, p21. Available at www.biomedcentral.com/1471-2431/10/21.

48   D Lawton, *Complex numbers: families with more than one disabled child*, Social Policy Research Unit, University of York, 1998; R Tozer, *At the double: supporting families with two or more disabled children*, National Children's Bureau, 1999.

49   D Gordon, R Parker and F Loughran with P Heslop, *Disabled children in Britain: a re-analysis of the OPCS disability surveys*, TSO, 2000.

50   C Blackburn, N Spencer and J Read, 'Prevalence of childhood disability and the characteristics and circumstances of disabled children in the UK: secondary analysis of the Family Resources Survey', (2010) *BMC Pediatrics* 10, p21, available at www.biomedcentral.com/1471-2431/10/21; E Emerson and C Hatton, 'The socio-economic circumstances of children at risk of disability in Britain', (2007) 22 *Disability and society*, pp563–580; T Burchardt, 'Changing weights and measures: disability and child poverty', (2006) 123 *Poverty*, pp6–9; Contact a Family, *Counting the costs: the financial reality for families with disabled children*, 2010, available at www.cafamily.org.uk/pdfs/CountingtheCosts2010.pdf.

51   Office for National Statistics, *The health of children and young people*, 2004.

52   C Blackburn, N Spencer and J Read, 'Prevalence of childhood disability and the characteristics and circumstances of disabled children in the UK: secondary analysis of the Family Resources Survey', (2010) *BMC Pediatrics* 10, p21. Available at www.biomedcentral.com/1471-2431/10/21.

impact on both income and expenditure of bringing up a disabled child in a household. Growing up with disability and caring for a disabled child involves the need for substantial additional expenditure. It has been estimated that families with disabled children need incomes 10–18 per cent higher than similar families with non-disabled children if they are to achieve the same standard of living.[53] Simultaneously, however, the demands of caring reduce the options available to the adults in the family, particularly mothers, to bring in income by undertaking paid work.[54] While state allowances and benefits may have originally been intended to cover the additional costs of living with disability, the shortfall between such costs and maximum benefit entitlement has been estimated at between 20 and 50 per cent depending on the age of the child.[55] Furthermore, many families simply do not receive their full benefit entitlements.[56]

1.32 Figures taken from the FRS indicate that when all groups in the population are taken together, the income[57] for a household with a disabled child is around 13 per cent lower than for households with non-disabled children. There are variations between some groups, however; the lowest incomes are to be found among lone parents, black and minority ethnic families and those with disabled parents and disabled children in the same household.[58]

53 J Bradshaw, 'The cost of necessities' in J Strelitz and R Lister (eds), *Why money matters: family income, poverty and children's lives*, Save the Children, 2008.

54 B Dobson and S Middleton, *Paying to care: the cost of childhood disability*, Joseph Rowntree Foundation/York Publishing Services, 1998; B Dobson, S Middleton and A Beardsworth, *The impact of childhood disability on family life*, Joseph Rowntree Foundation/York Publishing Services, 2001.

55 B Dobson and S Middleton, *Paying to care: the cost of childhood disability*, Joseph Rowntree Foundation/York Publishing Services, 1998.

56 Audit Commission, *Services for disabled children: a review of services for disabled children and their families*, Audit Commission Publications, 2003; G Preston, *Helter skelter: disabled children and the benefits system*, CASE Paper 92, Centre for the Analysis of Social Exclusion, London School of Economics, 2005.

57 Specifically, the median equivalised total weekly income. Equivalisation allows the living standards of households that vary in size and composition to be compared and is based on the common-sense notion that a family with several people requires a higher income than a single person to have the same living standard. Income was adjusted using the equivalisation variable available in the FRS data set, being the McClements equivalisation scales.

58 C Blackburn, N Spencer and J Read, 'Prevalence of childhood disability and the characteristics and circumstances of disabled children in the UK: secondary analysis of the Family Resources Survey', (2010) *BMC Pediatrics* 10, p21. Available at www.biomedcentral.com/1471-2431/10/21.

1.33   The combination of all of these factors means that living standards in families with disabled children are lower than those of their non-disabled peers. Some disabled children and their families are living in conditions of extreme material hardship and poverty. Households with disabled children (26.5 per cent) are more likely than those with non-disabled children (16.2 per cent) to report one or more debts. The highest proportion of families reporting being behind with payments are those where there are both disabled children and disabled adults. The most common debts are in relation to council tax, water rates and telephone bills.[59] On almost every measure of material deprivation, disabled children are more likely than other children to live in households who are unable to afford items and activities generally regarded as important for children and those caring for them. It is important to recognise that deprivation indices are not concerned with a lack of luxury items or special treats that require lavish expenditure. They are things which most people would regard as reasonable in the twenty-first century: for example, a child having more than one pair of shoes, outside space where a child can play, being able to afford a leisure activity such as swimming once a month, having enough money to celebrate a birthday or buy some basic toys, being able to save £10 per month per family, to be able to afford household insurance, to replace items of furniture when they are worn out, or to decorate a room in the house once in a while.[60]

1.34   Standard consumer durables such as cars, central heating, washing machines, dryers and telephones are essential items for families with disabled children if they are to meet their children's needs and offset the additional demands of living with disability. For those on low incomes, they are expensive to buy and maintain. Heavy usage of some items may mean that running costs and wear and tear are likely to be high. Studies have found lower rates of ownership of these essential items among families with disabled children compared with the general population.[61]

59 C Blackburn, N Spencer and J Read, 'Prevalence of childhood disability and the characteristics and circumstances of disabled children in the UK: secondary analysis of the Family Resources Survey', (2010) *BMC Pediatrics* 10, p21. Available at www.biomedcentral.com/1471-2431/10/21.

60 C Blackburn, N Spencer and J Read, 'Prevalence of childhood disability and the characteristics and circumstances of disabled children in the UK: secondary analysis of the Family Resources Survey', (2010) *BMC Pediatrics* 10, p21. Available at www.biomedcentral.com/1471-2431/10/21.

61 B Beresford, *Expert opinions: a national survey of parents caring for a severely disabled child*, Policy Press, 1995.

Problems with housing

1.35 Restricted financial resources are also partly responsible for many disabled children and their families living in poor or unsuitable housing.[62] Disabled children are more likely to live in rented accommodation and with fewer rooms than non-disabled children. Lack of space and poor access both outside and within the home are commonly reported problems. Some of the most severe housing difficulties are among families with lowest incomes and those from black and minority ethnic groups. Even when families are living in accommodation that might be judged reasonable against general criteria, it is often unsuitable for disabled children and their carers. Physical barriers inside and outside the home can make it difficult for children to take part in ordinary childhood activities. Families who find themselves in unsuitable housing but who are unable to access financial assistance for adaptations frequently overstretch themselves by moving house or by undertaking building work at their own expense. In a 2002 national survey of 3,000 households with disabled children, nine in ten identified at least one problem that made the house unsuitable for a disabled child and one in four identified six or more problem areas.[63] See chapter 6 for the obligation on local authorities to ensure disabled children live in suitable housing adapted to their needs.

Living and growing with disability: parents' and children's experience

At home

1.36 In addition to managing the higher costs of living with often very limited resources, families also have to meet their disabled children's needs for care. Bringing up children can always be taxing but the care

---

62 C Blackburn, N Spencer and J Read, 'Prevalence of childhood disability and the characteristics and circumstances of disabled children in the UK: secondary analysis of the Family Resources Survey', (2010) *BMC Pediatrics* 10, p21, available at www.biomedcentral.com/1471-2431/10/21; E Emerson and C Hatton, *The socio-economic circumstances of families supporting a child at risk of disability in Britain in 2002*, Institute of Health Research, University of Lancaster, 2005; B Beresford and D Rhodes, *Housing and disabled children: round-up: reviewing the evidence*, Joseph Rowntree Foundation, 2008.

63 B Beresford and C Oldman, *Housing matters: national evidence relating to disabled children and their housing*, The Policy Press, 2002.

of a disabled child frequently makes demands that exceed what is required of parents of non-disabled children. Studies record the on-going and long-term nature of the caring commitments and describe the often high levels of personal and practical care and assistance being provided by parents to their disabled sons and daughters.[64] While needs vary according to the individual child and their circumstances, age and impairments, care provided by parents may include help with bathing, washing, eating, toileting, mobility and communication. Parents may also be responsible for particular dietary requirements, administering medication, using technological equipment or procedures and undertaking physiotherapy and other interventions designed to keep a child well or to help their development. Some children need careful supervision if they are to be safe while others need a great deal of attention and stimulation if frustration is to be kept at bay. For some children, the need for care and assistance will lessen as they get older, but for many this is not the case.[65] As some children gain in height and weight, the physical demands on carers become greater. Parents often report that with an older and bigger child, any behavioural, social and communication difficulties can be harder to accommodate and manage. The impact that this may have on daily living routines and activities can also be more marked.

1.37   Getting out and about and doing things that others regard as ordinary often needs a great deal of planning, organisation and energy for disabled children and their families. Going shopping, getting a haircut or having a day out can be made difficult by a combination of such things as transport problems, an inaccessible physical environment, a restricted budget and the need to transport bulky equipment as well as parental fatigue. It is also quite common for parents and children to have to face negative or insensitive reactions by other members of the public or to find that public spaces and arrangements that may suit the majority are not designed to include them (see chapter 9 for the duties under the Equality Act 2010 to end this discriminatory treatment of disabled children and their families).[66]

---

64 B Beresford, *Expert opinions: a national survey of parents caring for a severely disabled child*, Policy Press, 1995; K Roberts and D Lawton, 'Acknowledging the extra care parents give their disabled children' (2001) 27 *Child: care, health and development*, pp307–319; S Kirk, C Glendinning and P Callery, 'Parent or nurse? The experience of being the parent of a technology-dependent child', (2005) 51 *Journal of Advanced Nursing*, pp456–464.

65 B Beresford, *Expert opinions: a national survey of parents caring for a severely disabled child*, Policy Press, 1995.

66 B Dobson, S Middleton and A Beardsworth, *The impact of childhood disability on family life*, Joseph Rowntree Foundation/York Publishing Services, 2001;

1.38   Caring for a disabled child is a workload undertaken in private, day after day, and for some children, during the night too.[67] Often it has to be accomplished by parents who also have to attend to the needs of other family members, particularly other children. Parents of disabled children may find that informal arrangements with family and friends such as 'child-swaps' or babysitting are less easy to come by. Formal childcare, as we shall see later, is also not easily available. If money is very tight, as is the case in many households, parents do not have the option of paying for some extra help or buying in something that makes life a little easier or more enjoyable for the children and adults. Instead, in order to get by, family members have only their own muscle-power, energy and ingenuity to fall back on, unless they are provided with support from statutory services.

1.39   The patterns of care in households with a disabled child tend to reflect childcare arrangements in families more generally. In both lone-parents and two-parent households, the caring workload overall tends to be weighted towards mothers and this has an impact on their employment and career opportunities. Women with disabled children are less likely than other mothers to be in paid work. When working, they are less likely to be employed full-time. Overall, couples with disabled children are less likely both to be in paid work compared with couples who have non-disabled children.[68] While fathers' employment rates are less affected than mothers', twice as many couples with a disabled child are jobless, compared to those who do not have a disabled child.[69] In addition, earlier research and anecdotal evidence point to the pressure to hold on to their jobs that is felt by men who are the single wage-earners in couple households. They also report tensions around having to take time off work to attend to matters related to their disabled child (see para 8.27 below for carers' employment rights).[70] For many, the lack of affordable and suitable childcare for disabled children of all ages, and a lack of

S Ryan, '"People don't do odd, do they?" Mothers making sense of the reactions of others towards their learning disabled children in public places', (2005) 3 *Children's Geographies*, pp291–306.

67 J Heaton, J Noyes, P Sloper and R Shah, 'The experience of sleep disruption in families of technology-dependent children', (2006) 20 *Children and Society*, pp196–208.

68 S McKay and A Atkinson, *Disability and caring among families with children*, Research Report No 460, Department for Work and Pensions, 2007.

69 S McKay and A Atkinson, *Disability and caring among families with children*, Research Report No 460, Department for Work and Pensions, 2007.

70 K Atkin, 'Similarities and differences between informal carers', in J Twigg (ed), *Carers: research and practice*, HMSO, 1992.

suitably trained staff to deliver it, are significant barriers to taking up work or, indeed, simply having time out from their caring responsibilities to attend to other important issues.[71] Families of children with complex care and support needs are known to have particular difficulties securing safe and appropriate care to meet their needs.[72]

1.40   Over the past few years, research has drawn attention to the particular barriers which disabled parents face and the difficulty of accessing services to assist them in their parenting roles.[73] Many report that their capacity as parents is questioned without their having been given the opportunity to have the supports that would enable them to care for their children successfully. Their difficulties are often exacerbated by the lack of effective collaboration between children's and adult social services (see chapter 10 on transition to adulthood). Given that recent research has highlighted a clustering of childhood and adult disability in a significant proportion of households,[74] it is reasonable to assume that many disabled parents and their disabled children are in a very vulnerable position and exist close to crisis point.

1.41   In addition to the work undertaken by parents, there has been growing recognition of the amount of care and support that some siblings offer to their disabled brothers and sisters. Sometimes they may provide help or assistance directly to their disabled brother or sister; at other times, they may do things to support a parent who is undertaking most of the care. In a survey of young people known to 'young carers' projects in the UK, 31 per cent reported offering care or assistance to a disabled sibling.[75] See paras 8.34–8.40 below for the law in relation to young carers.

---

71 C Kagan, S Lewis and P Heaton, *Caring to work: accounts of working parents of disabled children*, Family Policy Studies Centre, 1998; Audit Commission, *Services for disabled children: a review of services for disabled children and their families*, Audit Commission Publications, 2003; Daycare Trust, *Listening to parents of disabled children about childcare*, 2007.

72 S Kirk and C Glendinning, 'Developing services to support parents caring for a technology-dependent child at home', (2004) 30 *Child: care, health and development*, pp 209–218.

73 J Morris and M Wates, *Supporting disabled parents and parents with additional support needs*, SCIE Knowledge Review 11, Social Care Institute for Excellence, 2006.

74 C Blackburn, N Spencer and J Read, 'Prevalence of childhood disability and the characteristics and circumstances of disabled children in the UK: secondary analysis of the Family Resources Survey', (2010) *BMC Pediatrics* 10, p21. Available at www.biomedcentral.com/1471-2431/10/21.

75 J Dearden and S Becker, *Young carers in the UK: the 2004 report*, Carers UK, 2004.

1.42   While there is a great deal of evidence about the taxing workloads managed by parents and others in the household, it is important to stress that studies have indicated time and time again that parents are not prone to characterising their disabled children as burdensome. Research has repeatedly highlighted the strength of parents' understanding, love and appreciation of their children and the ways that they focus on personal and practical arrangements which would enable them and their children to achieve a reasonable quality of life. These studies also indicate that parents know only too well that many others do not see their children in the same way. Managing other people's misunderstanding of their children and hurtful attitudes towards them can be yet another problem to be dealt with.[76]

Dealing with services

1.43   In addition to the caring work and the practical and financial problems to be tackled at home, parents of disabled children have to have dealings with a wide range of health, education and social care agencies and professionals. Parents report that contact with these services often constitutes additional, tiring and frustrating work.[77] A number of themes consistently emerge from studies which explore parents' and children's experience as service users. There are high levels of unmet need for provision, with many finding that they are not eligible for services that would help them, or that the things that are provided are not suitable. Reports have highlighted the particular difficulties experienced by families from black and minority ethnic backgrounds and those on very low incomes. Services are delivered by specialists

76 B Dobson, S Middleton and A Beardsworth, *The impact of childhood disability on family life*, Joseph Rowntree Foundation/York Publishing Services, 2001; S Ryan '"I used to worry about what other people thought but now I just think ... well I don't care": shifting accounts of learning difficulties in public places', (2008) 23 *Health and Place*, pp199–210, 2008; J Read, *Disability, the family and society: listening to mothers*, Open University Press, 2000.

77 Audit Commission, *Services for disabled children: a review of services for disabled children and their families*, Audit Commission Publications, 2003; B Beresford, *Expert opinions: a national survey of parents caring for a severely disabled child*, Policy Press, 1995; S Kirk and C Glendinning, 'Developing services to support parents caring for a technology-dependent child at home' (2004) 30 *Child: care, health and development*, pp 209–218; R Townsley, D Abbott and D Watson, *Making a difference? Exploring the impact of multi-agency working on disabled children with complex healthcare needs and the professionals who support them*, Policy Press, 2003; HM Treasury and Department for Education and Skills, *Aiming high for disabled children: better support for families*, 2007; C Hatton, Y Akram, R Shah, J Robertson and E Emerson, *Supporting South Asian families with a child with severe disabilities*, Jessica Kingsley Publishers, 2004.

working in systems of baffling complexity. There are problems associated with co-ordination and joint planning between key agencies and disciplines at all levels, resulting in serious problems for children and their parents in relation to essential provision (see paras 2.34–2.36 below for the duties on services to co-operate to prevent these difficulties occurring). Only a minority of children and families have a key worker or lead practitioner (see paras 3.10–3.12 below) who acts as a point of contact to help them through the maze.[78]

1.44   The implications of this for children with complex support needs and their parents cannot be overstressed. It is not uncommon for families to have lengthy waiting times for an assessment and subsequently for the provision of basic equipment, adaptations and other services. Families sometimes report that by the time the provision reaches them, their child has outgrown it or that the opportunity to make full use of it has been missed. Parents also say that they have to be very persistent and active if they are to get provision that they feel would really help their child. While good services can be a powerful mediator of stress, parents report that dealing with poor ones and those that are difficult to access can be one of the most stressful aspects of bringing up a disabled child. These difficulties are exacerbated by a lack of knowledge in all parts of the system about what the law requires in terms of service provision to disabled children and their families – a problem this handbook aims to address.

Problems with information

1.45   Across the whole of childhood and through transition to adulthood, disabled children and their families say that they have difficulty in finding useable information at a time when they need it.[79] It is difficult for families to find essential information about such things as access and entitlements to services and benefits; approaches to managing aspects of a child's condition, development or behaviour; different services to meet different needs; the responsibilities of various organisations; and where to find key contacts. For whatever reason, it has proved difficult for service-providers to develop systems that

78 V Greco and P Sloper, 'Care co-ordination and key worker schemes for disabled children: results from a UK-wide survey', (2004) 30 *Child: care, health and development*, pp13–20.

79 W Mitchell and P Sloper, *User-friendly information for families with disabled children: a guide to good practice*, York Publishing Services, 2000; Audit Commission, *Services for disabled children: a review of services for disabled children and their families*, Audit Commission Publications, 2003.

are sufficiently sophisticated and user-friendly to cope with both the complexity of the information to be delivered and the diversity of circumstances of those needing it. Families for whom English is not a first language may have particular difficulty accessing information.

1.46   A number of studies have described what families regard as the key elements of effective information systems.[80] Parents say that they want short, clear, written guides to local services with more in-depth materials geared to key periods in their children's lives. They also need information on other important matters such as benefit entitlements and disabling conditions. Parents want information to be jargon-free and in different formats.

1.47   However, many parents say that the provision of information alone is not enough to make sure that they get what they and their children need. They stress the importance of having a person who can act as a key contact for information and other purposes. In recent years, service-providers and organisations for disabled children and their families have increasingly been using the internet to disseminate information. This is undoubtedly making a difference to many but families on low incomes may still have more limited access than others. It is, indeed, arguable that a reliance on the internet for information dissemination may exacerbate existing inequalities.[81] There are also issues of quality control in relation to information found online.

1.48   A time when information is particularly crucial is when children and families find themselves at a critical transition period – ie a stage when something important changes and a significant adjustment of circumstances and arrangements is required (see chapter 10 for the law on the key transition to adulthood). These transitional periods merit attention because of their potential to be hazardous and stressful for the children and adults concerned. They are sometimes related to a child's age or development, to external arrangements and services, to family circumstances or to a combination of some or all of these. The early time when disability is identified, accessing education and the transition to adulthood and to adult services are all

---

80   W Mitchell and P Sloper, *User-friendly information for families with disabled children: a guide to good practice*, York Publishing Services/Joseph Rowntree Foundation, 2000. See also Contact a Family, *We're listening*, 2003: www.cafamily.orguk/wmids/WeAreListeningFull.pdf.

81   C Blackburn and J Read, 'Using the internet? The experiences of parents of disabled children', (2005) *Child: care health and development*, pp507–515; K Baxter, C Glendinning and S Clarke, 'Making informed choices in social care: the importance of accessible information', (2008) 16 *Health and Social Care in the Community*, pp197–207.

predictable examples which affect most disabled children and their families. Typically at one of these points, the territory is unfamiliar and new knowledge and information have to be found, absorbed and applied to get a satisfactory outcome for the child and family.

Personal consequences

1.49   When all of these experiences and circumstances are taken together, it is not surprising that there can be personal consequences for the children and adults concerned. Many disabled children and their families face the restrictions commonly experienced by all who live on or near the poverty line. General poverty studies show how a lack of basic resources insidiously affects all aspects of the lives of the children and adults concerned and erodes their choices, opportunities and well-being.[82] For disabled children and their families, the level of social exclusion is magnified by the experience of growing up and living with disability. Many families who are not living on the lowest incomes nevertheless also deal with the increased demands of living with disability without sufficient human and material resources to offset them.

1.50   There is frequently a substantial gap between the aspirations and activities regarded as ordinary for non-disabled children and their disabled peers. Many disabled children are excluded from age-appropriate experiences that may be regarded as important for all children. Across their childhoods, they have a far greater chance of having someone making decisions on their behalf, of not being consulted about major decisions that affect them and of having a more restricted and confining social and personal life – despite all the legal obligations to the contrary. Children who do not use standard means of communication may find that others do not involve them or do not try to find out their ideas and wishes.[83] Leisure, play and time with friends are often more limited for disabled children and young people.[84] Childcare for disabled children of all ages has

---

82   D Gordon, L Adelman, K Ashworth, J Bradshaw, R Levitas and S Middleton, *Poverty and social exclusion in Britain,* Joseph Rowntree Foundation/York Publishing Services, 2000.

83   P Russell, *Having a say: disabled children and effective partnership in decision making,* Council for Disabled Children, 1998; J Morris, *Don't leave us out: involving children and young people with communication impairments,* York Publishing Services, 1998.

84   Audit Commission, *Services for disabled children: a review of services for disabled children and their families,* Audit Commission Publications, 2003; H Clarke, *Preventing social exclusion of disabled children and their families,* Research Report

frequently been unavailable to them, leaving them with fewer opportunities to mix with other children and benefit from the activities they enjoy.[85] Children and young people with complex impairments and high support needs will frequently experience a high degree of social exclusion.[86]

1.51   Parents often express concern about the limitations placed on their disabled children and are acutely aware of their isolation and restricted opportunities. Experiences that they regard as good for any child are often difficult to come by for their disabled children and can be arranged only at significant cost in terms of both time and money.[87] Many also express concern about the impact on their non-disabled sons and daughters of living with disability.[88] Studies which have consulted non-disabled siblings directly report mixed reactions to their situations.[89] Many speak positively about their relationship with their disabled brother or sister and have a straightforward attitude towards their impairments and support needs. Others, as might be anticipated, do not get on so well. Some report being upset by the attitudes of other people towards their brother or sister and it is also not uncommon for them to describe being teased or bullied themselves.

1.52   In some families, one consequence can be that the health of parents may suffer. As a group, parents of disabled children are reported to experience higher levels of stress and lower levels of well-being than those of non-disabled children.[90] Mothers of disabled children

RR782, DfES, 2006; G Bielby, T Chamberlain, M Morris, L O'Donnell and C Sharp, *Improving the wellbeing of disabled children and young people through improving access to positive activities*, Centre for Excellence and Outcomes in Children and Young People's Services, 2009.

85 See, for example, Council for Disabled Children, *Extending inclusion. Access for disabled children and young people to extended schools and children's centres: a development manual*, DCSF Publications, 2008; Daycare Trust, *Listening to parents of disabled children about childcare*, 2007.

86 J Morris, *That kind of life? Social exclusion and young disabled people with high levels of support needs*, Scope, 2001.

87 B Dobson and S Middleton, *Paying to care: the cost of childhood disability*, Joseph Rowntree Foundation/York Publishing Services, 1998.

88 Contact a Family, *Siblings*, 2008.

89 N Atkinson and N Crawforth, *All in the family: siblings and disability*, NCH Action for Children, 1995; K Stalker and C Connors, 'Children's perceptions of their disabled siblings: "She's different but it's normal for us"', (2004) 18 *Children & Society*, pp218–230.

90 P Sloper and B Beresford, 'Families with disabled children', (2006) 333 BMJ 928–929; M Hirst, 'Carer distress: a prospective, population-based study', (2005) 61 *Social Science and Medicine*, pp697–708.

have been found to be particularly vulnerable and some studies have suggested that their increased risk of poorer health and well-being may be attributed to their socio-economic disadvantage.[91] A recent American study investigated the levels of cortisol, a biological marker for stress, in mothers who had been caring long-term for their now adult sons and daughters with autistic spectrum disorders and challenging behaviour. The study found that that the mothers' cortisol profiles were similar to those of other groups experiencing chronic stress such as combat soldiers, Holocaust survivors and those with post traumatic stress disorder.[92]

The early years

1.53   For almost all parents, the time when their child was identified as being disabled is highly significant. This remains the case whether disability is identified in the early years of a child's life or later. Parents' accounts suggest that the process of finding out that they have a disabled child is experienced as exceptionally stressful by many.[93] In this section, we focus mainly on the experience of pre-school children and their families, given that improvements in diagnostic techniques means that more disabled children are being diagnosed at a younger age.

1.54   As negative perceptions of disability are so widespread, it is unsurprising that some parents initially approach the experience of finding that they have a disabled child with at least some negative attitudes that they later come to modify or reject. It is not uncommon for people to describe feeling shocked and overwhelmed.[94] Some may be unsure whether they can cope with what they think may be demanded of them and others may not wish their lives to change in ways that they assume will happen. Many of these concerns are of

91 E Emerson, C Hatton, G Llewellyn, J Blacker and H Graham, 'Socio-economic position, household composition, health status and indicators of well-being of mothers with and without intellectual disabilities', (2006) 50 *Journal of Intellectual Disability Research*, pp862–873.

92 M M Seltzer and others, 'Maternal cortisol levels and behavior problems in adolescents and adults with ASD', (2010) 40 *Journal of Autism and Developmental Disorders*, pp457–469.

93 B Dobson, S Middleton and A Beardsworth, *The impact of childhood disability on family life*, Joseph Rowntree Foundation/York Publishing Services, 2001; *Right from the start*, Scope, 2003.

94 B Dobson, S Middleton and A Beardsworth, *The impact of childhood disability on family life*, Joseph Rowntree Foundation/York Publishing Services, 2001.

course entirely rational, given the attitudes that many encounter and the scarcity and/or poor quality of service provision for disabled children in many areas. Personal reactions are diverse and complex but many parents report that getting to know their child through a loving, care-giving relationship means that their initial attitudes change. Some parents also report feeling distressed as they become exposed to the way that other people's attitudes about disability reflect on them. They find quite early on that they are perceived and treated differently and in ways that they regard as negative.[95]

1.55   In addition to any personal reactions they may have, studies have identified issues related to the nature and organisation of services that present problems for parents during the early years. Notwithstanding the positive support received by some, there are high rates of dissatisfaction with the services that many receive at this crucial time. Common problems include: insensitivity or inappropriate practice on the part of some professionals and service providers; a lack of information about key services and benefits; a lack of consistency and co-ordination between multiple service providers; exclusion from key mainstream and community service providers and facilities.[96] While some of these barriers are experienced by parents and their children throughout childhood, in the early years they are likely to be dealing with them for the first time and in a situation where both the idea and experience of living with disability are new. Many parents can spend a great deal of time and energy trying to find their way around the complex maze of unfamiliar services. Some studies point to the particular difficulties experienced at this time by families from minority ethnic groups and those whose first language is not English.[97] Although these issues have been at the heart of the highly praised Early Support Programme in England, there is evidence that all of these difficulties persist in many areas.

1.56   Depending on the child's condition, parents may also be extremely concerned about the child's health or even survival. As health and other professionals assess their child and plan and provide interventions, they may find themselves attending frequent appointments

95 B Dobson, S Middleton and A Beardsworth, *The impact of childhood disability on family life*, Joseph Rowntree Foundation/York Publishing Services, 2001.

96 Department for Education and Skills, *Together from the start: practical guidance for professionals working with disabled children (birth to third birthday) and their families*, 2003.

97 C Hatton, Y Akram, R Shah, J Robertson and E Emerson, *Supporting South Asian families with a child with severe disabilities*, Jessica Kingsley Publishers, 2004.

with a range of unfamiliar specialists in different settings. Some describe the feeling as 'of their lives being on hold'. Arrangements may be particularly demanding if the child has quite complex impairments. One report illustrated this with reference to the experience of the family of a 13-month-old child who had, over a nine-month period, attended a total of 315 service-based appointments in 12 different locations.[98] Parents may also have to learn new, sometimes highly technical skills for the first time as they begin to care for their child at home.[99]

1.57   As they undertake this taxing level of activity and try to test out the living arrangements that work for them, they may also find that money worries can be a further cause of stress. The impact of the higher costs of disabled living and reduced income can bite quite early.[100] There may be an immediate impact on parents', particularly mothers', choices about working outside the home. As we have seen, suitable and affordable daycare is often hard to come by and studies have shown how difficult it is for parents with disabled children to manage the demands of caring and working (see chapter 8).[101] As we noted earlier, considerable numbers of lone parents manage all of this unaided by a partner. We have also seen that the rate of lone parenthood increases during the first two years of a disabled child's life, suggesting that this is a time when some adult relationships may break down.[102]

Getting an education

1.58   Like all children, disabled children require and have a right to suitable education. A key issue remains the setting in which this education should be delivered. From the late 1970s onwards, there has

---

98 Department for Education and Skills, *Together from the start: practical guidance for professionals working with disabled children (birth to third birthday) and their families*, 2003.

99 S Kirk and C Glendinning, 'Developing services to support parents caring for a technology-dependent child at home', (2004) 30 *Child: care, health and development*, pp209–218.

100 B Dobson and S Middleton, *Paying to care: the cost of childhood disability*, Joseph Rowntree Foundation/York Publishing Services, 1998.

101 C Kagan, S Lewis and P Heaton, *Caring to work: accounts of working parents of disabled children*, Family Policy Studies Centre, 1998.

102 H Clarke and S McKay, *Exploring disability, family formation and break-up: reviewing the evidence*, Research Report No 514, Department for Work and Pensions, 2008.

been a growing challenge to the then established wisdom that it was both necessary and desirable for disabled children to be educated in separate schools from their non-disabled peers. By the mid-1990s, the inclusion of disabled children in mainstream schools had gained official support and recognition.[103] Those arguing for inclusion pointed to the part that a separate education system played in maintaining and reproducing the disadvantage experienced by disabled children and young people. It was suggested that the education that disabled children received was often of poorer quality and that it set them on a course of segregation and unequal opportunities that would continue for the rest of their lives. The major challenge in education was how the system as a whole, and schools within it, might change in fundamental ways in order to meet the needs of a more diverse population of children, and be the richer for it.[104] Increasingly, policy and practice assumes that mainstream schooling is the appropriate option for disabled children unless there is a particular reason why their needs cannot be met in this way. In recent times, inclusion in education has come to be seen as one important aspect of disabled children's right to social inclusion more generally.

1.59 As might be expected, there is variation in the reactions of disabled children and adults and their families to these shifts in thinking and to the experiences of both inclusive and separate education.[105] Some of these variations may be explained by the very different educational needs of different groups of disabled children; for instance, children with autistic spectrum disorders compared with children who have physical or sensory impairments. Parents of disabled children have to make difficult choices about what they regard as being in their children's interests at any particular time. They have to consider the information available to them, take all circumstances into account and decide on what seems to them to be the best option. The choices they make often have a strong element of pragmatism but this does not mean that they are not driven by deeply held ethical or moral beliefs.

103 Department for Education and Employment *Excellence for all children, meeting special educational needs*, The Stationery Office, 1998.

104 G Lindsay, 'Inclusive education: a critical perspective', (2003) 30 *British Journal of Special Education*, pp3–12; P Farrel and M Ainscow (eds), *Making special education inclusive*, David Fulton Publishers, 2002.

105 M Priestly and P Rabiee, 'Hope and fears: stakeholders' views on transfer of special school resources towards inclusion', (2002) 6 *Inclusive Education* pp371–390; C Rogers, 'Experiencing an "inclusive" education: parents and their children with "special educational needs"', (2007) 28 *British Journal of the Sociology of Education*, pp55–68.

Some parents make a considered and positive choice for mainstream school or simply assume that it is the obvious place for their sons and daughters to be. Others consider that that there are some forms of specialised and separate provision that can make a positive contribution to their children's development and well-being for at least part of their time at school. Others may have a commitment to inclusion in principle but cannot see how it can be made to work for their particular child as things stand. Some people make an 'on balance' decision where they see a particular placement as a trade-off.

1.60   The term 'special educational needs' (SEN) was introduced into policy and law in the early 1980s, following the seminal report by Mary Warnock.[106] The Education Act 1981 effected a major change in approach which remains the basis of law and policy today. The main principle behind this post-1981 system is that the educational needs of children who have a learning difficulty or who are disabled are determined and then provision is arranged that will meet those needs. It was the first example of an approach that set out to be 'needs-led', though others were to follow later. Those with higher levels of need that require the local authority to arrange additional or different educational provision may have a statement of SEN which is produced in accordance with prescribed statutory procedures. Just over 20 per cent of all children are deemed to have SEN and just under 3 per cent have a statement.[107] About a third of children with statements are educated in special schools.[108] The process of ensuring that a disabled child's SEN are properly addressed is considered in detail at chapter 4 below.

1.61   While the groups of children defined as SEN or disabled (according to the Equality Act 2010) are not the same,[109] many parents and their disabled children find themselves going through the formal 'statementing' process or one of the other procedures related to their educational needs. Practice in different localities varies and while some families undoubtedly have good experience, a range of recent

---

106 Department of Education and Science, *The report of the committee of enquiry into the education of handicapped children and young people* (the Warnock Report), Cmnd 7212, HMSO, 1978.

107 Department for Children Schools and Families, *Children with special educational needs 2009: an analysis*, 2009.

108 House of Commons Education and Skills Committee, *Special educational needs, third report of session 2005–06.*

109 J Porter, H Daniels, A Feller and J Georgeson, 'Collecting disability data from parents', (2009) *Research Papers in Education*, Routledge, November.

research studies[110] and official reports[111] indicate that many children and their parents experience serious problems as they try to navigate what is a very complex system.

1.62   There are common themes emerging from these sources. Parents report that it is stressful and difficult because of a lack of information, poor support and negative attitudes. While many value the confidence and security derived from a statement, they feel disadvantaged in a system that is unfamiliar and difficult to understand. Some parents and children have difficulty in finding the information they need, reading and commenting on professional reports and preparing written submissions about their children. Parents also complain that statements are vague, formulaic, lacking in specificity and not related to their child as an individual (in breach of legal requirements to the contrary). Being in disagreement with the school or the local authority and going through procedures to resolve disputes is also experienced as highly stressful.[112] Finally, there is a great deal of concern about the high rate of school exclusions among children and young people with SEN – an issue considered further at paras 4.114–4.123 below.[113]

1.63   In the end, the majority of parents with children with SEN report that they are happy with their children's educational provision.[114] Even when parents are satisfied with how processes work and with the outcomes, however, they generally report that they have to be engaged very actively with the system and work very hard to make progress for their child. Some professionals who have a key role in relation to a child, are reported not to have a thorough understanding

---

110 R Tennant, M Callanan, D Snape, I Palmer and J Read, *Special educational needs disagreement resolution services: national evaluation*, Research Report DCSF-RR054, DCSF, 2008. See also C Penfold, N Cleghorn, R Tennant, I Palmer and J Read, *Parental confidence in the special educational needs assessment, statementing and tribunal system: a qualitative study*, Research Report RR117, DCSF, 2009.

111 Lamb Inquiry, *Special educational needs and parental confidence*, DCSF, 2009. Available at www.dcsf.gov.uk/lambinquiry.

112 R Tennant, M Callanan, D Snape, I Palmer and J Read, *Special educational needs disagreement resolution services: national evaluation*, Research Report DCSF-RR054, DCSF, 2008; C Penfold, N Cleghorn, R Tennant, I Palmer and J Read, *Parental confidence in the special educational needs assessment, statementing and tribunal system: a qualitative study*, Research Report RR117, DCSF, 2009; Lamb Inquiry, *Special educational needs and parental confidence*, DCSF, 2009.

113 Disabled children are eight times more likely than their non-disabled peers to be excluded: Lamb Inquiry, *Special educational needs and parental confidence*, DCSF, 2009.

114 Lamb Inquiry, *Special educational needs and parental confidence*, DCSF, 2009.

of the SEN procedures.[115] These issues were recognised by the previous government in England in its response to the recent Lamb Inquiry, but the system reforms required to address them will take many years to work through. There is no credible 'quick fix' in a system which has to attempt to meet the differentiated needs of a complex population of disabled children within the resources that local and central government deem to be available.

Children who live away from home

1.64   While the majority of disabled children live with their families of origin and go to day schools, a minority live away from home for all or some of the year. Some are in boarding schools in term-time and go home to their families for holidays and some weekends; some stay at school 52 weeks a year (see paras 4.74–4.80 below); some are in healthcare settings and others are 'looked after' (see paras 3.84–3.87 below) by local authorities. These categories of placements and settings are not entirely separate as there may be some overlap, for example, a looked-after child (see para 3.84 below for the definition of 'looked after' status) may go to residential school.

1.65   Over a number of years, it has become apparent that we do not have enough information about this population of children: numbers, the pathways that take them to particular settings away from home, the educational and other personal outcomes, and what happens to them as they reach adulthood are all data that are lacking.[116] There is no doubt that for a long time, disabled children who live away from home were a very neglected group which did not feature in the main policy agendas.[117] In addition to a limited number of studies,[118]

---

115 C Penfold, N Cleghorn, R Tennant, I Palmer and J Read, *Parental confidence in the special educational needs assessment, statementing and tribunal system: a qualitative study*, Research Report RR117, DCSF, 2009.

116 Prime Minister's Strategy Unit, *Improving the life chances of disabled people*, TSO, 2005; Audit Commission, *Out of authority placements for special educational needs*, Audit Commission Publications, 2007; Department of Health, *Valuing people: a new strategy for learning disability for the 21st century*, TSO, 2001; Commission for Social Care Inspection, *Growing up matters: better transition for young people with complex needs*, 2007.

117 J Morris, *Gone missing? A research and policy review of disabled children living away from home*, Who Cares Trust, 1995.

118 D Abbott, J Morris and L Ward, *Disabled children and residential schools: a survey of local authority policy and practice*, Norah Fry Research Centre, University of Bristol, 2000; P Heslop and D Abbott 'Help to move on – but to what?

the most recent and comprehensive report on all of the children and young people was published by the then DfES in 2005. The report groups the children into those who are 'looked after' by local authorities, those in residential schools and those in health settings.[119]

1.66 As we have seen, children defined as having SEN and disabled children are not necessarily the same. It has been suggested, however, that among those in residential special schools, there is a large overlap between children who meet both definitions.[120] This may be attributable in part at least, to the fact that almost all children in residential special school have statements of SEN. The 2005 report records that at that time there were 1,320 looked after disabled children in residential settings. Of these, 595 are in residential schools and 620 in children's homes. The vast majority of looked after disabled children are between the ages of 10 and 15 years. There are about 10,500 children in residential special schools: 6,100 pupils are in maintained and non-maintained residential special schools and about 4,400 pupils in independent residential special schools. By far the biggest single group of children in residential special schools comprises teenage boys identified as having emotional and behavioural difficulties.

1.67 The 2005 report points out that data on hospital admissions does not identify disabled children as a group, but that some of the NHS classifications suggest that the children in those categories are disabled. The report indicated that over a three-year period, around 2,200 children had spent more than six months in hospital and, of these, 245 had spent more than five years there. The largest proportion of young people spending more than six months in hospital were aged between 15 and 19 years. The most common reason given for those spending long periods in hospital was that they had emotional and behavioural disorders. Other studies have identified the largest numbers of children in residential placements (as with those in special schools) to be teenage boys with emotional and behavioural disorders, children with complex needs and those with very challenging behaviour, including that linked to autistic spectrum disorders.[121]

Young people with learning difficulties moving on from out-of-area residential schools or colleges', (2009) 37 *British Journal of Learning Disability*, pp12–20.

119 A Pinney, *Disabled children in residential placements*, DfES, 2005.

120 A Pinney, *Disabled children in residential placements*, DfES, 2005.

121 N Pilling, P McGill and V Cooper, 'Characteristics and experiences of children and young people with severe intellectual disabilities and challenging behaviour attending 52-week residential special school', (2006) 51 *Journal of Intellectual Disability Research*, pp 184–196.

1.68   Some parents and children feel that a placement in residential
school, for example, is a positive choice and one which works to the
child's benefit. Unfortunately for others, however, a placement away
from home happens more by default or as a result of other, preferred
services and support not being available. We do not know enough
about what determines whether children leave home and live apart
from their families for some or all of the time. There are indications
that age may be a factor, as information on looked after children and
those in residential schooling shows that the majority are beyond
primary school age.[122] We have also seen the significant numbers
of teenage boys with emotional and behavioural disorders, challenging behaviour and autism in residential schools. Some research on
residential schooling as well as anecdotal accounts suggests that as
children get older, particularly if they have high support needs or
challenging behaviour, some families may not feel that they can continue to provide the levels of support and care that they require.[123]
This may be particularly the case if families have other stresses or
demands on their time and personal resources and if parents and
children have been offered little in the way of community care services. As we have seen, many families' resources are very stretched,
including in households where a lone parent is solely responsible
for the care of the children. There is also an over-representation of
children of lone parents in residential schools.[124]

1.69   It is often suggested that even when a child goes away from home
for primarily social or family reasons, some parents may find residential schooling a preferable and less stigmatising option to other
provision.[125] In some cases, including those on which the authors
have worked, residential schooling is required only because there is
no suitable educational provision to meet the child's needs in his
or her own locality. As rates of placement in residential school vary
substantially from one local authority to another,[126] it is reasonable

122 Lamb Inquiry, *Special educational needs and parental confidence*, DCSF, 2009.
123 D Abbott, J Morris and L Ward, *Disabled children and residential schools: a survey
     of local authority policy and practice*, Norah Fry Research Centre, University of
     Bristol, 2000.
124 D Gordon, R Parker and F Loughran with P Heslop, *Disabled children in
     Britain: a re-analysis of the OPCS disability surveys*, TSO, 2000.
125 D Abbott, J Morris and L Ward, *Disabled children and residential schools: a survey
     of local authority policy and practice*, Norah Fry Research Centre, University of
     Bristol, 2000.
126 D Abbott, J Morris and L Ward, *Disabled children and residential schools: a survey
     of local authority policy and practice*, Norah Fry Research Centre, University of
     Bristol, 2000.

to conclude that decisions have as much to do with local policy and resources as with children's educational needs. The same point may be made in relation to out-of-area services for looked after disabled children and young people. Some have argued that it is difficult to reconcile the aspiration for locally-based services with the need for specialist facilities that are only cost-effective when they are serving a wider geographical area.[127]

1.70   Earlier, attention was drawn to the inadequate child and family support services that are offered to many children and their families. The research is limited on the connection between stress on families, the shortage of flexible, community-based support to meet their needs and the use of substantial, sometime multiple provision away from home. However, some studies (of children with complex needs who spend long periods in healthcare settings) have suggested that a lack of adequate community-based services for them and their families contributes to their remaining in hospital for long stays.[128] Lengthy out-of-area placements are likely to result in some children and young people becoming cut off from their families.[129] It appears, however, that the majority of children in residential special schools go home regularly,[130] albeit that maintaining contact (eg due to distance, transport arrangements and expense) can particularly challenging for some.

1.71   While some children and young people may benefit overall from placements away from home, some may not. Some placements may deny a child the ordinary features of life which other children take for granted and in addition, there is concern that some groups of disabled children may be particularly vulnerable to abuse.[131] Disabled children in a large-scale US study were found to be 3.4 times more likely overall to be abused or neglected than non-disabled children, with similar

127 R McConkey, T Nixon, E Donaghy and D Mulhearn, 'The characteristics of children with a disability looked after away from home and their future service needs', (2004) *British Journal of Social Work*, pp561–576.

128 K Stalker, J Carpenter, R Phillips, C Connors, C MacDonald, J Eyre and J Noyes, *Care and treatment? Supporting children with complex needs in healthcare settings*, Pavillion Publishing, 2003.

129 D Abbott, J Morris and L Ward, *Disabled children and residential schools: a survey of local authority policy and practice*, Norah Fry Research Centre, University of Bristol, 2000.

130 A Pinney, *Disabled children in residential placements*, DfES, 2005.

131 M Stuart and C Baines, *Progress on safeguards for children living away from home: a review of action since the people like us report*, York Publishing Services, 2004; D Miller, *Disabled children and abuse*, NSPCC, 2002.

levels of mistreatment identified in smaller-scale UK studies.[132] In any event, being separated from family is clearly a significant matter for any child. This makes it crucial that it is not a placement that happens because of deficits in other community-based services or that arrangements do not isolate a child from significant family and community relationships. Some studies indicate that young disabled people are very likely to return to their family or area of origin after they have finished in residential school, making the maintenance of those personal links even more crucial.[133]

Transition to adulthood and adult services

1.72   Concern about the opportunities available to disabled young people in transition from childhood to adulthood is by no means new. In recent years, however, this crucial period in young people's lives has been given substantial attention in government policy.[134] Recent research continues to reflect earlier findings that this is a potentially hazardous time for the young people concerned and their families.[135] It is all too easy for young people to leave school and find themselves living a different life from that they would wish and one that is significantly more restricted than that of their non-disabled peers. There may be low expectations about what these young people have a right

132 National Working Group on Child Protection and Disability, *'It doesn't happen to disabled children': child protection and disabled children*, NSPCC, 2003, p20.

133 P Heslop and D Abbott, 'Help to move on – but to what? Young people with learning difficulties moving on from out-of-area residential schools or colleges', (2009) 37 *British Journal of Learning Disability*, pp12–20.

134 Prime Minister's Strategy Unit, *Improving the life chances of disabled people*, TSO, 2005; HM Treasury and Department for Education and Skills, *Aiming high for disabled children: better support for families*, 2007; Department for Children Schools and Families/Department of Health, *A transition guide for all services. Key information for professionals about the transition process for disabled young people*, DCSF Publications, 2007.

135 M Knapp, M Perkins, J Beecham, S Dhanasiri and C Rustin, 'Transition pathways for young people with complex disabilities: exploring the economic consequences', (2008) 34 *Child: care, health and development*, pp512–520; B Beresford, 'On the road to nowhere? Young disabled people and transition', (2004) 306 *Child: care, health and development*, pp581–587; L Ward, R Mallet, P Heslop and K Simons, 'Transition planning: how well does it work for young people with learning disabilities and their families?', (2003) 30 *British Journal of Special Education*, pp132–137; J Beecham, T Snell, M Perkins and M Knapp, *After transition: health and social care needs of young adults with long-term neurological conditions*, PSSRU Research Summary 48, London School of Economics, 2008.

to look forward to in the way of life as an adult and they will almost certainly come across problems as responsibilities for their support and assistance are transferred from children's to adult services. There is variation in practice in different areas, and young people and their parents often find that they have to be extremely active and informed to gain access to the supports that are needed.[136] It is often reported that there is a lack of adequate consultation with the young adults themselves and with their families and that they are not involved in a full and meaningful way in the decision-making that affects them so substantially.

1.73   Some common themes emerge from official reports and studies of the experience of young people and their families in transition. There is widespread under-recognition of need, inadequate planning and poor support at this vital time, despite the raft of legal duties intended to ensure assessment and planning take place in a timely fashion. Some services which young people have had as children are discontinued and are not replaced by an age-appropriate service for young adults. Important systems, organisations and funding streams are complex and information can be a problem. Social care support is often reported as being very low and adult health services often seem unequal to the task of co-ordinating and delivering healthcare to young people with complex needs. Opportunities for independence are severely restricted and many young disabled adults find that they are very dependent on their parents whatever everyone might otherwise wish.[137]

1.74   Some of these negative outcomes are likely to be related to disabled young people having had more limiting opportunities throughout their childhoods, including in education. The low educational qualifications of many disabled young people continues to be a cause for concern and many experience difficulties in the transition from school to further education.[138] Burchardt's work points to the encouraging way that disabled 16-year-olds' aspirations about post-school education and employment have risen and are now not significantly different from those of their non-disabled peers. Unfortunately, these aspirations are not translated into comparable attainments in

136 Audit Commission, *Services for disabled children: a review of services for disabled children and their families*, Audit Commission Publications, 2003.

137 J Beecham, T Snell, M Perkins and M Knapp, *After transition: health and social care needs of young adults with long-term neurological conditions*, PSSRU Research Summary 48, London School of Economics, 2008.

138 T Burchardt, *The education and employment of disabled young people*, Joseph Rowntree Foundation, 2005.

post-school education or employment. As a result, however positive their aspirations may be at 16, by the time disabled young adults have reached the age of 26, there is a widening gap between them and their non-disabled peers in terms of their subjective sense of well-being as well as their confidence about their abilities in relation to employment.[139] Long-term unemployment and reliance on benefits not only has a personal impact, it has financial consequences for disabled young adults and their families.[140]

1.75   Despite changes to the law and the development of policies on inclusion, many disabled young people still find that universal services are less responsive to them than they need.[141] While many disabled young people experience an unsatisfactory transition to adulthood and adult services, the experiences of three groups may merit particular attention on account of their circumstances or unmet needs. Firstly, because other people have a limited view of what is appropriate and possible, those with complex impairments and high support needs may be allowed only a restricted range of opportunities and aspirations and are likely to be offered only segregated services as young adults. On the other hand, young people who have lower support needs, including those with mild learning disabilities, may not be seen as eligible for support services.[142] Finally, there is a group of young people who have spent time in residential placements away from their families and neighbourhoods. As we have seen, the majority on leaving school return to their areas of origin. Most appear either to return to live with their families or to have some form of residential care and it is reported that choices offered to them are limited and frequently not well-planned. It cannot be assumed that they will be offered alternative choices of supported living which may accord better with their wishes and aspirations.

139 T Burchardt, *The education and employment of disabled young people*, Joseph Rowntree Foundation, 2005.

140 M Knapp, M Perkins, J Beecham, S Dhanasiri and C Rustin, 'Transition pathways for young people with complex disabilities: exploring the economic consequences', (2008) 34 *Child: care, health and development*, pp512–520.

141 Prime Minister's Strategy Unit, *Improving the life chances of disabled people*, TSO, 2005.

142 Prime Minister's Strategy Unit, *Improving the life chances of disabled people*, TSO, 2005; Commission for Social Care Inspection, *Growing up matters: better transition for young people with complex needs*, 2007.

Conclusion

1.76   This chapter has emphasised that disabled children and those close
to them are entitled to enjoy the same human rights as others and to
expect a quality of life comparable to that of their peers who do not
live with disability. However, as can be seen from the level of social
exclusion that they experience and the barriers they face, the aspiration of a more ordinary way of life is still beyond the reach of many
disabled children and their families. Challenging the social exclusion
and discrimination faced by these children and families and bringing
about positive change for their benefit is a considerable task requiring on-going political, social and legal action. This book focuses on
the contribution that the law can make towards the collective effort of
bringing about improvements in the lives of disabled children both
individually and as a group, and in particular how the law can be
used as a tool to help children and their families achieve the goals
that they value.

Legal fundamentals

Key points

- There is a wide range of domestic (UK) and international sources of law creating powers and duties in relation to disabled children.
- These powers and duties are influenced by an expanding range of international human rights conventions affecting disabled children.
- The extent to which services *must* be provided to disabled children will depend on whether there is a 'specific' or 'general' duty to do so.
- Where a public body has a power to provide services (rather than a duty to do so), that power must be exercised fairly, rationally and reasonably.
- Since the Children Act 2004, services for children (health, education, social care) are becoming more integrated.
- In particular, all the relevant agencies now have duties to co-operate to improve the well-being of all children (including disabled children).
- However, important separate legal duties remain in relation to children's services, education and health (see chapters 3, 4 and 5 respectively).
- Where agencies are or may be in breach of their duties, routes to redress include complaints processes, specialist tribunals and (where the problem is sufficiently serious and urgent) judicial review in the High Court.
- Funding through legal aid may be available for children and families when a legal challenge becomes necessary.

Introduction

2.1   There is a wide and expanding range of domestic and international sources of law affecting disabled children and their families, much of which has come into force in the last ten years. This chapter describes in outline terms the different sources of law and considers some of the most important powers and duties on public bodies (these are set out in more detail in the succeeding chapters). It explores the distinction between duties (things public bodies have to do) and powers (things public bodies may do), the line between which in many areas is becoming increasingly blurred. It further considers how the legal structures of the agencies providing services to disabled children and their families are changing, in many cases bringing agencies closer together. Finally, it sets out the different routes to redress for children and families who have been denied the services and support they need, including the potential for legal aid funding for some of these challenges.

2.2   In recent years, and most notably through the Human Rights Act (HRA) 1998, international human rights law has become as important a source of law for disabled children and their families as domestic legislation, regulations and statutory guidance. Each of these sources of law is explored in turn below.

International human rights conventions

European Convention on Human Rights

2.3   For the purposes of this book, the most important human rights convention is the European Convention on Human Rights (ECHR), because it has been incorporated into UK domestic law through the HRA 1998. Before the HRA 1998 came into force in 2000, individuals who felt that their ECHR rights had not been respected had to go to the European Court of Human Rights (ECtHR) in Strasbourg, a lengthy and time-consuming process. Now, cases alleging breaches of ECHR rights are routinely dealt with by the domestic courts.

2.4   Within the ECHR, the most relevant article to disabled children and their families is article 8, the right to respect for family, home and private life. Article 8 is what is termed a 'qualified' right. By this it is meant that although the state (for example a local authority, the police, etc) should not generally interfere with a person's privacy, their family life or their home, there may be situations where this is permitted (for example if a child is being abused or a home is being used for illegal purposes). The convention, however, stipulates that any such any interference with this right must be (among other things) 'proportionate' – or perhaps rather must not be 'disproportionate'. For example, in *Kutzner v Germany*[1] two sisters were taken into care because the parents had learning disabilities. The court held that this was a 'disproportionate' interference with the article 8 right to family life because, before taking this action, the government had failed to consider providing extra support to the family to enable them to remain living together.

1 (2002) 35 EHRR 25.

2.5   The courts have given a very broad meaning to the idea of 'private life'. They have held it to encompass not only the idea of having one's privacy respected – but also the notion of one's identity; one's 'ability to function socially';[2] one's 'physical and psychological integrity';[3] and of the right to develop one's personality and one's relations with other human beings 'without outside interference'.[4] Action by the state that may make a person unwell (for example through pollution[5]) will therefore engage the article 8 right as may a refusal to allow access to a person's social services file – if that contains information about his or her childhood (ie their 'identity').[6] The court has also held that creating barriers which restrict a disabled person's freedom of movement also interferes with a person's article 8 rights (the right to develop relations with one's environment/other people).[7] In this latter context, it has been argued that understanding of the nature of this right has, for disabled people, become aligned with many of the concepts associated with the social model of disability (see paras 1.5–1.7).[8]

2.6   ECHR article 8 places both a 'negative' and a 'positive' obligation on the state. The negative obligation is that the state must not interfere with the rights protected by article 8 unless it is pursuing one of the specified legitimate aims and even then it must not act in a disproportionate way – so the interference must be no more than strictly necessary. An example of a 'negative' interference would be taking away someone's home, or removing someone's children into care. But the state also has 'positive' obligations to take action in some cases – most obviously to protect those who are in some way vulnerable. *X and Y v Netherlands*,[9] for example, concerned a 16-year-old with learning difficulties who had been raped. The state failed to prosecute the rapist and the court held that this failure violated its positive obligations under article 8 to ensure 'practical and effective protection' of individual's personal integrity.

---

2   *R (Razgar) v Secretary of State for the Home Department* [2004] 2 AC 368 per Lord Bingham at [9].
3   *Pretty v UK* (2002) 35 EHRR 1.
4   *Botta v Italy* (1998) 26 EHRR 241.
5   *Hatton v UK* (2003) (Application No 36022/97).
6   *Gaskin v UK* (1989) 12 EHRR 36.
7   *Botta v Italy* (1998) 26 EHRR 241.
8   L Clements and J Read, 'The dog that didn't bark', in L Lawson and C Gooding (eds), *Disability rights in Europe: from theory to practice*, Hart Publishing, 2005.
9   (1985) 8 EHRR 235.

2.7   The positive obligations under the ECHR extend not merely to protecting vulnerable people from harm and prosecuting their abusers. There is also in certain circumstances a positive obligation on the state to take action to ensure the fulfilment of article 8 rights. For example, where a child's welfare is at stake, 'article 8 may require the provision of welfare support in a manner which enables family life to continue'.[10] Article 8 may also require states to take action to 'ameliorate and compensate' for the restrictions that disabled people experience – as Judge Greve of the ECtHR held in *Price v UK* (2002):

> In a civilised country like the United Kingdom, society considers it not only appropriate but a basic humane concern to try to improve and compensate for the disabilities faced by a person in the applicant's situation. In my opinion, these compensatory measures come to form part of the disabled person's physical integrity.[11]

2.8   It has been held that the 'very essence of the Convention is respect for human dignity'[12] and with this understanding comes an obligation on states to ensure that the supports made available to disabled people ensure they are not subjected to 'indignity'. In *R (Bernard) v Enfield LBC*[13] for example, the court found a violation of article 8 through the delay in provision of proper toileting – holding that providing accessible toileting facilities to a disabled woman 'would have restored her dignity as a human being'. Similarly, in *R (A, B, X and Y) v East Sussex CC and the Disability Rights Commission (No 2)*, Munby J (as he then was) held that the:

> Recognition and protection of human dignity is one of the core values – in truth the core value – of our society and, indeed, of all the societies which are part of the European family of nations and which have embraced the principles of the Convention.[14]

Other key conventions: children and disability

2.9   Alongside the ECHR, two other international human rights conventions are of direct relevance to disabled children. Firstly, the UN Convention on the Rights of the Child (UNCRC) creates a host of basic rights which should be enjoyed by all children. The UNCRC has

---

10 *Anufrijeva v Southwark LBC* [2004] QB 1124 per Lord Woolf at [43].

11 (2002) 34 EHRR 1285: a case that concerned article 3 – ie, the right not to be subjected to 'degrading treatment'.

12 *Pretty v UK* (2002) 35 EHRR 1 at [65].

13 [2002] EWHC 2282 (Admin); (2002) 5 CCLR 577 at [33].

14 [2003] EWHC 167 (Admin); (2003) 6 CCLR 194 at [86].

been ratified by every UN member state bar Somalia and the USA. It is therefore as close as possible to a universally agreed international human rights treaty. The ECtHR has held that the ECHR should be interpreted as far as possible in accordance with other rules of international law.[15] Furthermore, any ambiguity in the domestic legal framework affecting children should be resolved where possible through reference to the UNCRC.[16] In a 2006 judgment, Baroness Hale extended the obligation to read domestic legislation in accordance with the UNCRC still further:

> Even if an international treaty has not been incorporated into domestic law, our domestic legislation has to be construed so far as possible so as to comply with the international obligations which we have undertaken. When two interpretations of these regulations are possible, the interpretation chosen should be that which better complies with the commitment to the welfare of children which this country has made by ratifying the United Nations Convention on the Rights of the Child.[17]

2.10   Articles in the UNCRC of particular relevance to disabled children include:

- article 2 – non-discrimination;
- article 3 – the best interests of the child to be a primary consideration;
- article 4 – states to use the 'maximum extent' of available resources to realise children's economic, social and cultural rights;
- article 12 – the right to participation; and
- article 24 – the right to the 'highest attainable standard of health'.

2.11   Article 23 of the UNCRC relates specifically to disabled children. It requires states to recognise that disabled children should enjoy 'full and decent' lives. It further recognises the right of disabled children to 'special care'. Such support is to be provided to disabled children free of charge where possible, subject to resources. The aim of such support should be to allow every child to achieve 'the fullest possible social integration and individual development'.

2.12   The second international human rights convention of direct relevance to disabled children in the UK is the UN Convention on the Rights of Persons with Disabilities (Disability Convention) which the

---

15   *Forgarty v UK* (2001) 34 EHRR 302 at [35]–[36].

16   See, for example, *Mabon v Mabon* [2005] EWCA Civ 634; [2005] Fam 366.

17   *Smith v Smith and another* [2006] UKHL 35; [2006] 1 WLR 2024 at [78].

UK ratified in June 2009. In accordance with the general principles discussed above, the rights enshrined in the Disability Convention should be taken into account when there is any ambiguity in domestic law and in interpreting the ECHR, particularly article 8. The ECtHR has already recognised that the Disability Convention is an important reference point for the interpretation of article 8.[18]

2.13　Important articles in the Disability Convention for disabled children include:

- article 3 – general principles, including 'respect for inherent dignity' and 'full and effective participation and inclusion in society';
- article 9 – accessibility; and
- article 19 – independent living and inclusion in the community.

2.14　As with the UNCRC, there is a specific article in the Disability Convention (article 7) relating to disabled children. Article 7(1) requires states to:

> Take all necessary measures to ensure the full enjoyment by children with disabilities of all human rights and fundamental freedoms on an equal basis with other children.

2.15　Article 7(2) reinforces the UNCRC article 3 requirement that in all actions concerning a disabled child, the child's best interests shall be a primary consideration. Similarly, article 7(3) reinforces the right to participation under UNCRC article 12, requiring states to provide 'disability and age-appropriate assistance' to help disabled children realise this right.

2.16　Furthermore, article 23(3) specifically requires that disabled children have equal rights in respect of family life, and requires states to provide 'early and comprehensive information, services and support' to prevent 'concealment, abandonment, neglect and segregation' of disabled children. Under article 23(5), where the immediate family is unable to care for a disabled child, the state must make 'every effort' to find alternative care within the wider family or in a family setting in the community.

2.17　Article 24 of the Disability Convention concerns education. In particular, it requires states to establish an 'inclusive education system'. Disabled people have a right to be educated 'on an equal basis with others in the communities in which they live': article 24(2)(b).

18　See *Glor v Switzerland*, Application no 13444/04, 30 April 2009 and *Alajos Kiss v Hungary*, Application no 38832/06, 20 May 2010.

2.18   The UK government has entered a reservation to article 24 in relation to residential education[19] in the following terms:

> The United Kingdom reserves the right for disabled children to be
> educated outside their local community where more appropriate
> education provision is available elsewhere. Nevertheless, parents
> of disabled children have the same opportunity as other parents to
> state a preference for the school at which they wish their child to be
> educated.[20]

2.19   The UK government has also made a declaration in relation to article
24 to provide a definition of the meaning of 'inclusion':

> The United Kingdom Government is committed to continuing to
> develop an inclusive system where parents of disabled children have
> increasing access to mainstream schools and staff, which have the
> capacity to meet the needs of disabled children.
>
> The General Education System in the United Kingdom includes
> mainstream and special schools, which the UK Government under-
> stands is allowed under the Convention.[21]

2.20   This declaration reflects the government's position that the law relating to special educational needs in Part IV of the Education Act 1996
(as amended by the Special Educational Needs and Disability Act
2001) establishes an 'inclusive education system' while preserving a
role for special schools to meet the needs of children with more complex needs. This question is further considered at paras 1.58–1.59 and
more fully in chapter 4.

2.21   The UK has also ratified the Optional Protocol to the Disability
Convention, which permits individuals and groups to petition the
UN Disability Committee in Geneva where there are alleged viola-
tions of rights protected by the Disability Convention. As is normal
with international conventions there is a prior requirement to exhaust
domestic remedies before sending a 'communication' to the Disability Committee.[22] However, this still raises the prospect that where the
rights enshrined in the Disability Convention are not incorporated
into domestic law and cannot properly be read into the ECHR, then
a remedy may be obtained through the Disability Committee.

---

19 The issue of residential special school provision is discussed further at paras
    4.74–4.80.
20 Accessible at www.un.org/disabilities/default.asp?id=475.
21 Accessible at www.un.org/disabilities/default.asp?id=475.
22 Optional Protocol, article 2(d).

The hierarchy of domestic law

2.22   The simplest model for expressing the domestic law in relation to disabled children is to think of a pyramid, with a relatively small set of primary statutes at the top, a larger set of subordinate legislation – regulations, orders and rules – in the middle and a still larger group of statutory guidance documents at the base. Each layer of the pyramid provides greater detail as to the powers and duties of the different agencies involved with disabled children and families. Under HRA 1998, the entire pyramid must be interpreted as far as possible to achieve compatibility with ECHR rights, which in turn are informed by the other international human rights conventions.

2.23   Statutes or 'primary' legislation such as the Children Act (CA) 1989, the Education Act (EA) 1996 and the Equality Act 2010 are the simplest layer of the pyramid to understand. Put simply, these are the most important of our 'laws'. The role of the courts is to interpret the intention of parliament when enacting these laws and to give effect to their ordinary meaning: but also, in doing so, to endeavour to interpret them in a way that does not conflict with international human rights standards. Subordinate or secondary legislation (for example the Education (Special Educational Needs) (England) (Consolidation) Regulations 2001) has the same legal force as primary statutes. These rules and regulations are made under a specific statute by the relevant government minister and are subject to approval by parliament. Rules and regulations will normally go into more detail than the statute under which they are made, prescribing such matters as processes to be followed, timescales and so on.

2.24   At the bottom of the pyramid, guidance is – essentially – advice issued by government to explain what the law requires and to suggest how it may be complied with. Unlike the law (which we must all obey) guidance does not have to be followed slavishly if there are good reasons to depart from it. Problematically, however, there are two types of guidance and one ('statutory guidance') is much more binding than the other (often called 'practice guidance').

2.25   Statutory guidance is issued under a specific statutory provision, most frequently in relation to disabled children under section 7 of the Local Authority Social Services Act (LASSA) 1970. The courts will therefore expect decision-makers to treat the guidance in whatever way the primary statute requires. Sometimes the duty will be to 'act under' or to act 'in accordance' with the guidance, in which case the courts are unlikely to tolerate much deviation from it. For other guidance the duty set out in the primary statute is merely to 'have regard' to it. When this is the duty, decision-makers are generally expected to follow the guidance unless there is good reason not to do so. In *R v Islington LBC ex p Rixon*[23] the court set out precisely what local authorities have to do with guidance issued under LASSA 1970 s7:

> Parliament in enacting s 7(1) did not intend local authorities to whom ministerial guidance was given to be free, having considered it, to take it or leave it ... Parliament by s7(1) has required local authorities to follow the path charted by the Secretary of State's guidance, with liberty to deviate from it where the local authority judges on admissible grounds that there *is* good reason to do so, but without freedom to take a substantially different course.

2.26   It is often in statutory guidance that we find the most important duties in relation to disabled children – for instance, the duty to assess needs and produce a 'realistic plan of action' to meet those needs under CA 1989 s17.[24] Some of the most important examples of statutory guidance referred to in detail later in this book are:

- Framework for the Assessment of Children in Need and their Families (see, for example, paras 3.14–3.24);
- Special Educational Needs Code of Practice (see para 4.9);
- Improving Behaviour and Attendance (the school exclusions guidance, see para 4.114).

2.27   Where government issues 'practice guidance', for instance the *Assessing children in need and their families* (2000) practice guidance (see para 3.18 onwards), it is less coercive and public bodies have more freedom to deviate from it – where they have sound reasons for so doing. Nevertheless the advice it contains is something that must be taken into account when that body makes a decision and if the decision is at significant variance from the approach required in the guidance, the courts may (in the absence of compelling reasons) be prepared to find the decision to be made unlawfully.[25]

---

23 (1997–98) 1 CCLR 119 at [123].
24 Department of Health, *Framework for the assessment of children in need and their families*, 2000.
25 *R v Islington LBC ex p Rixon* (1997–98) 1 CCLR 119 at 131E.

Powers and duties

2.28 Public bodies such as local authorities are 'creatures of statute'. This means that they can only do things that they are permitted or required to do by Acts of parliament and secondary legislation. There is at present no 'general power of competency' (as some people say there should be) for local authorities to act outside of the statutory framework. There is, however, an important broad power in the Local Government Act (LGA) 2000 s2 for any local authority to do anything which is likely to promote the well-being of their area. This section looks at the different types of duties and powers, because understanding how these duties and powers operate is critical to determining whether disabled children and families have an entitlement to a particular service or benefit. In general terms, 'a power need not be exercised, but a duty must be discharged',[26] but as is set out below the nature of an individual power or duty is often much more subtle and nuanced.

2.29 First, legislation frequently places mandatory duties on public bodies, signified by the use of language such a 'shall' and 'must'. Some of the things parliament requires public bodies to do are expressed as 'specific' duties; a key example of this is CA 1989 s20(1), which requires local authorities to provide accommodation to *every* child who meets the qualifying criteria. Where a specific duty arises, it is appropriate to speak of the child as having a 'right' to a service.

2.30 Other duties are expressed in more general terms; for instance, CA 1989 s17(1), which creates a general duty to assess and provide services for children 'in need' (see chapter 3). This duty has been held by the courts not to be owed to each individual child in need but generally to all children in need in the local authority's area. Therefore, a child in need cannot rely on section 17 alone to claim a right to a service, although this right may be found in other legislation and statutory guidance (see paras 3.25–3.77). General duties are also often described as 'target' duties, meaning that parliament has set local authorities a 'target' but has not intended a failure to meet that target to give rise to a legal challenge for an individual aggrieved person. Target duties are essentially 'aspirational' in nature, so that the public body subject to the duty can take resource factors into account in determining how best to meet the aspiration.[27] Target duties cannot be ignored but generally require a public authority only

---

26 *R (G) v Barnet LBC* [2003] UKHL 57; [2004] 2 AC 208 per Lord Nicholls at [12].
27 C Callaghan, 'What is a "target duty"?', (2000) 5 *Judicial Review*, pp184–187.

to 'do its best',[28] not to achieve compliance with the duty in every individual case.

2.31   Parliament also gives local authorities 'powers', essentially a discretion to do something (eg to provide a service) but no duty (general or specific) to do so – frequently signified in legislation by the use of the word 'may'. An example is the power in the LGA 2000 s2 set out above. No individual can claim a right to a service which a public body only has a power to provide. However, public bodies must exercise their powers rationally, reasonably and fairly and it may be that certain powers have to be exercised in certain situations (for example, the power for local authorities to accommodate families together under CA 1989 s17(6) if the family are homeless and cannot access other accommodation by reason of their immigration status). What public bodies cannot do is to decide never to use a power, or decide only to use it in a specific way: this is known, in legal jargon, as 'fettering a discretion'. So if parliament has given a public body a power to do something, then each time the opportunity arises when it could use this power, it must consider whether or not to exercise it. The public body cannot decide never to use the power, or never to use it for the benefit of certain groups of people, for to do so would be to act against the will of parliament.

Key local structures/processes

2.32   In England, the Children Act (CA) 2004 radically transformed the structures of the agencies responsible for delivering services to children and families. In particular, the CA 2004 created:

- a Children's Commissioner for England, to promote 'awareness of the views and interests of children in England'[29] (Wales has had a Children's Commissioner for several years longer as a result of the Children's Commissioner for Wales Act 2001);
- lead Members for Children's Services – elected councillors in every children's services authority with direct responsibility for children's services, reporting to the council leader;[30]
- Directors of Children's Services – senior officers (replacing Directors of Education and the children's services role of Directors

---

28 *R v Radio Authority ex p Bull* [1998] QB 294 at 309.

29 CA 2004 s2(1).

30 CA 2004 s19.

of Social Services) with management responsibility for all children's services;[31] and

- the requirement for every children's services authority to produce a children and young people's plan.[32]

2.33 The coalition government in England has announced its intention to row back on some of these developments, for instance the requirement to produce a children and young people's plan and the requirement for local areas to organise themselves into Children's Trusts (see para 2.36).[33] However, such changes require either primary or secondary legislation and until this legislation comes into force the CA 2004 scheme continues to apply.

2.34 Chapter 1 has described the difficulties that families have in finding their way around complex services that do not co-operate effectively with one another: see paras 1.43–1.44. While the importance of effective collaboration between different services has long been recognised, research and official reports testify to the fact that it has proved difficult to achieve.[34] In an attempt to deal with this problem, the CA 2004 imposed important interlocking duties on relevant agencies to safeguard and promote the well-being of children. Under CA 2004 s10, each children's services authority is required to make arrangements to co-operate with its relevant partners. The list of relevant partners is extensive and includes all the local health agencies and the youth offending team.[35] Relevant partners are required to co-operate with the authority in the making of these arrangements and

---

31 CA 2004 s18.

32 CA 2004 s17. See the Children and Young People's Plan (England) Regulations 2005 SI No 2149, as amended by the Children and Young People's Plan (England) (Amendment) Regulations 2007 SI No 57, for what is required to be covered in each plan.

33 Department for Education news article, 'Reform of children's trusts', 22 July 2010.

34 Audit Commission, *Services for disabled children: a review of services for disabled children and their families*, Audit Commission Publications, 2003; V Greco and P Sloper, 'Care co-ordination and key worker schemes for disabled children: results of a UK-wide survey', (2004) 30 *Child: care, health and development*, pp13–20; R Townsley, D Abbott and D Watson, *Making a difference? Exploring the impact of multi-agency working on disabled children with complex healthcare needs, their families and the professional who support them*, Policy Press, 2003.

35 From 12 January 2010, the list of relevant partners in CA 2004 s10 includes the responsible body for schools, this requirement having been inserted by Apprenticeships, Children, Skills and Learning Act 2009 s193. However, the forthcoming Education Bill 2010 may seek to remove this requirement.

the aim of these arrangements must be to improve the well-being of children in terms of the five 'Every Child Matters' outcomes.[36]

2.35   The authority and its relevant partners are each required by CA 2004 s11 to make arrangements to ensure that 'their functions are discharged having regard to the need to safeguard and promote the welfare of children'.[37] This convoluted wording has some similarities to the general equality duty under the Equality Act 2010: see paras 9.73–9.85. What it means in practice is that in carrying out any functions, whether at a strategic or an individual case level, public bodies such as local authorities and primary care trusts must do so having regard to the need to promote children's welfare. Any agency taking a decision not to provide services to an individual disabled child or to tighten eligibility to services generally must be able to show how such a decision fits with this duty.

2.36   The duty to co-operate in CA 2004 s10 has been strengthened by statutory guidance re-issued in November 2008[38] which requires local areas to establish Children's Trusts. The guidance defines a Children's Trust as 'local area partnership led by the local authority bringing together the key local agencies' to improve the well-being of children. The Apprenticeships, Children, Skills and Learning Act 2009 envisages that Children's Trust Boards will be placed on a statutory footing, inserting a new section 12A into CA 2004. However, it is unclear whether this development will survive the focus on greater local autonomy which is central to the new coalition government in England.

2.37   The intended effect of all these changes is to create greater accountability and a more seamless delivery of services to children, including disabled children. It remains to be seen the extent to which these new general duties make a real difference to the lives of disabled children and whether they will be taken seriously by the courts. To date, there are only a handful of reported cases where the court has considered the CA 2004 duties: see, for example, *R(B) v Barnet LBC*,[39] a case where the local authority was held to have breached the CA 2004 s11 duty in relation to a severely disabled child with inappropriately sexualised behaviour. It therefore falls to families

---

36   CA 2004 s10(2), see para 5.10.
37   CA 2004 s11(2), see para 3.27. The education functions of a children's services authority are excluded from the CA 2004 s11 duty, because this duty is mirrored in relation to those functions by Education Act 2002 s175.
38   Department for Children, Schools and Families (DCSF) *Children's Trusts: Statutory guidance on inter-agency co-operation to improve well-being of children, young people and their families.*
39   [2009] EWHC 2842 (Admin); (2009) 12 CCLR 679.

and their legal advisers to make sure that the duties in CA 2004 are taken seriously by children's services authorities, their partners and if necessary the courts.

Routes to redress

Judicial review

2.38   The courts will take action if a public body (eg a local authority or NHS Trust) is in breach of its legal obligations. Generally this is achieved by way of a individual bringing a 'judicial review' action before the High Court – essentially asking the court to 'review' whether a decision, action or inaction by a public body is lawful. Such cases normally take place either in London or (if the case concerns a failure by a Welsh authority) in Cardiff. However, the courts are now keen to see such applications brought in the English regions and judicial review proceedings should now be issued in the regional centre with which the child and family have the closest connection. The High Court has various 'divisions' and most commonly cases of this nature come before what is known as the Administrative Court. The willingness of the court to intervene if public bodies are acting unlawfully is shown by the large number of cases cited in this book. However, judicial review is intended to be a remedy of last resort and before launching judicial review proceedings, it is essential to consider if there are any other alternative remedies which are *'convenient and effective'*.[40] It is also essential to ensure that any application for judicial review is brought 'promptly' and in any event no later than three months after the relevant decision has been taken.[41] Judicial review proceedings are issued using a claim form (N461) and it will often be necessary in cases involving a disabled child to ask the court to give 'urgent consideration' to the application using a form N463.

2.39   A vital issue to consider prior to commencing any application for judicial review is costs. At present,[42] the general rule in civil litigation applies to judicial review, so that the loser has to pay the winner's

---

40   *Kay v Lambeth LBC* [2006] UKHL 10; [2006] 2 AC 465 per Lord Bingham at [30].
41   Civil Procedure Rules 1998 (CPR) 54.5.
42   The Jackson Review of the costs of civil litigation has made recommendations which, if adopted, would generally prevent claimants in judicial review proceedings facing the risk of having to pay the defendant's costs. See Jackson LJ, *Review of Civil Litigation Costs*, The Stationery Office, December 2009, chapter 30.

costs. This means that if a family sought judicial review of a local authority's failure to properly assess their disabled child's needs and the court held that what the authority had done was in fact lawful, the family could be ordered to pay the authority's legal costs, which would be likely to amount to tens of thousands of pounds. The main way to avoid any risk of costs being awarded against a family is to obtain 'legal aid' funding, as legal aid brings with it 'costs protection', so that any costs awarded to the authority in the above scenario would be payable by the Legal Services Commission, not the family.

2.40   The further problem which then arises is that eligibility for civil legal aid has been substantially restricted so that many 'ordinary' families will not meet the financial eligibility criteria. However, in cases involving disabled children it may be possible to make the application for funding in the child's name, so that the child's financial means are taken into account rather than the parents. Individuals who want to know if they are financially eligible for legal aid can use the calculator on the Community Legal Advice website.[43] However, anyone who is seriously considering whether they can and should bring judicial review proceedings should contact a specialist solicitor at the first available opportunity. Solicitors will be able to advise in more detail on eligibility for legal aid and will often offer a low fixed fee for an initial consultation before legal aid is in place.

Children Act 1989 complaints procedures

2.41   Where a disabled child or his or her family wish to challenge a decision by a public body (for example, a local authority or an NHS body) then formal complaints procedures exist to ensure that these complaints are processed properly. Frequently, however, effective redress can be achieved more quickly through the political process – for example, by finding out who the 'lead member' (councillor) is for children's services and complaining to him or her – or by meeting the local MP at his or her constituency surgery. Additionally, however, public bodies are required to operate formal complaints procedures to allow aggrieved persons to seek redress from the body in question. For disabled children who are 'looked after', CA 1989 s26 mandates a procedure for case reviews when there are issues with the quality of provision being made.

2.42   As a result, in England and Wales similar procedures exist by which disabled children and their families are enabled to complain

43   Available at www.communitylegaladvice.org.uk/en/legalaid/index.jsp.

about the way a council has acted in relation to their social care needs. In each case the procedures are detailed in regulations[44] which are then amplified in statutory guidance.[45] Complaints concerning social care services (or the lack of them) are dealt with under a three-stage process, as set out below. Councils should respond to any complaint by sending a letter explaining how the process operates and providing the names and addresses of key contacts. The three stages comprise:

Stage 1 – local resolution

The aim of a good complaints system is to resolve complaints as quickly, informally and as 'locally' as possible. At the first stage, therefore, the complaint would be considered by the local manager of the service subject to the complaint, who would then be expected to respond within ten working days – although this can be extended for a further ten days if the complaint is complex.

If for any reason a satisfactory response is not provided within the above timescales, or the response is not acceptable, then the complaint can (if a request is made) be moved to the second stage.

Stage 2 – investigation

At the second state the local authority must undertake an investigation (by a nominated complaints officer) and an independent person it appoints. These investigators will meet with all relevant persons and view all relevant materials and will meet with the individual to discuss his or her complaint and the outcomes he or she would like to see. A report is then prepared detailing their findings and making any relevant recommendations. The investigation should be completed within 25 working days although it may be extended to a maximum of 65 days.

Stage 3 – review panel

If the complainant remains dissatisfied a request can be made for the complaint to be considered by a review panel. In England this will involve the council appointing three independent people to convene

44 Children Act 1989 Representations Procedure (England) Regulations 2006 SI No 1738 and, in Wales, the Representations Procedure (Children) (Wales) Regulations 2005 SI No 3365 (W262).

45 In England, Department for Education and Skills, *Getting the best from complaints: social care complaints and representations for children, young people and others*, 2006; in Wales, Welsh Assembly, *Listening and learning: a guide to handling complaints and representations in local authority social services in Wales*, 2006.

a meeting with the relevant persons at which they review the way the complaint has been conducted and its findings and then the panel make recommendations. In Wales the review stage is conducted by an independent panel appointed and administered by the Assembly.

2.43   A sample complaint letter which can be adapted for use by parents dissatisfied with their local authority's approach is provided below. Further precedent letters will be provided alongside the online version of this book.

Sample local authority complaint letter

From: [name and address]

To: Director of Children's Services, [name and address]

Date

Dear [name]

Formal Complaint

[Name and date of birth of child]

I ask that you treat this letter as a formal complaint concerning the discharge by your authority of its functions in respect of myself and my above named [son/daughter].

I require the complaint to be investigated under the formal complaints process under the Children Act 1989 (as amended). My complaint is:

[Here set out as precisely as possible

(a) what it is that is being complained about

(b) the names of the key social workers [etc] who the complaints investigator will need to speak to;

(c) the dates of the relevant acts/omissions.]

[If possible also enclose copies of any relevant papers.]

What I want to achieve by making this complaint is [here set out as precisely as possible what you want to be the result of your complaint: ie an apology, a changed service provision, an alteration to practice, compensation, etc].

[If relevant include – I do not, however, wish this complaint to in any way undermine my good working relationship with [name of social worker etc].]

I understand that your complaints receiving officer will wish to contact me in order to investigate this complaint. I suggest that this be done by [here give a telephone contact number and the time/days you are normally available or some other convenient way you can be contacted]. I also understand that in investigating this complaint you may need to share information with other relevant parties/agencies and also to access my [daughter's/son's] records. I confirm that I am in agreement to you taking this action – so far as it is strictly necessary, and accordingly give my consent to this, under the Data Protection Act 1998.

Yours ...

2.44   If complainants remain dissatisfied with the outcome of a complaint after the final stage, they are permitted to take the matter further – either by way of a complaint to the relevant ombudsman or by way of a judicial review (see above). However, judicial review remains available prior to complaints being made or dealt with if the situation is sufficiently urgent and there is a clearly arguable error of law in the approach of the authority.

NHS complaints procedures

2.45   The procedures for making a complaint against the NHS (a GP, a hospital or any other NHS body) are stipulated in regulations made in England[46] and Wales[47] as a result of the Social Care (Community Health and Standards) Act 2003 s113. Guidance has also been issued in England[48] and Wales[49] on the procedural requirements – but in

46 National Health Service (Complaints) Regulations 2004 SI No 1768 as amended by the National Health Service (Complaints) Amendment Regulations 2006 SI No 2084.

47 Welsh Assembly, *Directions to NHS trusts and local health boards on hospital complaints procedures* and *Directions to local health boards on dealing with complaints about family health service practitioners, providers of personal medical services and personal dental services other than personal dental services provided by NHS Trusts*, 27 March 2003, accompanied by guidance, *Complaints in the NHS – a guide to handling complaints in Wales*.

48 Department of Health, *Guidance to support implementation of the National Health Service (Complaints) Regulations*, 2004.

49 Welsh Assembly Government, *Complaints in the NHS: a guide to handling complaints in Wales*, 2003.

essence there are two stages in both countries: the first being an investigative stage and the second the possibility of a review panel hearing. In every case, when a complaint is made, the health body must respond – explaining the procedures that will be followed, the statutory timescales and who the key contact person/investigator is with whom the complainant should liaise. The precedent complaint letter (above) can be adapted to be used in such complaints (being addressed to the 'Complaints Manager') within the relevant health body. The same point applies about the availability of judicial review in urgent and serious health cases as made above in relation to children's services.

Ombudsman

2.46   The local government ombudsmen in England (the Public Services Ombudsman in Wales) investigate allegations of 'maladministration' by local authorities. The Parliamentary and Health Service Ombudsman investigates complaints in relation to NHS bodies and government departments. Unlawful actions by public bodies are highly likely to involve maladministration, but acts of maladministration will not necessarily be unlawful. This means that significant incompetence and/or ineptitude which may not be sufficient to establish unlawfulness in the High Court through judicial review can nonetheless found a successful claim to the relevant ombudsman.

2.47   Complaints to the ombudsman need to be made within 12 months of the date on which the person making the complaint knew of the problem. The local authority must have been given an opportunity to remedy the alleged maladministration before a complaint is made to the ombudsman. This means in normal circumstances the applicant must have gone through the relevant formal complaints process (unless, for example, the council has failed to investigate the complaint properly or with proper 'expedition'). Further information is on the ombudsmen's website at www.lgo.org.uk. Information on the Parliamentary and Health Service Ombudsman for complaints in relation to NHS bodies in England is at www.ombudsman.org.uk and in Wales at www.ombudsman-wales.org.uk.

2.48   The ombudsman can and does make powerful rulings in relation to maladministration affecting disabled children and these are illustrated throughout this text. Ombudsman reports frequently result in recommendations for significant remedial action by public bodies, including payment of compensation, and these recommendations are almost always complied with. However, a complaint to the ombudsman is necessarily a lengthy process and will not result in the immediate provision of services which may be required. As such, where disabled children and/or their families are in urgent need of services, it is more likely that the most appropriate course of action will be a judicial review application in the High Court rather than an ombudsman complaint (see paras 2.38–2.40).

Tribunals

2.49 In certain specific areas, parliament has established tribunals to resolve disputes between individuals and public bodies. The vast majority of these tribunals in England have now been unified into a single Tribunals Service. Of most relevance to disabled children is the First-tier Tribunal (Special Educational Needs and Disability), formerly and still commonly known as the Special Education Tribunal or 'SENDIST'. In Wales, the tribunal remains known as the Special Educational Needs Tribunal for Wales.[50] This tribunal deals with disputes between parents, schools and local authorities in relation to special educational needs provision and disability discrimination in education. It is discussed in more detail in chapters 4 and 9. For the majority of cases, the tribunal will provide the appropriate forum for disputes to be resolved. However, for exceptional cases where interim relief is required, it may still be appropriate to issue judicial review applications even if the case is within the scope of SENDIST. The issue is always whether the alternative remedy (in this case the tribunal) is 'convenient and effective' (see para 2.38).

---

50 See http://wales.gov.uk/sentwsub/home/?lang=en.

CHAPTER 3

Children's services

continued

Key points

- All 'disabled' children are children 'in need'.
- The primary duty on children's services authorities is to assess the needs of children in need, including disabled children.
- Once needs have been assessed, a children's services authority has a duty to provide services to meet the assessed needs if certain conditions are met.
- Once needs have been assessed, the children's services authority must put in place a care plan, amounting to a 'realistic plan of action, including services to be provided'.
- Where the criteria in Children Act 1989 s20(1) are met, disabled children must be accommodated.
- Accommodated disabled children have additional rights while 'looked after' and on 'leaving care'.
- Decisions not to assess, provide support or accommodate disabled children can be challenged through the complaints procedure, and (where sufficiently urgent) by judicial review.

Introduction

3.1   Disabled children are children first, and as such should be able to access all the services available to all children. These should include nurseries, playgroups, playgrounds, leisure services, children's centres and mainstream schools. The duties on service-providers to make mainstream and universal services accessible to disabled children are discussed in chapter 9 (equality and non-discrimination). There are also now specific obligations to ensure a sufficient supply of certain services for disabled children, for instance childcare; under the Childcare Act 2006 s6(5),[1] the duty on local authorities to secure sufficient childcare for working parents applies in relation to disabled children up to the age of 18. Duties towards carers and young carers are dealt with in chapter 8.

3.2   This chapter is concerned with the provision of additional services to disabled children by children's services authorities (in Wales still referred to as social services authorities, and sometimes given slightly different names in England, for instance 'Children and Learning Directorate' or similar). It sets out the duties to assess the needs

1   Section 22(5) in Wales: the Childcare Act 2006 is considered further at para 8.26.

of disabled children and discusses the complex issue of when the authority has a duty to provide services to meet the child's assessed needs. It also deals with duties on authorities to accommodate disabled children and the additional rights which should be enjoyed by disabled children who are 'looked after' as a result of being accommodated or who are 'leaving care'. Disabled children's rights to health services, including NHS continuing care, are considered in chapter 5.

3.3   This chapter, like all those that follow, should be read with the realities described in chapter 1 in mind. As we have noted (see paras 1.43–1.44 above), for many families the social care system is one of baffling complexity and dealing with it amounts to additional, tiring and frustrating work. Not infrequently the system requires parents to attend multiple meetings where they repeat the same information to a range of unfamiliar specialists in different settings. As we noted, in one case a family of a one-year-old child attended (over a nine-month period) 315 service-based appointments in 12 different locations (see para 1.56).

Statutory scheme: disabled children as 'children in need'

3.4   The key legislation governing the provision of additional services to disabled children is the Children Act (CA) 1989 (in particular Part III, 'Local authority support for children and families') and the Chronically Sick and Disabled Persons Act (CSDPA) 1970. The Chronically Sick and Disabled Persons Act 1970 establishes the duty to provide most of the services which disabled children will need. The Children Act 1989 establishes the assessment duty and also requires the provision of certain specific services, particularly residential and foster care short breaks. Assessments made under CA 1989 should also determine whether a child is eligible for support under CSDPA 1970.[2]

3.5   The Children Act 1989 s17(1) creates a general duty on children's services authorities to safeguard and promote the welfare of children within their area who are 'in need'. So far as is consistent with this duty, children's services authorities must promote the upbringing of such children by their families.[3] Children's services authorities

---

2   As specifically provided for by CA 1989 Sch 2 para 3(a).
3   CA 1989 s17(1)(b).

are empowered to provide 'a range and level of services' to meet the needs of 'children in need'. The work of authorities under CA 1989 Part III should be directed at (among other things) avoiding the need for care proceedings under CA 1989 Part IV by providing effective family support.[4]

3.6 The definition of 'children in need' is to be found at CA 1989 s17(10), which provides that a child is to be taken as 'in need' if:

(a) he is unlikely to achieve or maintain, or to have the opportunity of achieving or maintaining, a reasonable standard of health or development without the provision for him of services by a local authority . . .; or

(b) his health or development is likely to be significantly impaired, or further impaired, without the provision for him of such services; or

(c) he is disabled.

3.7 At subsection (11) the definition of 'disabled' for the purposes of CA 1989 Part III is given as follows:

For the purposes of this Part, a child is disabled if he is blind, deaf or dumb or suffers from mental disorder of any kind or is substantially and permanently handicapped by illness, injury or congenital deformity or such other disability as may be prescribed.

3.8 This definition is closely related to the definition of a disabled adult in the National Assistance Act 1948 s29. It is outdated and excessively medical in its approach; however, it has the practical advantage of being extremely broad. In particular, the phrase 'mental disorder of any kind' encompasses a wide range of conditions, including Asperger syndrome/high-functioning autism, attention deficit hyperactivity disorder (ADHD) and attention deficit disorder (ADD) as well as impairments such as learning disability, mental illness and personality disorder. All such conditions fall within the Mental Health Act 1983 s1(2), which defines 'mental disorder' as including 'any disorder or disability of mind'. Additionally, a mental disorder will generally amount to a disability within the definition in the Equality Act 2000 s6,[5] and accordingly any difference in treatment of such persons will be liable to challenge as unlawful disability discrimination – see, for example, *Governing Body of X School v SP and others*.[6]

---

4   CA 1989 Sch 2 para 7(a)(i).
5   Formerly Disability Discrimination Act 1995 s1.
6   [2008] EWHC 389 (Admin) and see also chapter 9 below regarding the definitions of 'disability' and 'discrimination' under the Equality Act 2010.

3.9   In the absence of any confirmed diagnosis, a child may still be a 'child in need' by virtue of requiring services for the reasons specified in section 17(10)(a) or (b). Moreover, any insistence on a medical diagnosis by a children's services authority before a child is deemed to be 'disabled' within section 17(10)(c) might be considered anomalous given the professed universal social work commitment to the 'social model' of disability (see paras 1.5–1.7). In any event, there is a low threshold for social care assessments,[7] which should be carried out if a child *may be* 'in need' (one of the potential outcomes of the assessment being a decision that he or she is not in fact 'in need').

Social work service/key workers

3.10   Although the policy guidance[8] (see para 3.14) expects that social workers will take the lead in assessing children in need, this is not a statutory requirement and a child's needs must be assessed even if the child (or the child's family) has no social worker assigned to them. Local authorities must, however, ensure that they 'secure the provision of adequate staff'[9] to discharge these various roles and where harm results from delay caused by staff shortages, it will constitute maladministration.[10]

3.11   Given the difficulties that parents and children have in obtaining information and accessing fragmented and unco-ordinated services, it is little wonder that many families value the allocation of a particular worker to them and refer to the positive impact that a capable and conscientious key worker can have on their lives.[11] Models of service and

7   See *R v Bristol CC ex p Penfold* (1997–98) 1 CCLR 315 in relation to the duty to assess adults who may be in need of community care services.

8   Department of Health, *Framework for the assessment of children in need and their families*, 2000, pp30 and 39; and Welsh Assembly, *Framework for assessing children in need and their families*, 2001, pp32 and 41.

9   Local Authority Social Services Act 1970 s6(6).

10 Report on complaint no 05/C/18474 against Birmingham City Council, 4 March 2008, where the ombudsman referred to Birmingham's 'corporate failure to ensure adequate resourcing and performance of its services to highly vulnerable people' (para 55).

11 S Mukherjee, B Beresford and P Sloper, *Unlocking key working: an analysis and evaluation of keyworker services for families with disabled children*, Policy Press, 1999; Audit Commission, *Services for disabled children: a review of services for disabled children and their families*, Audit Commission Publications, 2003; R Townsley, D Abbott and D Watson, *Making a difference? Exploring the impact of multi-agency working on disabled children with complex healthcare needs, their families and the professional who support them*, Policy Press, 2003; P Sloper,

the recommended roles for key workers vary, but central key worker tasks include being the single point of contact for the family, the key source of information and guidance, the mediator and facilitator with other professionals across agency boundaries and the co-ordinator of provision, as well as acting as an advocate and source of personal support. An individual in this position is well-placed not only to provide essential information but also to act as a guide through complex service structures, to take the strain of negotiation from the parents and to help them to access services. Key workers can be effective in relieving the stress often experienced by parents. While the first official recommendation that children and their families should have a single professional to act as their main point of contact was made in 1976,[12] research over subsequent decades has highlighted how patchy developments have been in this respect.[13] The government in England has long professed a commitment to key workers and has issued a range of guidance documents on the role of the 'lead professional'.[14]

3.12   In the following paragraphs, we detail the legal duties of local authorities in relation to assessment. There are, however, some very basic principles which should underpin all assessments of disabled children and their families.[15] Assessments should be needs-led rather than dictated by available provision. In consultation with all the children and adults concerned, the assessment process should identify first, the barriers that inhibit the child and family living an ordinary life and second, what can be done by the support agencies to tackle them.[16] Assessment should take account of the needs of the whole family and individuals within it; while some services may be provided directly to a disabled child, others may be offered to parents or siblings (see chapter 8 for duties to adult and child carers). The agreed

P Greco, V Beecham and R Webb, 'Key worker services for disabled children: what characteristics of services lead to better outcomes for children and families?', (2006) 32 *Child: care, health and development*, pp147–157.

12   Court Report, *Fit for the future: report of the committee on child health services*, Cmnd 6684, HMSO, 1976.

13   V Greco and P Sloper, 'Care co-ordination and key worker schemes for disabled children: results of a UK-wide survey', (2004) 30 *Child: care, health and developments*, pp13–20.

14   See, for example, Children's Workforce Development Council, *Lead professional: practitioners' and managers' guides*, 2007, refreshed March 2010.

15   For a more detailed discussion of good assessment practice, see J Read, L Clements and D Ruebain, *Disabled children and the law: research and good practice*, 2nd edn, Jessica Kingsley Publishers, 2006.

16   See, for example, Department for Education and Skills, *Together from the start: practical guidance for professionals working with disabled children (birth to third birthday) and their families*, 2003.

provision or arrangements following assessment may not necessarily take the form of what are usually seen as social care services.[17] There has also been a growing emphasis on assessment practice that adopts an outcome focus. This means that the practitioner undertaking the assessment, together with the children and adults in the family, identifies a range of outcomes that are important to help the family to live a more ordinary life. All involved then agree on the provision that could make those outcomes happen.[18] The effectiveness of any intervention is then judged on the extent to which the identified outcomes are achieved. Assessments should be undertaken and provision put in place promptly and children and their families should not have to wait for essential services. Early intervention is regarded as important in order to avoid families reaching crisis point.[19] Finally, because children grow and develop and family circumstances change, assessment of need should not be seen as a one-off event but should be repeated as required, while avoiding the burden that unnecessary repetitious assessments impose on families.

Duty to assess

3.13   Although CA 1989 contains no explicit duty on children's services authorities to assess the needs of disabled children and their families,[20] the House of Lords in *R (G) v Barnet LBC and others*[21] held that such a specific obligation to assess under CA 1989[22] did exist.

17 Department of Health, *Carers and Disabled Children Act: practice guidance*, TSO, 2001.

18 See Department of Health, *Carers and Disabled Children Act: practice guidance*, TSO, 2001; J Cavet and P Sloper, 'Participation by disabled children in individual decisions about their lives and in public decisions about service development', (2004) 18 *Children and Society* pp278–290; P Rabiee, P Sloper and B Beresford, 'Desired outcomes for children and young people with complex health care needs and children who do not use speech for communication', (2005) 135 *Health and Social Care in the Community* pp478–487.

19 HM Treasury and Department for Education and Skills, *Aiming high for disabled children: better support for families*, 2007.

20 There is such an express duty to assess in the primary legislation for adult social care: see NHS and Community Care Act 1990 s47.

21 [2003] UKHL 57; (2003) 6 CCLR 500 – the view was expressed by Lords Hope, Nicholls and Scott and influenced in part by the requirement in CA 1989 Sch 2 para 1 that 'Every local authority shall take reasonable steps to identify the extent to which there are children in need within their area'.

22 The issue in *R (G) v Barnet* was whether CA 1989 s17 created a specific duty to provide services, in particular accommodation. Lord Nicholls was in the

3.14 Any doubt as to whether there is a duty to assess the needs of children who are or may be 'in need' is resolved by the relevant statutory guidance, *Framework for the assessment of children in need and their families* ('the Assessment Framework')[23] which requires children's services authorities to undertake assessments adopting a child- and family-centred approach. The Assessment Framework is statutory guidance (see paras 2.24–2.27) issued under Local Authority Social Services Act (LASSA) 1970 s7 and as such children's services departments are bound to follow it unless there is good reason not to do so.[24] It is over 100 pages in length and has annexed to it model care plans which themselves occupy 40 pages. The Assessment Framework is the product of considerable research and seeks to ensure that social workers when undertaking an assessment address all aspects of the child's life. Its purpose is therefore to ensure that provision for children in need is not arbitrary or left to chance.

3.15 The Assessment Framework sets out mandatory requirements of the assessment process, including the following:

- A decision as to whether to assess should be made within *one working day* of a referral being received. A referral is defined as a request for services to be provided by the children's services/social services department, and may be made by the family, a professional or indeed anyone involved in or concerned about the care of a disabled child. A decision following a referral may be to take no action, but this remains a decision and should be recorded as such. All decisions should be communicated, with reasons, to the referrer, the parents or caregiver and the child, if appropriate (Assessment Framework, para 3.8).

- If there is a need to gather more information, an initial assessment must be completed *within a maximum of seven working days*. An

minority who held that such a duty did arise; however, his view that there was also a duty to assess was shared by Lord Hope and Lord Scott, who were in the majority. Lord Hope referred (at [77]) to CA 1989 Sch 2 para 3, which allows a children's services authority to assess the needs of a child who appears to be in need at the same time as any assessment under CSDPA 1970 and EA 1996 Part IV (a special educational needs assessment: see paras 4.28–4.44 below).

23 Department of Health, Department for Education and Employment and Home Office, *Framework for the assessment of children in need and their families (policy guidance)*, TSO, 2000: very similar guidance has been issued in Wales by the Welsh Assembly, *Framework for assessing children in need and their families*, TSO, 2001; Welsh Assembly, *Assessing children in need and their families: practice guidance*, 2001 although in this chapter, reference is made to the English guidance.

24 *R v Islington LBC ex p Rixon* (1997–98) 1 CCLR 119 at 123 J–K.

initial assessment can be brief if the child's circumstances allow, but must address all the 'dimensions' set out in the Assessment Framework (see para 3.16 below). It should determine whether the child is 'in need', the nature of any services required, who will provide these services and within what timescales. It should also state whether a further, more detailed core assessment should be undertaken. As part of any initial assessment, the child should be seen (Assessment Framework, paras 3.9–3.10).

• A core assessment is an in-depth assessment which 'addresses the central or most important aspects of the needs of a child'. Although led by children's services, it will invariably involve other agencies (in the case of a disabled child, most often the Primary Care Trust, or in Wales the Health Board). The conclusion of a core assessment should involve analysis of the findings to inform planning, case objectives and service provision. The entire process should be completed within a *maximum of 35 working days* (from the date the initial assessment ended). Appropriate services should be provided while awaiting the completion of the core assessment (Assessment Framework, para 3.11).

• At the conclusion of the assessment the child or the parent should be asked to record their views and comment on the assessment (Assessment Framework, para 3.13).

• Direct work with the child is 'an essential part of assessment'. Assessments of disabled children may therefore require more preparation, more time and potentially specialist expertise in communication (Assessment Framework, para 3.41).[25] This obligation to engage with the child in the assessment process is reinforced by CA 1989 s17(4A),[26] which requires an authority to ascertain and give due consideration to a child's wishes and feelings before deciding what (if any) services to provide to that child. The High Court has stressed that even if a disabled person was felt to be 'completely' prevented from communicating their wishes and feelings, the assessors had a duty to ascertain those wishes and feelings by any possible means.[27] See paras 1.21–1.24 for more on

---

25 Para 3.128 of both Department of Health, *Framework for the assessment of children in need and their families practice guidance*, TSO, 2000 and Welsh Assembly, *Assessing children in need and their families: practice guidance*, TSO, 2001. Also, Welsh Assembly, *Framework for assessing children in need and their families policy guidance*, TSO, 2001, para 3.42.

26 As inserted by CA 2004 s53.

27 *R (A and B) v East Sussex CC* [2003] EWHC 167 (Admin); (2003) 6 CCLR 194.

the fundamental duty to consult with disabled children on decisions about their lives.

3.16 Both an initial assessment and a core assessment must cover the three 'domains' and 20 'dimensions' set out in the Assessment Framework. The 'domains' are (i) the child's developmental needs, (ii) parenting capacity and (iii) family and environmental factors. Important 'dimensions' within these domains for a disabled child are likely to include health, education, emotional and behavioural development and self-care skills (child's developmental needs), ensuring safety (parenting capacity) and housing, family's social integration and community resources (family and environmental factors). 'Involving disabled children in the assessment process' is also listed as a separate 'domain' under family and environmental factors, demonstrating the importance of a genuinely participatory approach to assessment.

3.17 The Assessment Framework is a very prescriptive document and has been criticised for seeking to 'micro-manage' the assessment process. There is an obvious danger that form may trump substance, ie that a document which has all the correct headings for the different 'dimensions' may be produced but there may still be no proper assessment of the child's needs. This is the opposite of the intention of the Assessment Framework and any such document will be unlawful. What is therefore important is not that the assessment *looks* like an initial or core assessment, but that it carefully and accurately sets out and evaluates all the child's needs so a proper decision can be made as to what services (if any) are required to be provided to the child and/or family to meet those needs (see paras 3.45–3.46 on the duty to provide services to meet assessed needs).

3.18 To ensure that assessments addressed the particular needs of specific groups, practice guidance[28] was published at the same time as the Assessment Framework. This practice guidance includes a chapter entitled 'Assessing the needs of disabled children and their families', written by practitioners and containing guidance to ensure that the Assessment Framework is used sensitively and appropriately with disabled children. The practice guidance is a widely overlooked resource and should be consulted more frequently, particularly if the Assessment Framework appears not to address the particular needs of disabled children on a specific issue.

---

28 *Assessing children in need and their families: practice guidance*, Department of Health, 2000 and published in Wales by the National Assembly for Wales (2001).

3.19   As all 'disabled' children are children 'in need', then any referral of a disabled child to children's services should result in an initial assessment. The only time an initial assessment will not be required is if the family are satisfied by services being provided informally through some form of 'local offer'; but if an initial assessment is requested there is no legitimate way for an authority to avoid carrying one out if it accepts that the child is 'disabled' or otherwise 'in need' (see para 3.6).

3.20   The Assessment Framework is silent as to precisely when children's services authorities should move from an initial assessment to a core assessment. The presumption seems to be that if a child has needs which require the involvement of more than one agency, then a core assessment should be carried out. However, as even an initial assessment requires a consideration of the three 'domains' and 20 'dimensions' and must result in a care plan (see para 3.33), there may be little practical difference between the outcome of these different types of assessment – other than that a core assessment should result in much more input from other agencies (eg health) than an initial assessment.

3.21   It is clear from reading the Assessment Framework and its accompanying practice guidance that its primary focus is on the needs of children 'in need' as a result of environmental factors or difficulties within their families, rather than due to disability. In practice, disabled children are the only group of children 'in need' where some sort of parental 'deficit' is not assumed. However, the Assessment Framework clearly applies to *all* assessments of children in need and there is no reason in practice why it cannot be made to work for disabled children, if applied sensitively by professionals who have the necessary expertise. It is also important to recognise that disabled children are vulnerable to abuse and neglect and may therefore be 'in need' for the same reason as other children. Indeed the prevalence of abuse against disabled children and the degree to which is recognised have given rise to concern for some time (see para 1.71).[29]

3.22   The duties under the Assessment Framework have been the subject of significant litigation, which has reinforced their nature as being 'substance' rather than 'form'. In *R (AB and SB) v Nottingham CC*[30] it was held that a failure by an authority to have in place a

---

29   See, for example, H Westcott, 'Disabled children and child protection', in C Robinson and K Stalker (eds), *Growing up with disability*, Jessica Kingsley Publishers, 1998; D Miller, *Disabled children and abuse*, NSPCC, 2002.

30   [2001] EWHC 235 (Admin); (2001) 4 CCLR 294 at 306G–I.

'systematic approach' for conducting a core assessment was an 'impermissible departure from the guidance'. The High Court held further that at the end of the assessment process 'It should be possible to see what help and support the child and family need and which agencies might be best placed to give that help'. The High Court has also established that assessments must address foreseeable future needs as well as present needs; *R (K) v Manchester CC*.[31]

3.23   A failure to carry out a lawful assessment according to the Assessment Framework may result in the court requiring that a new assessment be undertaken.[32] A failure to involve a disabled child in his or her assessment may also render the process unlawful, as was the case in *R (J) v Caerphilly CBC*[33] where it was held that severely challenging behaviour exhibited by a young man did not absolve the authority of its duties to engage him in the assessment.

3.24   Since the Assessment Framework was published, there has been an attempt by central and local government to move away from detailed assessments of 'children in need' towards a more flexible approach, often using what has been termed the 'Common Assessment Framework' (CAF).[34] For younger children, the Early Support Programme and its family support plan, which also applies a simplified assessment process, have had a generally positive response.[35] The idea behind these developments is to streamline the assessment process so it can be used (and shared) by all professionals who have involvement with the relevant child. While such an approach has practical advantages, the fundamental legal duty towards 'children in need' (including disabled children) is to assess their needs in a manner consistent with the Assessment Framework. If families are happy with a less rigorous approach, this may be acceptable in practice. However, any

31 [2006] EWHC 3164; (2007) 10 CCLR 87.
32 *R (G) v Barnet LBC* [2003] UKHL 57; (2003) 6 CCLR 500 per Lord Nicholls at [32].
33 [2005] EWHC 586 (Admin); (2005) 8 CCLR 255. This case is discussed in detail at para 10.73.
34 Department for Children, Schools and Families, *Common assessment framework (CAF)*, 2006, at www.dcsf.gov.uk/everychildmatters/strategy/deliveringservices1/caf/cafframework/.
35 Department for Children, Schools and Families, *Early Support*, 2004, at www.dcsf.gov.uk/everychildmatters/healthandwellbeing/ahdc/earlysupport/home/ – but see P Gilligan and M Manby, *The common assessment framework: does the reality match the rhetoric?* (2008) 32 Child and Family Social Work, pp177–187; S White C Hall and S Peckover, *The descriptive tyranny of the common assessment framework: technologies of categorization and professional practice in child welfare*, (2009) 39 British Journal of Social Work, pp1197–1217; H Bonnick, 'Framework for optimism', (2010) *Community Care* 8, p8.

authority that neglects its assessment duty where a family is less than happy with the approach is likely to find itself criticised by the High Court or the Ombudsman and potentially required by a mandatory order to conduct a lawful initial or core assessment.

Duty to provide services

3.25   There is an expectation in the law and guidance that where disabled children are assessed as having substantial needs, these needs will be met through the provision of services. However, given the longstanding gulf between need and available resources, it is important for families to know when there is a *duty* on a children's services authority to meet need following assessment. This section seeks to answer this unhelpfully complex question.

3.26   In relation to the general expectation that assessed needs will be met, the general duty (see para 2.30) on authorities is to provide services so as to minimise the effects of disabled children's disabilities and give them the opportunity to lead lives which are 'as normal as possible'.[36] Furthermore, the clear expectation of the Assessment Framework is that an initial assessment or core assessment will generally lead to the provision of services. This is demonstrated by para 4.1 (emphasis added):

> The conclusion of an assessment should result in:
> • an analysis of the needs of the child and the parenting capacity to respond appropriately to those needs within their family context;
> • identification of whether and, if so, where intervention will be required to secure the wellbeing of the child or young person;
> • a *realistic plan of action (including services to be provided)*, detailing who has responsibility for action, a timetable and a process for review.

3.27   The duties under CA 1989 s17 and the Assessment Framework are reinforced by the general duty to safeguard and promote the welfare of all children in the authority's area under Children Act (CA) 2004 s11.[37] The statutory guidance[38] to the 2004 Act deals with the application of the duty to individual cases and describes the 'key functions of an effective system' as including that:

36   CA 1989 Sch 2 para 6.
37   Section 28 in Wales.
38   Department for Education and Skills, *Statutory guidance on making arrangements to safeguard and promote the welfare of children under section 11 of the Children Act 2004*, TSO, 2005.

Following assessment, relevant services are provided to respond to the identified needs of children and to support parents/carers in effectively undertaking their parenting roles.[39]

3.28 It is not, however, necessarily the case that services must be provided to meet *every* assessed need. Whether a children's services authority has to provide services following assessment is dependent upon the nature and extent of the need assessed and the consequences of not providing the service. It is also important here not to confuse the decision that a need must be met with the decision on the way to meet the need. For example, a local authority may conclude that there is a need for a child and his or her carers to have a short break from each other. This need can be met in a variety of ways – eg by a way of a sitting service in the child's home, by the child attending a day service or activity away from the home and so on.

The nature of the duty

3.29 The issue of when a specific duty (see para 2.29) arises to provide a service to meet an individual disabled child's identified needs is discussed in detail below. In short, the key issue is whether the criteria for the specific duties in CSDPA 1970 s2 (a duty which is often neglected but is of critical importance, see paras 3.48–3.57) or CA 1989 s20 to arise are met or, if not, whether 'intervention is required' under CA 1989 s17 to 'secure the well-being of the child'. An overview of the service provision decision process is provided first by diagram 1 overleaf.

3.30 Situations where the disabled child's needs require the provision of accommodation will be relatively infrequent. Much more frequently, the local authority will be under a specific duty to provide support in one of the ways identified in CSDPA 1970 s2. Where a child needs a service which is not listed in section 2 of the 1970 Act (for instance a residential short break outside the family home), then the duty is to provide it under CA 1989 s17 to the extent necessary to secure the child's well-being. Whether it is 'necessary' to provide a service to secure an individual disabled child's well-being is entirely case-specific – albeit that it may well be difficult for an authority to justify a decision to provide *no* services following an assessment of a child with moderate or complex disabilities.

39 See guidance at 2.15. For young disabled children under five, the duty to improve the well-being of young children and reduce inequalities between young children in Childcare Act 2006 s1(1) also applies.

Diagram 1: Assessment and service provision decision: stages and questions

Assessment

If a child presents who may be 'in need' (for example, they may be disabled – see para 3.7) , the local authority must undertake an assessment and identify what needs for support or services the child and/or the family have (see paras 3.13–3.15).

Following the assessment, the local authority must decide which of the various needs that have been identified it is 'necessary' to respond to, ie where an 'intervention will be required' (see para 3.26 above). This decision must then be set out in a care plan, amounting to a 'realistic plan of action'. While what is 'necessary' will vary for each individual child, it is highly likely that it will be 'necessary' to provide a service where a failure to so would cause significant harm to the child (and/or the family) – see para 3.43. 'Significant harm' means harm that is more than minor or trivial.

Service provision

If the local authority decides that its support must be provided, for example because a failure to do so is likely to cause significant harm to the child and/or the family, then the following questions should be asked in sequence:

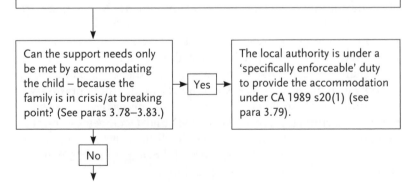

Can the support needs only be met by accommodating the child – because the family is in crisis/at breaking point? (See paras 3.78–3.83.) → Yes → The local authority is under a 'specifically enforceable' duty to provide the accommodation under CA 1989 s20(1) (see para 3.79).

No

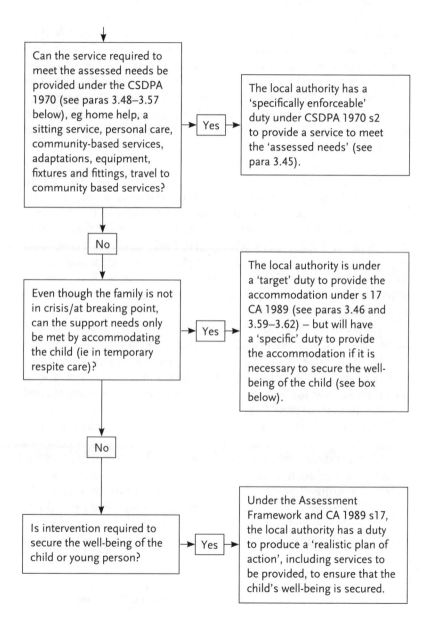

3.31   Unfortunately as a matter of law, the relationship between the 1970 and 1989 Acts is even more perplexing than outlined above. Thankfully this is a technical complexity that is not of relevance in practice. The difficulty arises from the references in CSDPA 1970 s2(1) to National Assistance Act (NAA) 1948 s29, one of the key legislative provisions for adult social care. In essence CSDPA 1970 requires that any services that are provided under section 2(1) are to be provided in the 'exercise of [the authority's] functions' under NAA 1948 s29. In relation to disabled children, this raises two difficulties. The first is that although services under CSDPA s2 can be provided to disabled children,[40] services under NAA 1948 s29 can only be provided to disabled adults. The second concerns the fact that the duty to provide services under NAA 1948 s29 is generally considered to be a 'target' duty whereas the duty to provide under section 2 has been held to be 'specifically enforceable' (see paras 2.28–2.31). In a series of cases the courts have sought to make sense of this drafting minefield[41] and *R (Spink) v Wandsworth LBC*[42] held that: (1) services provided under section 2 of the 1970 Act are in fact provided by a local authority in the 'exercise of their functions' under Part III of the 1989 Act and (2) such services when so provided are provided under a specifically enforceable duty.

3.32   Complex as the legal distinction may be between services provided under the 1970 and 1989 Acts, in practice there is generally going to be little difference in outcomes, since even if a service is provided pursuant to the 'less enforceable' provisions of the 1989 Act, a local authority's scope for declining to provide it are severely constrained (see the analysis at para 3.46).

3.33   Regardless of which duty a local authority is providing services under, it is essential that the nature and extent of the services to be provided are clearly set out in a care plan.[43] The importance of the assessment leading to a 'realistic plan of action' where a child's wellbeing so requires has been demonstrated in a number of cases. In *R (J) v Caerphilly CBC*,[44] the court held that a 'detailed operational plan' should result from the assessment process (in that case the pathway planning process for a young person leaving care, see paras

---

40   CSDPA 1970 s28A.
41   For a review and analysis of the relevant case-law, see L Clements and P Thompson, *Community care and the law*, 4th edn, LAG, 2007, paras 9.134–9.136.
42   [2005] EWCA Civ 302; (2005) 8 CCLR 272 at [34]–[35].
43   See Assessment Framework, 4.32–4.37, 'Plans for children in need'.
44   [2005] EWHC 586 (Admin); (2005) 8 CCLR 255.

10.71–10.73). Similarly, in *R (AB and SB) v Nottingham CC*[45] the council's assessment and care plan were struck down by the court because 'there was no clear identification of needs, or what was to be done about them, by whom and when.'[46] The same approach was followed by the court in *R (S) v Plymouth CC*,[47] where the assessments were quashed because they failed to result in a 'realistic plan of action' to meet the child's needs in relation to housing and respite care.

The service provision decision

3.34   As we have seen above, while children's services authorities are obliged to assess disabled children in accordance with the mandatory requirements of the Assessment Framework, they are not obliged to provide services as a consequence, unless a decision is reached that this should happen (ie because the duty under CSDPA 1970 s2 arises, or under CA 1987 s17 'intervention will be required' to secure the well-being of the child).[48]

3.35   The process of 'so deciding' requires that authorities act rationally, follow agreed procedures which are explained to the child/family in question and produce a decision for which clear and logical reasons are provided. At law, therefore, there are two distinct issues: (1) the process of deciding what services are required (referred to in this chapter as the 'service provision decision'); and (2) the legal consequences that flow once an authority decides that services are required (essentially the enforceability of that decision).

The use of eligibility criteria

3.36   Sadly these distinct processes (the service provision decision and the consequences of the decision) are sometimes confused. The confusion relates to the notion of 'eligibility criteria' – which in itself is not surprising, since as Lord Laming observed in his Victoria Climbié Inquiry Report[49] their use 'to restrict access to services is not found either in legislation or in guidance, and its ill-founded application is

---

45 [2001] EWHC 235 (Admin); (2001) 4 CCLR 294.
46 [2001] EWHC 235 (Admin); (2001) 4 CCLR 294 at [43].
47 [2009] EWHC 1499 (Admin).
48 If a negative service provision decision is made, there is no obligation on the authority to specify what services would have met the assessed needs.
49 Lord Laming, *The Victoria Climbié Inquiry: Report of an Inquiry*, Cm 5730, TSO, 2003.

not something I support'. Eligibility criteria are, of course, criteria which are used to determine eligibility, and the confusion relates to the question: 'eligibility for what?'

3.37 As we have seen above, children's services authorities are under a statutory duty to assess all children in need. Accordingly, it would be unlawful for a local authority to impose its own 'eligibility criteria' for assessments. This would constitute an extra-statutory hurdle for a child to cross. However, once a child has been assessed, the law does not require that services be provided in every case.

3.38 Various statutory provisions require social services/children's services departments to provide support for disabled children. The most important of these comprise CA 1989 and CSDPA 1970 s2. However, other provisions do exist and one of these, Mental Health Act 1983 s117, is considered briefly at para 5.82.

3.39 The general duty[50] to provide support services under CA 1989 Part III (see para 3.58) is triggered by the authority 'determining' (s17(4A) that the provision of services is 'appropriate' (s17(1)). The specifically enforceable duty[51] under CSDPA 1970 s2 (see para 3.48), is triggered by the authority being 'satisfied' the services are 'necessary'.[52] Arguably there is very little, if any, difference between these two tests. In practice, a local authority could (and perhaps 'should')[53] decide that it will only 'determine' that the provision of services is 'appropriate' under CA 1989 Part III when it is satisfied these are necessary (ie the test for accessing support under the 1970 Act). If this is right then the same decision must effectively be made regardless of which Act the decision is being taken under.

3.40 It follows that it is reasonable for an authority to state that a disabled child will not as a general rule be 'eligible' for support services unless the authority is satisfied that these are necessary. This then requires that the authority explains the process by which it will decide whether or not a child is 'eligible' – ie the criteria it uses to make this judgment. The use of 'eligibility criteria' in this context has been held to be lawful by the courts.[54]

---

50 See para 2.30 for an explanation as to the nature of a 'general' or 'target' duty.
51 See para 2.29 for an explanation as to the nature of a 'specifically enforceable' duty.
52 *R v Gloucestershire CC ex p Barry* [1997] AC 584; (1997–98) 1 CCLR 40.
53 Not least, because CA 1989 Sch 2 permits an authority to assess a child's needs for the purposes of CSDPA 1970 s2 at the same time as assessing under CA 1989.
54 *R v Gloucestershire CC ex p Barry* [1997] AC 584; (1997–98) 1 CCLR 40.

3.41 Such criteria must, however, promote the objects of the legislation, ie that so far as possible disabled children be brought up by their families[55] and that the services provided should seek to minimise the effects of their disabilities and give them the opportunity to lead lives which are 'as normal as possible'.[56] Given that resources are limited, the criteria should also contain an element of 'prioritisation' – ie it is legitimate for authorities to target those in most need and to devote resources where they can have the most positive impact.[57] While the use of such criteria is well developed in relation to adult care law[58] this is not so for children's services. In *R (JL) v Islington LBC*,[59] Black J stressed the 'pressing need' for government guidance on eligibility criteria for children services, given that many local authorities have, at best, imperfect, and, at worst, unlawful criteria. As Clements and Thompson observe (para 24.36), all too often these:

> are poorly publicised and formulated with little or no consultation. It appears that in many cases, access to support services is measured largely by assessing the imminence of family breakdown. Thus if it is imminent or has occurred, resources can be accessed, but not otherwise. Clearly such criteria cater for the needs of children suffering abuse or neglect but are likely to be inappropriate for many families with disabled children or young carers. In practice such policies deny support to families until such time as they fall into (or are at severe risk of falling into) the child protection regime: effectively therefore they cater, not for CA 1989 Part III (provision of services for children and their families) but for Part VI (child protection).

3.42 It is permissible therefore, for children's services authorities to operate eligibility criteria to limit access to services. However, the principles of public law and departmental guidance[60] demand that there must be a rational process for deciding which children are eligible for services and which are not. Eligibility criteria must therefore:

---

55 CA 1989 s17(1)(b).

56 CA 1989 Sch 2 para 6.

57 In this context see also L Clements and P Thompson, *Community care and the law*, 4th edn, LAG, 2007 ('Clements and Thompson'), paras 24.35–24.36.

58 See for example, Department of Health, *Prioritising need in the context of putting people first: a whole system approach to eligibility for social care. guidance on eligibility criteria for adult social care, England 2010*; and the equivalent Welsh Assembly Government policy guidance, *Creating a unified and fair system for assessing and managing care*, 2002. See also L Clements and P Thompson, *Community care and the law*, 4th edn, LAG, 2007, para 3.163.

59 [2009] EWHC 458 (Admin); (2009) 12 CCLR 322.

60 See in this context, Department for Children, Schools and Families, *Aiming high for disabled children: core offer*, 2008.

- be transparent (because both of the policy expectation – see, for example, the Aiming High for Disabled Children 'core offer'[61] – and to comply with public law duties and an authorities' obligations under ECHR article 8);[62]
- explain in clear 'everyday language' how services are allocated on the basis of need;
- take account of the impact of disability on children and families; and
- have been the subject of consultation which has taken into account (among other things) the relevant equality duties, particularly the duty under the Equality Act 2010 s149[63] (see paras 9.73–9.85).

3.43   The human rights obligations on public bodies (particularly article 8: see para 3.46) additionally require that any criteria they operate must not be so strict as to deny support where there is a real risk of significant harm[64] to the child or family if support is not provided (being harm that is more than minor or trivial).[65]

3.44   The lawfulness of one example of eligibility criteria for disabled children's services was tested in *R (JL) v Islington LBC* (2009)[66] where

---

61   Department for Children, Schools and Families, *Aiming high for disabled children: core offer*, 2008.

62   If a local authority operated 'secret' criteria or otherwise refused to make their criteria transparent, this would not be 'in accordance with law', which is one of the requirements of ECHR article 8.

63   Formerly Disability Discrimination Act 1995 s49A; see paras 9.73–9.85.

64   'Significant harm' is not defined in the CA 1989, but does not include 'minor shortcomings' or 'minor defects' in care being provided; CA 1989 Guidance and Regulations, Volume 1, Court Orders (1991) Department of Health, para 3.12. See R White, A P Carr and N Lowe, *The Children Act in practice*, 4th edn, LexisNexis, 2008, paras 8.43–8.44 and HM Government, *Working together to safeguard children: a guide to inter-agency working to safeguard and promote the welfare of children*, 2010, paras 1.26–1.31 for more on the 'significant harm' threshold.

65   In *R v Gloucestershire CC ex p Mahfood* (1997–98) 1 CCLR 7, DC (a pre-Human Rights Act 1998 judgment), McCowan LJ expressed this proposition in the following way: 'I should stress, however, that there will, in my judgment, be situations where a reasonable authority could only conclude that some arrangements were necessary to meet the needs of a particular disabled person and in which they could not reasonably conclude that a lack of resources provided an answer. Certain persons would be at severe physical risk if they were unable to have some practical assistance in their homes. In those situations, I cannot conceive that an authority would be held to have acted reasonably if they used shortage of resources as a reason for not being satisfied that some arrangement should be made to meet those persons' needs.'

66   [2009] EWHC 458 (Admin); (2009) 12 CCLR 322.

the court held the criteria to be unlawful for a variety of reasons, including that i) they sought to limit access to services regardless of the outcome of the assessment (through imposing an upper maximum limit on the support that could be provided – in this case respite care) and ii) in formulating the criteria the council had failed to have proper regard to its general disability equality duty under (what is now) the Equality Act 2010 s149[67] (see paras 9.73–9.85).

Duty to meet 'assessed needs'

3.45 Once it has been decided that a child's or family's needs are sufficient to meet the statutory tests under CSDPA 1970 s2 or the Assessment Framework/CA 1989 s17, as set out locally in the authority's eligibility criteria, then there is an obligation on the authority to provide services and support to meet the assessed need(s). Generally, but not always, this is a straightforward legal obligation. The complication arises from the nature and the 'enforceability' of the legal duties underlying the obligation. Put simply, the duty to provide a service under the CA 1989 is generally less 'enforceable' than the duty to provide a service under CSDPA 1970 s2. The services available under the 1970 and 1989 Acts are considered separately below, but certain general points can be made:

- Services assessed as required under the 1970 Act must be provided – regardless of resources. Once a child/family has been assessed as eligible for support under the 1970 Act there is a specific duty (see para 2.29) to provide them with services to meet their assessed needs, a duty which cannot be avoided because of lack of resources.[68] As the court stated in *R v Kirklees MBC ex p Daykin* (1998):[69]

  Once needs have been established, then they must be met and cost cannot be an excuse for failing to meet them. The manner in which they are met does not have to be the most expensive. The Council is perfectly entitled to look to see what cheapest way for them to meet the needs which are specified.

  It follows that councils cannot, in such situations, seek to delay or attempt further rationing – for instance by placing a person

---

67 Formerly Disability Discrimination Act 1995 s49A; see paras 9.73–9.85.

68 *R v Gloucestershire CC ex p Mahfood* (1997–98) 1 CCLR 40 at 15K and 16D–H per McCowan LJ

69 (1997–98) 1 CCLR 512 at 525D.

on a waiting list[70] or suggesting that the case needs to go to a 'panel'.[71]

• If a service can be provided under either CA 1989 or CSDPA 1970, then it is provided under the 1970 Act.[72] In essence, the reason for this is that the more enforceable duty under the 1970 Act trumps the lesser duty under the 1989 Act – or put another way, a local authority cannot escape its obligations by choosing to provide a services under a less enforceable provision.

• As will be seen below, the broad range of services available under the 1970 Act means that most services for disabled children and their families are therefore provided under the 1970 Act.

3.46   Even if a service is assessed as needed under the 1989 Act (ie because it cannot be provided under the 1970 Act) this does not mean that a local authority need not provide it. Although in such cases there is a target duty[73] not a specific duty (see paras 2.29–2.30) it is important to distinguish this from a mere 'power'. When 'intervention is required', the obligation under the Assessment Framework requires that the local authority produce a 'realistic plan of action (including services be provided)'. Furthermore, local authorities should meet their duties unless they have good reasons for failing so to do. The key considerations in such are likely to be:

1) As above, local authorities must have clear, published criteria explaining how they will decide who should get support services; these criteria must have been the subject of consultation and have been subjected to a rigorous assessment of their potential impact on disabled people as required by the Equality Act 2010 s149.[74]

2) Local authorities cannot adopt general exclusions or rigid limits or lists of services that will not be provided – for example, excluding all children with Asperger syndrome from disabled children's services, having caps or ceilings on the amount of service to be provided (eg a maximum of 100 hours per year of short breaks), or

---

70 See, for example, Local Government Ombudsman Complaint no 00/B/00599 against Essex, 3 September 2001.

71 See L Clements and P Thompson, *Community care and the law*, 4th edn, LAG, 2007, para 3.183 for further discussion about the questionable legality of such 'allocation or funding' panels.

72 *R v Bexley LBC ex p B* (2000) 3 CCLR 15 and see also *R (Spink) v Wandsworth LBC* [2005] EWCA Civ 302; (2005) 8 CCLR 272.

73 *R (G) v Barnet LBC and others* [2003] UKHL 57; (2003) 6 CCLR 500.

74 Formerly Disability Discrimination Act 1995 s49A: see paras 9.73–9.85.

stating that 'out of county residential respite will not be provided'. To do any of these things would, in public law terms, be to 'fetter their discretion' to meet their general duties in such cases.[75]

3) A local authority that is not providing a service to meet a need, must be able to demonstrate that it has complied in all material respects with the relevant guidance,[76] eg the Assessment Framework policy and practice guidance.

4) The more severe the consequences of not meeting a need, the more 'anxiously' will the courts and the ombudsmen scrutinise the reasons given by the council for not responding to that need,[77] any actions taken in trying to meet the needs[78] and the process by which the council arrived at its decision.[79]

5) Where a fundamental human right is likely to be violated by a failure to provide support – such as in particular the right to respect for personal dignity[80] or family life[81] under article 8 of the ECHR – the 'positive obligations' of the state may mean that an authority has no choice but to meet its general duty and provide the service: see para 2.7.[82]

3.47 It should be emphasised that it will only be in rare cases that the service required cannot be provided under CSDPA 1970: see below. Furthermore, in all cases, if the authority considers that it is necessary to provide services to secure the child's well-being, the general duty under CA 1989 s17 is made into a specific duty to provide services by the Assessment Framework: see para 3.33.

---

75 See, for example, *R v Bexley LBC ex p Jones* [1995] ELR 42 at 55.
76 See, for example, *R v Birmingham CC ex p Killigrew* (2000) 3 CCLR 109 and *R v Lambeth LBC ex p K* (2000) 3 CCLR 141.
77 See, for example, *R v Lambeth LBC ex p K* (2000) 3 CCLR 141.
78 *R v Islington LBC ex p Rixon* (1998) 1 CCLR 119.
79 *R v Ealing LBC ex p C* (2000) 3 CCLR 122.
80 *R (A and B, X and Y) v East Sussex CC* [2003] EWHC 167; (2003) 6 CCLR 194.
81 *R (Bernard) v Enfield LBC* [2002] EWHC 2282 (Admin); (2002) 5 CCLR 577.
82 See *Anufrijeva v Southwark LBC* [2004] 1 QB 1124 at [43], where the Court of Appeal stated that: 'Article 8 may more readily be engaged where a family unit is involved. Where the welfare of children is at stake, article 8 may require the provision of welfare support in a manner which enables family life to continue.' The authors would suggest that this will particularly be so where the family includes a disabled child.

Services under the Chronically Sick and Disabled Persons Act 1970

3.48   CSDPA 1970 s2 provides a list of services that councils must make available to disabled people (children[83] or adults). In practice this includes services of great importance, such as short breaks (also known as 'respite care', although many disabled people object to this language), day activities, equipment, adaptations and so on. As noted above, if a service can be provided to meet an assessed need under CSDPA 1970 s2, there is a specific duty to provide it which cannot be avoided by an authority claiming to be acting under CA 1989 s17. The list of services which can be provided under CSDPA 1970 s2 is summarised below.

Practical assistance in the home

3.49   The provision covers a very wide range of home-based (sometimes called 'domiciliary') care services, although it does not cover health-care services even if these do not have to be provided by qualified health professionals.[84] In practice the services provided under this provision include personal care in the home such as bathing, help using the toilet, moving and helping with feeding and routine household chores. Importantly, this provision also includes respite/short break care if provided as a sitting-type service in the home or through home-based child support or play workers.

Home-based respite care/short breaks

3.50   Short break or respite care is a 'highly valued' service[85] – giving families and the disabled child the chance to have time apart – or at least time when the family is not providing care or supervision. It is identified in policy documents as well as by families themselves as one of the most important support services that can be provided.[86] The key element of good practice is that a service is arranged that is of benefit to all family members, including the disabled child. Home-and

---

83   CSDPA 1970 s28A.

84   *R (T, D and B) v Haringey LBC* [2005] EWHC 2235 (Admin); (2006) 9 CCLR 58.

85   For example: Contact a Family, *What makes my family stronger*, 2009, accessible at www.cafamily.org.uk/pdfs/wmmfs.pdf; Contact a Family, *No time for us: relationships between parents who have a disabled child – a survey of over 2,000 parents in the UK*, 2004; Mencap, *Breaking point: families still need a break*, 2006; Shared Care Network, *Still waiting*, 2006.

86   H M Treasury/Department for Education and Skills, *Aiming high for disabled children*, 2007.

community-based short breaks take a wide variety of forms such as sitting-in and befriending schemes for children and young people of all ages. Home-based short breaks are provided under section 2(1)(a) of the 1970 Act (ie as 'practical assistance in the home') and community-based support is provided under section 2(1)(c) (ie as recreational/educational facilities 'outside his home' – see below). Some short breaks are linked to a disabled child's preferred leisure activities, for instance a play scheme at a local football club, horse riding, swimming etc. If a child has a need for short break/respite care which cannot be provided in their own home or a community-based setting and which has to be provided in a care home or foster placement (ie away from the child's home) then it cannot be provided under the 1970 Act and will generally be provided under CA 1989 (see paras 3.59–3.62).

Wireless, television, library, 'or similar recreational facilities'

3.51   The use of the phrase in CSDPA 1970 s2 of 'or similar recreational facilities' means that in today's electronic age, this provision could include such things as a computer, gaming consoles and other recreational equipment.

Recreational/educational facilities

3.52   As with 'practical assistance in the home' above, this provision is particularly wide in its potential scope – covering community-based activities such as day centres and after-school or school holiday clubs as well as specific recreational/educational support activities that the assessment of need identifies as of importance to the child's development and sense of well-being. Clearly services under this provision may also include an element of respite/short break, since if the child is being provided with care and support in the community, then he or she is having a short break from his or her family (and in this context see para 3.50).

3.53   While local authorities fund the attendance of many disabled children at community-based day centres, play schemes, holiday clubs etc, not infrequently these facilities are used by other disabled children whose parents pay for the service themselves (ie without any local authority support). While this may be because their needs have been held to be insufficiently great to be eligible for support (see paras 3.45–3.46) it can be because there has been no proper assessment – and if this is the case, a request should be made for the authority to undertake one. A not uncommon indication that such an assessment is required is when the community-based service decides that it is unable to meet the child's needs because they are so demanding (for example, that there is a need for 1:1 care).

3.54   Services under this provision include those which assist the disabled person 'in taking advantage of educational facilities' that are available to him or her. Although this does not cover the actual provision of education, it is aimed at providing support that enables the disabled person to access education – for example, help with their personal care requirements while they pursue their studies,[87] as well as escorted travel to and from it and possibly the provision of additional facilities at the institution[88] (although these might also be required under the Equality Act 2010[89] – see paras 9.55–9.72 below).

Travel and other assistance

3.55   Councils must, when assessing a disabled person's need for community-based support, also consider that person's travel needs to enable him or her to access that service. It is not acceptable for a local authority to have a blanket policy that it will not provide such transport – or for it to state that a disabled person's mobility component of disability living allowance should be used to cover this. While councils are permitted to charge for services under the 1970 Act (see paras 3.92–3.93 below) the law requires that in assessing the charge, entitlement to the mobility component of disability living allowance must be ignored.[90]

Home adaptations, fixtures and fittings

3.56   This provision covers situations where an authority assesses a disabled person (child or adult) as needing adaptations to the home in which they live, or the provision of additional fixtures and fittings. These can include such things as ramps, grab handles, wheelchair accessible showers and can extend to major works such as through floor lifts and ground-floor extensions. Frequently the authority may ask the family to apply for a Disabled Facilities Grant to meet some or all of the cost of this work – and these grants are considered further below (see chapter 6). It is, however, important to note that the fact that a grant

---

87   See Department of Health LAC(93)12 – Further and Higher Education Act 1992.

88   *R(M) v Birmingham CC* [2009] EWHC 688 (Admin).

89   Formerly the Disability Discrimination Act 1995.

90   Social Security Contributions and Benefits Act 1992 s73(14) and see also the Local Government Ombudsman Report Case no B2004/0180 against Newport City Council, 31 August 2006.

may be available does not detract from the core duty under the CSDPA 1970 – so (for example) if the cost of the works that are required exceeds the current maximum mandatory grant (see para 6.34), then the council will have to consider making the additional sums available to comply with its duty under section 2 of the 1970 Act.[91]

Holidays, meals and telephones

3.57 Once satisfied that the child meets the authority's eligibility criteria for support, the authority must consider if this need for support can and should be met by the provision of (or assistance in obtaining) a holiday, meals and/or a telephone (including any special equipment necessary to enable it to be used including such things as minicoms and other electronic items). While it might be seen as anomalous to include such items, it is arguable that holidays – in particular – are of great importance to a child's development and a family's sense of well-being.[92]

Services under CA 1989 Part III

3.58 Although the range of services which can be provided under the 1970 Act is very wide, there are some services that disabled children and their families need that do not fall within the terms of that Act. One such service is the provision of accommodation for children and families together – for which a power is expressly provided in CA 1989 s17(6).[93] However, a more commonly encountered support service which cannot be provided through the 1970 Act is residential short breaks (still frequently referred to as 'respite').

Respite care/short breaks away from the home

3.59 As noted above, while much short break/respite care is provided under the 1970 Act in the home or community (or via Direct Payment (see paras 3.63–3.66 below), it may also be provided in residential

---

91 See, for example, local government ombudsman reports on complaints 02/C/8679, 02/C/8681 and 02/C/10389 against Bolsover DC, 30 September 2003 and complaint no 05/B/00246 against Croydon LBC, 24 July 2006, para 37.

92 One week's holiday a year away from the home is a core criteria within the Townsend Deprivation Index – see P Townsend, P Phillimore and A Beattie, *Health and deprivation: inequality and the North*, Croom Helm, 1988.

93 As inserted by Adoption and Children Act 2002 s116. Guidance on the operation of this power is given in England through LAC (2003)13. See chapter 6 for further information on housing and disabled children.

units, in hospices or by foster carers. In *R (JL) v Islington LBC*[94] the court confirmed that residential and other overnight short break care (eg with a short-term foster carer) could not be provided under the 1970 Act and that as a general rule such support is provided by councils pursuant to their powers under CA 1989 s17(6) or s20(4).[95] When determining whether such care should be provided to meet an assessed need, the authority must comply with the obligations detailed above (see paras 3.45–3.46).

3.60   The duty to provide respite care under the CA 1989 has been reinforced by an amendment[96] such that CA 1989 Sch 2 para 6(c), when the amendment comes into force,[97] will require authorities to:

> Assist individuals who provide care for such children to continue to do so, or to do so more effectively, by giving them breaks from caring.

3.61   In the *Islington* judgment, the judge (Black J) considered that in limited circumstances residential and other overnight short breaks care might be provided because of a council's duty under CA 1989 s20(1) (see below, paras 3.78–3.83). This is of importance, since the duty under section 20(1) is not a power or 'target duty' but one that is specifically enforceable (see para 2.29). In the judge's opinion, however, the section 20(1) duty would only arise to when a parent was 'immediately' prevented from providing a disabled child with suitable care and accommodation.[98]

3.62   Any placement made under CA 1989 s20 must accord with the requirements of the Arrangements for Placement of Children (General) Regulations 1991 (see para 3.86).[99] These regulations will be replaced in England from 1 April 2011 by the Care Planning, Placement and Case Review (England) Regulations 2010,[100] which have far

---

94 [2009] EWHC 458 (Admin); (2009) 12 CCLR 322.

95 Which reads; 'A local authority may provide accommodation for any child within their area (even though a person who has parental responsibility for him is able to provide him with accommodation) if they consider that to do so would safeguard or promote the child's welfare'.

96 Introduced by Children and Young Persons Act 2008 s25.

97 As at the date of writing this book (July 2010) this provision had not been brought into effect. It is understood that it should come into force in April 2011.

98 [2009] EWHC 458 (Admin); (2009) 12 CCLR 322 at [95]–[96].

99 1991 SI No 890. Regulation 2(1)(a) states that the regulations apply to placements by a local authority of any child. In Wales, the 1991 Regulations were amended by the Arrangements for Placement of Children (General) and the Review of Children's Cases (Amendment) (Wales) Regulations 2002 SI No 3013, particularly in relation to health assessments.

100 SI No 959.

more detailed requirements in relation to placements of children in need, including disabled children.

Direct payments

3.63 Instead of the authority arranging for services to be provided to a disabled child, the parents (or the child if aged 16 or 17) can generally insist on having the support by way of a 'direct payment' and can then use that payment to buy the necessary services (including periods of residential short breaks/respite care away from the child's own home). The right to insist on a direct payment applies regardless of whether the support is provided under the CSDPA 1970 or the CA 1989.[101] The statutory scheme governing direct payments derives from CA 1989 s17A and has been fleshed out by regulations[102] and detailed guidance[103] issued under the Health and Social Care Act (HSCA) 2001 which place a duty on children's services authorities to make a direct payment in certain situations.[104] The conditions are that:

- the person appears to the responsible authority to be capable of managing a direct payment by themselves or with such assistance as may be available to them;
- the person consents to the making of a direct payment;
- the responsible authority is satisfied that the person's need for the relevant service can be met by securing the provision of it by means of a direct payment; and
- the responsible authority is satisfied that the welfare of the child in respect of whom the service is needed will be safeguarded and promoted by securing the provision of it by means of a direct payment.

3.64 The regulations[105] restrict the use of direct payments to pay a relative who lives in the same household as the disabled child. There is,

---

101 This derives from the fact that services provided under section 2 of the 1970 Act are technically provided in discharge of a local authorities functions under CA 1989 Part III – see para 3.31.

102 Community Care, Services for Carers and Children's Services (Direct Payments) (England) Regulations 2009 SI No 1887 and the Community Care, Services for Carers and Children's Services (Direct Payments) (Wales) Regulations 2004 SI No 1748 (W185).

103 Department of Health, *Guidance on direct payments for community care, services for carers and children's services England*, 2009 and, in Wales, *Direct payments guidance community care, services for carers and children's services (direct payments) guidance*, 2004.

104 Regulation 7(1)(c).

105 Regulation 11 in England and regulation 7 in Wales.

however, no restriction if the relative lives elsewhere. Accordingly paying such a relative, who may well know and have a good relationship with the child, to provide care may be a very attractive option for families. However, if the relative lives in the same household, the presumption is that he or she may not be paid with the direct payment – unless the authority 'is satisfied that securing the service from a family member is necessary for promoting the welfare of the child'. In simple English, this means that the council can agree to such a payment, if it is satisfied that it is necessary – ie the threshold for reversing the presumption against such an arrangement is a relatively low one.

Direct payments and respite care/short breaks

3.65   Where a disabled person has been assessed as needing a service, then in general there is a duty to make the provision by way of a direct payment if so requested. In this context the ombudsman has held it be maladministration for a local authority:

- to require a parent carer to give reasons why he wanted a direct payment in lieu of a service, and for the authority to state 'that direct payments would not be paid for childcare and that childcare was the responsibility of the parents, whether or not children have a disability';[106] and
- to have a policy of refusing direct payments for certain services – such as short (overnight) breaks.[107]

3.66   Although direct payments cannot be used to purchase prolonged periods of residential respite care (being capped at a maximum of four consecutive weeks in any period of 12 months)[108] in practice as long as the residential care periods are less than four weeks long and are separated by at least four weeks of non-residential care, then successive such periods are permitted.[109]

---

106 Public Service Ombudsman (Wales) Complaint No B2004/0707/S/370 against Swansea City Council, 22 February 2007 – see in particular paras 78, 133 and 137.

107 Complaint no 08 005 202 against Kent CC, 18 May 2009 para 39 – in this case the council had refused on the grounds that it was able to provide these 'in house'.

108 Community Care, Services for Carers and Children's Services (Direct Payments) (England) Regulations 2009 SI No 1887 reg 13 and the Community Care, Services for Carers and Children's Services (Direct Payments) (Wales) Regulations 2004 SI No 1748 (W185) reg 8.

109 Department of Health, *Guidance on direct payments for community care, services for carers and children's services England 2009*, 2009, paras 101–103 and *Direct payments guidance community care, services for carers and children's services (direct payments) guidance Wales*, 2004, paras 76–77.

Independent user trusts

3.67 Although the Direct Payment Regulations[110] permit payments to be made to persons with parental responsibility for a disabled child, such arrangements must come to an end when the child becomes 18. At this stage, the payment must either be paid to the disabled person (if he or she wishes to continue with a direct payment) or if he or she lacks sufficient mental capacity to consent to the payment, then it can (in England)[111] be paid to someone on his or her behalf – if (among other things) that third party agrees. It follows that on a child becoming an adult, a significant change in the payment arrangements has to take place. One way of seeking to avoid such disruption is for the carers of the disabled child to create a trust (or a company limited by guarantee) – variously called an 'Independent User Trust', 'User Independent Trust' and a 'Third Party Scheme'. The trust then assumes responsibility for ensuring that services are provided to meet the assessed needs of the disabled person – for example, by employing care assistants and/or paying an independent agency etc. Not infrequently the parents of a disabled child will be the initial trustees of such a trust. Such arrangements, which the courts have held to be lawful,[112] have a number of practical benefits over and above securing continuity of care arrangements during the transition into adulthood (see paras 10.49–10.60 below) – and these include the fact that the NHS is also permitted to make payments to such a trust (see para 5.64 below).[113]

Individual budgets and personalisation

3.68 Many children and families will now be told that their entitlement to services will take the form of an 'individual budget' or 'personal budget'. This is a core part of the 'personalisation' agenda, which is

---

110 Community Care, Services for Carers and Children's Services (Direct Payments) (England) Regulations 2009 SI No 1887 and the Community Care, Services for Carers and Children's Services (Direct Payments) (Wales) Regulations 2004 SI No 1748 (W185).

111 Health and Social Care Act 2008 s146 and the Community Care, Services for Carers and Children's Services (Direct Payments) (England) Regulations 2009: as at the date of writing this book (July 2010) s146 had not been brought into effect in Wales.

112 *R (A and B) v East Sussex CC No 1* [2002] EWHC 2771; (2003) 6 CCLR 177.

113 For further consideration of such trusts, see L Clements and P Thompson, *Community care and the law*, 4th edn, LAG, 2007, paras 12.64–12.70.

starting to take hold in children's services. However, it is essential to note that the only legal basis for 'personalisation' is the Direct Payments legislation (see paras 3.63–3.66), and any attempt to use personalised approaches to avoid the assessment and service provision duties set out above will be unlawful.

3.69   Adult care services in England have been the subject of the Department of Health's personalisation agenda since 2005. The programme seeks to make services and supports more responsive to the needs of disabled people by putting them at the centre of the process – and if possible by giving them a direct payment so they can be in control of their care arrangements. Since many disabled people consider that managing a direct payment is too onerous an undertaking, the English government has proposed an intermediate arrangement, whereby the disabled person is advised how much the local authority is devoting to his or her care and then encouraged to decide[114] what other ways the money could be spent to maximise their sense of independence and well being. In this intermediate phase, instead of a direct payment being made to the disabled person the monies are retained by the local authority and referred to as a 'personal budget': with the disabled person or their parents (if a child) encouraged to exercise as much control as they wish over directing how the budget is used. Ultimately the government in England would like these budgets to include not only social services monies but other funds the disabled person receives (such as funding from the Independent Living Fund as well as income received from the Supporting People's scheme, Disabled Facilities Grants, Access to Work monies and so on): these budgets are referred to as 'Individual Budgets'. The personalisation programme is still only being piloted in relation to children's services, but councils in England are being encouraged to find ways of incorporating its aims in their commissioning arrangements.[115]

3.70   While many of the principles underpinning the personalisation agenda are admirable, it has had its critics[116] and the implementation has caused not insignificant difficulties – particularly in relation to what are termed 'Resource Allocation Systems/Schemes' (RAS).

---

114 Sometimes referred to as 'Self Directed Support' (SDS).

115 See, for example, M Prabhakar, G Thom, J Hurstfield and U Parashar, *Individual budgets for families with disabled children*, Research Report DCSF–RR057, DCSF, 2008.

116 See, for example, I Ferguson, 'Increasing user choice or privatizing risk? The antinomies of personalization', (2007) 37 *British Journal of Social Work*, pp387–403, 2007 and L Clements, 'Individual budgets and irrational exuberance', (2008) 11 CCLR 413–430.

These are crude systems that endeavour to give a disabled person an indication of the resources that the council would be prepared to expend on his or her care – before the care planning process has been completed. They are sometimes referred to as 'upfront allocations' or 'indicative amounts'. The calculation is generally based on a questionnaire that the disabled person has completed. This awards 'points' which are then converted into an indicative financial amount. The idea is that disabled people may opt for this sum – and then make their own arrangements – without having to go through the whole care planning process, which would involve the detailed assessment of the actual cost of a real care package.

3.71   Admirable as this may sound, in practice the process is often disempowering – so that disabled people do not appreciate that they have a choice to have a direct service instead of a personal budget (for, as noted above, the 'personalisation' programme is underpinned by no law). Children and families may be given to believe that they have little or no option but to accept the 'indicative amount' even though this may be less than they are presently receiving or insufficient to enable them to have their care needs addressed satisfactorily.[117] In law, individuals are entitled to decline having a personal budget and to insist that their care package be provided by the local authority or that any sum they have (eg as a direct payment) be sufficient to purchase a satisfactory package of care to meet their needs. The fact that the local authority advises them that their care costs are above the 'indicative amount' generated by a RAS is simply irrelevant: the legal duty remains (as indicated at paras 3.45–3.46) to meet eligible assessed needs.

Timescales for assessments and providing services

3.72   As noted above (para 3.15) the Assessment Framework lays down detailed and tight timescales for the completion of assessments – just eight working days for an initial assessment and accompanying care plan. Where delay occurs either in the assessment or the provision of services then the complaints process may be invoked (see paras

117 This was found by Black J to be the case in *R (JL) v Islington LBC* [2009] EWHC 458 (Admin), where (at [39]) she observed that she found it 'hard to see how a system such as this one, where points are attributed to a standard list of factors, leading to banded relief with a fixed upper limit, can be sufficiently sophisticated to amount to a genuine assessment of an individual child's needs'; and see also *R (Savva) v Kensington & Chelsea RLBC* [2010] EWHC 414 (Admin); (2010) 13 CCLR 227.

2.41–2.44) since this will at least put the process on a fixed timescale (ie that for investigating the complaint).

3.73   In relation to the provision of services, the law requires that these be provided within a 'reasonable time'; the Assessment Framework expresses this obligation in terms of the plan of action being 'realistic'. What is a 'reasonable time' is a question of fact, depending on the nature of the obligation and the purpose for which the decision is to be made.[118] Generally the disabled child and/or the family will have a good idea of what is reasonable and what is not unreasonable (for example, how urgent the need is and what steps the council has actually taken to meet its obligations). Where the period seems excessive then the reasons why this is thought to be the case should be explained, in ordinary language, in any complaint.

3.74   The local government ombudsman has investigated a considerable number of complaints concerning delayed assessments relating to home adaptations (see chapter 6). In a 1996 report,[119] for example, a delay of six months in assessing a disabled person's needs was held to be maladministration, and another 1996 report found seven months for an assessment and a further four months' delay by the authority in processing the disabled facilities grant approval to be maladministration.[120] In this complaint the local ombudsman reiterated her view that if the authority has a shortage of occupational therapists, it should not use them for assessment purposes if this will result in unreasonable delay, stating, '[i]f such expertise is not available, councils need to find an alternative way of meeting their statutory responsibilities'. Where a delay arises because there is a physical shortage of services (for example, no place available at a day centre) the court will require that short-term alternative arrangements be made to meet the identified need as well as steps taken by the council to address the structural 'supply side' problem, if there is one (eg the shortage is not a 'one-off' but a chronic problem).[121]

3.75   In general if the shortage is due to a budgetary problem it will not be an acceptable excuse – as the court has noted:[122]

118   See, for example, *Re North ex p Hasluck* [1895] 2 QB 264; *Charnock v Liverpool Corporation* [1968] 3 All ER 473.

119   Complaints nos 93/B/3111 and 94/B/3146 against South Bedfordshire DC and Bedfordshire CC.

120   Complaints nos 94/C/0964 and 94/C/0965 against Middlesbrough DC and Cleveland CC.

121   *R v Islington LBC ex p Rixon* (1997–98) 1 CCLR 119 at 128.

122   *R v Gloucestershire CC ex p Mahfood* (1997–98) 1 CCLR 7, DC, per McCowan LJ; and see also *R v Kirklees MBC ex p Daykin* (1997–98) 1 CCLR 512 at 525D.

Once a local authority has decided that it is necessary to make the arrangements, they are under an absolute duty to make them. It is a duty owed to a specific individual and not a target duty. No term is to be implied that the local authority are obliged to comply with the duty only if they have the revenue to do so. In fact, once under that duty resources do not come into it.

Conclusion: the need for services to promote dignity

3.76 To conclude on the duty to provide services, it should be remembered that in keeping with the state's obligations under the European Convention on Human Rights (ECHR), the purpose of assessment and care planning must be to promote and protect the inherent dignity of disabled children. In *R (A, B, X and Y) v East Sussex CC*[123] the High Court stated (at [86]) that:

> The recognition and protection of human dignity is one of the core values – in truth the core value – of our society and indeed all societies which are part of the European family of nations and which have embraced the principles of the [European Convention on Human Rights].

3.77 The obligations on children's services authorities to provide services to meet disabled children's assessed needs must therefore be seen in the context of the state's convention obligations, and in particular the positive obligations under ECHR article 8, to ensure decent and dignified standards of living for disabled children, where possible with their families. The service provision decision therefore needs to be taken with due regard to all the general principles and human rights standards set out in chapters 1 and 2.

Duty to accommodate disabled children

3.78 As noted above, in general where a local authority facilitates short break/respite care in a way which involves the child spending a period in a residential care (or substitute family) placement, then this care is considered to be provided as a general support service under CA 1989 s17. However, if the placement arises because 'the person who has been caring' for the disabled child is 'prevented ... from providing him with suitable accommodation or care' for whatever reason, then the care is provided under a different section of CA

123 [2003] EWHC 167 (Admin); (2003) 6 CCLR 194.

1989, being section 20(1). This distinction is important, because the duty to provide accommodation under CA 1989 s20(1) is a 'specifically enforceable' duty[124] and a child accommodated under this duty is considered to be 'looked after' by a local authority.[125] Residential short breaks may also be provided under the authority's power to accommodate pursuant to section 20(4) of CA 1989 – but only if the qualifying criteria for the section 20(1) duty are not met on the facts of the individual case.

3.79   In *R (G) v Southwark LBC*,[126] the House of Lords confirmed that where the qualifying criteria in CA 1989 s20(1) are met, an authority is under a specific duty to accommodate a child under that section. This duty trumps the power to accommodate a child under CA 1989 s17(6) and children's services authorities cannot avoid their section 20(1) obligations by referring children in need of accommodation to housing authorities or providing 'help with accommodation' under CA 1989 s17.

3.80   As noted above (see para 3.61), Mrs Justice Black held in *R (JL) v Islington*[127] that the 'prevention' referred to in CA 1989 s20(1)(c) had to be current, and that the duty only arose (in effect) at the point of crisis. Where a disabled child is placed away from home, including at a residential special school (see paras 4.74–4.80), it will therefore be a question of fact as to whether the placement is made pursuant to CA 1989 s20(1)(c).

3.81   It follows that the section 20(1) duty to accommodate may not be triggered until a family is close to 'breaking point' and the parents at risk of no longer being able to provide the necessary care to the disabled child (and potentially any non-disabled siblings). The precise wording of the relevant limb of the section 20(1) duty states that the duty to accommodate arises where the child requires accommodation as a result of:

> (c) the person who has been caring for him being prevented (whether or not permanently, and for whatever reason) from providing him with suitable accommodation or care.

---

124 See para 2.29.
125 This arises if the child is in local authority care by reason of a court order or is being accommodated under CA 1989 s20, regardless of whether under subsection (1) or (4) for more than 24 hours by agreement with the parents (or with the child if aged over 16).
126 [2009] UKHL 26; (2009) 12 CCLR 437.
127 [2009] EWHC 458 (Admin); (2009) 12 CCLR 322.

3.82   It is important to bear in mind that accommodation under CA 1989 s20(1) is *voluntary*, in other words that a child cannot be accommodated under this duty if a person with parental responsibility who is willing and able to provide accommodation objects (CA 1989 s20(7)).[128] Before providing accommodation an authority must give due consideration to the wishes and feelings of the child, although these may not be determinative.[129] Authorities must additionally consider the child's wishes and feelings throughout any placement. Accordingly in *R (CD) v Anglesey CC*[130] the High Court criticised the respondent council for attempting to end a successful fostering arrangement for a 15-year-old severely disabled girl and requiring her to reside at an establishment 'to an extent substantially contrary to her wishes and feelings'.

3.83   In relation to children accessing overnight or residential short breaks, it should be remembered that these arrangements only engage the CA 1989 s20(1) duty if all the qualifying criteria are met. In particular, if the parents are not 'prevented' from providing suitable accommodation and care but the short breaks are being provided to promote the child's well-being and support positive family life, then the service is being provided under CA 1989 s17 or s20(4). The *Care matters: time for change* white paper emphasised that 'looked after' status 'should not be an automatic response to the use of [respite care]'.[131]

Duties towards accommodated disabled children

3.84   Any disabled child who is accommodated under CA 1989 s20(1) duty (or indeed the section 20(4) power)[132] is a 'looked after' child for the purposes of CA 1989: see CA 1989 s22(1)(b). For this to apply, the accommodation must be provided for a continuous period of more than 24 hours (CA 1989 s22(2)). A children's services authority does not acquire parental responsibility for children it is voluntarily accommodating; responsibility remains with the child's mother or parents (CA 1989 s2).

128 Unless the child is 16 or over and agrees to be provided with accommodation under this section: CA 1989 s20(11).

129 *R (Liverpool CC) v Hillingdon LBC* [2009] EWCA Civ 43 per Dyson LJ at [32], approved by Baroness Hale in *R (G) v Southwark LBC* [2009] UKHL 26; (2009) 12 CCLR 437 at [28].

130 [2004] EWHC 1635 (Admin); (2002) 7 CCLR 589.

131 Cm 7137, TSO, 2007, para 2.33.

132 But not under CA 1989 s17.

3.85　　Children's services authorities do, however, have additional duties towards disabled children who are 'looked after' (as they do to all 'looked after' children), including the provision of accommodation and maintenance.[133] Furthermore, once amendments made in 2008 come into force, under CA 1989 s22C[134] authorities will have to:

- place the child in what is, in their opinion, the most appropriate placement available;[135]
- place the child within the local authority's area, unless that is not reasonably practicable;[136] and
- ensure so far as is reasonably practicable that the placement is close to the child's home, does not disrupt the child's education or training and is suitable to the child's particular needs as a disabled child.[137]

3.86　Placements of children away from home are currently governed by the Arrangements for Placement of Children (General) Regulations 1991.[138] These regulations impose additional duties on children's service's authorities in respect of 'looked after' children, including requirements to have regard to a series of health and educational considerations set out at Schedules 2 and 3 to the regulations respectively. These regulations will be replaced in England from 1 April 2011 by the Care Planning, Placement and Case Review (England) Regulations 2010,[139] which have far more detailed requirements in relation to placements of children in need, including disabled children.

3.87　　Children's services authorities are also required to ensure that a health assessment (including physical and mental health) is undertaken as soon as possible after a child becomes 'looked after' and that this is reviewed at least annually.[140] In relation to education, concerns about the low attainment of 'looked after' children led to the amendment to CA 1989 s22(3)(a) by section 52 of the Children Act 2004, which aims to ensure that particular attention is given to the educational implications of decisions in relation to children's welfare.

133　CA 1989 s23.

134　Substituted, together with ss22A, 22B, 22D–22F, for s23 as originally enacted, by Children and Young Persons Act 2008 s8(1). Parts of CA 1989 s22C as amended remain not yet in force.

135　CA 1989 s22C(5).

136　CA 1989 s22C(9).

137　CA 1989 s22C(8).

138　SI No 890.

139　SI No 959.

140　Review of Children's Cases Regulations 1991 reg 6 (as amended by Children Act (Miscellaneous Amendments) (England) Regulations 2002 SI No 546.

Duties towards disabled children 'leaving care'

3.88   In recognition of the unacceptably poor outcomes for formerly 'looked after' children, the Children (Leaving Care) Act 2000 created a new scheme to oblige children's services authorities to continue to provide assistance to young people whom they had formerly been looking after, both disabled and non-disabled. The duties are in respect of 'eligible', 'relevant' and 'former relevant' children.

3.89   'Eligible' children are those who are 16 or 17 years old and have been 'looked after' for 13 weeks, either continuously or in total. In respect of 'eligible' children, children's services authorities are required to:

- assess the young person's needs and then prepare a 'pathway plan' to meet those needs;[141]
- appoint a personal adviser to co-ordinate services, who must be independent of the authority and not the person with responsibility for the assessment or pathway plan; *R (J) v Caerphilly CBC.*[142]

3.90   'Relevant' children are children aged 16 or 17 years old who have ceased to be 'looked after' but otherwise would have been 'eligible'.[143] Children's services authorities have a duty to 'keep in touch' with relevant children and prepare pathway plans for them.

3.91   'Former relevant' children are young people who are over 18 but were previously 'eligible' or 'relevant' children.[144] Duties towards former relevant children are discussed in paras 10.64–10.76, where the 'leaving care' scheme is generally given more detailed consideration.

Charging for children's services

3.92   Children's services authorities have the power to charge for services provided under the CA 1989. Authorities may recover 'such charge as they consider appropriate' (CA 1989 s29(1)) and in so doing, if the child is under 16, can take into account of the financial circumstance of the parents, and if 16 or over, can take into account the child's

---

141   CA 1989 s19B. The assessment should be completed within three months of the child reaching 16: Children (Leaving Care) (England) Regulations 2001 SI No 2874 reg 7.

142   [2005] EWHC 586 (Admin); (2005) 8 CCLR 255.

143   CA 1989 s23A.

144   CA 1989 s23C.

means (section 29(4)). However, no person can be charged while in receipt of income support or a range of other benefits (section 29(3)). Furthermore, an authority cannot require a person to pay more than he or she can reasonably be expected to pay (section 29(2)).

3.93   Children's services authorities can also charge for services provided under CSDPA 1979 s2. In practice, few authorities do charge parents or children for services provided either under CA 1989 Part III or CSDPA 1970 s2.[145]

Safeguarding and child protection

3.94   Local authorities have extensive powers and duties under CA 1989 to protect children from harm, including the power to intervene and remove children into their care. The fact that these powers and duties are not considered in detail in this book should not be taken to indicate that effective and appropriate measures to safeguard disabled children are anything other than crucial. In addition, as with any children, decisions about protecting disabled children from harm are often complex. A small number of recent cases indicate, however, that the existence of these powers may give rise to fear among parents that if they find themselves disagreeing with or complaining about the council, or taking action of which the council disapproves, then they may find themselves the subject of child protection proceedings. For a local authority to misuse their powers in this way, would of course, run contrary to the entire object and purpose of CA 1989 Part III, which is that 'local authorities should provide support for children and families'.[146]

3.95   In *A Local Authority v A (A Child)*[147] Munby LJ made a number of observations and findings of considerable relevance to this power imbalance. The case concerned two families who each had a disabled child with Smith Mangenis Syndrome: a condition which, at times, resulted in hyperactive behaviour characterised by the person not sleeping. In order to cope and for the children to be safe, their parents (who the court held to be exemplary carers) locked them in their rooms at night. The court found that this did not amount to a 'deprivation of liberty' – indeed that what was occurring was of a quite

---

145   See L Clements and P Thompson, *Community Care and the Law*, 4th edn, LAG, 2007, paras 24.68–24.73 and chapter 10 for further information on charging.

146   *R (M) v Gateshead Council* [2006] EWCA Civ 221 per Dyson LJ at [42].

147   [2010] EWHC 978 (Fam); (2010) 13 CCLR 536.

different nature and was not even close to a deprivation of the children's liberty. This finding was important, since if it were otherwise, there would have been a duty on the local authority to take action to bring this state of affairs to an end – or at least to formalise the situation (under the Mental Capacity Act 2005) – and the court gave helpful guidance as to what an authority ought do in such cases.

3.96   Lord Justice Munby also took the opportunity to make some very general – and important – observations about heavy handed interventions by local authorities in cases of this nature: of an attitude (which he considered [at para 50]) was 'shared by too many other local authorities': that they were not merely 'involved' with such families but that that they had 'complete and effective control ... through [their] assessments and care plans' [at para 51]. Of this attitude Munby LJ observed that 'it needs to be said in the plainest possible terms that this suggestion, however formulated – and worryingly some local authorities seem almost to assume and take it for granted – is simply wrong in law.' He continued:

> 52 Moreover, the assertion or assumption, however formulated, betrays a fundamental misunderstanding of the nature of the relationship between a local authority and those, like A and C and their carers, who it is tasked to support – a fundamental misunderstanding of the relationship between the State and the citizen. People in the situation of A and C, together with their carers, look to the State – to a local authority – for the support, the assistance and the provision of the services to which the law, giving effect to the underlying principles of the Welfare State, entitles them. They do not seek to be 'controlled' by the State or by the local authority. And it is not for the State in the guise of a local authority to seek to exercise such control. The State, the local authority, is the servant of those in need of its support and assistance, not their master. ...
>
> 53 This attitude is perhaps best exemplified by the proposition that 'in the event that the parents were to disagree with the *decisions* of the local authority (which will always be based upon the opinion of relevant professionals) it would seek to *enforce its decisions* through appropriate proceedings if necessary' (emphasis added). This approach, ..., though reflecting what I have come across elsewhere, reflects an attitude of mind which is not merely unsound in law but hardly best calculated to encourage proper effect being given to a local authority's procedural obligations under Article 8 of the Convention ... . Moreover, it is likely to be nothing but counter-productive when it comes to a local authority 'working together', as it must, with family carers. 'Working together' involves something more – much more – than merely requiring carers to agree with a local authority's 'decision' even if, let alone just because, it may be backed by professional opinion.

3.97   Munby LJ referred to a number of other cases considered by the courts where a local authority had acted in such a high handed way (see para 55 of the judgment). The local government ombudsman has also expressed concern about local authorities seeking to use their child and adult protection powers inappropriately. A 2008 ombudsman complaint[148] concerned a local authority in dispute with a disabled child's family over a care plan. The disagreement centered on the use of a hoist that the council considered necessary, but the family were not satisfied with the proposed arrangements and continued to carry the young man upstairs to be bathed. Although it was accepted that his family were devoted to him, nevertheless the local authority made an adult protection referral – asserting that this was putting him at risk. The ombudsman (at para 37) held that it 'beggars belief that the referral was made at all'. In similar vein a 2009 ombudsman complaint[149] concerned a mother who (because of a service failure by the council) had no option but to hose her sons down in the back garden to keep them clean. Instead of providing adequate bathing facilities, she was warned by the social services panel that cleaning them this way was 'abusive' – something that the ombudsman considered to be of 'breathtaking insensitivity' by a council that (in her opinion) exhibited an 'institutionalised indifference' not only to the disabled children's needs and the mother's plight but also to the council's duties and responsibilities (paras 40 and 43).

3.98   The proper procedures to be followed in relation to safeguarding disabled children in England can be found in statutory guidance entitled *Working together to safeguard children,*[150] revised in 2010. It sets out how organisations and individuals should work together to safeguard and promote the welfare of children and young people in accordance with the CA 1989 and the CA 2004. The general principles in the statutory guidance are also supplemented by specific practice guidance in relation to disabled children.[151] The statutory guidance emphasises the need to work sensitively with disabled children where there are concerns about their welfare, including drawing upon the expertise of specialist disability workers in any child protection investigations.[152] *Working together to safeguard children* also

---

148 Complaint no 07/B/07665 against Luton Borough Council, 10 September 2008.
149 Complaint no 07/C/03887 against Bury MBC, 14 October 2009.
150 HM Government, *Working together to safeguard children: A guide to inter-agency working to safeguard and promote the welfare of children,* 2010 ('*Working together*').
151 DCSF, *Safeguarding disabled children – Practice Guidance,* 2009.
152 *Working together,* 1.31.

contains a specific section on 'abuse of disabled children'[153] which requires that 'expertise in both safeguarding and promoting the welfare of child and disability has to be brought together to ensure that disabled children receive the same levels of protection from harm as other children'.[154] The guidance highlights the increased risk of abuse (particularly of disabled children away from home) and requires agencies to promote 'a high level of awareness of the risks of harm and high standards of practice' and strengthen 'the capacity of children and families to help themselves'.[155] This brings us back to the core purpose of CA 1989 Part III – to provide support to children and families to help them lead ordinary lives.

153 *Working together*, 6.43–6.48.
154 *Working together*, 6.46.
155 *Working together*, 6.45.

Education

continued

Key points

- Disabled children have a right to suitable, effective and appropriate education.
- A large proportion of disabled children have 'special educational needs' (SEN).
- Local education authorities (LEAs) have general duties to promote the welfare of disabled children and children with SEN and to promote the fulfilment by every child of his or her educational potential.
- There is a legal presumption in favour of mainstream education for disabled children and children with SEN.
- Most children with SEN in mainstream schools will have their needs met at 'school action' or 'school action plus', the school-based stages of the SEN Code of Practice.
- The law permits disabled children to be educated in specialist provision where specific criteria are met.
- The route to specialist or significant additional provision is through a statutory assessment which may lead to a statement of special educational needs (SSEN).
- Residential placements are usually only funded by the LEA when the child needs a 24-hour 'waking day' curriculum.
- Residential placements may also be co-funded by the social care budget of the children's services department and/or the NHS in addition to funding from the LEA (now also part of children's services).
- Children, including children with complex needs, can also be educated at home.
- Children with SEN should not be excluded from school except as a 'last resort'; where they are excluded, their parents can appeal to a governors' committee and an independent appeal panel or to SENDIST (see below) in some cases where disability discrimination is alleged.
- Local authorities owe a specific duty to children (including disabled children and children with SEN) who are out of school to offer suitable alternative provision.
- Disputes between parents and local authorities in relation to specific aspects of the SEN system can be resolved through an appeal to the independent tribunal generally known as SENDIST.

Introduction

4.1   Getting the right education for a disabled child (as for any child) is crucial. This is particularly so for those disabled children who have special educational needs (SEN) – which means that they have a learning difficulty calling for special educational provision.[1] 'Learning difficulty' typically means a significantly greater difficulty in learning than the majority of children of a child's age.[2] 'Special educational provision' means provision which is additional to, or otherwise different from, educational provision made generally for children of the relevant age in local schools.[3] Just over 20 per cent of children are identified as meeting this definition and having SEN; just under three per cent of all children have more complex needs which require the local education authority (LEA) to maintain a statement of SEN (see paras 4.45–4.60).[4]

4.2   Unfortunately, and primarily because of resource constraints, special educational provision is frequently a battlefield between parents and LEAs. Many families find that they only obtain adequate support by challenging or appealing LEA decisions, potentially through multiple tribunal appeals during a child's school years. Even then, families routinely experience frustrating delay, for example, when LEAs resist appeals and then concede shortly before hearing

---

1   Education Act (EA) 1996 s312(1).

2   EA 1996 s312(2). The definition also includes a disability which affects the child's ability to make use of educational facilities in the child's area. However, this must be read in the context of the Disability Discrimination Act 1995 and (once fully in force) the Equality Act 2010 (see chapter 9). It is therefore much more likely that the first category of the definition will apply to any given individual child. In addition, a child under five has a learning difficulty if he or she is likely to fall into either of these categories when he or she reaches five, whether or not special educational provision is made for the child before his or her fifth birthday.

3   EA 1996 s312(4); for children under two, 'special educational provision' means educational provision of any kind.

4   Lamb Inquiry, *Special educational needs and parental confidence*, DCSF, 2009 (Lamb Inquiry Report), p16. The report was commissioned by the then secretary of state in England to look into improving parental confidence in the SEN system. It is available at www.dcsf.gov.uk/lambinquiry/. The DfE Statistical First Release, *Special educational needs in England: January 2010* states that in January 2010 some 220,890 (or 2.7% of) pupils across all schools in England had statements of SEN, the same percentage as in January 2009. There were 1,470,900 pupils with SEN without statements in England in January 2010, representing 18.2% of pupils across all schools, an increase of 0.4% from 2009.

(a practice which has attracted criticism from the local government ombudsman[5]). As we noted in chapter 1 (see paras 1.61–1.63 above) the research suggests that parents find the process stressful and difficult, even though the majority of those who are able to see it to the end report that they are ultimately happy with their children's educational provision. However, the system still fails many, as the recent Lamb Inquiry[6] concluded:

> Educational achievement for children with SEN is too low and the gap with their peers too wide. This is a hangover of a system, and a society, which does not place enough value on achieving good outcomes for disabled children and children with SEN.

4.3   The Lamb Inquiry also reported 'extreme variation' in the quality of SEN provision and the outcomes achieved by children with SEN.[7] The Lamb Inquiry (at 2.5, p21) described the 'wider outcomes' as follows:

a)   46 per cent of primary and 42 per cent of secondary persistent absentees are recorded as having SEN, more than double the rate across the whole school population;

b)   overall exclusion rates for children with SEN are currently eight times higher than for those without; and

c)   61 per cent of pupils with a learning difficulty have been bullied, compared with 48 per cent of all pupils.

4.4   The Lamb Inquiry identified these as systemic problems, concluding that we are still 'living with a legacy of a time when children with SEN were seen as uneducable'. It called for 'major reform of the current system' with a 'radical recasting of the relationship between parents, schools and local authorities to ensure a clearer focus on the outcomes and life chances for children with SEN and disability'.[8] Until such radical change is achieved, parents will continue to have to fight (where necessary through legal routes) to ensure their children get the special educational provision they need. Indeed, unless any system change is accompanied by significantly more resources and/or

---

5   See, for example, Local Government Ombudsman's *Digest of Cases (Education) 2006/07*, Report 05/A/13627.

6   Lamb Inquiry Report, p2.

7   Lamb Inquiry Report, p4. See also 4.1, p52: 'Throughout the Inquiry one of the most striking features of the SEN system has been the variation we have seen. We have seen widely varying levels of parental confidence and there is variation at local authority level in a wide range of different indicators: from overall levels of SEN and the SEN–non-SEN attainment gap, to levels of exclusions, the number of statements issued and the time in which they are issued'.

8   Lamb Inquiry Report, p2.

those resources which are available are targeted more effectively, conflicts are likely to remain and parents and children will continue to need to use legal routes, in particular tribunal appeals, to get the right education.

4.5 This chapter considers the duties owed to disabled children with SEN. Disabled children, including children with specific learning difficulties (for example, dyslexia and dyspraxia) or conditions such as attention deficit hyperactivity disorder (ADHD), will have SEN if their learning difficulties are significantly greater than other children, as opposed to only marginally greater.[9] There is significant overlap between the duties to children with SEN and the important duties on schools and LEAs under the Equality Act 2010, which are set out in chapter 9: see paras 9.55–9.65. The new coalition government in England has begun to consider significant reforms to the SEN system, but as any reforms are likely to require primary legislation and may be hotly contested this chapter deals with the law as it is now, not as it may become in the future. Similarly, although the extent to which the statutory SEN framework will apply to future academies and 'free schools' remains unclear, it is likely that these duties will continue to apply to most if not all schools for the foreseeable future.

The human right to education

4.6 Disabled children, like other children, have a human right to education. The Council of Europe has also identified education as a *'basic instrument of social integration'* for disabled children.[10] This right is contained in a number of international treaties,[11] but most importantly within the first sentence of article 2 of Protocol 1 to the European Convention on Human Rights ('A2P1'), which states simply that 'no-one shall be denied the right to education'. The right under A2P1 is to an 'effective'[12] education in accordance with the education system

---

9 EA 1996 s312(2).
10 Council of Europe *Action Plan to promote the rights and full participation of people with disabilities in society: improving the quality of life of people with disabilities in Europe 2006–2015.*
11 See, for example, article 26 of the Universal Declaration of Human Rights, article 13 of the International Covenant on Economic, Social and Cultural Rights, articles 28 and 29 of the UN Convention on the Rights of the Child and article 24 of the UN Convention on the Rights of Persons with Disabilities.
12 *Belgian Linguistic Case (No 2)* 1 EHRR 252.

'prevailing in the state'.[13] The question which must be asked to determine whether the A2P1 right to education has been breached is:

> Have the authorities of the state acted so as to deny to a pupil effective access to such educational facilities as the state provides for such pupils?[14]

4.7　The Supreme Court recently considered the scope of the A2P1 right to education in relation to disabled children in *A v Essex CC and the National Autistic Society (Intervener)*.[15] In this case, lawyers acting for A brought a damages claim under A2P1 in relation to a period of 18 months during 2002 and 2003 when A was effectively without any education, apart from irregular speech and language therapy sessions and access to some educational toys. A had and continued to have complex needs, including severe learning disabilities, autism and epilepsy. His needs were ultimately met successfully in a residential special school placement. The Supreme Court held by a majority of 3–2 that it was not arguable that A2P1 gave A an absolute right to education to meet his special needs during the 18 months he was out of school. However, a different 3–2 majority of the Justices found that it was arguable that Essex had failed to provide educational facilities that were available that might have mitigated the consequences of the failure to meet A's special needs during this period.[16] Despite this, the Supreme Court declined to extend time to allow this part of A's claim to proceed to trial. This judgment is complex, with all five Justices giving separate speeches, but it clearly demonstrates that at the very least local authorities must not neglect the educational needs of children with even the most complex SEN and must do what is possible to provide these children with some education, even if less than suitable education, while a suitable placement for them is being found.

4.8　In relation to children with SEN like A who are out of school, the A2P1 right to education is supplemented by the powerful duties contained in EA 1996 s19 which require suitable alternative education

---

13　*Ali v Governors of Lord Grey School* [2006] 2 AC 363 per Lord Bingham at [24].
14　*Ali v Governors of Lord Grey School* [2006] 2 AC 363 per Lord Bingham at [24].
15　[2010] UKSC 33; (2010) 13 CCLR 314.
16　See speech of Lord Phillips at [89]: 'it is possible, indeed likely, that the failure over 18 months to meet [A's] needs might have been mitigated by the provision of significantly more educational assistance than was in fact provided. I agree with Lord Kerr that there might, dependent upon facts that have not been explored, be a case for saying that, during this 18-month period, A was deprived of such educational provision as could have been made available and that this deprivation violated [A2P1]'.

to be provided regardless of resource difficulties – see below, paras 4.124–4.130. It should also be remembered that it was only the Education (Handicapped Children) Act 1970 which ended the classification of some disabled children as 'unsuitable for education in school', demonstrating the relatively recent focus on this fundamental human right for disabled children (see also paras 1.58–1.60).

The statutory scheme for SEN

4.9 The statutory scheme for SEN in England and Wales is set out in Part 4 of the EA 1996, as amended by the Special Educational Needs and Disability Act 2001. This scheme is fleshed out by regulations,[17] which detail the requirements for statutory assessments and statements of SEN and by a Special Educational Needs Code of Practice issued by the Department for Education and Skills in England in November 2001 and by the National Assembly for Wales in 2004. The code of practice is statutory guidance issued under EA 1996 s313 which states on its face that LEAs, schools, early education settings and other relevant bodies must have regard to it.[18] LEAs have the overall responsibility for making sure that children's SEN are met and the funding relationship between maintained schools and the LEA should be explained in the SEN information which LEAs must publish under the relevant regulations.[19]

4.10 Beneath this primary statutory scheme sits a substantial body of policy and practice guidance intended to support good practice in the provision of education for children with SEN.[20] While this chapter highlights the key documents and provisions, there is insufficient space to detail the full extent of this guidance.

4.11 In carrying out their functions towards children with SEN, LEAs must also have regard to their general duties under the Education Acts. In particular, they must have regard to:

---

17 In particular, the Education (Special Educational Needs) (England) (Consolidation) Regulations 2001 SI No 3455 and the Education (Special Educational Needs) (Wales) Regulations 2002 SI No 152 (W20).

18 Special Educational Needs Code of Practice ('SEN CoP'), p5.

19 Special Educational Needs (Provision of Information by Local Education Authorities) (England) Regulations 2001 SI No 2218 – see in particular para 1 in the schedule.

20 See, for example, S Oliver, *Special educational needs and the law*, 2nd edn, Jordans, 2007, pp12–15.

a) promoting the fulfilment by every child concerned of his educational potential;[21] and

b) the need to safeguard and promote the welfare of children.[22]

4.12 A number of other important duties also apply generally to relevant bodies in relation to children with SEN. These include:

- a new duty on the chief inspector to have particular regard to the education provided to disabled pupils and pupils with SEN during school inspections in England;[23]
- a duty on LEAs, when carrying out their duties to secure the provision of sufficient schools, to have regard to the need to secure suitable provision for pupils with SEN;[24]
- a duty on health authorities and other local authority departments to co-operate with LEAs in relation to SEN provision;[25] and
- a duty on governing bodies of schools to use their best endeavours to make any special educational provision that a pupil requires.[26]

4.13 Children with SEN are generally educated in either mainstream or special schools. Mainstream schools are those catering for the needs of all children in their area. A 'special school' is, essentially, a school whose primary purpose is to cater for children with SEN. They may be maintained by the state or be private schools where fees must be paid (independent and non-maintained special schools).[27] Special schools are approved by the secretary of state under EA 1996 s342. Some children with SEN will, however, be educated at home: see paras 4.88–4.91.

---

21 EA 1996 s13A(1)(c), as inserted by Education and Inspections Act 2006 s1.
22 Education Act (EA) 2002 s175(1). This mirrors the safeguarding duty imposed on children's services' authorities in carrying out their non-educational functions under Children Act 2004 s11 (in England) and s28 (in Wales).
23 Children, Schools and Families Act 2010 s1, amending Education Act 2005 s5. In force from 1 September 2010: the Children, Schools and Families Act 2010 (Commencement No 1) Order 2010 SI No 1817 article 3.
24 EA 1996 s14(6)(b).
25 EA 2002 s322.
26 EA 1996 s317(1)(a).
27 SEN CoP, p204.

Children under five years of age

Early intervention and pre-school provision

4.14   The duty to get the right education for children with SEN arises as soon as the need is identified. Where a child is not in any educational or early years 'setting' (see below) and a potential SEN is identified, parents can approach the LEA for a statutory assessment to ensure their child's SEN, if any are identified and met (see below, paras 4.28–4.41). Chapter 4 of the SEN Code of Practice outlines what should happen in such cases for children between the ages of three and five. To make sense of the code, it is necessary to understand some of the basic terms used. For example, the action required at this stage is known as 'early years action'; this applies to children in any 'setting' which include, for example, a nursery, family centre, playgroup and other establishments that receive government funding.[28] The duty rests on the person in charge of the establishment, but there is also an obligation that such 'settings' (1) identify a member of staff to act as the special educational needs co-ordinator (SENCO)[29] and (2) work closely with parents to help children develop in six areas of learning:

a) personal, social and emotional development;
b) communication, language and literacy;
c) mathematical development;
d) knowledge and understanding of the world;
e) physical development;
f) creative development.[30]

4.15   The code of practice requires a 'graduated response' through close monitoring of the progress of individual children.[31] Once it is clear that a child is not making progress, this indicates a requirement for special educational provision.

4.16   Once a child has been identified as having special educational needs, the setting should intervene through 'early years action'. This is provision devised and implemented solely within the setting. A staff member or the SENCO is required to collate all information about the child (and this may involve liaising with health and social services professionals, including educational psychologists who the

28   SEN CoP, 1:23.
29   SEN CoP, 4:15.
30   SEN CoP, 4:6.
31   SEN CoP, 4:9.

guidance stresses 'can have a key role'), and then to decide with the parents on the action needed to help the child make progress.[32] The agreed plan of action should be recorded through an individual education plan (often referred to as an IEP).[33]

4.17   Where intervention at 'early years action' does not lead to the child catching up with his or her peers, intervention may move to 'early years action plus', where advice and support is sought from external agencies.[34] At this stage external specialists may assist with devising a new individual education plan which may include setting targets, developing specialist strategies or providing specialist assessments.[35]

4.18   Where a child continues to fall behind even after a period of intervention at 'action plus', then the setting or the parent should request a statutory assessment from the LEA (see paras 4.28–4.41). It is important to note that if a child's needs are particularly significant and/or complex, a statutory assessment can be requested before any early education intervention has been attempted.[36] The procedure for statutory assessment of children under compulsory school age but over two is the same as for children of school age. Any statement issued following a statutory assessment will also follow the same format as for children of school age. Parents of children under school age but over two may request a preference for a maintained school, and as with school age children the LEA must agree to this preferred school being named in the statement so long as the criteria in Schedule 27 to the EA 1996 are met (see para 4.62).

Children under two years of age

4.19   Statutory assessments of children under two need not follow the general statutory assessment procedures.[37] An LEA must make an assessment of a child under two if a parent requests it and the LEA believes the child may have special educational needs for which the LEA should determine special educational provision.[38] LEAs are encouraged to consider meeting the special educational needs of very

---

32   SEN CoP, 4:20–4:26.
33   SEN CoP, 4:27.
34   SEN CoP, 4:11.
35   SEN CoP, 4:29.
36   SEN CoP, 4:36.
37   EA 1996 s331 and SEN CoP, 4:47.
38   EA 1996 s331.

young children with home-based programmes.[39] The requirements of any statement issued for a child under two are set out in the code of practice at para 4:49.

Children of school age

Education in school

4.20   By the time a child joins an infant or primary school, the expectation is that any SEN the child may have will already have been identi-fied.[40] Governing bodies of maintained schools must use their best endeavours to ensure these SEN are met[41] and must inform parents that special educational provision is being made.[42] Regulations[43] re-quire governing bodies to publish information about a wide range of matters in relation to the school's special educational provision. However, too often needs will not be identified prior to a child reach-ing school age, so schools are also obliged to have systems in place that identify as well as assess and provide for SEN.

4.21   The code of practice stresses that SEN is a whole school responsi-bility and all teachers are teachers of children with SEN.[44] At primary level, the expectation is that most children with SEN will learn and progress through the 'continuous cycle of planning, teaching and assessment' which forms the heart of every primary school class.[45] Schools now have significant funds 'delegated' to them by the LEA to enable them to meet needs without a statement of SEN.[46] Schools also have a duty to inform the child's parents that special educational provision is being made to meet the child's SEN.[47]

4.22   For children starting school with recognised SEN, schools are advised to undertake a baseline assessment to focus on the child's

---

39   SEN CoP, 4:48.
40   SEN CoP, 5:1.
41   EA 1996 s317(1).
42   EA 1996 s317A.
43   Education (Special Educational Needs) (Information) (England) Regulations 1999 SI No 2506.
44   SEN CoP, 5:2.
45   SEN CoP, 5:3.
46   Under Apprenticeships, Skills Children and Learning Act 2009 s251, LEAs must produce information about how their education funding is delegated. The previous statutory provision, School Standards and Framework Act 1998 s52, continues to apply in Wales.
47   EA 1996 s317A.

skills and highlight areas for further action.[48] As in the early years, schools are required to adopt a graduated response, trying an array of strategies to meet the range of SEN. Schools are further required to make full use of classroom and school resources before calling in outside support, other than in exceptional cases.[49] In this way, the code of practice emphasises that meeting SEN and making special educational provision is primarily a responsibility of schools.

SENCOs

4.23 To deliver on their SEN responsibilities, schools are required to appoint SEN co-ordinators (SENCOs) who should be given sufficient time for their SEN co-ordination role.[50] Regulations set out the requirements of the SENCO role, including that SENCOs must be qualified teachers.[51]

'School action' and 'school action plus'

4.24 The school-based stages of the code of practice are described as 'school action' and 'school action plus'. Provision at the 'school action' stage should be made by the class teacher with support from the SENCO and the support should be delivered in a way that is additional to or different from the school's usual differentiated curriculum.[52] Intervention at this stage is particularly important where there are signs of developmental delay, emotional and behavioural difficulties and other problems despite the child having access to differentiated learning opportunities.[53] The responsibility for further assessment and planning for support at the 'school action' stage rests with the SENCO.[54] The action planned may include additional staff support, different learning materials or special equipment.[55] Individual education plans should be developed and reviewed at least twice each year for every child at the 'school action' stage.[56]

---

48 SEN CoP, 5:10.
49 SEN CoP, 5:20.
50 SEN CoP, 5:30–5:36.
51 Education (Special Educational Needs Co-ordinators) (England) Regulations 2008 SI No 2945 reg 3.
52 SEN CoP, 5:43.
53 SEN CoP, 5:44.
54 SEN CoP, 5:46.
55 SEN CoP, 5:49.
56 SEN CoP, 5:50–5:53.

4.25   Where a child continues to make little or no progress or struggles in other ways despite intervention at 'school action', external support should be brought in to advise, assess and provide support under 'school action plus'.[57] External specialists can act in an advisory capacity or provide direct support.[58] A new individual education plan should be developed which sets out fresh strategies to ensure the child makes progress.[59]

4.26   Where significant cause for concern remains that a child at 'school action plus' is not making adequate progress, the school can request a statutory assessment by the LEA. Parents can also request a statutory assessment.[60] The requirements for information that schools will need to provide when requesting a statutory assessment are set out in the code of practice at para 5:64. LEAs should be able to decide 'relatively quickly' whether a statutory assessment is necessary if their support services have been involved at the school-based stages.[61] Following a request for a statutory assessment and/or while the assessment is underway, the child should continue to be supported at 'school action plus'.

4.27   The school-based stages at secondary age operate in the same way as for infant and primary schools. Secondary schools are reminded to look for children entering Year 7 who may have unidentified SEN,[62] although the expectation is that a child's SEN should have been identified and addressed well before secondary years. Again, secondary schools are reminded that SEN is a whole school responsibility[63] and that baseline assessments will need to be carried out on entry to the school.[64] The code of practice also calls for a graduated response at secondary level, using interventions at 'school action' and 'school action plus', but recognises the need for a greater degree of flexibility at secondary stage so long as core principles of appropriate provision and accurate record-keeping are followed.[65] The role of the SENCO in mainstream secondary schools is given particular focus in the code of practice.[66]

57   SEN CoP, 5:54–5:61.
58   SEN CoP, 5:58.
59   SEN CoP, 5:59.
60   EA 1996 ss329 and 329A.
61   SEN CoP, 5:65.
62   SEN CoP, 6:1.
63   SEN CoP, 6:2.
64   SEN CoP, 6:6–6:9.
65   SEN CoP, 6:25.
66   SEN CoP, 6:32–6:40.

Statutory assessment and statements of SEN

Statutory assessment

4.28 Despite the focus in the code of practice on meeting children's SEN within the resources available to schools, the statutory scheme recognises that some children's needs will be so extensive that it is appropriate for it to be the responsibility of the LEA to ensure that they are met. The duty on the LEA to arrange a child's special educational provision arises once a child is the subject of a statement (see para 4.45). The route to such a statement is through a statutory assessment by the LEA.

4.29 The duty to undertake a statutory assessment of a child's SEN arises when it is more likely than not to be necessary for the LEA to determine the child's special education provision by making a statement of SEN.[67] The principles of a statutory assessment of SEN are broadly similar to those for assessing 'children in need' (see paras 3.13–3.24) – meaning among other things that the child should be at the centre of the assessment, that the child's views, wishes and feelings should be properly considered and that there should be a careful process of identifying and assessing needs.[68] A refusal by an LEA to carry out an assessment can be appealed to the tribunal (see para 4.131).

4.30 Statutory assessment will not always result in a statement of SEN being issued for the child, as the information gathered during an assessment may show how the child's needs can be met effectively at 'school action plus'. A decision not to issue a statement following assessment can also form the subject of an appeal to the SEN tribunal (see para 4.131).

4.31 Requests for a statutory assessment can be made by a parent,[69] the child's school or setting or another agency,[70] for instance an NHS body. Parents and schools may also request a re-assessment of a child with an existing statement under the same statutory provisions. It will be maladministration for councils to fail to respond appropriately to requests by parents and/or professionals (eg teachers, health and/or social services staff) that a child's SEN be assessed.[71]

---

67 EA 1996 s323; SEN CoP, 7:4.
68 SEN CoP, 7:3.
69 EA 1996 s328 or s329.
70 EA 1996 s329A.
71 Local Government Ombudsman's *Digest of Cases (Education) 2003/04* Report 02/C/2543 – where a catalogue of failures by the LEA led to prolonged delay in the child receiving appropriate SEN support and resulted in a compensation recommendation of £8,000.

4.32   Schools should consult parents before requesting an assessment. An LEA must comply with a request for an assessment from either a school or a parent unless it has made an assessment within six months of the date of the request or it concludes that a statutory assessment is not necessary.[72] Where a parental request is made without the request of the school (or, for example, where the child is being home-educated), LEAs must take this request seriously and take appropriate action.[73] If the child is on a school roll, the LEA must inform the head teacher of a parental request for a statutory assessment.[74]

4.33   Prior to deciding whether to assess, an LEA must issue a statutory notice[75] which gives parents certain specified information about the assessment process, including the statutory timescales[76] and the name of an officer of the LEA from whom further information may be obtained (generally known as the 'named LEA officer'[77]). It will be maladministration to fail to identify a named officer – even if the council has difficulties in identifying suitable people.[78] The notice must also be copied to all other relevant agencies, including health agencies.[79] Parents must be given at least 29 days to make representations as to whether or not their child needs a statutory assessment.[80]

4.34   LEAs must decide within six weeks whether to carry out a statutory assessment,[81] although the decision should be taken as quickly as thorough consideration of all the issues allows.[82] This suggests that where parents and relevant professionals are in agreement that a child needs a statutory assessment, LEAs should decide to assess well before the six-week time limit is reached. LEAs should certainly not

---

72 SEN CoP, 7:11 and 7:21.
73 SEN CoP, 7:22.
74 SEN CoP, 7:27.
75 Under EA 1996 s323(1) or s329A(3).
76 SEN CoP, 7:16.
77 Defined by the code of practice at page 204 as 'the person from the LEA who liaises with parents over all the arrangements relating to statutory assessment and the making of a statement'.
78 Local Government Ombudsman, *Digest of Cases (Education) 2002/03* Report 01/C/5192: in this case the ombudsman observed that the council could have suggested that the parents contact organisations such as the British Dyslexia Association or the Independent Panel for Special Education Advice, although of course the duty to have a 'named officer' remains with the LEA.
79 SEN CoP, 7:19.
80 SEN CoP, 7:16v.
81 SEN CoP, 7:26.
82 SEN CoP, 7:29.

use the six weeks provided simply to delay the process of issuing a statement if it is obvious that one will be required. LEAs are required to make consistent decisions on requests for assessment and then reach open and objective judgments as to whether a statement of SEN should be issued.[83]

4.35   In deciding whether to assess, the code of practice describes the 'critical question' to be whether there is convincing evidence that the child's difficulties may require the LEA to determine his or her special educational provision, despite the best efforts of the school or setting.[84] LEAs are required to take account of all relevant evidence and exercise judgment on the facts of each individual case.

4.36   The code of practice provides for immediate referrals for statutory assessment for children whose needs are such that the full assessment process would be inappropriate.[85] Where children need a 'quick response' from the LEA, the code suggests that the time limits which generally apply can be shortened.[86] There is also a power[87] to place a child who is undergoing a statutory assessment in a special school. All parties, including parents, must agree to such a placement, which may be in the child's interests to avoid permanent exclusion (see below, paras 4.114–4.123).[88]

4.37   No later than six weeks after the request for a statutory assessment, the LEA must tell the parents and the school or setting (if they made the request) whether it will assess.[89] A decision not to carry out an assessment must be in writing with reasons and should set out the provision the LEA considers would meet the child's needs appropriately without a statutory assessment or statement.[90] A refusal to assess can be appealed to the tribunal: see para 4.131.

4.38   If the LEA decides to assess, it must then seek advice from the child's parents and educational, medical, psychological and 'social services' advice.[91] If the child is to be assessed or examined, parents must be told of their right to be present.[92] Copies of representations or evidence provided by the child's parents must be given

---

83   SEN CoP, 7:29.
84   SEN CoP, 7:34.
85   SEN CoP, 7:30–7:32.
86   SEN CoP, 7:30.
87   Under EA 1996 s316A(2).
88   SEN CoP, 7:31–7:32.
89   SEN CoP, 7:68.
90   SEN CoP, 7:69.
91   SEN CoP, 7:74.
92   SEN CoP, 7:75.

to all professionals asked for advice.[93] The advice must relate to the child's current and future educational needs. Those giving advice can comment on the amount of provision they consider appropriate and should not be barred from doing so by the LEA.[94] However, advice should not be influenced by a potential school or setting and specific schools must not be suggested.[95] The code of practice emphasises the importance of involving the child in the assessment process, in particular by ascertaining the child's views about his or her needs and aspirations (see also paras 1.21–1.24).[96]

4.39   LEAs have ten weeks from serving the notice agreeing to assess the child to decide whether or not to make a statement of SEN or amend an existing statement.[97] Again, this is a maximum time limit, not an excuse for an LEA to delay unreasonably in deciding whether or not a statement is required. If all the evidence is available sooner, it may well be reasonable for the LEA to make a decision well within this timeframe. If the LEA decides to make or amend a statement, it must send a draft of what it proposes to the child's parents within two weeks of the decision.[98] All advice received as part of the assessment process should be attached to the draft statement.

4.40   If the LEA decides *not* to make or amend a statement, it must notify the parents and the school, giving reasons, within two weeks.[99] It will be maladministration for an LEA to fail to inform a parent of their right to appeal against its refusal to undertake a SEN assessment.[100] The code of practice states that it is preferable that LEAs should issue a 'note in lieu' of a statement if deciding not to make a statement. However, 'notes in lieu' are unenforceable and as such are no substitute for a statement. They do provide a summary of the additional knowledge gained about a child's SEN during the assessment process[101] which would enable staff at the school to augment their strategies for meeting the child's SEN. However, it is unlikely that parents will be satisfied with a note in lieu if they have felt that

93 SEN CoP, 7:78.
94 SEN CoP, 7:79.
95 SEN CoP, 7:79.
96 SEN CoP, 3:18 and 7:85.
97 SEN CoP, 7:86.
98 SEN CoP, 7:87.
99 SEN CoP, 7:88.
100 Local Government Ombudsman's *Digest of Cases (Education) 2002/03* Report 01/C/5192, where it was recommended that compensation of £12,000 be paid for the failure of support.
101 SEN CoP, 8:17.

their child's needs were sufficient to require a statutory assessment or if parents have experience of the school being reluctant or resistant to implementing a range of strategies to meet their child's needs. Where an LEA decides not to make or amend a statement, parents can exercise their right of appeal to the tribunal (see para 4.131).

4.41 Whether or not a statement is to be made or amended, parents should know the outcome of the assessment process and where necessary be informed of their right of appeal to the tribunal within 12 weeks of the referral for an assessment.[102]

Timescales for statutory assessments

4.42 As noted above, the statutory regime places a number of specific time limits by which the LEA must undertake and/or complete various procedures – resulting in an overall *six-month limit* for the production of a statement of SEN. In this context the code of practice (para 7:16) requires that LEAs:

> explain the precise timing of each of the various stages of the assessments within the overall six-month time limit, indicate ways in which the parents can assist the LEA in meeting the time limits, and explain the exceptions to the time limits.

4.43 Despite the statutory force of the relevant timescales, delay remains a feature of the process, and has been the subject of many critical local government ombudsman reports. A 2003 report,[103] for example, concerned an LEA that had taken a year to produce a statement, rather than the required six months. In her report the ombudsman: (1) criticised the council for having financial procedures that created delay (eg procedures that required specific officer/member/'panel' authority to incur additional expenditure); and (2) noted that some delay was attributable to the failure of NHS professionals to provide reports promptly – but considered that the council's system for following up late responses was inadequate.

4.44 Delay can cause hardship, not only during the initial statementing process, but also in relation to necessary amendments and subsequent revisions to the statement. In a 2003 report,[104] for example, the

---

102 SEN CoP, 7:90.

103 Local Government Ombudsman's *Digest of Cases (Education) 2002/03* Report 02/C/2968; and see also the *Digest of Cases (Education) 2003/04* Report 01/CB/6663, where maladministration was found for a process that took nine months longer than the statutory six-month period.

104 Local Government Ombudsman's *Digest of Cases (Education) 2002/03* Report 01/B/16041, where it was recommended that compensation of over £3,000 be paid in consequence.

ombudsman held that a delay of seven months in the issuing of an amended statement amounted to maladministration. The negative consequences of such delays are obvious, and include those discussed in paras 1.61–1.62. It is therefore imperative that LEAs use their best endeavours to complete the assessment and statementing process as quickly as possible and treat the specific and overall time-scales as maximums, not targets.

Statements of SEN

4.45   The duty on LEAs to 'make and maintain' a statement of SEN arises when following assessment, it is necessary for the LEA to 'determine' the special educational provision which the child's learning disability 'calls for'.[105] The code of practice suggests that this means that the 'degree of the child's learning difficulty' and 'the nature of the provision necessary' are such that the LEA is required to determine the provision for itself.[106] The code obliges the LEA to make and maintain a statement when the required provision 'cannot reasonably be provided within the resources normally available to mainstream schools and early education settings in the area'.[107]

4.46   The code of practice notes (at 8:5) that resources to maintain statements of SEN are now routinely 'delegated' or 'devolved' to schools. While this may assist in having needs met within the setting, there remains an absolute duty on LEAs both to 'make and maintain' the statement *and* to ensure that the provision set out in part 3 of it (see para 4.47) are in fact delivered, regardless of whether the school has received the funding to do this. This second duty stems from EA 1996 s324(5)(a)(i), which states that:

> Where a local education authority maintain a statement ..., then unless the child's parent has made suitable arrangements, the authority shall arrange that the special educational provision is made for the child.

4.47   The duty to arrange the special educational provision specified in a statement applies whatever the setting in which the child is educated and is not qualified by any resource considerations. Any breach of this duty can be remedied through judicial review. In the recent case of *R (N) v North Tyneside Borough Council (IPSEA Intervening)*,[108] the Court of Appeal overturned a decision of the High Court which would

---

105   EA 1996 s324(1).
106   SEN CoP, 8:1.
107   SEN CoP, 8:2.
108   [2010] EWCA Civ 135; [2010] ELR 312.

have allowed the authority unilaterally to vary the statement as and when it appeared to be appropriate. The Court of Appeal reiterated that provision identified in part 3 of a statement must be actually provided, absent any formal amendment to the statement. Sedley LJ reminded local authorities that 'there is no best endeavours defence in the legislation' in relation to any failure to implement the provisions of a statement.[109]

4.48 Given the importance and legal enforceability of a statement, it is essential that it specifies and quantifies with precision the SEN provision that an individual child requires. 'Vague' statements, which do not specify provision appropriate to the identified needs of the child, do not comply with the law and any flexibility built into the statement must be there to meet the needs of the child and not the needs of the system.[110] So, a statement may need to say that the child will have a certain number of hours of teaching assistant support, or it may need to require that all staff working with the child have particular training or expertise relating to the child's needs. It follows that it will be maladministration for an LEA to have a policy of not specifying in statements the number of hours support a child requires, as the ombudsman has held in relation to a child of secondary age.[111]

4.49 The 'non-resource-dependent' nature of the duty to meet a child's SEN identified in a statement is illustrated by a 2003 local government ombudsman report[112] which concerned a statement that required the provision of '12 hours a week help from a non-teaching assistant; and information technology support and appropriate alternative arrangements to record his work'. In the ombudsman's opinion the pupil in question, if given this support was perfectly capable of keeping pace with his peers – but that without this support he was 'critically disabled'. Due to resource difficulties, the school advised the parents that he could have the 12 hours' extra help or a laptop – but not both. The ombudsman considered it unacceptable for anyone acting on behalf of a council to suggest to parents that they must choose one element of provision in the statement over others due to insufficient resources. This meant that 'councils have a duty to make resources available to meet the whole provision' identified by a statement.

109 [2010] EWCA Civ 135; [2010] ELR 312 at [17].
110 *R (IPSEA) v Secretary of State for Education and Skills* [2003] EWCA Civ 07; [2003] ELR 393.
111 See, for example, Local Government Ombudsman's *Digest of Cases (Education) 2004/05* Report 03/A/9667.
112 Local Government Ombudsman's *Digest of Cases (Education) 2002/03* Report 01/C/5192.

4.50   Even where the 'resource' problem is not directly financial (for
example, arising from a staff shortage) the ombudsman will require
a local authority to put in place contingency plans to address this.
A 2010 ombudsman report,[113] for example, concerned a registered
blind student's statement of SEN that required the provision of ten
hours per week input from a qualified teacher for the visually impaired. However, due to staff shortages this was not provided over
an extended period. In finding maladminstration the ombudsman
accepted that it was 'difficult for the council to provide any cover at
short notice for unexpected absences. But absences of more than a
day or two could have been covered'.

4.51   LEAs can only avoid the obligation to 'arrange' the provision for
a child with a statement if the parents have made suitable arrangements themselves. The code of practice at para 8:97 states that
'Parents should not be treated as having made suitable arrangements
if the arrangements do not include a realistic possibility of funding
those arrangements for a reasonable period of time'. Although this
is in relation to part 4 placements (see para 4.52 below), the principle
clearly applies to whether the parents have made suitable arrangements in relation to part 3 provision. Parents should never be forced
to make their own arrangements by the availability of only inappropriate provision for their children by LEAs.

4.52   Statements themselves must be in the form prescribed by the
schedule to the regulations,[114] the format being:[115]

a) Part 1: Introduction (Child's details)
b) Part 2: Special Educational Needs (learning difficulties), includ-
    ing details of *each and every one* of the of the child's special educa-
    tional needs as identified through the statutory assessment (em-
    phasis added)
c) Part 3: Special Educational Provision, including objectives, provision
    required to meet needs and objectives (facilities, equipment, staff-
    ing arrangements and curriculum) and monitoring arrangements
d) Part 4: Placement, being the type and name of school or the LEA's
    arrangements for provision to be made otherwise than in school

---

113 Local Government Ombudsman's Report No 09 001 513 against the Isle of
     Wight Council, 27 May 2010: compensation of £3,500 was recommended to
     provide additional help to enable the child to make up for the provision she
     has lost and of £1,500 to the mother as compensation for her distress, time
     and trouble in making the complaint.
114 Education (Special Educational Needs) (England) (Consolidation) Regulations
     2001 Sch 2.
115 SEN CoP, 8:29.

e) Part 5: Non-Educational Needs
f) Part 6: Non-Educational Provision

4.53 Because only parts 2, 3 and 4 of the statement fall within the jurisdiction of the tribunal, these are the parts that parents should focus on.[116] The school to be named in part 4 should if possible be able to deliver all the provision set out in part 3, where necessary with the assistance of the LEA. In *R v Kingston-upon-Thames Council and Hunter*,[117] McCullough J emphasized the importance of the 'flow' of a statement:

> Part 4 cannot influence part 3. It is not a matter of fitting part 3 to part 4 but of considering the fitness of part 4 to meet the provision in ... part 3.

4.54 The code of practice has a section on 'writing the statement'. Relevant provisions of this section include:

* statements should be 'clear' and 'unambiguous' (8:31);
* part 2 should describe all the child's learning difficulties (8:32);
* part 3 must specify the special educational provision to meet identified needs in part 2 (8:33);
* the LEA is responsible for arranging the provision in the statement, irrespective of who actually delivers it, unless the LEA is satisfied that the child's parents have themselves made suitable arrangements (8:34b);
* part 3 should detail appropriate provision to meet each identified need (8:36);
* part 3 provision should normally be quantified (8:37);[118] and
* speech and language therapy should be recorded as educational provision unless there are exceptional reasons for not doing so (8:49).

4.55 All the advice obtained and considered during the assessment must be attached as appendices to the statement. The code (at para 8:3) specifies that, at minimum, this must include (a) parental evidence; (b) educational advice; (c) medical advice; (d) psychological advice; and (e) social services advice.

---

116 See SEN CoP, 8:47 for the requirement on LEAs to explain this legal position to parents.
117 [1997] ELR 223 and see also *A v Barnet* [2003] EWHC 3368 (Admin) where the court spoke of the process requiring the completion of part 2 before part 3 and only then moving on to part 4..
118 See also *L v Clarke and Somerset CC* [1998] ELR 129.

4.56   The total length of time from a request for a statutory assessment until the issuing of the final statement of SEN should be no more than 26 weeks.[119] Statements must not suggest that provision to be made under part 3 will be quantified and specified after future assessments have been carried out, but must specify and quantify the provision to be made according to the information available when they are finalised.[120]

'Educational' and 'non-educational' provision

4.57   As noted above (see para 4.54) the statutory scheme distinguishes between 'educational' needs (set out in part 2 of the statement) and 'non-educational' needs (part 5), and states that only educational provision specified in part 3 is 'legally binding' (whereas non-educational provision in part 6 cannot be enforced).[121] The question then arises as to what precisely constitutes 'educational' needs and provision. The code of practice explains that educational needs are those that arise from a child's learning difficulties and educational provision is the provision required to meet those needs.[122] This formula was adopted in *X v Caerphilly CC*[123] where it was held that:

> Since the form of therapy recommended by Ms Kelly related to Y's poor social interaction, independence and self-help skills, and since those skills were regarded by the LEA as learning skills for which educational provision had to be made (see part 2 of the statement), the tribunal should have held that the therapy which was needed to improve those skills should have been included in part 3 of the statement, and not part 5.

4.58   If therapeutic provision of any kind is necessary to meet a child's educational need, it should be quantified and specified in part 3 of the statement. In particular, the code of practice states (at 8:49) that speech and language therapy should be treated as educational provision unless *exceptional* reasons exist not to do so.

4.59   The crucial importance of such therapies to some disabled children is illustrated by a 2003 Local Government Ombudsman report[124]

---

119 SEN CoP, flowchart at 8:134.
120 *C v SENT and LB Greenwich* [1999] ELR 5.
121 SEN CoP, 8:47.
122 SEN CoP, 8:32–8:33.
123 [2005] ELR 78 at [27].
124 Local Government Ombudsman's *Digest of Cases (Education) 2002/03* Report 00/B/18517 and see also Local Government Ombudsman's *Digest of Cases (Education) 2005/06* Report 04/B/07871.

which concerned a statement of SEN that required a 'structured language programme implemented on a daily basis with advice and input from a speech and language therapist, and intensive support from the speech and language therapy service'. Since this provision was included in part 3 of the statement, it was the LEA's duty to ensure it was provided. The LEA agreed with the local NHS that their therapist would provide this support, but she then left such that the child's support fell from 60 sessions a term to only 10. Although the ombudsman considered that initially it was reasonable for the council to hope that the NHS would be able to recruit a replacement, when after a term this was not the case, the council should have (for example) contracted with a private therapist. What the council could not do was to 'wash its hands of its responsibilities, even though the problems arose in a service which the council did not itself run'.

4.60   LEAs will be obliged to arrange the provision of any therapies specified in part 3 of the statement which amount to provision to meet educational needs identified in part 2. This could include other common therapies such as occupational therapy and physiotherapy, all of which are capable of being educational provision.[125] Whether in fact they are 'educational' or 'non-education' will depend in every case on the needs of the individual child. Whether the LEA will actually have to *fund* these therapies will depend on what relationships it has in place with health bodies and/or other parts of the children's services authority. However, LEAs cannot arrange part 3 provision in a way which requires parents to fund it.

Placements

4.61   In some cases, the most important part of a child's statement of SEN will be part 4 – in which the school or other provision which the child will attend is named. This is particularly so where the child's needs are such that a special school, whether day or residential, is felt by his or her parents to be required. Placement is understandably often the most contested part of a statement, as this is where most of the expenditure for an LEA arises (albeit that therapeutic and other provision specified in part 3 can also result in significant costs). When statements are published in draft, parents will have the opportunity to express a preference for their child's placement. The law governing different types of placement (maintained and non-maintained,

125 *Bromley LBC v SENT* [1999] ELR 260.

mainstream and special) is set out below. During the negotiations on a draft statement, parents who are unhappy with the stance of the LEA will have to take a proactive approach to identifying alternative suitable placements and may need to contact the advice organisations listed at the end of this chapter for assistance with this. On an appeal by a parent, the tribunal will consider any placement a parent puts forward, from home education to a residential special school (so long as it meets the legal criteria, see below), but will not play any part in helping the parent find the placement their child needs. A child with SEN must be admitted to any school named in part 4 of his or her statement.[126]

Maintained placements

4.62   Under EA 1996 Sch 27, a parent may express a preference during the statementing process for any maintained school (ie, a school maintained by an LEA), whether mainstream or special. The LEA *must* comply with this preference unless one of the following specific reasons apply:

a) the school is unsuitable to the child's age, ability, aptitude or special education needs;

b) the placement would be 'incompatible' (see below) with the efficient education of other children; or

c) the placement would be 'incompatible' (see below) with the efficient use of resources.

4.63   Furthermore, by virtue of the EA 1996 s316, an LEA must ensure that a child is educated in a *mainstream* school unless:

a) a parent indicates (in whatever way) that they do not wish the child to be in a mainstream school; or

b) the placement is incompatible with the efficient education of other children.

4.64   Parents therefore have an almost unqualified right to a maintained mainstream placement for their child with SEN. The only qualification (if the parents want such a place) is that it must not be 'incompatible' with the efficient education of other children.[127] However,

---

126 School Standards and Framework Act 1998 s98.

127 See the recent decision of the Upper Tribunal in *NA v Barnet LBC* [2010] UKUT 180 (AAC) for the proper approach to this test (judgment at [34]) and that it must be applied by reference to the circumstances only of the child in question and other children who are already known or predicted to be educated with the child (judgment at [36]).

that qualification has to be considered in the light of both the Equality Act 2010 and the specific duty to consider what reasonable steps the LEA might take to remove the incompatibility.[128]

4.65 Parents who are seeking a maintained *special school* placement for their child or a specific mainstream school placement should be successful unless any of the exceptions in Schedule 27 are triggered (see para 4.62 above). By way of example, *Hampshire CC v R and SENDIST*[129] concerned a dispute as to the suitability of two different maintained special schools. The mother considered the school named by the LEA to be unsuitable and the LEA considered that a placement in the school preferred by the mother would be incompatible with the provision of efficient education to other children. The tribunal found in the mother's favour and on appeal the High Court held that the impact of the child attending the preferred school must be so great as to be incompatible with the efficiency of the education of other children in the school (a very high threshold); ie 'incompatible' was not the same as saying 'there would be some impact'. It followed that if there is not found to be such incompatibility, the preferred school must be named. However, if there was such an incompatibility, then the tribunal still retained a discretion as whether it remained appropriate to name the school.[130]

Non-maintained/independent placements

4.66 When LEAs send parents a copy of the proposed statement, they must be told that they have the right to make representations in favour of a non-maintained or independent school.[131] If a parent wants their child to attend an independent school other than those approved under EA 1996 s347, the consent of the secretary of state must be obtained. When a parent is seeking a placement other than at an LEA-maintained school, the relevant statutory provision is EA 1996 s9 which provides as follows:

> **9 Pupils to be educated in accordance with parent's wishes**
> ... Local education authorities shall have regard to the general principle that pupils are to be educated in accordance with the wishes of their parents, so far as that is compatible with the provision of efficient instruction and training and the avoidance of unreasonable public expenditure.

128 SEN CoP, 8:58.
129 [2009] ELR 371.
130 This discretion arising from EA 1996 s324(4).
131 SEN CoP, 8:69.

4.67   The section 9 duty applies to parental preferences for independent special schools;[132] where the parental choice is for such a school, the LEA (and ultimately the tribunal) is required to balance the educational advantages of the place preferred by the parents to the extra cost of it to the LEA.[133] In *Ealing LBC v SENDIST and K and K*[134] the court held that public expenditure may be considered unreasonable 'if it is disproportionate to the educational advantages of the placement preferred by the parents'. In this case the court contrasted the test under section 9 (reasonableness) with the test under Schedule 27, which requires consideration of whether the increased costs would be so substantial as to be incompatible with the efficient use of resources.[135]

4.68   It follows that where parents are seeking independent or non-maintained provision, a crucial issue to determine is whether the alternative provision proposed by the LEA is appropriate to meet the identified needs of the child. Only if this can be established should the LEA (or the tribunal) name this provision in part 4 instead of a more expensive independent provision preferred by the parents. As Sedley LJ confirmed in *Oxfordshire CC v GB and others*,[136] 'where the state system simply cannot provide for the child's needs, there will be no choice: The LEA must pay the cost [of whatever suitable provision is sought by the parent]'.

4.69   Even if the LEA's provision is held to be suitable for the child, following the *Ealing* judgment (see para 4.67) the parent's chosen provision should still be ordered unless the cost is disproportionate to the educational advantages of the placement to the child. Guidance in these situations was provided by Sedley LJ in the *Oxfordshire* case (see para 4.68) (at [15]), stating that this means 'an undue or disproportionate burden on the education budget'. In effect, if the parent's chosen non-maintained school costs significantly more than the LEA's proposed placement and the LEA's placement is suitable, the parent will lose any appeal to the tribunal.

4.70   It then becomes important to work out exactly which costs should enter into the 'balance sheet' in relation to the LEA's proposed provision. The short answer is that those costs which are incurred

---

132 *C v Buckinghamshire CC and SENT* [1999] ELR 179.

133 *Oxfordshire CC v GB and others* [2002] ELR 8.

134 [2008] ELR 183 at para 14.

135 Schedule 27 has no application to situations such as this where the parents' preference is for an independent school and the LEA propose to name a maintained school: *C v Buckingham CC and SENT* [1999] ELR 179.

136 [2002] ELR 8.

with or without the placement of the child at the maintained school are *ignored* when calculating the placement costs. Only extra costs incurred by the placement of the individual child at the maintained school are taken into account. This remains the case whether the additional expenditure is direct by the LEA or from the school's delegated budget; *Coventry CC v SENDIST and Browne.*[137]

4.71 An issue which frequently arises is whether the costs of non-educational provision which a child will require if they attend the LEA's proposed placement should be taken into account when assessing the relative costs of the placements. The short answer to this question is yes, as was made clear in *O v Lewisham LBC.*[138] In this case, the court held firstly that the tribunal should take account of any social services expenditure likely to be incurred alongside the educational placement proposed by the LEA, and secondly that where the exact nature of this expenditure was uncertain or likely to change, the tribunal should do its best to assess the position at the date of the hearing. The judgment in *O v Lewisham* focussed solely on social services expenditure, but there is no good reason to suggest that the court (or now the Upper Tribunal, see below) would take a different approach to other aspects of public spending that would differ between different placements, for instance by a health body.

4.72 The 'unreasonable public expenditure' provisions outlined above are complicated and may be made clearer through the following examples:

- In a SENDIST appeal, the parents want their child to attend school A, an independent special school where the placement would cost £40,000 per year. The LEA proposes school B, a maintained special school, which the parents accept is suitable (but still prefer school A). The only costs of placing the child at school B which are *specific to that child* are a part-time teaching assistant at £10,000 per year and provision of various therapies at £5,000 per year. If this case went to tribunal, it would almost certainly be held that school B should be named in part 4 of the child's statement because the difference in costs between the schools (being £25,000) would mean placing the child at school A would be a 'disproportionate burden on the education budget'.

- However, following *O v Lewisham* (see para 4.71), if in the above scenario the child would also be receiving a package of short breaks costing £25,000 per year if she attended school B, and if

137 [2008] ELR 1.
138 [2007] EWHC 2092 (Admin).

this package would not be required at school A because it operated an extended day, then the tribunal should name school A in part 4 of the statement. This is because there would be no difference in costs and therefore the duty to comply with parental wishes in EA 1996 s9 would require school A to be named.

4.73   The Court of Appeal has recently held in *Slough BC v SENDIST and Others*[139] that where an independent school discounts its fees for an individual child, in that case in recognition of fundraising efforts undertaken by the parents, then the reduced fee can be taken into account by the tribunal rather than the full fee when determining the placement cost. The Court of Appeal left open the question as to whether it would be permissible for parents simply to make a part-payment of fees to bring the remaining costs of the independent placement below that of the maintained school. This judgment is clearly problematic as many children with SEN will not have parents who can fundraise on behalf of their chosen school, but it is a welcome sign that the courts are prepared to take a flexible approach to the test set out in EA 1996 s9. Another welcome feature of this judgment for parents is that the Court of Appeal rejected the argument advanced by the LEA that the cost of its maintained school placement was just the cost of 1:1 support for the child and upheld the tribunal's finding that the true cost, including therapeutic input and other supplementary spending, would exceed the cost of the independent placement sought by the parents. The Court of Appeal's judgment in *Slough* may therefore make it somewhat easier for parents to obtain placements in the independent sector than has been the case since the court's judgment in the *Oxfordshire* case (see above, para 4.68).

Residential placements

4.74   Children with complex needs may at some stage require residential schooling – whether as a result of the complexity of their needs or as a result of family breakdown, or indeed a combination of the two. Residential school placements are usually only funded solely by an LEA when the child needs a 24-hour 'waking day' curriculum, and in *R (M) v (1) Wiltshire CC (2) SENDIST*[140] the court held that in these cases SENDIST must consider the educational reasons why a waking day curriculum was said to be required before determining

---

139 [2010] EWCA Civ 668.
140 [2006] EWHC 3337 (Admin); [2007] ELR 171.

placement. When considering whether 'waking day' provision is required, the focus must be on whether or not the child requires educational programmes continuing after the end of the school day.[141]

4.75 Arguments over whether residential provision is required arise frequently in cases involving children with autism. *S v Solihull MBC*[142] is one of many cases reflecting the fact that an 'inability to generalise [skills is an] educational need' for children with autism. The concept of generalisation was held to mean the ability of a child to 'translate into his home and social and indeed all areas of his life and functioning, the skill which he learns within the school and school room'.[143] This is of course only one example of an educational need which may require residential provision.

4.76 In *R (TS) v Bowen and another*,[144] the High Court further considered the issue of when a waking day curriculum was needed. The appellant, TS's father, submitted that there was overwhelming expert evidence that TS required a waking day curriculum, available only in the residential school. The judge dismissed the appeal, agreeing with the local authority that the fact that a tribunal identifies that a consistency of approach is required, going beyond the school day does not mean either that that is necessarily an educational need, or that it can only be met by residential provision. The judgment illustrates how high the hurdle is that parents have to cross to establish that their child has an *educational* need for residential provision (but see below in respect of wider needs for residential provision). Not infrequently a more productive line of argument is that no local provision exists which is capable of meet the child's needs, such that the LEA is required to fund residential provision whatever the cost, relying on the judgment of Sedley LJ in the *Oxfordshire* case (see above, para 4.68).

4.77 The 'waking day' requirement does not, however, apply where the need for a residential placement arises out of a combination of factors – for example, the child's educational, social and/or healthcare needs or family breakdown. In such cases it is important that all agencies focus on the wider issues – such as the well-being of the wider family, as is well illustrated by a 2009 local government ombudsman

141 *The Learning Trust v SENDIST and MP* [2007] EWHC 1634 (Admin); [2007] ELR 658.

142 [2007] EWHC 1139 at [19].

143 *S v Solihull MBC* [2007] EWHC 1139 at [17].

144 [2009] EWHC 5 (Admin); [2009] All ER (D) 56 (Jan).

report.[145] The complaint concerned a family with two children, one of whom had learning disabilities and very aggressive behaviour, which impacted particularly badly on his parents and his younger sister. The parents and social services believed that the family would benefit from the son having a residential placement but social services were unable to agree joint funding of such a placement with the LEA, since the education officers believed they could meet the son's SEN educational needs with local provision and support (ie without a residential school placement). Ultimately this proved disastrous, particularly for the daughter who developed significant mental health difficulties. The ombudsman found the council guilty of maladministration, since (1) by concentrating on the son's needs it lost sight of the need to provide effective support and respite care for the family; and (2) it should have undertaken separate social care assessments of the needs of the parents as carers and of each child as children in need in their own right (see paras 3.13–3.24 above for assessments of children in need).

4.78   A similar failure was identified by the local government ombudsman in a 2008 report.[146] The complaint concerned a family with three children, one of whom (L), was severely autistic with associated communication difficulties and had a statement of special educational needs. At an annual review, the professionals unanimously recommended that L should attend a residential school from the point of transfer to secondary education, as her needs could not be met locally. This was supported by a social care assessment (see paras 3.13–3.24) which recommended that her needs should be met outside the home, in a setting where she would receive 24-hour supervision and care, with an educational programme integrated into her life both at school and outside. Not only did the LEA fail to provide the agreed support, it failed to explain how the need for a 24-hour curriculum could be met without a residential school placement. L remained at home for eight months during which time the family received no respite care – despite this having been identified as an assessed need. The ombudsman found these systemic failings to be maladministration noting that 'education and social care professionals did not work together effectively with one another and with the

---

145 Complaint No 07B 04696 and 07B10996 against Croydon LBC, 16 September 2009.

146 Local Government Ombudsman's *Digest of Cases (Education) 2008/09* Report 06B04654, where it was recommended that compensation of £10,000 be paid for the failure of support.

healthcare professionals involved, to ensure that not only [L]'s needs, but those of her parents and siblings were met'.[147]

4.79   Where a child is placed in a residential special school solely funded through a statement, the placement is not ordinarily made under Children Act (CA) 1989 s20(1) and the child will therefore not be 'looked after' within the meaning of CA 1989 s22.[148] However, where a child is placed in a residential school with the intention that he or she should remain there for longer than three months, the LEA must notify the director of children's services, or in Wales the lead director for children and young people.[149] The director must then 'take such steps as are reasonably practicable to enable them to determine whether the child's welfare is adequately safeguarded and promoted' and consider whether to exercise any of their functions under CA 1989 in relation to the child.[150]

4.80   It is highly unsatisfactory that despite the Children Act 2004, LEAs and the tribunal are only required to consider a child's educational needs for residential provision under the EA 1996. However, children's services authorities (of which LEAs are part) must take a holistic view to meeting disabled children's needs and cannot rely on the fragmented legislation to avoid providing a residential placement to meet a disabled child's education and care needs if that is what is required (see chapter 3 for the wider duties of children's services authorities to disabled children).

Children placed out-of-authority

4.81   Some, but by no means all, children in residential schools will be placed outside of their 'home' LEA. Other children will be placed outside their authority by children's services, either as a result of family breakdown or to meet their social care needs (see chapter 3). Where any child is placed away from their family home and the criteria under the CA 1989 s20(1) are met (see para 3.78), the child will become 'looked after' and the placing authority will continue to have responsibilities towards them.

---

147 See also Local Government Ombudsman's *Digest of Cases (Education) 2008/09* Report 06B04654, pp14–15, where the failure of social services and education to work together to prepare a 'full social and educational assessment' was held to constitute maladministration.

148 *R (O) v East Riding of Yorkshire CC* [2010] EWHC 489 (Admin); [2010] ELR 318 per Cranston J at [70].

149 CA 1989 s85.

150 CA 1989 s85(4).

4.82   As a group, 'looked after children' (see paras 3.84–3.87) are nine times more likely to have a statement of SEN than the general pupil population; 28 per cent of looked after children have a statement of SEN, with 60 per cent of all looked after children having some form of SEN.[151] Because these children are frequently placed 'out-of-authority' (for example, with foster parents) there can sometimes be confusion as to the responsibilities that LEAs have towards the child if the child needs to be assessed for a statement of SEN. This has prompted the DCSF (now the Department for Education (DfE)) to produced clear guidance on in relating to meeting the SEN of looked after children who are placed out-of-authority.[152]

4.83   For the purposes of the EA 1996 an LEA is responsible for a child if he or she is in their area. The term 'in their area' is not defined by the Act. The DCSF construes this phrase to mean 'ordinarily resident in their area'. This means that an SEN assessment must be carried out by the authority where the child is ordinarily resident. 'Ordinary residence' is similarly not defined in the EA 1996; however, the concept of 'ordinary residence' was held by the House of Lords in *R v Barnet LBC ex p Shah*[153] to imply the following:

> Ordinary residence is established if there is a regular habitual mode of life in a particular place 'for the time being', 'whether of short or long duration', the continuity of which has persisted apart from temporary or occasional absences. The only provisos are that the residence must be voluntary and adopted for 'a settled purpose'.

4.84   Accordingly, and in line with the guidance referred to above, where a looked after child is in a settled placement, for example, with foster parents, then the authority where the foster parents are resident will be the authority responsible for carrying out the SEN assessment. Similarly if the child is resident in a children's home the local authority where the home is situated bears the responsibility.

4.85   When an out-of-authority placement is made for a child who already has a statement of SEN, that statement should transfer to the authority where the child will be living. The transfer of the statement is provided for by the Education (Special Educational

---

151 Department for Children, Schools and Families (DCSF), *Guidance on looked after children with special educational needs placed out-of-authority*, 2009, p3.

152 DCSF, *Guidance on looked after children with special educational needs placed out-of-authority*, 2009.

153 [1993] 1 All ER 226.

Needs) (England) (Consolidation) Regulations 2001[154] and the new authority should treat such a transfer in the same way as any other. The placing authority will retain its obligations under CA 1989: see chapter 3.

Moving school

4.86 The need to finalise[155] or update/amend a statement of SEN is particularly important when a child is approaching a transitional period – for example, a move from primary to secondary schooling. In the local government ombudsman's opinion it is vital that any revisions to a statement occasioned by such a transfer should be made in good time (for example, no later than the spring term preceding the transfer to secondary school) so as to allow time for any appeal that made be made over the school to which the child will transfer.[156]

4.87 The timescales laid down by the legislation and the duty to act without delay and with diligence also apply where a child arrives in the LEA's area from another area (or indeed another country[157]). This is also the case where a child who is accommodated (see paras 3.78–3.87 above) by an adjoining local authority moves into the LEA's area.[158]

Education otherwise than at school

4.88 Like all children, children with SEN can be educated at home.[159] In addition, however, the LEA can decide to fund home education for children with SEN where it considers that it would be inappropriate for some of all of the provision required by a child to be made in a

---

154 Regulation 23.

155 See, for example, Local Government Ombudsman's *Digest of Cases (Education)* *2003/04* Report 02/B/11771.

156 See, for example, Local Government Ombudsman's *Digest of Cases (Education)* *2004/05*, Report 03/B/8725.

157 See, for example, Local Government Ombudsman's *Digest of Cases (Education)* *2006/07* page C4 and also the digest of cases (education) 2007/08, Reports 06A11234 and 14354, where the delay concerned the failure to readmit a child after a failed move abroad.

158 See, for example, Local Government Ombudsman's *Digest of Cases (Education)* *2008/09*, p13.

159 EA 1996 s7.

school.[160] This was confirmed by the Court of Appeal in *TM v Hounslow LBC*,[161] where it was held that:

> Where the LEA is considering what special educational provisions the child needs ... the local education authority has to ask whether it is satisfied that it would be 'inappropriate' for the special educational provision which a learning difficulty of a child in their area calls for, or any part of it, to be made in a school. This is where s319 comes in.

4.89   EA 1996 s319 specifically envisages that *part* of the provision required by a particular child may be made out of school. So for example, a child may attend a mainstream school but may have a type of therapy specified in part 3 of her statement which cannot be delivered in the school but which the LEA has the obligation to ensure is delivered elsewhere. Where this power does not arise and parents are making arrangements to educate their child at home, the statement can (and it is submitted should) specify any provision that the LEA have agreed to make under EA 1996 s319 to help parents provide suitable education at home.[162]

4.90   If the provision made by parents at home is not suitable and does not meet the child's SEN, then the LEA is not absolved of its responsibility to arrange the provision in the statement. The LEA should make attempts to ensure the provision can be made suitable by working with the parents. If this is not possible then the LEA must carry out its duty to ensure the child's SEN are met and it may be necessary to issue a school attendance order.[163]

4.91   LEAs' duties towards home educated children with SEN in England were further clarified by a guidance letter for directors of children's services produced by the DCSF (now DfE) in February 2010. This was in order to fulfil a commitment made by the government in their response to the Badman review[164] to support home educators and further to make clear the responsibilities of local authorities towards home educated children.

---

160 EA 1996 s319, which reads: '(1) Where a local education authority are satisfied that it would be inappropriate for – (a) the special educational provision which a learning difficulty of a child in their area calls for, or (b) any part of any such provision, to be made in a school, they may arrange for the provision (or, as the case may be, for that part of it) to be made otherwise than in a school. (2) Before making an arrangement under this section, a local education authority shall consult the child's parent.'

161 [2009] EWCA Civ 859 at [24].

162 SEN CoP, 8:96.

163 Under EA 1996 s437.

164 Graham Badman, *Report to the secretary of state on the review of elective home education in England*, June 2009.

Transport

4.92   Transport for children with SEN but without a statement will be governed by the local authority's general school transport policy. The statutory provisions in relation to school transport in England are found in EA 1996 ss508A–509A. LEAs must arrange suitable home-to-school travel arrangements for eligible children,[165] eligibility generally being determined by distance from school. However, children who are unable to walk because of SEN, a disability or mobility problems and children who cannot reasonably be expected to walk because of the nature of the route will also be eligible. If a child is not eligible for free home-to-school transport, the local authority may still make transport arrangements for them. Such arrangements do not have to be free of charge, but whether or not there will be a charge should be made clear in the authority's school travel policy. The school transport duties on local authorities in England are further explained in the relevant government guidance.[166]

4.93   The SEN Code of Practice gives advice as to the transport arrangements to be made for children with statements of SEN (paras 8:87–8:90). In particular, it advises (para 8:90) that where the LEA names a residential provision at some distance from the parents' home the LEA should provide transport or travel assistance (for example, through the reimbursement of public transport costs, petrol costs or provision of a travel pass). Where transport arrangements are not specified or the disabled child does not have a statement, the council will have to consider its general education (and possibly social care – see chapter 3) duties and its specific duties under the Disability Discrimination Act 1995 and (once fully in force) the Equality Act 2010 (see chapter 9) in determining whether to provide transport.[167]

4.94   Where a parent chooses to send his or her child to a school which is not the nearest appropriate school and is not named as the 'appropriate school' in the child's statement, the LEA may choose not to

---

165   EA 1996 s508B(1).

166   Department for Education and Skills, *Home to school travel and transport guidance*, 2007.

167   See, for example, Local Government Ombudsman's *Digest of Cases (Education) 2007/08*, Report 06C02934, which concerned a child who became disabled and as a consequence unable to catch a bus to a school outside her area. The ombudsman found maladministration in the way the council dealt with requests by the family for help with transport – not least because it failed to apply its own education transport policy properly and failed to consider its duties to the child under the Disability Discrimination Act.

provide assistance with transport.[168] The school named in a child's statement must be capable, however, of meeting the child's SEN: see paras 4.61–4.73 above. LEAs should not, therefore, promulgate general transport policies that seek to limit the schools for which parents of children with statements may express a preference if free transport is to be provided. In most cases LEAs will have clear general policies relating to transport for children with statements of SEN; these should be made available to parents and more often than not are well publicised on LEA websites.

4.95   However, it is acceptable for the LEA to name the school preferred by the child's parents in part 4 of the statement on condition that the parents agree to meet all of or part of the transport costs.

4.96   Home-to-school transport should not cause the child undue stress, strain or difficulty that would prevent the child benefiting from the education the school has to offer.[169] Disputes in relation to school transport will generally be resolved by local education transport panels, such panels being required to act fairly and to take into account any educational needs an individual learner may have.[170]

4.97   For looked after children placed out-of-authority, the Inter-Authority Recoupment Regulations provide that for children with SEN statements, the local authority to which the child belongs must pay to the providing authority such amounts as the authorities agree or as the secretary of state directs; this will generally include the costs of transport. Where the statement does not expressly cover the provision of transport or where the placing authority expresses a preference for a school further away and beyond reasonable walking distance, then the placing authority will be financially responsible for the transport costs.

Re-assessments

4.98   EA 1996 s323 requires there to be an annual review of all statements. A refusal by an LEA to amend a statement following an annual review can now be appealed to the First-tier Tribunal: see para 4.132 below. Outside of the annual review, a parent may request a reassessment at any time,[171] and the LEA must comply with that request if (1) there has been no reassessment within the preceding six months

---

168   SEN CoP, 8:87.
169   *R v Hereford and Worcester CC ex p P* [1992] 2 FCR 732; [1992] 2 FLR 207.
170   *A v North Somerset CC* [2009] EWHC 3060 (Admin); [2010] ELR 139.
171   Pursuant to s328(2)(a).

and (2) it is necessary for there to be a further assessment. In deciding whether re-assessment is 'necessary', the code of practice advises that LEAs should consider whether there have been changes which have impacted significantly on the child's special educational needs since the last assessment.[172] So if a child's behaviour or ability to concentrate have significantly deteriorated, it may well be necessary for a reassessment to take place. Any refusal to reassess can be challenged by an appeal to the tribunal, see para 4.131 below.

Transition planning

4.99   At the first annual review of a statement of SEN after a young person's 14th birthday and any subsequent reviews until the child leaves school, there should be a transition plan which draws together information in order to plan coherently for the young person's transition to adult life. The first annual review after a child's 14th birthday must seek information from social services departments as to whether a child with a statement is disabled and requires services from the local authority when leaving school. The critical importance of SEN transition planning is considered further in chapter 10: see paras 10.19–10.26.

Ceasing to maintain a statement

4.100   Once a statement is made, the local authority must maintain it[173] unless it is satisfied that 'it is no longer necessary' to do so.[174] The code of practice requires[175] that if an LEA decides to cease to maintain a statement, it must explain its reasons to the child's parents. There is a right of appeal to the tribunal against a decision by an LEA to cease to maintain a statement.[176] In such an appeal, the tribunal has a wide range of powers – for example, to order that the statement be maintained with or without amendment[177] and the tribunal's powers on a 'cease to maintain' appeal also extend to the naming a school in

---

172   SEN CoP, 7:96.
173   In accordance with EA 1996 Sch 27 para 11.
174   EA 1996 Sch 27 para 11(1).
175   Para 7:96.
176   EA 1996 Sch 27 para 11(2)(b).
177   EA 1996 Sch 27 para 11(3)(b).

part 4 of the statement.[178] The statement will remain in force pending the outcome of the tribunal appeal.

4.101   The circumstances when a local authority may lawfully cease to maintain a statement are considered in the code of practice at 8:117–8:124. At 8:117, the code states that 'a decision to cease to maintain a statement should be made only after careful consideration by the LEA of all the circumstances and after close consultation with parents', and at para 8:118, it advises that:

> The LEA should always, therefore, consider whether, notwithstanding the achievement of some, or even all, of the objectives in the statement, the child's progress will be halted or reversed if the special educational provision specified in the statement or modified provision which justified the maintenance of a statement were not made.

4.102   Para 8:119 of the code of practice provides a list of factors for an LEA to consider when deciding whether or not to maintain a statement. These include:

a) Can the child's needs be met in future within the resources of a mainstream school?

b) Do the child's SEN no longer significantly impede access to the National Curriculum?

c) Can the child cope with everyday social interaction at school?

d) Has the child no significant self-help difficulties that require more provision than is normally available within school?

4.103   Paragraph 8:121 of the code confirms that a statement will lapse[179] automatically if a young person moves into further or higher education (FE) (see para 10.18 below). Importantly, the code at para 8:123 deals with a situation where a parent wants their child to remain at school post-16, while the LEA considers that a further education institution is more appropriate. The code confirms that the LEA:

> cannot know whether the child still requires a statement until it has contacted the FE institution in question and confirmed that it is both able to meet the young person's needs and has offered a place.

178 Tribunal's decision in *J* (appeal 002435, April 2003) where, in reaching this conclusion, the tribunal read across to s324(3)(b) of the Act, which states that the statement must 'specify the special educational provision to be made for the purpose of meeting those needs, including the particulars required by subsection (4)'. Subsection 4 includes the school or type of school appropriate for the child.

179 However, in *R (Hill) v Bedfordshire CC* [2008] EWCA Civ 661, the Court of Appeal held (at [109]) that the relevant provisions of the EA 1996 'do not use the language of "lapse". They assume that in all cases the local education authority will determine whether or not to cease to maintain a statement'.

4.104 Paragraph 8:123 continues that 'it is not sufficient for LEAs to have a general expectation that an FE institution should be able to meet a young person's needs'. Finally, at para 8:124, the code states that where a school does not provide for young people post 16, the LEA should consider: 'whether to amend the statement to name another school or cease the statement if an appropriate FE course is identified.'

4.105   It will be maladministration for an LEA to allow a statement to lapse where it has given insufficient attention to the young person's social needs and has failed to resolve a conflict between its officers and his parent as to where his post-16 educational needs could be best met. This maladministration will be compounded if the evidence suggests that the council failed to explain in writing, in advance, that the statement would lapse and the consequences of this lapse.[180]

4.106   In *Wolverhampton v SENDIST and Smith*[181] the High Court ruled that a right of appeal continues to exist to the tribunal for young people over the age of 16 who are not registered at schools and in such cases that the tribunal has the power to order an LEA to continue to maintain a statement.

School admissions for non-statemented children with SEN

4.107 A child with SEN but without a statement of SEN (or a disabled child without SEN) must apply for school admission in the normal way. Where the parents want the child to attend a school which is over-subscribed, as high-performing schools generally are, the application will only be successful if the parents can establish that the child meets one of the relevant over-subscription criteria. This is because admissions authorities are absolved of their duty to comply with parental preference under School Standards and Framework Act (SSFA) 1998 s86(2) if the school's admission number is exceeded.

4.108   Parents can appeal to the independent appeal panel responsible for their particular admissions authority[182] to seek a place for their child at the school of their choice. Such appeals in relation to disabled children are more likely to succeed if the parent can establish that their child has an 'exceptional social or medical need' to attend

---

180 Report 03/B/16496-7, reported in the Local Government Ombudsman *Digest of Cases 2005/6* at A13.

181 [2007] ELR 418.

182 Generally the LEA or governing body.

a particular school, as this will place their child in a higher category than children appealing (for example) under the criterion relating to the distance from the school at which they live.

4.109   School admissions procedures are regulated by two statutory codes of practice, issued under SSFA 1998 s84. These are the School Admissions Code ('the Admissions Code') and the School Admission Appeals Code ('the Appeals Code'). Relevant bodies, including admissions authorities and independent appeal panels must 'act in accordance' with the codes.[183]

4.110   The two-stage appeals process is set out in the Appeals Code at 3.1 as follows:

> **First Stage: establishing the facts**, at which the panel considers whether the school's published admission arrangements:
> i. comply with the mandatory requirements of the School Admissions Code and Part 3 of the SSFA 1998.
> ii. were correctly applied in the individual's case, and decides whether 'prejudice' would arise were the child to be admitted. If this is proved, the panel moves on to the second stage
> **Second Stage: balancing the arguments**, at which the panel exercises its discretion, balancing the degree of prejudice to the school against the appellant's case for the child being admitted to the preferred school, before arriving at a decision.

4.111   Taking the key elements of these stages in turn, the Appeals Code is clear (at 3.2a) that where the relevant oversubscription criteria were not applied 'correctly and impartially', and where if they had been the child would have been offered a place, the panel must uphold the appeal at this first stage, except where a significant number of children are affected and admitting them all would cause serious prejudice. Only if the panel is satisfied (among other things) that the criteria were correctly and impartially applied should the panel move on to consider 'prejudice' (the second part of the first stage, see below).

4.112   The first stage also requires the school to demonstrate 'prejudice' if the child were to be admitted, which must be more than the simple fact that ths school is full. If some 'prejudice' to the school in admitting the child is shown (ie the test in the second part of the first stage is met), the panel should then move on to the second stage, and consider 'whether the appellant's grounds for the child to be admitted outweigh any prejudice to the school' (Appeals Code at 3.6). The panel is required to take into account the appellant's reasons for expressing a preference for the particular school.

---

183 SSFA 1998 s84(3).

4.113   The provisions of the Appeals Code were considered by Lord Carlile of Berriew QC (sitting as a deputy judge of the High Court) in *R (M) v Independent Appeal Panel of Haringey*.[184] Lord Carlile held that the appeal panel had failed to properly apply both the first and second stage tests in the code. However, the panel's appeal to the Court of Appeal against the decision of Lord Carlile was successful and the judgment of the Court of Appeal should be handed down before the end of 2010. The Court of Appeal's judgment should provide much needed clarity about the precise requirements of the code in school admissions.

Exclusion from school

4.114   It is of grave concern that children with SEN remain eight times more likely than other children to be permanently excluded from school.[185] This statistic alone suggests, at the very least, indirect discrimination against disabled children contrary to the Equality Act 2010.[186] Exclusion, particularly for disabled children and children with SEN, should be regarded as 'a draconian remedy of last resort',[187] as made clear by the relevant statutory guidance in England.[188] In particular the guidance states that:

- schools 'should try every practicable means to maintain the pupil in school', including where appropriate asking the LA to consider carrying out a statutory assessment (para 64);
- permanent exclusion is 'an acknowledgment by the school that it has exhausted all available strategies for dealing with the child' (para 16); and
- pupils with statements of SEN should not be excluded 'other than in the most exceptional circumstances', and that schools should make 'every effort' to avoid excluding pupils being supported at

184 [2009] EWHC 2427 (Admin).
185 Lamb Inquiry Report, 2009, p21.
186 See in this context, the Local Government Ombudsman's *Digest of Cases (Education) 2007/08*, Report 06C06190, concerning an exclusion of a young person with SEN and the ombudsman's finding that the LEA had failed to have regard to the likelihood that the case facts engaged its general duties under the Disability Discrimination Act 1995.
187 J Ford et al, *Education law and practice*, 3rd edn, Jordans, 2010, para 8.38.
188 DCSF, *Improving behaviour and attendance: Guidance on exclusion from schools and pupil referral units*, 2008. The Education (Pupil Exclusions and Appeals) (Maintained Schools) (England) Regulations 2002 reg 7(2) requires head teachers, LEAs and IAPs to 'have regard' to the guidance.

'school action' or 'school action plus' (para 64). This may include considering the various alternatives to exclusion set out in the guidance at para 11.

4.115   At para 13, the English exclusions guidance states that a decision to exclude a pupil permanently should only be taken in response to serious breaches of the school's behaviour policy *and* if allowing the pupil to remain in school would seriously harm the education or welfare of the pupil or others in the school. By using the word 'only', the guidance creates a discrete and exclusive test for when a permanent exclusion is a justified and a lawful response. When asking whether the pupil acted as alleged, the standard of proof is the balance of probabilities and this means whether something is 'more likely than not' to have occurred.[189]

4.116   Despite the very high threshold for lawful exclusion of children with SEN, the guidance confirms (at para 63) that 'over two-thirds of all permanently excluded pupils have been identified as having SEN'. As such, it is essential that schools and LEAs comply with their duties to children with SEN after exclusion. Where a child is permanently excluded, the headteacher and teacher in charge should use the period between his or her initial decision and the meeting of the governing body to work with the LEA to see whether more support can be made available or whether the statement can be changed to name a new school. If either of these options is possible, the headteacher and teacher in charge should normally withdraw the exclusion.

4.117   For both fixed period and permanent exclusions, there is a duty to provide alternative education for the pupil from the sixth day of the exclusion. For children with statements of SEN, such provision must be appropriate to their special educational needs as set out in their statement (see the English exclusions guidance at paras 38a and 52). If a child with SEN is permanently excluded, within the first five days the LA should arrange to assess the pupil's needs and how to meet them, including their SEN (guidance at para 52).

4.118   Notwithstanding these time-specific duties, it is still all too often the case that provision of education for excluded children is inadequate. A 2004 local government ombudsman report,[190] for example,

189   *Re B (Children) (Sexual Abuse: Standard of Proof)* [2009] 1 AC 11.
190   Local Government Ombudsman's *Digest of Cases (Education) 2003/04*, Report 01/B/6663, where it was recommended that compensation of over £2,000 be paid for the failure of support. See also the *Digest of Cases (Education) 2007/08*, Report 06C06190, which concerned the exclusion (for behavioural reasons) from a mainstream school of a young person with a statement of SEN. The ombudsman found there to be maladministration, not least because requests

concerned a child who was excluded for violent and disruptive behaviour while the LEA was in the process of assessing his SEN. He was out of school for over a year. For the first half term no education was provided and after this he received tuition which varied between six and 12 hours a week. In the ombudsman's opinion this was grossly inadequate and could not be described as 'suitable education'.

4.119   A similar finding emerges from a 2010 report,[191] which concerned a six-month exclusion of a child who had mental health difficulties (and for whom an application for a statement of SEN was then made). The ombudsman found that during the exclusion period the education provided 'was well below the requirements of the statutory guidance', and observed (para 30):

> According to Section 19 of the Education Act 1996, the Council was responsible for this once it became impossible for [the child] to attend School A .... Therefore, it is not sufficient for the Council to say that [she] remained on the school roll and so the local authority was not responsible for her education. That fails to reflect the reality of the situation: that the school had become unsuitable for [her] and it was impossible for her to attend. Accordingly, the Council was responsible for arranging suitable educational provision.

4.120   Longer fixed-term exclusions and all permanent exclusions must be reviewed by the school's governing body, normally by the governor's disciplinary committee. Parents of children who are permanently excluded can also appeal to the independent appeal panel (IAP). The IAP is required to consider whether the exclusion is a proportionate response by the headteacher, and any failure to properly address a pupil's SEN will be a relevant factor when the IAP is considering this question. Similarly the panel should consider the basis of the exclusion and the procedures followed having regard to the school's published SEN policy (as per the guidance at 156(b)).

4.121   An example of the IAP considering proportionality is found in *W v Bexley LBC Independent Appeal Panel*,[192] a case in which the IAP accepted the school's evidence that W had cut another student's folder with a knife and sliced this student's shirt with the knife while the student was wearing it. However, despite making this finding, the IAP concluded that permanent exclusion was a disproportionate

for a reassessment of his needs were ignored by the LEA because he was approaching Year 11. The ombudsman also noted the failure of the LEA to have regard to the likelihood that these facts engaged its general duties under the Disability Discrimination Act 1995.

191 Complaint no 07A14912 against Barnet LBC, April 19 2010.
192 [2008] EWHC 758 (Admin).

response and that a fixed-term exclusion would have been more appropriate. As the IAP had no power to order a fixed-term exclusion, reinstatement was ordered.

4.122   IAPs must also consider whether the exclusion amounts to disability discrimination. Disability discrimination is further considered at chapter 9. Claims of disability discrimination in relation to fixed-term exclusions must be brought to the tribunal: see paras 9.95–9.96 below.

4.123   The inappropriate exclusion of disabled children not only occurs in relation to education provision: it is also evident in health and social care settings – and in this context it is considered further at chapter 3 and chapter 5.

Duties to children who are out of school

4.124   Any child (regardless of disability or SEN) who is out of the education system for any reason is owed the duty in EA 1996 s19 by their LEA. This duty is to 'make arrangements for the provision of suitable education at school or otherwise' for such a child. 'Suitable education' means 'efficient education suitable to his age, ability and aptitude and to any special educational needs he may have'.[193] As a consequence, a failure to provide adequate home tuition while a child is not in mainstream schooling will be maladministration.[194]

4.125   Given the number of children with SEN who are, for one reason or another 'out of the education system' it is of no surprise that there has been considerable attention as to the nature, extent and enforceability of the section 19 duty on LEAs. Any failure to comply with the section 19 duty will generally need to be remedied through judicial review, given the urgency of getting the child back into education. The nature of the section 19 duty has been clarified by a number of court and local government ombudsman decisions. These have established in particular that LEAs cannot plead a 'shortage of resources' as a reason for not making suitable arrangements for disabled children in such cases. More importantly still, in the landmark case of *Tandy*,[195] the House of Lords held that the duty under EA 1996 s19 is owed to each individual child who falls within the definition in the

---

193 EA 1996 s 19(6).
194 See, for example, Local Government Ombudsman's *Digest of Cases (Education) 2007/08*, Report 05A15425 5192, where it was recommended that compensation of £7,000 be paid for the failure of support.
195 *R v East Sussex CC ex p Tandy* [1998] AC 714.

section and that 'suitable education' must be determined purely by educational considerations, disregarding any resource constraints an LEA may face.

4.126 In England, statutory guidance[196] entitled *Guidance for local authorities and schools – PRUs and alternative provision*[197] emphasises that any provision made for a child under EA 1996 s19 must be suitable for their needs, stating:

> 3.5 It is not an option for local authorities to decide not to arrange any education, or to make arrangements that do not provide suitable education for pupils out of school who are resident within the local authority area. Although the nature of these arrangements will vary from local authority to local authority depending on local circumstances and policies, there are minimum standards that all local authorities are expected to meet. This is particularly important when making arrangements for pupils in vulnerable groups or for pupils whose previous family, social or educational experience has been characterised by difficulties. This may mean taking additional steps to ensure that the individual needs of pupils are met or providing access to appropriate support services.

4.127 There will of course be a degree of leeway available to the LEA as to what constitutes 'suitable education' and this may mean that attendance at the Pupil Referral Unit (PRU)[198] may be deemed to be reasonable, depending upon the precise facts of each case and provided that the LEA is not operating a rigid policy in this regard.[199]

4.128 Many disabled children are failed by their schools either due to bullying or due to the inability of the school to provide suitable education. On occasions this results in their parents withdrawing them and subsequently making a complaint to the courts or local government ombudsmen. In *R (G) v Westminster CC*,[200] however, the Court of Appeal held that a father had not acted reasonably in withdrawing his son from school on the grounds he was being bullied when the school was taking reasonable steps to address his bullying. The court did hold that where a child was not receiving suitable education

196 Issued under EA 1996 s19(4A).
197 DfES, January 2005, LEA/0024/2005.
198 PRUs are alternative provision established to cater for children who are outside mainstream education, generally by reason of exclusion. In England, PRUs are now known as 'short stay schools', although the term PRU remains used in Wales.
199 See, for example, *R (C) v Brent LBC* [2006] ELR 435, albeit that this involved a non-disabled child.
200 [2004] 1 WLR 1113.

and there was no suitable education available that was reasonably practicable for the child, the authority would be in breach of EA 1996 s19.[201]

4.129   The ombudsman has, however, held in a different case that parents acted reasonably in removing their son from a school (and educating him at home) when the LEA and the school had comprehensively failed to comply with his statement of SEN, and indeed their associated SEN obligations under the EA 1996.[202] Likewise in a 2007 complaint[203] the local government ombudsman considered that a mother's removal of her disabled son due to bullying was not unreasonable, given the LEA's maladministration in failing to use its mediation process to help to address the bullying and its failure to provide assistance to reintroduce child to his school or to find an alternative.

4.130   The EA 1996 s19 duty has been considered by the High Court in two recent cases involving children with SEN. In *R (B) v Barnet*,[204] the court held that it was not reasonably practicable for a child to attend a school which the headteacher had said was unsuitable for her and as such there had been a breach of the section 19 duty. In a case such as this, there is then a duty on the LEA to make alternative provision which the court enforced in relation to B by way of a mandatory order.[205] By contrast, in *R (HR) v Medway*,[206] the court approved the *Barnet* case but held that on the facts, the LEA had discharged its EA 1996 s19 duty by offering a placement in a hospital special school, even though an independent educational psychologist has said that this school was not suitable for HR. This was essentially because it was not sufficiently obvious that the school was unsuitable, given the LEA's evidence to the contrary. These two cases together suggest that even where a disabled child is out of school for a significant period the court will only intervene when it is obvious that the LEA has not offered 'suitable' education, particularly if there is an ongoing tribunal appeal pending (as there was in relation to both B and HR).

---

201 *R (G) v Westminster CC* [2004] 1 WLR 1113 at [46].

202 Local Government Ombudsman's *Digest of Cases (Education) 2003/04*, Report 02/A/13068.

203 Local Government Ombudsman's *Digest of Cases (Education) 2006/07*, Report 05/B/11513.

204 [2009] EWHC 2842 (Admin).

205 [2009] EWHC 2842 (Admin) at [39].

206 [2010] EWHC 731 (Admin).

Appeals to the tribunal

First-tier Tribunal

4.131 The First-tier Tribunal (Special Educational Needs and Disability) (still routinely referred to as the SEN Tribunal or 'SENDIST') hears appeals in relation to specified SEN matters and claims of disability discrimination (see paras 9.95–9.96 below) in relation to schools in England. In Wales, the tribunal continues to be known as the SEN Tribunal for Wales (SENTW). The rights of appeal under the SEN framework are in relation to:

a) refusals to assess;
b) refusals to make a statement;
c) the contents of a statement (any or all of parts 2, 3 and 4);[207]
d) refusals to reassess;
e) refusals to change the school named in part 4; and
f) decisions to cease to maintain a statement.

4.132 A further right of appeal, against a decision by an LEA not to amend a statement following an annual review, has been created by the Children, Schools and Families Act 2010 s2.[208] SENDIST has no jurisdiction in relation to any other matters than those specified above.

4.133 Only a person with parental responsibility has the right of appeal to the tribunal, although the government has recently consulted on extending a limited right of appeal to children in certain specific circumstances.[209] This is particularly important to deal with the situation where the child is 'looked after' by the same authority as is responsible for meeting his or her SEN. However, it will also have important consequences for funding since at present it is the parent's income that is taken into account for the purposes of calculating legal aid eligibility, by contrast to judicial review proceedings which can generally be brought in the name of the child.

---

207 There are three occasions when a parent can appeal against the contents of an SSEN: (i) when the SSEN is first made, (ii) when parts 2 and/or 3 are amended by the LEA, and (iii) when, after an assessment under EA 1996 s323, the LEA decides not to amend the SSEN.

208 Introducing new section 328A into the EA 1996. In force from 1 September 2010: the Children, Schools and Families Act 2010 (Commencement No 1) Order 2010 SI No 1817 article 3.

209 A right of appeal for children was another recommendation of the Lamb Inquiry (recommendation 47). In Wales, a pilot scheme is in place whereby children can bring appeals to the Welsh tribunal in their own name.

4.134   The role of the tribunal in relation to an SEN appeal is essentially to 'stand in the shoes' of the LEA and take the relevant decision for itself.[210] Therefore, a tribunal may decide that a child does in fact need to be assessed, or that the results of the assessment indicate that it is in fact necessary for the LEA to determine the required provision through making and maintaining a statement. Similarly, the tribunal can and does rigorously examine parts 2, 3 and 4 of a statement and will order specific amendments to some or all of these sections. The principles the tribunal will apply on an appeal are those the LEA should apply, summarised under the relevant sections above.

4.135   Application forms, the relevant Rules[211] and guidance notes are all available on the tribunal website, www.sendist.gov.uk. Appeals in relation to SEN must be brought within two months of the date on the letter from the LEA setting out the decision which is under appeal. The tribunal has a discretion to extend time if just and equitable to do so. Different and somewhat more generous time limits apply to disability discrimination appeals: see para 9.95. SENDIST is expected to undertake active case management and has a wide range of powers to ensure that its overriding objective, that cases are dealt with fairly and justly, is achieved.

4.136   Given the length of time it can take to resolve tribunal appeals (potentially over a year in some cases where multiple hearings are required), parents may wish to ask SENDIST to order expedition so that the appeal can be heard as quickly as possible. The forms to be used to make applications to SENDIST are available on its website, www.sendist.gov.uk. Parents should also be careful to make sure they make the correct appeal; in particular, given that the school named in part 4 of the statement will result from the needs and provision identified in parts 2 and 3, parents will generally need to appeal all three parts to the tribunal, not simply part 4. Any errors made by parents can and should be corrected with the assistance of the tribunal judge allocated to the appeal during the case management process.

4.137   One area of contention at the tribunal is often the treatment of expert witnesses.[212] Good expert evidence is often vital to a parent's

---

210   The root of this approach seems to be a Practice Direction from the former SENDIST President in 1995, reported at [1995] ELR 335, but this is now simply general practice: see S Oliver, *Special educational needs and the law*, 2nd edn, Jordans, 2007, 15.7.

211   Tribunal Procedure (First-tier Tribunal) (Health, Education and Social Care Chambers) Rules 2008 SI No 2699.

212   In wider public law challenges involving children, the High Court has held that experts should be careful to limit themselves to their area of

case, but the courts have accepted that, as an expert tribunal itself, the tribunal is well fitted to decide which expert evidence to accept or reject. The High Court has, however, shown itself willing to quash decisions made by SENDIST where it has, for example, not shown due regard to expert evidence before it or failed to appreciate the full import of its content.[213] Accordingly in *Jones v Norfolk CC*[214] it was held that the tribunal had failed to deal properly with the evidence from three expert witnesses, the judge, Crane J observing (at para 36):

> I do not consider that the Tribunal's reference to a conclusion unhesitatingly reached saves its decision, since that begs the question as to why the Tribunal rejected the views as to placement of the three expert witnesses.

4.138 In *R (L) v Waltham Forest LBC*,[215] it was held that:

a) a tribunal's reasons must cover the substantial points raised so parties could understand why decision was reached;

b) if SENDIST rejected expert evidence it should state so specifically and in some cases should state why;

c) mere recitation of evidence is no substitute for giving reasons; and

d) where SENDIST uses its own expertise to decide an issue it should give parties an opportunity to comment on its thinking and to challenge it.

4.139 If SENDIST upholds an appeal, it will generally order the LEA to do what the parent has requested – carry out a statutory assessment, make and maintain a statement, amend the contents of the statement and so on. In appeals against the contents of a statement, it is not uncommon for the tribunal to order only some of the amendments to the statement contended for by the parent. Any order made by SENDIST must be complied with within a specified timeframe.[216]

expertise: (*R (A) v Liverpool CC* [2007] EWHC 1477). Furthermore, in *Shala v Birmingham CC* [2007] EWCA Civ 624, the Court of Appeal quashed a decision by a local authority officer on the basis that insufficient consideration had been given to two reports from medical experts and criticised the defendant for relying on an expert who had not actually seen the individual who they were claiming to assess.

213 See, for example, *D v SENDIST and others* [2006] ELR 370.

214 [2006] All ER (D) 111 (Jul).

215 [2004] ELR 161.

216 As specified for each different type of appeal by the Education (SEN England Consolidation) Regulations 2001 reg 25.

4.140   SENDIST has the power to award costs against a losing party (LEA or parent) in certain limited circumstances, most frequently if they have 'acted unreasonably' in the proceedings.[217] Costs applications must be made within 14 days of the date the tribunal sends its final decision letter. However, costs remain unlikely to be awarded in SENDIST proceedings, particularly against parents. LEAs who use the tribunal proceedings simply as a way of delaying (for example) the placement of a child at expensive provision may, however, find themselves penalised by costs orders made against them in favour of parents.

Upper Tribunal

4.141   Appeals from SENDIST on a point of law now go to the Upper Tribunal,[218] with the permission of either SENDIST or the Upper Tribunal. This is part of the overall reforms to the tribunal system which are aimed and reducing the burden on the High Court and creating a better and more uniform approach to administrative appeals. Although only a few cases have as yet been reported, the Upper Tribunal seems to be taking a more robust approach to overturning SENDIST decisions than was previously the case when appeals went to the High Court. For example in *Hampshire CC v JP*,[219] the LEA's appeal was upheld on the basis that the SENDIST:

a) misunderstood expert evidence on the child's need or otherwise for residential education; and

b) gave inadequate reasons for its conclusion that the child required residential provision.

4.142   Similarly, in *MW v Halton BC*,[220] the parents' appeal succeeded because the SENDIST had failed to give sufficient reasons and failed to have proper regard to expert medical evidence advanced by the parents. Both the *MW* and *JP* cases show that the Upper Tribunal is prepared to examine SENDIST decisions in significant detail and consider carefully for itself whether expert evidence (which is critical

---

217 Tribunal Procedure (First-tier Tribunal) (Health, Education and Social Care Chambers) Rules 2008 r10. SENDIST also has the power to order wasted costs against a representative.

218 Under Tribunals, Courts and Enforcement Act 2007 s11. For more information on the Upper Tribunal (Administrative Appeals Chamber), see http://www.osscsc.gov.uk.

219 [2009] UKUT 239 (AAC).

220 [2010] UKUT 34 (AAC).

in such cases) has been treated properly by the SENDIST panel. In *MW*, Upper Tribunal Judge Ward also made clear that (i) a detailed and overt fact-finding process is required in SENDIST appeals[221] and (ii) that the need to show deference to expert tribunals should not constrain the Upper Tribunal in considering whether there are any errors of law in SENDIST decisions.[222]

Other enforcement methods

Judicial review

4.143 Where a child is suffering an ongoing disadvantage as a result of a school or LEA's breach of duty, for instance the duty on LEAs to provide suitable education for children out of school, it may be possible to achieve a remedy through an application for judicial review in the High Court. Care must be taken, however, to ensure that no other effective remedy can be obtained through another route, in particular through a SENDIST appeal, otherwise the High Court is likely to either refuse permission for the judicial review to proceed or refuse to grant any relief at the end of the proceedings.

Complaint to secretary of state

4.144 Alternatively, a parent or child may make a complaint to the secretary of state if an LEA or governing body of a maintained school in England has acted unreasonably[223] or is in breach of its duties.[224] It is usually necessary to follow all internal complaints procedures before making a written complaint to the secretary of state. An investigation by the secretary of state can take in excess of six months so this should not be used as a remedy in urgent cases. If the complaint is upheld, however, the secretary of state can issue directions to require the LEA or school to carry out its legal obligations properly.[225]

---

221 [2010] UKUT 34 (AAC) at [39].
222 [2010] UKUT 34 (AAC) at [43]. A further recent decision, *NA v Barnet LBC* [2010] UKUT 180 (AAC), saw the Upper Tribunal overturn SENDIST's finding in relation to the 'efficient education of other children' exemption to the duty to comply with a parental choice of mainstream school: see above, fn 123.
223 Education Act 1996 s496.
224 Education Act 1996 s497.
225 See Disability Law Service, *How and when to complain to the Secretary of State for Education and the Local Government Ombudsman*, available at www.dls.org.uk.

Complaint to ombudsman

4.145   Complaints in relation to maladministration by LEAs can also be made to the local government ombudsman (www.lgo.org.uk). A number of examples of successful ombudsman complaints are given throughout this chapter.

Further advice and support

4.146   Special education law is notoriously complex and even in this relatively lengthy chapter we have not been able to cover all relevant issues. Parents and others are strongly advised to seek independent advice on their own case, including from the following sources:

a)   IPSEA (Independent Parental Special Education Advice) – www.ipsea.org.uk.

b)   ACE (Advisory Centre for Education) – www.ace-ed.org.uk.

c)   Contact a Family – www.cafamily.org.uk.

d)   National Autistic Society Advocacy for Education Service – www.nas.org.uk/nas/jsp/polopoly.jsp?d=143.

e)   Down's Syndrome Association – www.downs-syndrome.org.uk/contact-us/education-advice.html.

4.147   The English government's advice on SEN issues is available at the following link: www.direct.gov.uk/en/Parents/Schoolslearningand development/SpecialEducationalNeeds/DG_4000690.

4.148   The local government ombudsman in England has published a Factsheet for parents and young people who are experiencing problems about school-related matters: 'Complaints about schools'.[226]

4.149   All LEAs are obliged (under EA 1996 s332A) to make arrangements for parent partnership services (PPS) to provide independent advice and support to parents whose children have SEN. The PPS can put parents in touch with an independent parental supporter who can give information and attend meetings with them. Contact details for local parent partnership services are available from the National Parent Partnership Network: www.parentpartnership.org.uk.

4.150   A number of solicitors' firms specialise in education work, including SEN issues (SENDIST appeals, judicial review applications, school exclusions). Although paying privately for legal advice and representation can be very expensive, parents who qualify for legal

---

226   See www.lgo.org.uk/publications/fact-sheets/complaints-about-schools/.

aid will be able to access free advice through the Legal Help scheme and solicitors can also find trainee and junior barristers who are willing to represent parents *pro bono* where funding is not available (for instance at SENDIST appeals or exclusions appeal panels). We cannot recommend specific solicitors' firms but the advice agencies above may hold lists of firms that they recommend, or who at least are known to work in this area.

4.151   Legal practitioners with a particular interest in SEN law may wish to join the Education Law Association, which has a SEN special interest group. See www.educationlawassociation.co.uk for further information.

Health

continued

Key points

- Disabled children have the same right as other children to access universal health services.
- NHS bodies have a duty to engage disabled children and their families in decisions about the planning and delivery of health services.
- NHS bodies and local authorities have duties to co-operate to ensure that disabled children's health needs are met.
- The key standards for disabled children's health services in England are those set by the Children's National Service Framework (NSF).
- Within the English Children's NSF, Standard 8 sets out the expectations for the health services to be provided to disabled children.
- Disabled children may require a range of specialist health services, including therapy services and equipment.
- Where disabled children have particularly severe and/or complex health needs, the NHS will have the primary responsibility for providing them with 'continuing care'.
- Many disabled children may also require Child and Adolescent Mental Health Services (CAMHS) input.
- It is always essential to determine whether a disabled child can and does consent to treatment, and to know if a child cannot or does not consent what the appropriate legal route is in each individual case.
- Children with life limiting conditions will require high quality palliative care.
- The transition from children's to adult health services is vital for the well-being of disabled young people and must be properly planned.

Introduction

5.1   Health services are critically important for many disabled children. It is often health services such as GPs, hospital-based services and health visitors that first identify that a child may have an impairment. Obviously, disabled children also need to access the same range of universal health services provided for other children. However, many disabled children also require additional specialist health services.

These will range from therapeutic services such as physiotherapy to equipment and technology which may assist severely disabled children to lead more ordinary lives.

5.2　In a clear break with the past, the NHS Operating Frameworks in England for 2008/09 and 2009/10 explicitly state that children should be one of four national priorities for the NHS in England, alongside cancer, stroke and maternity. The health and well-being of children was also shown to be a priority with the publication in February 2009 of 'Healthy lives, brighter futures', the English government's first-ever strategy for children and young people's health. This new emphasis on the healthcare needs of disabled children is underpinned by international obligations – particularly those enshrined in article 25 of the UN Convention on the Rights of Persons with Disabilities and article 24 of the UN Convention on the Rights of the Child.

5.3　However, despite this recent clear focus, health outcomes for disabled children remain problematic. The UN Committee on the Rights of the Child has found that inequality in access to health services remains in the UK, with disabled children in particular facing barriers to the realisation of this basic right.[1] The 2006 Parliamentary Hearings on Services for Disabled Children found that almost half of disabled children's parents (48 per cent) and over a third of professionals (35 per cent) described health services for disabled children as poor.[2] This perception was mirrored by a 2006 Disability Rights Commission investigation[3] which revealed 'an inadequate response from the health services and governments in England and Wales to the major physical health inequalities experienced by some of the most socially excluded citizens: those with learning disabilities and/or mental health problems'. Importantly, the investigation also found that the least satisfied parents were usually those of children with the most complex multiple impairments. In 2008, the Healthcare Commission[4] described the reality for disabled children and their families as follows:

> Children and young people with complex needs, including children with disabilities or those in situations that make them vulnerable, do not always get the attention and care from healthcare services that they need ... the funding and provision of services for children and young

---

1　UN Committee on the Rights of the Child, *Concluding observations 2008*.

2　Every Disabled Child Matters, *Disabled children and health* (2009), p11, available from www.ncb.org.uk/edcm/edcm_disabled_children_and_health.pdf.

3　Disability Rights Commission, *Equal treatment: closing the gap – a formal investigation into physical health inequalities experienced by people with learning disabilities and/or mental health problems*, 2006.

4　Healthcare Commission, *State of healthcare 2008* (2008).

people with learning and/or physical disabilities varies throughout the country.

5.4   In addition to concerns about inadequate access to healthcare generally, since the 1980s there has been considerable public, professional and legal debate about decisions to withhold or withdraw medical treatments which save or extend the lives of disabled children. Prior to that time, it was common practice to bring about the deaths of some infants with learning disabilities and physical impairments and decisions about 'selective non-treatment' were largely confined to the domain of medical practice and conduct. Without doubt, some decisions and associated protocols were underpinned by the assumption that disabled children's lives were of less value than their non-disabled peers. In the early 1980s, a number of landmark legal judgments confronted this practice and established that the courts were the proper place to determine issues of principle in relation to the right to life of disabled children.[5] Since that time, disabled people and parents of disabled children have written extensively about the value accorded to disabled children's lives and the implications of this for medical and healthcare decisions.[6]

5.5   There continue to be cases brought before the courts by healthcare providers and parents seeking judgments on practice which may result in the death of a child. Where these challenges concern decisions as to the cost effectiveness of embarking on expensive treatments the courts have held that these are primarily for the NHS and not for courts to make.[7] However, when the NHS seeks to withdraw life sustaining treatment (or to embark on a treatment regime that may accelerate death) then if there is a dispute between the medical professionals and the parents – or others[8] – then the court should adjudicate.[9] In such cases the test will be the child's 'best interests' – which must be given a wide interpretation, and although the guiding

5   For a detailed discussion of these issues, see J Read and L Clements, 'Demonstrably awful: the right to life and the selective non-treatment of disabled babies and young children', (2004) 31 *Journal of Law and Society*, pp482–509 and L Clements and J Read (eds), *Disabled people and the right to life: the protection and violation of disabled people's most basic human rights*, Routledge, 2008.

6   See for example, J Campbell 'It's my life–it's my decision?: assisted dying versus assisted living', in L Clements and J Read (eds), *Disabled people and the right to life: the protection and violation of disabled people's most basic human rights*, Routledge, 2008.

7   *R v Cambridge Health Authority ex p B* [1995] 1 WLR 898, CA.

8   See, for example, *Re B (a minor)(wardship: medical treatment)* [1981] 1 WLR 1421; [1990] 3 All ER 927.

9   *Glass v UK* (2004) Application No 61827/00, 9 March 2004.

principle will be to prolong life, other factors are relevant including the pain and suffering caused by the treatment and the quality of the life which will be prolonged. Where this is considered to be intolerable, from the point of view of the person concerned, then life-prolonging treatment may not be in their best interests.[10]

5.6 This chapter sets out the duties and powers governing the provision of health services to disabled children, both in terms of universal and specialist services. It also considers the duties to provide specific services, whether by way of continuing care to disabled children with severe and/or complex health needs, mental health services or palliative care for children with life-limiting conditions. Although the Secretary of State for Health in England has published outline proposals for a major re-organisation of the NHS,[11] the changes (which may include the abolition of Primary Care Trusts, see para 5.18 below) will be the subject of significant consultation, the outcome of which cannot yet be known. This chapter therefore reflects the present law in relation to the health services that disabled children need.

5.7 The two principal statutes that place obligations on health bodies to provide services, are not (unlike those that govern social care and education rights – see chapters 3 and 4 above) drafted in specific and individualistic terms. Nevertheless, they have been held by the courts to place fundamental and enforceable obligations on health bodies. The two statutes comprise an overarching Act – the National Health Service Act (NHS Act) 2006 – and one that is specific to Wales, the NHS (Wales) Act (NHS(W) Act) 2006. This means that some provisions that relate to Wales, for example, the duty on NHS bodies to co-operate with local authorities, are found in the NHS Act 2006 (in this case at section 82) since it is a common obligation that affects both nations.

Children and families' views to inform health services

5.8 NHS bodies have a duty under NHS Act 2006 s242(2)[12] to make arrangements to ensure that users of services are, either directly or through representatives, involved in:

10 See, for example, *Portsmouth NHS Trust and Derek Wyatt and Charlotte Wyatt* [2004] EWHC 2247 (Fam).
11 Department of Health, *Equity and excellence: liberating the NHS*, 12 July 2010, Cm 7881.
12 In Wales, NHS(W) Act 2006 s183(1).

a) planning of the provision of health services;

b) the development and consideration of proposals for changes in the way those services are provided, if implementation of the proposal would have an impact on the manner in which services are provided or the range of services available; and

c) decisions to be made by the NHS body affecting the operation of those services, if the decision would have an impact on the manner in which services are provided or the range of services available.

5.9 The views of disabled children, young people and their families are therefore expected to inform local design and delivery of health services. Frequently however, disabled children have been found to be less actively involved in decisions about both their treatment and service development than children who are not disabled. Under Standard 8 of the English National Service Framework (NSF) for Children (see below), local authorities, Primary Care Trusts (PCTs) and other NHS trusts are required to ensure disabled children and their parents are routinely involved and supported in making informed decisions, that there is an ongoing user involvement programme for disabled children and young people in line with the wider patient and public involvement programmes and that facilities, equipment and skilled workers are available to enable children who communicate differently to others to participate in assessment and decision-making processes.[13] The involvement of children and families in decision making has been reinforced in England by the *Aiming high for disabled children* review[14] and in the Local Government and Public Involvement in Health Act 2007, which allows for the establishment of Local Involvement Networks, set up to scrutinise and monitor health services and represent users' views.

Co-operation between PCTs and local authorities

5.10 An important issue for many disabled children and their families is which body will take the lead responsibility for meeting their needs – the local authority or the health body, for example, a PCT in England or its equivalent in Wales, a Health Board (HB)? The answer to this question is that health bodies and local authorities are expected

13 Disabled Child Standard, Children's NSF, p30.
14 HM Treasury/DfES, 2007.

to work together to meet the health needs of disabled children. This expectation comes from (among other sources):

- NHS Act 2006 s82, which states that in exercising their respective functions NHS bodies and local authorities must co-operate with one another in order to secure and advance the health and welfare of the people of England and Wales; and
- Children Act 2004 s10,[15] which requires local authorities to co-operate with their 'relevant partners', including health bodies, to safeguard and promote the welfare of children in their area.

5.11   For children 'in need' generally, including disabled children, local authorities have a clear obligation to take the lead in ensuring their needs are met, bringing in different agencies (including health) where necessary. However, for children with particularly severe and/or complex health needs, the NHS may be the lead agency – for example, when a child is eligible for 'Continuing Care' funding (see paras 5.53–5.64).

5.12   To deliver co-operation and joint working on the ground, 'key workers' or 'care co-ordinators' are essential (see paras 3.10–3.12). In England, Standard 8 of the Children's NSF states that the key workers should be 'the main point of contact with the family' and should take responsibility for co-ordinating review meetings and liaising with professionals to ensure all agreed support is delivered.

5.13   A multidisciplinary approach requires co-ordinated assessment, planning and commissioning. The English guidance publication *Healthy lives, brighter futures: The strategy for children and young people's health*[16] advises how agencies should work together and reinforces the requirements of Standard 8 of the Children's NSF. Additionally the English *Joint planning and commissioning framework for children, young people and maternity services*[17] introduces a framework to help local commissioners (both PCTs and local authorities) to design a unified system in each local area to achieve a joined-up picture of children and young people's needs and for collaboration to achieve the best use of joint resources for 'better outcomes'.[18]

---

15 In Wales, Children Act 2004 s25.
16 *Healthy lives, brighter futures: the strategy for children and young people's health*, English Guidance, February 2009.
17 HM Government, *Joint planning and commissioning framework for children, young people and maternity services*, 2006.
18 This is reinforced in Department of Health/Department for Children Schools and Families, *Securing better health for children and young people through world class commissioning: a guide to support delivery of healthy lives, brighter futures*, 2009, and Department of Health, *The commissioning framework for health and well-being*, 2007.

5.14 Since there is no explicit statutory obligation on the NHS or the local authority to act as the lead agency, there is obvious scope for a disabled child's needs to be allowed to 'drift' while each authority blames the other for a service failure. In such cases a complaint (or if sufficiently urgent, an application for judicial review: see paras 2.38–2.40) should be made against both authorities and framed, not only in terms of the failure to meet the specific need but also in terms of the authorities' failure to 'work together' as required by section 82 of the 2006 Act and section 10 of the 2004 Act.[19] The ombudsmen in general expect the authority that is in touch with the child to 'grasp the nettle' and secure the provision, before entering into protracted negotiations with the other authority on liability for the care costs.[20]

5.15 Such a complaint will also be appropriate when the dispute is between different NHS bodies. The NHS Ombudsman in England and the Public Services Ombudsman in Wales have found maladministration[21] where disputing health bodies have, in such a case, failed to agree which one of them would accept funding responsibility on an interim basis.

Health services – fundamental duties

5.16 Section 1(1) of the NHS Act 2006 requires the secretary of state to continue the promotion in England[22] of a comprehensive health service, designed to secure improvement:

(a) in the physical and mental health of the people of England, and
(b) in the prevention, diagnosis and treatment of illness.

5.17 Under section 3 of the 2006 Act, the secretary of state is also under a duty to provide throughout England,[23] to such extent as he considers necessary to meet all reasonable requirements:

(a) hospital accommodation,
(b) other accommodation for the purpose of any service provided under this Act,

19 In Wales, Children Act 2004 s25.
20 Complaint no 96/C/3868 against Calderdale MBC.
21 Report by the Public Services Ombudsman for Wales and the Health Service Ombudsman for England of an investigation of a complaint about the Welsh Assembly Government (Health Commission Wales) Cardiff and Vale NHS Trust and Plymouth Teaching Primary Care Trust, Third Report, Session 2008–2009 HC 858, TSO, 2009.
22 NHS(W) Act 2006 s1 places an identical obligation on the Welsh ministers.
23 NHS(W) Act 2006 s3 places an identical obligation on the Welsh ministers.

(c) medical, dental, ophthalmic, nursing and ambulance services,

(d) such other services or facilities for the care of pregnant women, women who are breastfeeding and young children as he considers are appropriate as part of the health service,

(e) such other services or facilities for the prevention of illness, the care of persons suffering from illness and the after-care of persons who have suffered from illness as he considers are appropriate as part of the health service,

(f) such other services or facilities as are required for the diagnosis and treatment of illness.[24]

5.18   The 2006 Acts require therefore that there be a 'comprehensive' health service which all can access – including disabled children. These statutory functions are in practice delegated by a plethora of regulations and orders to the local NHS bodies – ie PCTs in England[25] of which there are currently about 150, and HBs in Wales[26] of which there are seven.[27]

5.19   Health services can be categorised into those delivered as 'primary care' and 'secondary care'. Primary care describes the health services that play a central role in local community including GPs, pharmacists, dentists and midwives. Primary care providers are usually the first point of contact for a patient and a continuing point of contact, even if the patient is receiving services from a hospital or from some other 'secondary' NHS facility. The NHS Acts 2006 require PCTs and HBs to meet all the reasonable requirements of a patient, and to exercise their powers so as to provide primary medical services within their areas.[28]

5.20   Secondary care is acute or specialist healthcare provided in a hospital or other secondary care setting. Patients are usually referred from a primary care professional – for example, a GP. Regulations[29] in England and Wales identify which PCT or HB is responsible for

24 NHS Act 2006 s3.

25 See, for example, the National Health Service (Functions of Strategic Health Authorities and Primary Care Trusts and Administration Arrangements) (England) Regulations 2002 SI No 2375.

26 See, for example, the Local Health Boards (Directed Functions) (Wales) Regulations 2009 SI No 1511 (W147).

27 The Local Health Boards (Establishment and Dissolution) (Wales) Order 2009 SI No 778 (W66).

28 NHS Act 2006 s83(1) and NHS(W) Act 2006 s41.

29 NHS (Functions of Strategic Authorities and Primary Care Trusts and Administration Arrangements) (England) Regulations 2002 SI No 2375 as amended by SI Nos 2002/2548, 2003/1497, 2006/359 and 2007/559; Local Health Board (Functions) (Wales) Regulations 2003 as amended.

the funding of a specific patient's needs. In England responsibility is primarily linked to registration with a GP, and for those who are not registered with a GP it is based on where they are 'usually resident'. In Wales, the responsible HB is the one where the person is 'usually resident' regardless of the address of their GP.

The responsibilities of GPs and other primary health services

5.21   As with all children, GPs act as the main point of access or referral to all appropriate medical and health services that a disabled child may need. At the primary care level, these may include: medical services provided directly by the GP, physiotherapy, speech and language therapy, occupational therapy, early intervention rehabilitation programmes, general community nursing and health visiting. The GP also is responsible for referring a child for services in the secondary healthcare sector (and liaising with other healthcare professionals in this respect).[30] This can include obtaining a 'second opinion' on a child's diagnosis and healthcare treatment – as well as referrals for in- and out-patient paediatric care in hospital settings and some interventions such as physiotherapy, speech and language therapy and occupational therapy which may also be provided in this sector as well as in primary care. Some children, particularly those with complex impairments, may require assessment, treatment and monitoring by a range of medical and healthcare specialists working in different in- and out-patient departments of hospitals.

5.22   The GP contract[31] requires, among other things, that they refer their patients for 'other services under the 2006 Acts'. Since the 2006 Act includes services provided by local authorities such as a home help service[32] (which would include a 'sitting service') it follows that GPs are also obliged to make referrals to local authorities where a need for such social care support may exist.

5.23   As noted above at para 1.56, disabled children – especially if their impairment is diagnosed in hospital at birth – may be subjected to

---

30 Regulation 15(4)(b) of the National Health Service (General Medical Services Contracts) Regulations 2004 SI No 291 (as amended).

31 Regulation 15 of the National Health Service (General Medical Services Contracts) Regulations 2004 SI No 291 (as amended).

32 NHS Act 2006 s254 and Sch 20 para 3 – which applies to both England and Wales and includes such a service for a disabled child.

multiple health assessments to diagnose their condition to the satisfaction of the medical practitioners. However, they may then be – in
effect – abandoned by the statutory services. This phenomenon has
been expressed in the following terms:[33]

> As soon as a condition or impairment has been identified or diag-
> nosed, service professionals may fade away without any support or
> significant information being provided for the family. All too often
> nothing further is done until a crisis develops.

5.24   The child may then be discharged with only limited liaison with the
local GP surgery and the health visitor and without any proper co-
ordination with the local authority concerning social care support
services. In such cases, immediate contact should be made with the
GP surgery to ensure that the child's and family's needs are addressed
and that timely referrals can then be made to the relevant expert services as and when a need arises (for example, physiotherapy, speech
and language therapy as well as social care support from the local
authority).

Duty to assess healthcare needs

5.25   Notwithstanding the absence of an explicit provision in the NHS
Acts 2006 requiring a health body to assess the healthcare needs of
a disabled child, there are a number of reasons why such a duty almost certainly exists. The first concerns the analogous findings of
the House of Lords in *R (G) v Barnet LBC and others*[34] that a duty to
assess exists under the Children Act (CA) 1989, despite it too lacking
an explicit obligation (see para 3.13 above). The second and more co-
gent reason concerns the demands of public law – essentially that in
order to exercise their duties towards disabled children, health bodies
must follow a process that is, by any other name, an assessment – ie
the gathering of all relevant information about the child and his or
her care needs and the determination of whether it is necessary to
provide services to meet these needs.[35]

---

33 J Read, L Clements and D Ruebain, *Disabled children and the law: research and
good practice*, 2nd edn, Jessica Kingsley Publishers, 2006, p116.

34 [2003] UKHL 57.

35 In effect 'asking themselves the right question', one of the fundamental public
law requirements on all public bodies, see *Secretary of State for Education and
Science v Tameside MBC* [1977] AC 1014.

5.26   Assessment is therefore the means by which the health body 'assembles the relevant information and applies it to the statutory ends, and hence affords good evidence to any inquirer of the due discharge of its statutory duties'.[36] Further evidence of such a duty to assess can be implied from the obligations created by CA 2004 s11,[37] which requires health bodies and others to safeguard and promote children's welfare and from the recent Child Health Strategy in England, which made a commitment that 'by 2010, all children with complex health needs will have an individual care plan' – a commitment which rests on there being a duty to assess a child's individual needs so that such a plan can be meaningfully drawn up.[38]

Children's health services – the children's NSF

5.27   In 2003, in an effort to drive up the standard of care provided to all children by the NHS and social services authorities in England, the government commenced publication of a *National service framework for children, young people and maternity services* ('the Children's NSF'),[39] which sets national standards and provides best practice guidance for children's health and social care. The Children's NSF, which comprises 11 separate documents focusing on distinct issues/disabling conditions, is best considered as 'practice guidance' (see para 2.24). As such it acts as a benchmark – setting a standard to which public bodies should aspire. A significant failure to reach the standards set out in the Children's NSF may be evidence of maladministration. Sadly, however, it appears that in relation to the improvement of health service standards of care, the NSF has had 'minimal' effect.[40]

5.28   Part 1 of the Children's NSF sets out five core standards concerning service provision for all children and young people and their parents and carers. Each of the standards is accompanied by a long-term vision, markers of good practice, the rationale and interventions required to meet the standard. Each core standard is summarised below.

---

36 *R v Islington LBC ex p Rixon* (1997–98) 1 CCLR 119 at 128.
37 CA 2004 s28 in Wales.
38 Department for Children Schools and Families/Department of Health, *Healthy lives, brighter futures*, 2009, p72 at 6.42.
39 Department of Health, *National service framework for children, young people and maternity services: core standards*, 2004.
40 EDCM, 'Disabled children and health', 2009, p4.

Standard 1: Promoting health and well-being, identifying needs and intervening early

The health and well-being of all children and young people is promoted and delivered through a co-ordinated programme of action including prevention and early intervention wherever possible, to ensure long-term gain, led by the NHS in partnership with local authorities.

As part of achieving Standard 1 a Child Health Promotion Programme has been introduced which offers a comprehensive system of care encompassing the assessment of the child and family's needs, health promotion, childhood screening, immunisations and early interventions to address identified needs. A marker of good practice is that the programme is offered to all children and young people and their families. Emphasis is placed on the importance of assessment of need and early intervention. To meet the standard, PCTs must ensure that a systematic assessment of each child's physical, emotional and social development and family needs is completed by the child's first birthday and in the absence of regular contact a review takes place when the child is aged between two and three. Key issues must be identified and interventions required documented.[41] In addition all professionals working with children and young people need to be aware of health and developmental problems and proactive in identifying opportunities to promote a child's health and well-being. Systems are needed to ensure that signs of physical or mental ill health or developmental difficulties are identified and appropriate referrals made.[42] PCTs and local authorities also have a responsibility to tailor health promotion services to the needs of disadvantaged groups, including children in special circumstances, identified through a local population needs assessment.[43]

Standard 2: Supporting parents or carers

Parents or carers are enabled to receive the information, services and support which will help them to care for their children and equip them with the skills they need to ensure that their children have optimum life chances and are healthy and safe.

The markers of good practice for this standard include the provision of information and services to support parenting through local multi-agency partnerships, that parents whose children are experiencing

---

41 Core Document, Children's NSF, p41.
42 Core Document, Children's NSF, p42.
43 Core Document, Children's NSF, p22.

difficulties receive early support and evidence-based interventions and that PCTs and local authorities ensure that local parents are involved in the planning and delivery of services, with representation from all local communities and groups.[44]

Standard 3: Child, young person and family-centred services

Children and young people and families receive high quality services which are co-ordinated around their individual and family needs and take account of their views.

This standard recognises that children have a right to be involved in decisions about their care. Particular effort should be made to ensure that children and young people who are often excluded from participation activities are supported in giving their views and that parents' views are considered in planning and service development.[45] Formal working arrangements need to be in place for the provision of link workers, advocates to support children and young people, interpreters and/or support workers for children in special circumstances or from minority groups, to represent their needs during individual consultations and on multi-disciplinary review and development groups.[46]

All children and young people have a right to care and support which meets their developmental needs and provides them with the opportunity to achieve, or maintain, their optimal standard of health, development and well-being, regardless of their individual circumstances or those of their families and communities.[47] To achieve this there needs to be a high degree of co-ordination between different children's service providers with the highest degree of integration and co-ordination required when a child or young person is suffering abuse or neglect and local safeguarding children procedures are being followed.[48]

Every organisation or service should identify a senior lead for children and young people to ensure that children and young people's needs are at the forefront of local planning and service delivery.[49] All staff working with children and young people must receive training and be skilled in the common core of skills, knowledge and competencies which enable them to communicate with children and

---

44 Core Document, Children's NSF, p66.
45 Core Document, Children's NSF, p91.
46 Core Document, Children's NSF, p92.
47 Core Document, Children's NSF, p93.
48 Core Document, Children's NSF, p99.
49 Core Document, Children's NSF, p112.

young people and their parents, and assist them to achieve their full potential.[50]

Standard 4: Growing up into adulthood

All young people have access to age-appropriate services which are responsive to their specific needs as they grown into adulthood.

This standard is considered in chapter 10, see para 10.79.

Standard 5: Safeguarding and promoting the welfare of children and young people

All agencies work to prevent children suffering harm and to promote their welfare, provide them with the services they require to address their identified needs and safeguard children who are being or who are likely to be harmed.

Safeguarding and promoting children's welfare must be a priority. All agencies should ensure that the Local Safeguarding Children Board (LSCB), is effective in safeguarding and promoting the welfare of children and young people through the provision of adequate financial and human resources, senior management representation and adherence to its policies and procedures (see also the *Working together to safeguard children* guidance, paras 3.98–3.99). Agencies must work in partnership within the framework of multi-agency public protection arrangements (MAPPA) to safeguard and promote the welfare of children and young people. All organisations must have safe-recruitment practices in place, robust complaints and whistle-blowing policies and procedures for addressing allegations against staff which take account of the recommendations from *Lost in care*, the inquiry into the abuse of children in care in North Wales.[51]

Disabled children's health services and the NSF

5.29   While the core standards of the NSF apply to all children, the needs of disabled children and their families are specifically addressed in Standard 8, the headline standard within which reads as follows:

Children and young people who are disabled or who have complex health needs receive co-ordinated, high quality child and family

---

50   Core Document, Children's NSF, p114.
51   Core Document, Children's NSF, p150.

centred services which are based on assessed needs, which promote social inclusion and where possible, enable them and their families to live ordinary lives.

5.30   When read with the five core standards of the Children's NSF, Standard 8 provides comprehensive best practice guidance on the provision of health and related services to disabled children.

Identification of disability and the NSF

5.31   Standard 8 of the Children's NSF requires that local authorities, PCTs, NHS Trusts and schools ensure that children with possible impairments have prompt access to a diagnostic assessment facility, that diagnosis is followed quickly by a multi-agency comprehensive needs assessment following the *Framework for the assessment of children in need and their families* (see para 3.14) and that the assessment includes the parents' and siblings' needs for support.

Hospital services and the NSF

5.32   Disabled children's need to attend hospital appointments can be disruptive to school and family life. Under Standard 8 of the Children's NSF, PCTs and NHS Trusts should ensure that hospital departments and clinics synchronise their appointment systems as far as possible, so that families make a minimum number of visits and that systems are in place to ensure that children and young people who find it hard to wait, eg those with autistic spectrum disorders, do not have to wait unduly at out-patient clinics or general practice surgeries. Children and young people with complex healthcare needs who are prone to health crises must be seen urgently on request.[52]

5.33   The Standard for Hospital Services for Children in the Children's NSF, applicable to every department and service within a hospital that delivers care to children and young people, aims to deliver hospital services that meet the needs of children, young people and their parents, and provide effective and safe care, through appropriately trained and skilled staff working in suitable, child-friendly and safe environments.[53]

5.34   The above requirement for the standard of hospital based care is considered by the NSF to comprise three distinct elements, namely:

---

52 Disabled Child Standard, Children's NSF, p12.
53 Standard for Hospital Services, Children's NSF, p8 at 2.1–2.2.

1. *Child-centred hospital services*[54]
Children and young people should receive care that is integrated and co-ordinated around their particular needs, and the needs of their family. They, and their parents, should be treated with respect, and should be given support and information to enable them to understand and cope with the illness or injury, and the treatment needed. They should be encouraged to be active partners in decisions about their health and care, and, where possible, be able to exercise choice.

'Child-centred hospital services' are described in the Standard (at 2.5) as services that:

- consider the 'whole child', not simply the illness being treated;
- treat children as *children*, and young people as *young people*;
- are concerned with the overall experience for the child and family;
- treat children, young people and parents as partners in care;
- integrate and co-ordinate services around the child and family's particular needs;
- graduate smoothly into adult services at the right time;
- work in partnership with children, young people and parents to plan and shape services and to develop the workforce.

2. *Quality and safety of care provided*[55]
Children and young people should receive appropriate high quality, evidence-based hospital care, developed through clinical governance and delivered by staff who have the right set of skills.

3. *Quality of setting and environment*[56]
Care will be provided in an appropriate location and in an environment that is safe and well suited to the age and stage of development of the child or young person.

5.35   In meeting these three elements of the standard, hospitals need to recognise and meet the very particular needs of disabled children and involve them and their parents in the planning of services.[57] Disabled children, young people and their parents need to know that staff understand how to support them and have a sound knowledge of the needs of disabled children. Where necessary, this includes how to communicate, support with eating and drinking, the use of specialised aids and equipment, and the delicacy required in dealing with ethical issues, such as consent to intensive therapy. Staff need competencies in supporting children with a range of disabilities, including

---

54 Standard for Hospital Services, Children's NSF, p13.
55 Standard for Hospital Services, Children's NSF, p21.
56 Standard for Hospital Services, Children's NSF, p36.
57 Standard for Hospital Services, Children's NSF, p32 at 4.52.

those with learning disabilities or autistic spectrum disorders. There should be procedures for managing challenging behavior and suitable equipment should be available.[58]

5.36   A multi-agency plan developed and agreed with the disabled child or young person and their parents should be put in place while they are in hospital. For disabled children with complex health needs, this should be expanded into a personal record with a clinical summary of what they require, for example, therapies and equipment, support with eating and drinking, going to the toilet or communicating.[59]

5.37   Sadly however, the reality of hospital services for children (including disabled children) remains very different from the NSF's vision. In February 2009, the Healthcare Commission published a report on the care provided to children in NHS hospitals outside of specialist paediatric settings.[60] This reported the need for 'significant improvement' in areas such as child protection, managing children's pain, life support and skills of surgeons and anaesthetists. Specifically, it found almost two-thirds of health trusts did not train enough nurses to administer pain relief to children, and that there was 'very limited progress' in training staff to provide life support to children, with 94 per cent failing to provide basic resuscitation training to surgeons. These are all areas of poor practice that disproportionately affect disabled children.

NHS therapy services

5.38   The importance of disabled children receiving appropriate and timely therapies – such as speech and language therapy or physiotherapy – is emphasised in a number of official documents[61] – not least the NSF (see para 5.39). As noted above (para 4.58) speech and language therapy should generally be considered as special educational provision and accordingly provided by the local education authority where a statement of SEN exists. Where there is no such statement, or when the child has a need other than an educational need for therapy, then

---

58 Standard for Hospital Services, Children's NSF, p32 at 4.54.
59 Standard for Hospital Services, Children's NSF, p33 at 4.55.
60 Healthcare Commission, *Improving services for children in hospital*, 2009.
61 HM Treasury and Department for Education and Skills, *Aiming high for disabled children: better support for families*, 2007 and Department for Children Schools and Families, *The Bercow report: a review of services for children and young people (0–19) with speech, language and communication needs*, 2008.

these crucial services must be accorded a high priority by the relevant health body – not least in relation to speech and language therapy since the positive obligation on a state to facilitate a child's right of expression comes within the sphere of fundamental human rights.[62] If delay in providing these supports occurs due to a dispute between an education authority and the NHS, then consideration should be given to making a joint complaint about the failure of these bodies to work together (see para 5.14).

5.39　Despite the vital importance of such healthcare supports, children and young people's access to rehabilitation and therapy services is inconsistent across regions, with long waits in some areas. In meeting standard 8 of the Children's NSF local authorities and PCT's are expected to review local therapy services in order to:

- promote self-referral, simplifying the care pathway, and reduce excessive waits that may affect a child's development;
- improve administrative systems and processes for referral and discharge, and the effectiveness of outcomes of different therapeutic regimes, such as group sessions; and
- ensure that the supply of timely therapy services is sufficient to meet the needs of children and young people who require it, based on assessed needs. This may involve increased capacity to ensure that all children and young people attending early education settings and mainstream or special schools have equal access to therapy.[63]

5.40　Ultimately local authorities and PCTs need to ensure that:

- parents or carers, children and young people are active partners in decisions about rehabilitation or therapy services, with agreed goals for what it is intended to achieve and how they can help;
- therapeutic interventions are agreed and overseen by specialist paediatric therapists; and
- therapy is delivered in the most appropriate setting, which may include the home or educational settings.[64]

62　For example, articles 8 and 10 of the European Convention on Human Rights: this assertion is made by J Morris, *Accessing human rights: Disabled children and the Children Act*, The Who Cares? Trust, London, 1998, p20, and accepted by the Department of Health: see Department of Health, *Assessing children in need and their families: practice guidance*, HMSO, 2000, para 3.125.

63　Disabled Child Standard, Children's NSF, p15.

64　Disabled Child Standard, Children's NSF, p15.

NHS equipment provision

5.41 Section 3 of the NHS Act 2006 and the NHS(W) Act 2006 requires the NHS to provide – among other things – services and facilities to address people's healthcare needs. The NHS's equipment provision obligations are broad and complimentary to those on local authorities concerned with social care support (see chapter 3). They include, for example, providing specialist beds for children living at home, ceiling rails for hoists, refrigerators for medicines, walking frames, wheelchairs and so on. The provision of such equipment may have to be sanctioned by the local health body (such as a PCT or HB) although GP's are authorised to provide a wide range of 'appliances', eg medical aids, dressings, pads etc as well as basic equipment to help overcome the effects of disability.[65]

5.42 Because of concerns over the inadequate nature of equipment services[66] steps have been taken in England and Wales (accompanied by not inconsiderable funding support) to require local health bodies and councils to establish joint 'integrated equipment services'.[67] Paragraph 7 of the English guidance[68] provides an illustrative list of the type of equipment that might be available from such an integrated service:

> *Community equipment* is equipment for home nursing usually provided by the NHS, such as pressure relief mattresses and commodes, and equipment for daily living such as shower chairs and raised toilet seats, usually provided by local authorities. It also includes, but is not limited to:
> - minor adaptations, such as grab rails, lever taps and improved domestic lighting;
> - ancillary equipment for people with sensory impairments, such as liquid level indicators, hearing loops, assistive listening devices and flashing doorbells;
> - communication aids for people with speech impairments;

---

65 NHS (General Medical Services Contracts) Regulations 2004 SI No 291 reg 39 and National Health Service (General Medical Services Contracts) (Wales) Regulations 2004 SI No 478 (W48).

66 See, for example, Audit Commission, *Fully equipped: the provision of equipment to older or disabled people by the NHS and social services in England and Wales,* 2000.

67 Department of Health, *Community equipment services guidance,* HSC 2001/0: LAC (2001)13 (2001).

68 Department of Health, *Community equipment services guidance* HSC 2001/0: LAC (2001)13 (2001) and Welsh Assembly Government, *Guidelines for developing and integrating community equipment services in Wales,* 2008.

- wheelchairs for short-term loan, but *not* those for permanent wheelchair users, as these are prescribed and funded by different NHS services;[69]
- telecare equipment such as fall alarms, gas escape alarms and health state monitoring for people who are vulnerable.

5.43   Notwithstanding the aim of making equipment an integrated support services, disputes will inevitably arise as to which authority is responsible for provision. This may be a dispute between a council and a PCT/HB – but disputes can also arise between health bodies themselves – for example, where a disabled child is attending a school in an area outside his or her home PCT/HB[70] and the equipment is needed at the school (for example, an additional walking frame). If hardship is caused by such a dispute then a joint complaint or application for judicial review about the failure of these bodies to work together should be considered (see para 5.14 above). A 2007 ombudsman's report[71] concerned such a case, where the patient required a specialist profiling bed and a specialised seating system. The ombudsman considered that one of the health bodies should have funded the necessary equipment as an interim measure, pending the resolution of the dispute – and that a failure to do this amounted to maladministration.

Wheelchair provision

5.44   The provision of publicly funded wheelchairs is an NHS responsibility under section 3 of the NHS Act 2006 and NHS(W) Act 2006.[72] The need for a suitable wheelchair will often be capable of being expressed in the language of human rights, for example, in terms of a right under article 8 European Convention on Human Rights (ECHR) for a child to be enabled to interact with other people and the environment.[73] Not infrequently considerable hardship and pain

---

69 See para 5.44.

70 In such cases guidance exists as to how to decide the 'responsible commissioner' – see para 5.13.

71 Public Services Ombudsman for Wales, Complaint against Bro Morgannwg NHS Trust, Cardiff & Vale NHS Trust, Vale of Glamorgan Council and Vale of Glamorgan Local Health Board, Case Ref 200501955, 200600591 and 200700641, 28 November 2007 – see pp28 and 30.

72 See, for example, Department of Health/Care Services Improvement Partnership, *Out and about: Wheelchairs as part of a whole-systems approach to independence*, 2006, p30.

73 See, for example, *Botta v Italy* (1998) 26 EHRR 241 at [32] and see also paras 2.5–2.8 above.

(particularly postural pain) will be caused by the use of an unsuitable wheelchair such that this could be expressed as degrading treatment contrary to article 3[74] or contrary to article 8 in relation to the impact on the person's physical and psychological integrity.[75]

5.45 Assessments for wheelchairs and their provision are the responsibility of local NHS wheelchair services in England, and the Artificial Limb and Appliance Service in Wales. Assessments are undertaken by specialists, usually an occupational therapist or physiotherapist, although GPs should support children in seeking such equipment and provide advice on the process.

5.46 In England brief guidance on wheelchair provision was issued in 1996[76] albeit that it concentrates on the provision of electrically powered indoor/outdoor wheelchairs (EPIOCs). A voucher scheme also exists that gives the option of purchasing a non-motorised wheelchair from an independent supplier – although in such cases the user will be responsible for its maintenance and repair. In some cases powered wheelchairs/scooters can also be purchased through the Motability Scheme by surrendering the high rate mobility component of the disability living allowance (DLA).

5.47 In Wales no specific guidance exists[77] and the provision of wheelchairs is the responsibility of five specialist centres.[78]

5.48 The English guidance concerning EPIOCs gave as suggested criteria for their provision that the person is:[79]

• unable to propel a manual chair outdoors;
• able to benefit from the chair through increased mobility leading to improved quality of life; and
• able to handle the chair safely.

---

74 *Price v UK* (2002) 34 EHRR 1285.
75 See again *Botta v Italy* (1998) 26 EHRR 241 at [32] and *R (Bernard) v Enfield LBC* [2002] EWHC 2282 (Admin); (2002) 5 CCLR 577.
76 HSG (96)34, *Powered indoor/outdoor wheelchairs for severely disabled people* and HSG(96)53, *The wheelchair voucher scheme.*
77 Welsh Health Circular (2003) 63, *Planning and commissioning guidance,* refers to wheelchairs as being the responsibility of the (now-disbanded) Health Commission Wales – but the commission effectively delegated responsibility to five specialist providers.
78 The Cardiff and Wrexham Artificial Limb and Appliance Service Centres and the Rehab Engineering Units in Swansea, Cardiff and Llanfairfechan.
79 NHS Executive, *Powered indoor/outdoor wheelchairs for severely disabled people,* HSG (96)34, May 1996.

5.49   In practice there have been severe concerns about the adequacy of the NHS wheelchair services in England and Wales[80] – and these concerns continue.[81] This has resulted in many families seeking charitable and other support in order to address their child's mobility needs – for example, from the Whizz-Kidz charity.[82]

Short breaks

5.50   Although short breaks, or respite care, are services most commonly provided by local authorities – and are considered at paras 3.50 and 3.59–3.62 above – the NHS also has important responsibilities to provide such support. The NHS duty was recognised in *R (D) v Haringey LBC*[83] (see 5.54 below) and is highlighted in a number of important NHS guidance documents.[84] Where therefore the child would need access to healthcare supports during a period of respite the NHS should ensure that this service is available. It can do this by providing or funding the short break/respite care or working with the local authority to ensure that the service is available. In the *Haringey* case the PCT was responsible for the service by providing a respite care service in the children's home (or paying a private agency to do this). Sometimes, however, the provision of short breaks will be a joint initiative under the 'working together' duty (see para 5.14). For example, a respite care centre run by a local authority may not have

---

80   See, for example, Audit Commission, *Fully equipped 2002: assisting independence*, 2002; Department of Health, *Evaluation of the powered wheelchair and voucher system 2000*, 2002; emPower, *NHS wheelchair and seating services mapping project: final report*, Limbless Association, 2004; and Prime Minister's Strategy Unit, *Improving the life chances of disabled people*, 2005.

81   See, for example, N Sharma with J Morrison, *Don't push me around! Disabled children's experiences of wheelchair services in the UK*, 2006, a joint report published by Barnardo's and Whizz-Kidz and endorsed by the UK's four Children's Commissioners; the 2010 Inquiry commissioned in Wales – Welsh Assembly Government (2010) Health, Wellbeing and Local Government Committee: Ministerial Evidence session HWLG(3)-04-10-p4: 4 March 2010 and Every Disabled Child Matters, 'Disabled children and health', 2009, p13.

82   See www.whizz-kidz.org.uk.

83   [2005] All ER (D) 256.

84   See, for example, Department of Health, *The national framework for NHS continuing healthcare and NHS funded nursing care in England*, 2009, para 104; Department of Health *NHS continuing healthcare practice guidance*, March 2010, para 11.1; Welsh Assembly Government WHC (2004)54: NAFWC 41/2004, *NHS Responsibilities for meeting continuing NHS health care needs: guidance 2004*, 2004, para 10; and Welsh Assembly Government *The continuing NHS health care framework for implementation in Wales 2004*, 2004, para 2.1.

staff trained to deliver certain healthcare support (such as administering rectal valium) which as a consequence might make the service unavailable to children with certain disabling conditions. Such an impasse could be resolved, if a care assistant at the centre was willing to take on this role and be trained by the NHS in the procedure (and when administering the valium he or she would be doing this as an agent of the NHS).

5.51 In England, short breaks have been identified as a key priority for NHS delivery and investment in both 'Aiming high for disabled children' and 'Healthy lives, brighter futures', with a clear expectation that both local authorities and PCTs will deliver additional and better quality short breaks services for disabled children and their families.[85]

Continence services

5.52 Achieving continence is a central goal for many disabled children and their families. Yet even when continence assessments are available, parents report real problems in securing the supply of the right sort of continence products for their child, with many experiencing a 'one size fits all' service. NHS guidance in the Children's NSF recommended 'an integrated community based paediatric continence service' in every area. In 2007 the Department of Health issued the Children's Continence Exemplar to support the development of child-centred local delivery.[86]

5.53 Detailed practice guidance concerning the organisation and range of continence services that should be made available has been issued in England.[87] This advises that the nature and quantity of continence supplies made available should be determined as a result of an individual assessment of need in every case. Research suggests,[88] however, that despite the need for pads to be available on the basis of clinical need, almost 75 per cent of PCTs operate a fixed policy which stipulates a maximum number of continence pads that can be provided

---

85 Department for Children Schools and Families/Department of Health, *Aiming high for disabled children: short breaks implementation guidance*, 2008.

86 Despite these recommendations, the *Every disabled child matters* campaign describes integrated paediatric continence services as 'virtually non-existent': EDCM, 'Disabled children and health', 2009, p30.

87 Department of Health, *Good practice in continence services*, April 2000.

88 Royal College of Physicians, *National audit of continence care for older people*, November 2006, accessible at www.rcplondon.ac.uk/news/news.asp?PR_id=331.

over a specified period. The research concerned older people but the experience of disabled children is similar: such policies are, however, contrary to the guidance, fetter the authorities' discretion and, where individual hardship results, constitute maladministration.

Continuing care

5.54   Although (as noted above, see para 5.11) the local authority will generally be the lead agency in co-ordinating the support services for a disabled child, frequently the package will have funding support from the NHS and the education department (in relation to SEN needs – see chapter 4) as well as from the children's services authority. In some cases, however, the child's needs are such that the NHS may not only become the lead agency, but it may also assume sole responsibility for funding the child's health and social care needs. In such situations the child is held to be eligible for 'NHS Continuing Care'. However, it should be noted that the English guidance on Continuing Care for disabled children (see para 5.55 below) assumes that for virtually all children there will be input from agencies other than health – in contrast to the position for adults.

5.55   *R (T, D and B) v Haringey LBC*[89] is an example of a case involving severely disabled children and young people with complex health needs. The judgment related to the younger child (aged 3 at the hearing) who had a complex medical condition which required a tracheostomy (a tube in the throat) which needed regular suctioning, without which there was a severe risk to life. The child was discharged from hospital and cared for at home, with her mother being trained to manage the tracheostomy with regular back up from the district nurses. The issue in the case was which authority – the PCT or local authority – was responsible for providing the respite care that the mother required – since when she was attending to the tracheostomy she had to be awake through the night. The court held that in such a situation, the NHS was responsible – meaning that the same principles as applied to adults, applied to children. In the judge's opinion the 'scale and type of nursing care' was such that it was outside that which could be provided by the local authority.

5.56   In England the Department of Health has issued guidance specifically concerned with the assessment of children's eligibility for NHS Continuing Care – *The National Framework for Children and*

89 [2005] EWHC 2235 (Admin); (2006) 9 CCLR 58.

Young People's Continuing Care ('the Continuing Care Framework'). In Wales the NHS Continuing Care guidance only applies to adults – although the Welsh Assembly Government has indicated that it also proposes to publish separate guidance relating to children.[90]

5.57　The English Continuing Care Framework sets out the process for arranging packages of continuing care for children and young people who have health needs that cannot be met by existing universal and specialist services.

English Framework – assessment and the Decision Support Tool

5.58　The English Continuing Care Framework (in the remainder of this section referred to as 'the Framework') requires that every child or young person referred to the NHS with possible continuing care needs should be offered a comprehensive assessment[91] by a nominated children and young people's health assessor.[92] The assessment should (among other things):

a) consider the preferences of the child or young person and his or her family;

b) be holistic – considering the needs not only of the child or young person but also of his or her family, and where relevant should include a carer's assessment (see paras 8.5–8.22 below);

c) consider all relevant reports and risk assessments from the multidisciplinary team (health, social and education).

5.59　The Framework contains a Decision Support Tool which is based on a tool widely used for adults,[93] and brings together needs from across ten care domains: challenging behaviour, communication, mobility, nutrition food and drink, continence and elimination, skin and tissue viability, breathing, drug therapies and medicines, psychological and emotional and seizures. It describes five levels of need, from low to priority, and provides descriptors to assess the level of need for each of the care domains. The Framework indicates that three 'high'

---

90 Welsh Assembly Government (2010), *Continuing NHS Healthcare: The national framework for implementation in Wales*, May 2010, Welsh Assembly Government Circular: 015/2010 paras 1.6 and 9.6.

91 *Continuing Care Framework*, p50.

92 *Continuing Care Framework*, p51.

93 For detailed consideration of these tools see L Clements and P Thompson, *Community care and the law*, 4th edn, LAG, 2007, chapter 14 and L Clements, 'NHS funding for continuing care in England the revised (2009) guidance', (2009) 1 *Journal of Social Care and Neurodisability*, pp39–47.

ratings, one severe rating or one priority rating is likely to indicate that the child or young person has continuing care needs.[94]

5.60   The Framework stresses that the Decision Support Tool is not prescriptive and the importance of exercising evidence-based professional judgment in all cases. Following assessment the Framework indicates that a decision as to whether or not the child has a continuing care need should be made by a multidisciplinary or multi-agency forum or panel and, where a decision is made regarding a package of continuing care, processes undertaken to put it in place.

5.61   The Framework requires PCTs to have a local complaints procedure in place to respond to any disagreements voiced by the child or their family about any aspect of the continuing care process. In addition once a continuing care package is put in place regular reviews must be carried out. The Framework recommends that a review takes place three months after initial assessment and then annually or more frequently depending on the specific case.

The continuing care pathway

5.62   Included in the Framework is a continuing care pathway (Annex B), which shows how the continuing care process should look from the perspective of child or young person and their family.[95] The pathway specifies:

a) three phases – assessment, decision-making and arrangement of provision;

b) seven discrete stages within these phases – identify, assess, recommend, decide, inform, deliver and review;

c) key actions to be undertaken at each stage; and

d) timescales, which should see the child and family informed of the continuing care service provision decision within 28 working days of the referral.

Continuing care and direct payments/personal budgets

5.63   Where a disabled child is deemed eligible for NHS Continuing Care funding it means that the care provided is subject to the provisions of the NHS Acts 2006 and not the social services statutes (such as

94 *Continuing Care Framework*, Annex A, p35.
95 *Continuing Care Framework*, Annex B, p57.

CA 1989 and CSDPA 1970, see chapter 3). In some cases this is problematic – particularly in that there is no duty on the NHS to provide its support by way of direct payments –and in some cases there is not even a power so to do.

5.64 In *R (Harrison) v Secretary of State for Health and others*[96] the High Court held that there was no power under the NHS Acts to make direct payments. The courts have, nevertheless, held that NHS bodies are permitted to make payments to Independent User Trusts[97] (see para 3.67 above). Such a trust could be created by the family of a disabled child and would then be capable of receiving monies from a PCT or HB. As noted above, however, the Continuing Care Framework in England does not envisage that a child will ever be 100 per cent NHS funded and in such situations, where both the local authority and the NHS are contributing to a care packages, there appears to be nothing in principle under the CA 1989 or the NHS Acts to stop the NHS body transferring its contribution to the local authority via NHS Act 2006 s256 (or in Wales the NHS(W) Act 2006 s194) and for the local authority funding the support by way of a direct payment to the parent.

5.65 Section 12A of the NHS Act 2006[98] empowers PCTs in England to make direct payments to patients along similar lines to those paid by social services. At the time of publication these are being piloted in eight regions, with seven having power to make direct payments and/or children in transition payments.[99] All other PCTs have the power to assist by contributing to a 'personal budget' (see paras 3.68–3.71) for a disabled child.

Child and adolescent mental health services (CAMHS)

5.66 Many disabled children will experience episodes of mental ill-health, or indeed their disability could be a mental illness. These children will need support from CAMHS, which promote the mental health and psychological well-being of children and young people. The intention of CAMH services can be stated as 'to provide high quality, multi-disciplinary mental health services to all children and young people with mental health problems and disorders to ensure effective

---

96 [2009] EWHC 574 (Admin).
97 *Gunter v SW Staffordshire PCT* [2005] EWHC 1894 (Admin).
98 Inserted by the Health Act 2009 s11.
99 Announcement on 28 June 2010 at www.dh.gov.uk/en/mediacentre/pressreleases/DH_117020.

assessment, treatment and support, for them and their families'.[100] The term 'CAMHS' can be used widely to refer to all services which play a part in promoting children's mental well-being, or narrowly to refer to specialist mental health services for children. The narrow meaning of the term is used in the remainder of this section, recognising the critical importance of wider health and other services in achieving good mental health for disabled children – and their families.

5.67　There is no specific statutory framework for CAMHS. Therefore, community-based CAMH services will be provided under the NHS Acts and the Mental Health Act (MHA) 1983. Provisions in relation to detention in hospital and compulsory treatment will be found in the MHA 1983, for children as for adults. All issues in relation to mental health treatment should be informed by the Mental Health Act Code of Practice ('MHA Code'), revised in 2008, which has statutory force.[101] Particular regard should be had to chapter 36 of the English MHA Code, 'Children and young people under the age of 18' (chapter 33 of the Welsh Code).

5.68　Input into CAMHS from children's services within local authorities will be governed by the Children Acts 1989 and 2004, the Chronically Sick and Disabled Persons Act 1970 s2 (see chapter 3) and the MHA 1983 s117 (see para 5.81).

5.69　CAMH services are not governed by a single statutory provision and are in large part shaped by government policy initiatives and targets. These targets and polices are relevant in that they give an indication of the nature and quality of services that disabled children and their families should expect to receive if they need the help of a specialist mental health service. It is for this reason that the following paragraphs provide a brief overview of the structure of local CAMH services, their guiding principles and the services that they should be able to provide.

5.70　Many disabled children will require input from CAMHS, whether because their primary need is a mental health need or because of secondary mental health problems associated with their disabilities, which may sadly emerge as a result of their needs not being addressed properly. The expectation is that all such children will have 'access to timely, integrated, high quality, multi-disciplinary mental

---

100　Department for Children Schools and Families, *Services supporting the emotional wellbeing and mental health of children and young people*, 2010.

101　*R (Munjaz) v Mersey Care NHS Trust* [2006] 2 AC 148.

health services to ensure effective assessment, treatment and support'[102] and that these CAMHS will provide for four levels of service:

Tier 1 A primary level of care.

Tier 2 A service provided by specialist individual professionals relating to workers in primary care.

Tier 3 A specialised multi-disciplinary service for more severe, complex or persistent disorders.

Tier 4 Essential tertiary level services such as day units, highly specialized out-patient teams and in-patient units.

A comprehensive CAMHS

5.71   *Improvement, expansion and reform*[103] set the expectation that a comprehensive CAMHS would be available in each locality in England by 2006. This has proved to be aspirational, in that it is debatable whether such a service has as yet been achieved.[104]

5.72   In 2004 a specific Children's NSF Standard was published to address the 'Mental Health and Psychological Well-being of Children and Young People[105] which required that CAMHS should ensure, as part of their underpinning principles:

- access for all children and young people regardless of their age, gender, race, religion, ability, culture, ethnicity or sexuality;[106]
- multi-agency commissioning and delivery of services;[107] and
- participation of children and young people and their families at all levels of service provision.[108]

5.73   The NSF places great emphasis on early intervention,[109] by (among other things) requiring that health bodies and local authorities ensure CAMH workers are available and accessible within community

102 Department of Health/DfES, *National service framework for children young people and maternity services: the mental health and psychological well-being of children and young people: Standard 9*, 2004 ('NSF Standard 9'), p4.

103 Department of Health, *Improvement, expansion and reform: the next 3 years, priorities and planning framework 2003–2006*, 2003.

104 For analysis of what is meant by a 'Comprehensive CAMHS' and whether it has been achieved, see 11 Million, *Out of the shadows?* Children's Commissioner for England, 2008, p42 and the 2008 UK Children's Commissioners' *Report to UN Committee on the rights of the child*, p23.

105 NSF Standard 9, p49.

106 NSF Standard 9, p49.

107 NSF Standard 9, p49.

108 NSF Standard 9, p13.

109 NSF Standard 9, eg, pp8–9.

settings[110] and that all localities have specialist multidisciplinary teams with the resources and skills to provide:

- specialist assessment and treatment services;
- services for the full range of mental disorders in conjunction with other agencies as appropriate;
- a mix of short-term and long-term interventions and care;
- a full range of evidence-based treatments; and
- specialist services that are commissioned on a regional or multi-district basis, including in-patient care.[111]

5.74   Adequate services must be in place for emergencies, including policies that clarify the level of service provided and the criteria for referral. Arrangements need to be in place to ensure that 24-hour cover is provided to meet children's urgent needs and that a specialist mental health assessment is undertaken within 24 hours or during the next working day where indicated.[112]

5.75   Health Bodies and local authorities also need to develop a long-term strategy to ensure that young people[113] are provided with services which meet their developmental needs. This includes ensuring there are no gaps in service provision and that there is a smooth transition to adult services. The Care Programme Approach should be used on transition from child to adult services (see paras 10.77–10.87 below for more on transition to adult health services).[114]

5.76   It is the responsibility of Health Bodies and local authorities to ensure that children and young people with learning disabilities receive equal access to mental health services at all tiers of CAMHS. This includes:

- adequately resourced Tiers 2 and 3 learning disability specialist CAMHS with staff with the necessary competencies to address mental health difficulties in children and young people with learning disabilities; and
- access to Tier 4 services providing in-patient, day-patient and out-reach units for children and adolescents with learning disabilities and severe and complex neuro-psychiatric problems.[115]

---

110 NSF Standard 9, p11–12.
111 NSF Standard 9, p50.
112 NSF Standard 9, p19.
113 The Mental Health Act Code refers to 'child' or 'children' as under 16s and 'young person' or 'young people' in relation to those aged 16 or 17.
114 NSF Standard 9, p22.
115 NSF Standard 9, p24.

Admission to hospital for treatment of a mental disorder

5.77 The law relating to the admission and treatment of a child or young person with a mental health difficulty (whether 'informally', with parental consent or under the MHA 1983) is complex and is explained in detail with clarity in a 2009 Department of Health publication, *The legal aspects of the care and treatment of children and young people with mental disorder.*[116] A key complicating factor is the difficult relationship that exists between the detention and treatment powers under the 1983 Act, the Mental Capacity Act 2005 (which is of primary relevance for persons aged 16 and over) and the common law as it relates to children's powers to make their own decisions.

5.78 Detailed guidance on assessment and applications for detention in hospital under the MHA 1983 is set out in chapter 4 of the MHA Code[117] which in addition, at chapter 36, provides guidance on particular issues arising in relation to children and young people (chapters 5 and 33 respectively of the Welsh Code).[118] An application is usually made by the Approved Mental Health Professional (AMHP) and, save in cases of emergency, must be supported by two medical recommendations and only occur after agreement of the child or young person's 'nearest relative' and consultation with those who have parental responsibility for him or her.

Ensuring an age appropriate environment for CAMHS

5.79 MHA 1983 s131A requires that for mental health purposes the hospital environment in which a child or young person is to be accommodated is age appropriate. The requirement applies regardless of whether the admission is informal or formal and its primary purpose is to ensure that children and young people are not admitted inappropriately on to adult psychiatric wards. A detailed briefing published in 2010 by Young Minds[119] explains the nature of the obligation created by section 131A and the very limited circumstance

---

116 Department of Health, *The legal aspects of the care and treatment of children and young people with mental disorder*, 2009, accessible at www.iris-initiative.org.uk/silo/files/children-and-young-people-mh-legal-guide.pdf.

117 Department of Health, *Code of Practice: Mental Health Act 1983*, TSO, 2008.

118 Welsh Assembly Government, *Code of Practice: Mental Health Act 1983*, WAG, 2008.

119 C Parker, *Young Minds briefing on the responsibilities of NHS Trust Boards under section 131A of the Mental Health Act 1983*, Young Minds, 2010.

when an admission to a adult psychiatric ward would be permitted – and the obligations that are placed on the hospital in such cases.

Hospital discharge

5.80 The Children's NSF Standard for Hospital Services[120] provides general advice concerning the discharge of children from hospital care – including the need (where appropriate) for effective liaison with the social work service – to ensure (for example) that equipment is available and 'that rehabilitation programmes can be continued at home'.[121]

5.81 Good practice guidance is given in the Children's NSF Standard for Mental Health and Psychological Well-being of Children and Young People[122] where the discharge follows a period in an NHS mental health setting (or CAMHS arranged setting). The advice includes (para 9.14):

> The in-patient unit needs to be able to hand over to an appropriately equipped community service. There needs to be a shared understanding of the level of care required on discharge from inpatient services and if the appropriate resources are not available in community services, shared aftercare arrangements should be considered; there may be a continuing role for the in-patient team in the provision of outreach and after-care services.

5.82 Where (unusually) the discharge of the child or young person follows their formal detention under either section 3 or one of the criminal provisions of the 1983 Act, then they will be entitled to support services, not under the CA 1989 or the Chronically Sick and Disabled Persons Act 1970 (see chapter 3 above) but under MHA 1983 s117 ('section 117 services'). The fact that these services are provided under a distinct statutory provision should not in practice make any material difference to the child, young person or his or her family. Section 117 services do have certain distinct legal characteristics, for example, they are the joint responsibility of both the NHS and the local authority,[123] they must be provided free of charge[124] and can cover a wide spectrum

---

120 Department of Health, *Getting the right start: national service framework for children: standard for hospital services*, 2003, see para 3.27 onwards.

121 Department of Health, *Getting the right start: national service framework for children: standard for hospital services*, 2003, see paras 3.27 and 3.30.

122 NSF Standard 9, para 9.13 onwards.

123 *R v Mental Health Review Tribunal ex p Hall* (1999) 2 CCLR 361.

124 *R v Manchester CC ex p Stennett and others* [2002] UKHL 34; (2002) 5 CCLR 500.

of supports – both health and social care – albeit that they must be required because of a mental health need.[125] A detailed consideration of section 117 services is provided by the MHA 1983 Code of Practice[126] and in Clements and Thompson.[127]

Consent to mental health treatment

5.83 In all areas of healthcare, including mental health care and treatment, it will be unlawful to treat a disabled child unless the appropriate consent has been obtained or the treatment is otherwise authorised. Issues of capacity to consent to treatment generally are deal with below, but the flowchart overleaf summarises the approach that should be taken in relation to mental health treatment.

Consent to treatment

Children (under 16s)

5.84 Consent to treatment is a difficult issue for disabled children, as it can be for all children. Consent should be sought for each aspect of the child or young person's treatment as and when it arises, even if the treatment proposed could be given without consent under the MHA 1983.[128] In relation to mental health treatments, reference should be made to the Department of Health publication *The legal aspects of the care and treatment of children and young people with mental disorder.*[129]

5.85 Detailed guidance has been issued by the Department of Health concerning treatment decisions relating to children.[130] Children's capacity to consent to treatment is determined by individual assessment.

125 *R (Mwanza) v Greenwich LBC and Bromley LBC* [2010] EWHC 1462 (Admin); (2010) 13 CCLR 454.
126 Department of Health, *Code of Practice: Mental Health Act 1983*, TSO, 2008, chapter 27 and Welsh Assembly Government, *Code of Practice: Mental Health Act 1983*, WAG, 2008, chapter 31.
127 L Clements and P Thompson, *Community care and the law*, 4th edn, LAG, 2007, para 21.27 onwards.
128 Department of Health, *The legal aspects of the care and treatment of children and young people with mental disorder*, 2009, p56 at 4.3. Accessible at www.iris-initiative.org.uk/silo/files/children-and-young-people-mh-legal-guide.pdf.
129 Department of Health, *The legal aspects of the care and treatment of children and young people with mental disorder*, 2009.
130 Department of Health, *Reference guide to consent for examination or treatment*, 2nd edn, 2009.

Diagram 2: Capacity to consent

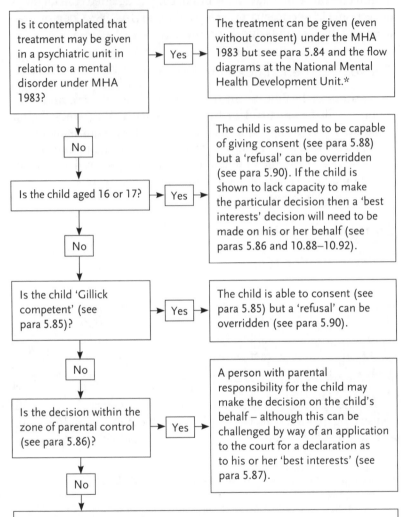

Children who are able to make decisions about their admission to hospital or treatment are referred to as being 'Gillick competent', a reference to the leading House of Lords authority.[131] A 'Gillick competent' child is a child who has attained sufficient understanding and intelligence to be able to understand fully what is involved in the proposed intervention. Such a child will be regarded as competent to consent to a particular intervention, such as admission to hospital or proposed treatment.[132]

5.86   If a child is not 'Gillick competent', those with parental responsibility may, as a general rule, consent if the decision falls within the 'zone of parental control'.[133] The zone of parental control is an artificial and elusive concept – but certain treatments are outside the 'zone' such as forced feeding and ECT. Even if the decision is normally one that lies within the zone, clinicians are advised to be cautious about relying on the consent of a parent if there is any indication that he or she is not acting in the best interests of the child or may lack capacity to make the decision in question.[134] The parent's consent should be sought for each aspect of the child or young person's care and treatment as it arises.[135]

5.87   The 'inherent jurisdiction' of the High Court can be invoked to make treatment decisions on behalf of all children, whether competent or otherwise and the court may override treatment consents or refusals if it considers it necessary to do so in the child's 'best interests'.[136] This jurisdiction has no limits other than the requirement to act in the child's best interests, although the House of Lords has held that the Family Division cannot compel a public authority to exercise its public law functions.[137]

---

131 *Gillick v West Norfolk and Wisbech Area Health Authority* [1986] AC 112.

132 Department of Health, *The legal aspects of the care and treatment of children and young people with mental disorder*, 2009, p18 at 2.10.

133 Department of Health, *The legal aspects of the care and treatment of children and young people with mental disorder*, 2009, p24 at 2.32–2.33.

134 See, for example, P Fennell, *Mental health: the new law*, 2nd edn, Jordans, 2010, chapter 11.

135 See the MHA Code 23.31–23.36, 23.37–23.41 and 36.53.

136 *Re W (A Minor) (Medical Treatment: Court's jurisdiction)* [1993] 1 Fam 64 and P Bowen, *Blackstone's guide to the Mental Health Act 2007*, OUP, 2007, para 9.33.

137 *A v Liverpool CC* [1982] AC 363. In addition to the High Court's inherent jurisdiction, courts also have jurisdiction under section 8 of the Children Act 1989 to make a 'specific issue order' for the purposes of determining a specific question, including a question relating to medical treatment. See P Bowen, *Blackstone's guide to the Mental Health Act 2007*, OUP, 2007, para 9.35.

Young people (16- and 17-year-olds)

5.88   The law on consent to treatment, including treatment for mental disorder, for young people (aged 16–17 years) is governed by the Mental Capacity Act (MCA) 2005 and Family Law Reform Act (FLRA) 1969 s8. The MCA 2005 creates a rebuttable presumption that all individuals aged 16 or over have capacity to make decisions for themselves.

5.89   MCA 2005 s3 provides that a person is deemed to be incapable of making a specific decision if they cannot understand the information about the decision, retain the relevant information in their mind, use or weigh the information as part of the decision-making process or communicate their decision.[138] A person may be incapable of 'understanding' relevant information due to a particularly severe intellectual impairment or because they have a completely distorted sense of reality – for example, a belief that they are obese, when they are in fact emaciated. Likewise a person's inability to weigh information in their mind as part of the decision-making process, might stem, not from profound cognitive impairment but from an obsessional or compulsive disorder – for example, an incontrollable phobia.[139]

5.90   For 16- to 17-year-olds, the MCA 2005 presumption of capacity to make decisions has to be considered in the context of FLRA 1969 s8. This provides that persons of this age can consent to any surgical, medical or dental treatment. The courts have, however, distinguished between the right to consent and the right to refuse – and held that in certain cases a court (or even a parent) can override a refusal by such a child.[140] While it is questionable whether the case law based on FLRA 1969 s8 is still good law (preceding as it did the enactment of MCA 2005), it is nevertheless the case that the courts, in the exercise of their wardship powers, can override certain treatment refusal decisions of 16- and 17-year-olds even if the young person is 'Gillick competent'. See in this respect the 2009 Department of Health guidance concerning treatment decisions relating to children.[141]

---

138 MCA 2005 s3.

139 See, for example, *Re MB (Caesarean Section)* [1997] 2 FLR 426; (1998) 38 BMLR 175.

140 See, for example, *Re: R (A minor) (Wardship: Medical Treatment)* (1991) 4 All ER 177 and *Re: W (A minor) (Wardship: Medical Treatment)* (1992) 4 All ER 627 – both cases decided before the MCA 2005 and so of uncertain status.

141 Department of Health, *Reference guide to consent for examination or treatment*, 2nd edn, 2009.

Emergency treatment

5.91 If there is no other lawful basis on which to give the treatment and if the failure to treat is likely to lead to the child or young person's death or to severe injury, it may be possible to treat without consent or formal authorisation. In this context, the 2009 Department of Health guidance concerning treatment decisions relating to children[142] advises:

> A life-threatening emergency may arise when consultation with either a person with parental responsibility or the court is impossible, or the person with parental responsibility refuses consent despite such emergency treatment appearing to be in the best interests of the child. In such cases the courts have stated that doubt should be resolved in favour of the preservation of life, and it will be acceptable to undertake treatment to preserve life or prevent serious damage to health.

Palliative care

5.92 A group of disabled children whose needs are frequently neglected are those with life-limiting conditions who require palliative care services. In accordance with Standard 8 of the Children's NSF, high quality palliative care services should be available for all children and young people who need them. As with CAMH services, there is no specific statutory basis for palliative care services, which are provided under the NHS Acts.

5.93 Since the publication of the Children's NSF in England, local authorities, PCTs and NHS Trusts have been required to ensure that:

- Palliative care services provide high quality, sensitive support that takes account of the physical, emotional and practical needs of the child and their family, including siblings. Services are sensitive to the cultural and spiritual needs of the child and family.
- Services maximise choice, independence and creativity to promote quality of life.
- Services are delivered where the child and family want.
- Services include the prompt availability of equipment to support care, access to appropriate translation services, and workers skilled in using communication aids.
- Services are regularly reviewed with parents or carers, children and young people, and gaps in provision identified and addressed.

142 Department of Health, *Reference guide to consent for examination or treatment*, 2nd edn, 2009, p35, para 18.

- Services are planned in partnership with voluntary sector providers and children and young people's hospices in localities where these exist.
- Provision of services includes, where appropriate:
  a) 24-hour access to expertise in paediatric and family care (often provided by local community children and young people's services to enable continuity of care) is available;
  b) 24-hour expertise in paediatric palliative care (provided by those with specialist palliative care training) is available;
  c) pain and symptom control;
  d) psychological and social support;
  e) spiritual support which takes account of the needs of the whole family;
  f) where required, formal counselling or therapy;
  g) arrangements to avoid unnecessary emergency admission to hospital are in place;
  h) protocols for immediate access to hospital, if needed, are in place; and
  i) a process for keeping the general practitioner informed.[143]

5.94   In recognition of the ongoing problems in children's palliative care, the recent government strategy document *Better care: better lives*[144] provides best practice guidance on children's palliative care services in England. The vision of the guidance is that every child with a life-limiting and life-threatening condition has equitable access to high quality, family centred care with services built around a philosophy of 'children first'.[145] To achieve the vision, the guidance recognises the need for a fully integrated approach among key delivery partners and for all services to be designed around the needs of children and their families.[146]

5.95   The guidance recognises that all children need to experience life as a child and as such all children with palliative care needs should have equal access to universal and generic services. These universal services should also be able to inform children and their families about what other support is available and work in partnership to ensure support is timely, accessible and effective. A flexible approach

---

143 Disabled Child Standard, Children's NSF, pp33–34.
144 Department of Health, *Better care: better lives: improving outcomes and experiences for children and young people and their families living with life-limiting and life-threatening conditions*, 2009.
145 *Better care: better lives*, p11.
146 *Better care: better lives*, p12.

should be adopted with recognition that traditional methods of service delivery may need to be reviewed and in some cases services may have to be taken to the child.[147] To achieve this there should be joint assessment and planning, joint funding or aligned budgets and an agreed decision-making formula such as the Decision Support Tool in the National Framework for the Assessment of Children's Continuing Care (see para 5.55).[148]

5.96　The guidance also aims to ensure that all children have a choice of location of care, 24-hour access to multidisciplinary community teams and, when needed, specialist care advice and services.[149] The independent review of children's palliative care services demonstrated that there is an overreliance on hospital-based care and that there needs to be an increased amount of community-based support through the use of multidisciplinary children's community teams.[150] Access to specialist end of life care is highlighted as a key component of palliative care services. At this stage families need access to the multidisciplinary community team working seven days a week as well as 24-hour specialist support and advice and specialist psychological, emotional and spiritual care and bereavement support.[151]

5.97　Co-ordination of transition between children's and adult services is as critical in palliative care as in every other aspect of disabled children's service provision. A transition support worker or named key worker should ideally be identified for each young person to oversee their transition, ensuring links with a counterpart within the receiving adult service.[152]

Transition from child to adult services

5.98　As set out in detail in chapter 10, the guidance (and in some contexts, the legislation) concerning the respective responsibilities of the NHS, social care and other services differ between children's and adult services. By way of example, the National Framework for NHS Continuing Healthcare and NHS-funded Nursing Care and the supporting guidance only applies to people aged 18 or over. The terms

---

147　*Better care: better lives*, p26.
148　*Continuing Care Framework*, Annex A.
149　*Better care: better lives*, p30.
150　*Better care: better lives*, p31.
151　*Better care: better lives*, p33.
152　*Better care: better lives*, p40.

'continuing care' (in relation to children's services) and 'NHS continuing healthcare' (in relation to adults) also have different meanings, as explained above. It is important that young people and their families are helped to understand this difference and its implications from the start of transition planning.[153] *Transition: moving on well*[154] sets out good practice for health professionals and their partners in transition planning for young people with complex health needs or disabilities and *A transition guide for all services*[155] explains how all relevant services should work together with a young person to identify how they can best support them to help achieve their desired outcomes. All transition planning for young people should take full account of the approaches set out in these documents.[156]

5.99   Children's continuing care teams should identify those young people for whom it is likely that adult NHS continuing healthcare will be necessary and notify the relevant PCT that will hold adult responsibility for them. Such young people should be identified when they reach the age of 14. This should be followed up by a formal referral for screening at age 16 to the adult NHS continuing healthcare team at the relevant PCT. By the age of 17, an individual's eligibility for adult NHS continuing healthcare should be decided in principle by the relevant PCT in order that, where applicable, effective packages of care can be commissioned in time for the individual's 18th birthday.[157]

5.100   Entitlement for adult NHS continuing healthcare should initially be established through use of the decision-making process set out in the National Framework for NHS Continuing Healthcare and NHS-funded Nursing Care. If a young person receiving children's continuing care has been determined by the relevant PCT not to be eligible for adult NHS continuing healthcare, they should be advised of their non-eligibility and of their rights to request an independent review on the same basis as NHS continuing healthcare eligibility decisions regarding adults.[158] Even where a young person is not

---

153 *Continuing Care Framework*, p26 at 79.

154 Department for Children Schools and Families/Department of Health, *Transition: moving on well – a good practice guide for health professionals and their partners on transition planning for young people with complex health needs or a disability*, 2008.

155 Department for Children Schools and Families/Department of Health, *A transition guide for all services: key information for professionals about the transition process for disabled young people*, 2007.

156 *Continuing Care Framework*, p26 at 80.

157 *Continuing Care Framework*, p27 at 83–85.

158 *Continuing Care Framework*, p27 at 87.

entitled to adult NHS continuing healthcare, they may have some health needs that fall within the responsibilities of the NHS. In such circumstances, PCTs should continue to play a full role in transition planning for the young person.[159]

5.101 Further information on the issues for disabled young people in transition to adult health services can be found in chapter 10.

159 *Continuing Care Framework*, p28 at 89.

Housing

Key points

- Disabled children need housing which is both generally suitable and specifically adapted to meet their individual needs.
- Housing authorities and other public bodies, including children's services authorities and health bodies, have duties to co-operate to ensure that disabled children's housing needs are met.
- Families with disabled children can benefit from the statutory protection for 'homeless' people, including in situations where they have accommodation but it is so unsuitable for their needs that it is impossible for them to continue to live there.
- The main route for families with disabled children to secure adaptations to make their home safe and accessible for their child is through a disabled facilities grant (DFG).
- DFGs must be paid to eligible individuals if the mandatory requirements for the grant are met.
- The maximum amount of a DFG is currently £30,000 in England and £36,000 in Wales.
- Housing authorities have powers to supplement the DFG to meet the cost of more expensive works or to pay for adaptations which fall outside the criteria for a DFG.
- If a disabled child has an assessed need for an adaptation to his or her home which costs more than the maximum amount for a DFG, the law may require the shortfall to be met by the children's services authority and/or the housing authority.
- It will not be lawful to refuse to make an adaptation to meet an assessed need solely by reason of resource shortfalls (costs or human resources).

Introduction

6.1   Appropriate housing is a foundation of the right to an ordinary life for disabled children. As with many areas covered in this book, disabled children have the same basic housing needs as their non-disabled peers. However, many disabled children also require adaptations to their homes to make them safe and reasonably accessible for them to live in. For some disabled children, for instance those with autism or who use bulky equipment, the need may simply be for more space than would be considered necessary for a non-disabled child. The practice guidance to the Children Act (CA) 1989 notes that 'when houses are well adapted for a particular child, the family's life can be transformed'.[1] Yet as has been noted in chapter 1 (para 1.35 above), many families with disabled children currently live in housing which is restrictive and unsuitable for both the child or children and their carers. These families also frequently suffer from a chronic lack of space or live in housing which is simply sub-standard.

6.2 This chapter does not attempt to set out all the duties owed to children and families under the Housing Act 1996 and related legislation. Not only would this be impossible given the limited space, but also a number of other excellent handbooks can provide this information.[2] This chapter instead focuses on the links between housing rights and duties and those rights and duties created by the community care scheme. Housing duties are owed by housing authorities, which will be part of the same (unitary) local authority as a children's services authority in some areas but in other areas will be a different authority; the housing authority will be the district council whereas the social services authority will be the county council. The particular focus of this chapter is on the duty to make adaptations to the home of a disabled child through a disabled facilities grant (DFG).[3] The chapter also looks specifically at the ways in which families with disabled children can qualify for assistance as 'homeless' if their accommodation is seriously unsuitable for their child's needs. The provision of accommodation under the Children Act 1989 to homeless children (section 20) is dealt with in chapter 3.

Responsibilities of housing authorities and duties to co-operate

6.3 In meeting their responsibilities to consider housing conditions and provision in their area, housing authorities are obliged under the Chronically Sick and Disabled Persons Act (CSDPA) 1970 s3[4] to have

---

1 Department of Health, *Assessing children in need and their families: practice guidance*, 2000, para 3.115.

2 See, for example, D Astin, *Housing law: an adviser's handbook*, LAG, 2008 and A Arden QC, E Orme and T Vanhegan, *Homelessness and allocations*, 8th edn, LAG, 2010.

3 This material draws heavily from L Clements and P Thompson, *Community care and the law*, LAG, 2007 ('Clements and Thompson'), chapter 15, which provides more detailed information on the DFG scheme as it applies to both children and adults.

4 As inserted by the Housing (Consequential Provisions) Act 1985 s4 and Sch 2 para 20.

specific regard to the needs of disabled people, including disabled children. This duty is exemplified in practice guidance issued in England in 2006[5] which calls for the 'social inclusion of all citizens' and requires housing authorities to counter 'disabling environments' through planning and housing design.

6.4   When deciding who would have priority for public housing in their area (known as an 'allocations scheme'), local authorities must give reasonable preference to individuals (including disabled children) who need to move on medical or welfare grounds.[6] When a family has had their has had their priority within their council's allocations scheme assessed[7] this becomes a material consideration in relation to any future community care assessment,[8] which would include a Children Act initial or core assessment (see para 3.15).

6.5   There is an obvious requirement on housing authorities and children's services authorities to co-operate to ensure that the housing needs of disabled children are met. This longstanding duty is presently to be found in Children Act 2004 s10 and Housing Act 1996 s213. In relation to this obligation, joint guidance issued by the then-Departments of Health and the Environment in 1992,[9] which is still in force, states (at [16]) that:

> Social services authorities and housing should construct an individual's care plan with the objective of preserving or restoring non-institutional living as far as possible, and of securing the most appropriate and cost-effective package of care, housing and other services that meets the person's future needs ...

6.6   Under section 3 of the Homelessness Act 2002, housing authorities must have a homelessness strategy which seeks to prevent homelessness, including arrangements for satisfactory provision of support for people at risk of homelessness. The Homelessness Code of Guidance[10] stresses the importance of social services authorities, including

---

5   Department of Communities and Local Government/Department for Education/Department of Health, *Delivering housing adaptations for disabled people: a good practice guide*, 2006.

6   Housing Act 1996 s167(2)(d) as amended. See also Housing Act 2004 (Commencement No 2) (England) Order 2005 SI No 1120.

7   Known as a 'housing needs assessment'.

8   *R (Ireneschild) v Lambeth LBC* [2006] EWHC 2354 (Admin); (2006) 9 CCLR 686. Approved by the Court of Appeal in [2007] EWCA Civ 234 at [64].

9   LAC(92)12/DOE Circular 10/92, *Housing and community care*.

10 Department of Communities and Local Government, *Homelessness code of guidance for local authorities*, 2006 and, in Wales, the Welsh Assembly Government *Code of guidance for local authorities on allocation of accommodation and homelessness*, 2003.

children's services authorities, working together to develop this strategy and prevent homelessness for specific groups, which would include families with disabled children.[11] Examples of collaborative working are listed at 5.6 of the Homelessness Code and include joint protocols for referral of clients between agencies – a matter recently stressed as critical by Baroness Hale in relation to homeless teenagers in *R (G) v Southwark LBC*[12] (see para 3.79).

6.7   Duties to co-operate with housing authorities also extend to health bodies: as we note above (see paras 5.10–5.15) NHS Act 2006 s82 places an obligation on NHS bodies and local authorities to co-operate with one another in order to 'secure and advance the health and welfare of the people of England and Wales'. Although this long-standing duty has been stressed in many policy documents,[13] the evidence suggests that its operation leaves much to be desired. By way of example, in 2008 the ombudsman criticised as 'appalling' the failure of Kirklees MBC to make suitable adaptations to the home of a quadriplegic young man following his discharge from hospital, with the result that he was confined to two unsuitable rooms without suitable facilities for washing for over 18 months.[14]

Families with disabled children becoming 'homeless'

6.8   Families with disabled children can come within the provisions of Part VII of the Housing Act 1996, which governs support for homeless people. In essence a housing authority is required to provide accommodation under these provisions if satisfied on four issues, namely: (1) that the person/family is homeless or threatened with homelessness; (2) that the person or a member of the family is

11 See, in particular, the English Code, 1.6 and the Welsh Code, page vii.

12 [2009] UKHL 57; (2009) 12 CCLR 437.

13 See, for example, the hospital discharge guidance in England, Department of Health, *Ready to go?* 2010, p8 and in Wales, NLIAH *Passing the baton*, 2008, para 3.26; Department of Communities and Local Government *Homelessness code of guidance for local authorities* (2006) para 5.14; and Welsh Assembly Government *Code of guidance for local authorities on allocation of accommodation and homelessness*, 2003, para 8.62.

14 Complaint No 07/C/05809 against Kirklees MBC, 26 June 2008. The ombudsman recommended a payment of £7,000 to the young man to reflect the unreasonable restriction on his day-to-day life, including his social contact, caused by its delay and also recommended further payments to the young man's parents.

'vulnerable' and so in 'priority need; (3) that the person/family has a 'local connection' with the council; and (4) that the person/family is not intentionally homeless.

6.9   Under section 175(3) of the 1996 Act, a person is considered to be homeless, not only if they lack a roof, but also if they have accommodation which for one reason or another it is not reasonable for them to live in. Furthermore, a family with a disabled child will be in 'priority need' for the purposes of Part VII and therefore will potentially qualify for homelessness assistance: see section 189(1)(c) of the 1996 Act.[15]

6.10   The duties under the homelessness scheme to families with disabled family members were considered in detail in *Birmingham CC v Ali and others*.[16] Baroness Hale, with whom the other Law Lords agreed, stressed that where a family are 'homeless' as a result of their accommodation being unsuitable, a housing authority may have an immediate duty to transfer the family to suitable accommodation.

6.11   The case concerned a number of large families who were unsuitably housed in accommodation that was seriously overcrowded.[17] Baroness Hale paid particular attention to the fact that under section 175(3) of the 1966 Act (as above):

> A person shall not be treated as having accommodation unless it is accommodation which it would be reasonable for him to continue to occupy.

6.12   In the court's opinion the duty under section 175(3) was a prospective and ongoing duty, ie one that had to be considered at all stages and kept under review.[18]

6.13   If a family is homeless, eligible for assistance and has a priority need, then a housing authority is under an interim duty to secure suitable accommodation for the family pending a final decision on entitlement (HA 1996 s188(1)). The housing authority must decide that the 'full' housing duty is owed where a family is homeless, in

---

15 It should, however, be noted that under the Homelessness (Priority Need for Accommodation) (England) Order 2002, young people aged 16 or 17 do not have priority need for Housing Act accommodation if they are owed a duty under CA 1989 s20: see paras 3.78–3.79. The precedence of the Children Act over the Housing Act in relation to homeless teenagers was confirmed by the House of Lords in *R (G) v Southwark LBC* [2009] 1 WLR 1299.

16 [2009] UKHL 36.

17 In the case of *Ali* itself, both the father and one of the children were disabled.

18 Speech at [20]. In the cases decided in *Ali* [2009] UKHL 36, Birmingham had accepted that the families were unintentionally homeless and in priority need by virtue of serious overcrowding.

priority need and is not homeless intentionally (HA 1996 s190(2) and (3)).[19] Regardless of whether the accommodation is secured under section 188(1) as interim accommodation or under the 'full' housing duty, a housing authority must ensure that the accommodation is 'suitable': section 206(1).

6.14   The issue that fell to be decided in *Ali and others* was whether a local authority can leave a family in unsuitable housing pending suitable housing becoming available. In Baroness Hale's judgment, although the question was primarily one for the local authority to determine, there would be situations when the courts would require the immediate provision of suitable accommodation. In her opinion:

> there will be cases where the court ought to step in and require an authority to offer alternative accommodation, or at least to declare that they are in breach of their duty so long as they fail to do so. While one must take into account the practical realities of the situation in which authorities find themselves, one cannot overlook the fact that Parliament has imposed on them clear duties to the homeless, including those occupying unsuitable accommodation. In some cases, the situation of a particular applicant in her present accommodation may be so bad, or her occupation may have continued for so long, that the court will conclude that enough is enough.[20]

6.15   Baroness Hale reinforced the potentially immediate nature of the duty on local authorities, stating, 'In any case where the applicant could not be expected to spend another night in her accommodation, the council would be obliged to provide her with new accommodation forthwith'. The proper route to determine whether this point has been reached for families with disabled children may well be as part of an initial or core assessment in relation to section 17 of the CA 1989, given that housing is one of the specific assessment domains that must be considered: see para 3.16 above.[21]

Housing adaptations – disabled facilities grants

6.16   The primary route through which families with disabled children can get public support to meet the costs of adaptations to their homes is

---

19 In that case a housing authority must secure accommodation for the family (HA 1996 s193(1) and (2)).

20 See para [51] of the judgment.

21 See also *R (S) v Plymouth CC* [2009] EWHC 1499 (Admin).

through a disabled facilities grant – known as a DFG.[22] Housing authorities are responsible for DFGs, although it is likely that a family
will be referred to their housing authority by their social worker or
other professional employed by health or children's services.[23] The
purpose of DFGs is to 'modify disabling environments in order to
restore or enable independent living, privacy, confidence and dignity
for individuals and their families'.[24] Blatant failures to take action to
ensure that a property is suitable for the needs of a disabled person
may result in a violation of both the private and family life rights
within European Convention on Human Rights (ECHR) article 8:
R (Bernard) v Enfield LBC.[25] They may also be evidence that the award
process for DFGs has not been subjected to a full impact review
under the Equality Act 2000 s149[26] (see paras 9.73–9.85 below).[27]

Statutory scheme

6.17   DFGs are made under Part 1 of the Housing Grants, Construction
and Regeneration Act (HGCRA) 1996. The duties and powers under
the 1996 Act are expanded upon by regulations, principally the Housing Renewal Grants Regulations 1996, which are updated annually
in both England and Wales.[28] Separate regulations are made to deal

---

22 Children can be eligible for a DFG if they meet the definition of disabled in
section 100(1) of the Housing Grants, Construction and Regeneration Act 1996
or if they are named in the register of disabled children maintained by their
local authority or if the local authority accepts that they are a disabled child for
the purposes of Part III of CA 1989 (see para 3.7 above); section 100(3) of the
1996 Act.

23 NHS bodies have extensive statutory powers to transfer funds to social services
authorities (including children's services authorities) and these can be used to
facilitate housing adaptations.

24 Department of Communities and Local Government/Department for
Education/Department of Health, *Delivering housing adaptations for disabled
people: a good practice guide,* 2006, para 1.6. The scheme covers mobile homes,
houseboats and caravans as well as housing: see Clements and Thompson,
paras 15.39–15.40.

25 [2002] EWHC 2282 (Admin); (2002) 5 CCLR 577, and see also Local
Government Ombudsman's Report on complaint no 07/A/11108 against
Surrey County Council, 11 November 2008, paras 48–49.

26 Formerly the Disability Discrimination Act 1995 s49A.

27 See Local Government Ombudsman's *Digest of Cases 2008/09* Section F,
Housing, p2.

28 The most recent updating regulations being the Housing Renewal Grants
(Amendment) (England) Regulations 2009 SI No 1807 and the Housing
Renewal Grants (Amendment) (Wales) Regulations 2010 SI No 297
respectively.

with the maximum amount of the grant,[29] currently set at £30,000 in England,[30] and for other related matters.

6.18 Guidance on the DFG scheme has been issued in both England and Wales. In England, detailed non-statutory practice guidance was issued in 2006,[31] referred to in the remainder of this chapter as 'the 2006 guidance'. Somewhat briefer guidance was issued in Wales in 2002.[32]

Grant-eligible works

6.19 Section 23 of the HGCRA 1996 sets out the purposes for which a grant must be approved, which can be summarised as follows:

a) facilitating access to the home;

b) making the home safe;

c) facilitating access to a room used or usable as the principal family room;

d) facilitating access to, or providing for, a room used or usable for sleeping;

e) facilitating access to, or providing for, a lavatory, or facilitating the use of a lavatory;

f) facilitating access to, or providing for, a bath or shower (or both), or facilitating the use of such;

g) facilitating access to, or providing for, a room in which there is a washbasin, or facilitating the use of such;

h) facilitating the preparation and cooking of food by the disabled occupant;

i) improving any heating system in the home to meet the needs of the disabled occupant or, if there is no existing heating system there or any such system is unsuitable for use by the disabled occupant, providing a heating system suitable to meet his or her needs;

---

29 Disabled Facilities Grants (Maximum Amounts and Additional Purposes) (England) Order 2008 SI No 1189 and Disabled Facilities Grants (Maximum Amounts and Additional Purposes) (Wales) Order 2008 SI No 2370.

30 Article 2 of both the Disabled Facilities Grants (Maximum Amounts and Additional Purposes) (England) Order 2008 SI No 1189 and the Disabled Facilities Grants (Maximum Amounts and Additional Purposes) (Wales) Order 2008 SI No 2370.

31 Department of Communities and Local Government/Department for Education/Department of Health, *Delivering housing adaptations for disabled people: a good practice guide*, 2006.

32 *Housing renewal guidance*, NAFWC 20/02.

j)   facilitating the use of a source of power, light or heat by altering the position of one or more means of access to or control of that source or by providing additional means of control;

k)   facilitating access and movement by the disabled occupant around the home in order to enable him or her to care for a person who is normally resident there and is in need of such care; and

l)   such other purposes as may be specified by order of the secretary of state.

6.20   Since May 2008 local authorities are also required to fund works which facilitate a disabled occupant's access to and from a garden or works which make access to a garden safe for a disabled occupant.[33]

6.21   Entitlement to a DFG arises following an assessment which identifies the need for one or more adaptations to be made (see below)[34] and the duty to make a DFG cannot be avoided by reason of a shortage of resources; *R v Birmingham CC ex p Taj Mohammed*.[35] The main purposes for which grants must be made to families with disabled children are discussed further in paras 6.22–6.26 below.

Facilitating access

6.22   This heading includes works which are intended to remove or help overcome obstacles to the disabled child moving freely into or around the home and accessing the facilities and amenities within it.[36] These include family rooms, bedrooms and bathrooms.

Making the home safe

6.23   Works under this heading may include adaptations to minimise the risk of danger posed by a disabled child's behavioural problems[37] as well as (for example) the installation of enhanced alarm systems for persons with hearing difficulties.[38] Any grant made under this heading must reduce any identified risk as far as is reasonably practicable, if it is not possible to entirely eliminate the risk.[39]

---

33   Article 3 of both the Disabled Facilities Grants (Maximum Amounts and Additional Purposes) (England) Order 2008 SI No 1189 and the Disabled Facilities Grants (Maximum Amounts and Additional Purposes) (Wales) Order 2008 SI No 2370.

34   *R (Fay) v Essex CC* [2004] EWHC 879 (Admin) at [28].

35   (1998) 1 CCLR 441.

36   2006 guidance, Annex B, para 16.

37   2006 guidance, Annex B, para 18.

38   2006 guidance, Annex B, para 19.

39   *R (B) v Calderdale MBC* [2004] EWCA Civ 134; [2004] 1 WLR 2017 at [24].

Room usable for sleeping

6.24 The building of a new room 'usable for sleeping' should only be grant funded if the adaptation of an existing room is not a suitable option.[40] Grants can be made to expand the size of a shared bedroom used by a disabled child and (for example) a brother or sister.

Bathroom

6.25 The HGCRA 1996 separates out the provision of a lavatory and washing, bathing and showering facilities in order to emphasise that a grant must be available to ensure that a disabled child has access to each of these facilities and is able to use them.[41] Any failure to ensure that a disabled child can access each of these facilities with dignity may be unlawful and/or constitute maladministration.[42] On some occasions an existing room may be capable of adaptation to provide such facilities – but the ombudsman considers it unreasonable for DFG grants officers to expect disabled persons and their families to give up a family room in order to make way for a ground floor shower/toilet.[43]

Fixtures and fittings

6.26 One potential problem with the DFG scheme is the lack of clarity as to whether fixtures and fittings, including items such as specialist equipment, come within its terms. The 2006 guidance is silent on this point. However, the previous practice guidance suggested that equipment which requires structural modifications to a building should come within the DFG scheme, with smaller items remaining the responsibility of children's services departments under the CSDPA 1970[44] (see paras 3.48–3.57 above). The 2006 guidance does, however, stress that where major items of equipment have been installed, arrangements for servicing and repairs should be made at the time of installation and the costs factored into the grant payable.[45]

---

40 2006 guidance, Annex B, para 21.
41 2006 guidance, Annex B, para 22.
42 See, for example, complaint nos 02/C/8679, 02/C/8681 and 02/C/10389 against Bolsover DC, 30 September 2003.
43 Local Government Ombudsman Complaint no 05/C/13157 (Leeds City Council), 20 November 2007.
44 See Clements and Thompson, paras 15.74–15.75.
45 2006 guidance, para 8.1.

Individual eligibility for DFGs

Main residence

6.27   Once an individual child has qualified as a disabled person,[46] DFGs will be available to make adaptations to the child's only or main residence.[47] If the child's parents are separated, this may cause difficulties since the mandatory DFG remains only available for the 'main' residence.[48] Adaptations to the home of the other parent may need to be carried out under CSDPA 1970 s2 if they are assessed as necessary: see para 3.56 above.

Tenure

6.28   A DFG is available where a disabled child's parents are owner-occupiers, tenants (of all forms) and licensees.[49] Where the applicant is a tenant the consent of the landlord will be required. Authorities should seek to obtain this consent from private landlords and should offer to 'make good' the adaptations once the family leave the home in appropriate circumstances.[50] The 2006 guidance is clear (at 3.21) that the nature of a person's housing tenure is irrelevant in relation to access to a DFG. Any material difference in treatment of applicants who have different tenure (for instance, council tenants and private tenants) would constitute maladministration.[51]

6.29   A problem with the DFG scheme which has been identified by the local government ombudsman is that it only applies to existing tenancies.[52] However, if a family with a disabled child propose to move house and therefore acquire a new tenancy, it would be unreasonable and maladministration for an authority not to expedite the works once the family have taken on the new tenancy.[53]

---

46 See fn 21 above.
47 HGCRA 1996 ss21(2)(b) and 22(2)(b).
48 Confirmed by the 2006 guidance, Annex B, para 50.
49 See HGCRA 1996 s19(5) re licensees.
50 2006 guidance, para 6.3.
51 See, for example, the Ombudsman reports on complaint 99/B/00012 against North Warwickshire DC, 15 May 2000 and 30 November 2000.
52 HGCRA 1996 s24(2).
53 See, for example, complaint no 00/C/19154 against Birmingham CC, 19 March 2002.

Occupancy requirements

6.30 DFGs are made subject to a requirement that the disabled person lives or intends to live in the accommodation as his or her only or main residence for the grant condition period.[54] This period is currently five years from the date certified by the housing authority as the date on which the works are completed to its satisfaction.[55] The 2006 guidance states that any belief by the assessor that the applicant may not be able to live in the property for five years as a result of their deteriorating condition should not be a reason for withholding or delaying grant approval.[56] However, the guidance somewhat qualifies this otherwise clear statement in a later paragraph which suggests that if the disabled person's 'degeneration' may be 'short-term', this 'should be taken into account when considering the eligible works'.[57] This may be read as little more than a reminder that each applicant's individual circumstances need to be taken into account.

Decisions on individual eligibility

6.31 The administration of the DFG scheme is the responsibility of the housing authority in whose area the relevant property is located. The housing authority is required to consult the relevant children's services authority (if it is not itself a children's services authority, as it will be in a unitary authority such as a London borough).[58] A housing authority may not approve a DFG application unless it is satisfied that:

a) the relevant works are necessary and appropriate to meet the needs of a disabled child; and

b) it is reasonable and practicable to carry out the relevant works, having regard to the age and condition of the home.[59]

6.32 The decision as to whether requested works are 'necessary and appropriate' must be taken with reference to the views of the relevant children's services authority on the adaptation needs of disabled people.[60]

---

54 Or for such shorter period as his health and other relevant circumstances permit: HGCRA 1996 ss21(2)(b) and 22(2)(b).
55 HGCRA 1996 s44(3)(a) and (b).
56 Para 6.7, and see also para 5.22.
57 2006 guidance, Annex B, para 29.
58 HGCRA 1996 s24(3). It is, however, a matter for the housing authority whether it accepts the children's services authority's advice following consultation: 2006 guidance, Annex B, para 34.
59 HGCRA 1996 s24(3). Guidance is given on the meaning of 'reasonable and practicable' in the 2006 guidance, Annex B, para 37.
60 HGCRA 1996 s24.

Although under the CSDPA 1970 all assessed needs must be met once a child is deemed eligible (see para 3.45 above), an authority is entitled to consider a range of ways of meeting the need.[61] The Court of Appeal has stressed that the question of whether the works are of a type which come within the provisions of the scheme must be answered separately and prior to the question of whether the specific works requested are 'necessary and appropriate'.[62]

6.33   A situation may arise where the housing authority would consider it to be more cost-effective to relocate a family with a disabled child, but accepts that otherwise the proposed adaptations were 'necessary and appropriate' and 'reasonable and practicable'. It is unclear whether a refusal to award a DFG to fund adaptations for this reason alone would be lawful; the answer to this question will depend to a very great extent on the individual circumstances of the case – especially the practical reality of an alternative property being available. The 2006 guidance[63] certainly suggests that this option should be considered where major adaptations are required and it is difficult to provide a cost-effective solution in the existing home.

Maximum grant

6.34   The maximum grant awarded as a DFG is now £30,000 in England[64] and £36,000 in Wales.[65] Local authorities are empowered to make higher awards as discretionary grants: see paras 6.42–6.44. Minor adaptations costing less than £1,000 are governed by a different scheme and are, in England, free of charge.[66] The previous government in England had a stated commitment dating from 2007[67] to seek to increase the maximum cap to £50,000. It remains to be seen whether the new coalition administration shares this intention.

---

61 *R v Kirklees MBC ex p Daykin* (1997–98) 1 CCLR 512.

62 *R (B) v Calderdale MBC* [2004] EWCA Civ 134; [2004] 1 WLR 2017.

63 Para 6.15.

64 Article 2 of the Disabled Facilities Grants (Maximum Amounts and Additional Purposes) (England) Order 2008 SI No 1189.

65 Article 2 of the Disabled Facilities Grants (Maximum Amounts and Additional Purposes) (Wales) Order 2008 SI No 2370.

66 Community Care (Delayed Discharges etc) Act 2003 ss15 and 16 make provision of such free supports in England and Wales (respectively); the provision has come into effect in England but not in Wales: see Clements and Thompson, paras 15.45–15.46.

67 *Disabled facilities grant programme: the government's proposals to improve programme delivery*, January 2007, para 31a.

6.35   If an adaptation is required to meet an assessed need and the cost of the works will exceed the maximum cap for a DFG, the remainder should be met either by the housing authority exercising its discretionary powers (see paras 6.42–6.44), the children's services authority meeting the additional costs pursuant to its duty under CSDPA 1970 s2 (see para 3.56) or by a combination of the two. It will not be lawful for an authority to refuse to make adaptations which have been assessed as necessary solely by reason of cost.

Means testing

6.36   Applications for a DFG for a disabled person under the age of 19 are no longer subject to a means test.

Timescales and grant deferment

6.37   Housing authorities must approve or refuse a DFG application as soon as reasonably practicable and no later than six months after the date of application.[68] The actual payment of the DFG, if approved, may be delayed until a date not more than 12 months following the date of the application.[69] If any hardship is caused by delay even within these timescales, the children's services authority should be pressed to carry out the works under their parallel duties under the CSDPA 1970: see para 3.56.

6.38   Despite these clear statutory provisions, housing authorities routinely adopt a range of extra-statutory procedures to delay the processing of DFG applications. For instance, authorities have been criticised for creating inappropriate administrative hurdles prior to applications being received[70] and for delaying preliminary assessments, citing a shortage of assessors.[71] The 2006 guidance is unhelpfully not as strong in calling for authorities to expedite grant applications as its predecessors.[72]

---

68 HGCRA 1996 s34. Any delay beyond six months from the referral by children's services to the execution of the works will generally be considered unjustified and will constitute maladministration: Complaint no 02/C/08679 against Bolsover DC, 30 September 2003.

69 HGCRA 1996 s36.

70 Complaint no 02/C/04897 against Morpeth BC and Northumberland CC, 27 November 2003.

71 Complaint no 90/C/0336, 9 October 1991: delay of nine months for an occupational therapist assessment constituted maladministration.

72 See Clements and Thompson, para 15.85 for references to the predecessor guidance documents.

6.39   The 2006 guidance accepts that some DFG applications will be prioritised ahead of others by housing authorities. Although particular priority should be given to those with deteriorating conditions,[73] authorities are also reminded to take a broader approach reflecting the social model of disability, which would consider wider risks to independence.[74] It would of course be unlawful for an authority to operate a blanket policy which discriminated against applications made by families with disabled children in comparison to those made by disabled adults, or to adopt any similar policy which penalised one group of disabled people in relation to any other as a matter of course.

6.40   The 2006 guidance provides a table which illustrates a 'possible approach' to target times for each stage of a DFG.[75] The indicative targets for the total process amount to 83 working days for high priority applications, 151 working days for medium priority applications and 259 working days for low priority applications.

6.41   Authorities also have a duty to make interim arrangements to ameliorate any hardship experienced by a disabled child between the assessment of the need for adaptations to their home and the completion of the works. The 2006 guidance states forcefully that it is 'not acceptable' for disabled people to be left for weeks or months without interim help.[76] Furthermore, children's services and housing authorities should consider meeting some or all of the costs occasioned if a family need to make other arrangements while work is being carried out, and should consider moving the family to temporary accommodation when major works are required.[77]

Discretionary grants

6.42   Housing authorities in both England and Wales have a wide discretionary power to give assistance in any form for adaptations and other housing purposes.[78] There is no financial limit on the amount

---

73   2006 guidance, para 4.8.
74   2006 guidance, para 5.21. See Clements and Thompson, paras 15.88–15.93 for further discussion of DFG prioritisation processes.
75   Para 9.3 p54. The table is reproduced in Clements and Thompson, p504, and is also accessible at www.communities.gov.uk/documents/housing/pdf/138595.pdf
76   Para 5.40.
77   2006 guidance, paras 5.43–5.44.
78   Article 3 of the Regulatory Reform (Housing Assistance) (England and Wales) Order 2002.

of assistance that can be given. Specific guidance on the exercise of this discretion was given by the government in England in 2003.[79] The 2006 guidance suggests that the types of assistance that can be provided under this power will include:

a) funding for small-scale adaptations not covered by mandatory DFGs, or to bypass the lengthy DFG timescales for minor works;

b) top-up funding to supplement a mandatory DFG where the necessary works will cost more than the maximum DFG cap; and

c) help to buy a new property where the authority considers that this will benefit the disabled child at least as much as improving or adapting the existing accommodation.[80]

6.43 Discretionary support offered by an authority can be in any form, for instance as a loan or an outright grant. Any discretionary loan made to an individual family will not affect their entitlement to a mandatory DFG.[81]

6.44 As with all discretionary powers, housing authorities must exercise their power to fund additional adaptations rationally and reasonably and must ensure like cases are treated alike. It would be unlawful for an authority to operate a blanket policy of refusing to make any discretionary payments to fund adaptations; each individual case must be considered on its merits.

79 Office of the Deputy Prime Minister, *Housing renewal*, Circular 05/2003, 2003.

80 2006 guidance, para 2.24.

81 2006 guidance, para 6.22.

CHAPTER 7

Welfare benefits

continued

Key points

- Disabled children and their families are potentially eligible for many different types of welfare benefits, each with their own rules and administration.
- Certain payments are made in accordance with legally binding rules, while others are awarded more flexibly on the basis of principles and guidance.
- Parents will often act as their children's 'appointees' in relation to benefit claims, applying for and managing the funds received.
- For many disabled children and their families, disability living allowance (DLA) is a key starting-point as it can provide both financial support and automatic entitlement to other benefits or payments.
- DLA is split into a care component for those with care needs and a mobility component for those who need help with getting around; children with both care and mobility needs can access both components.
- DLA is paid at various rates according to a child's needs: highest, middle and lowest (care component) and higher and lower (mobility).
- Carer's allowance (CA) is a benefit for people who look after a child with significant care needs.
- The Social Fund (community care grant), Independent Living Fund and Family Fund are grants available on a more flexible basis for particular needs.
- Benefits can interact, so that receipt of a particular benefit can entitle recipients to further support, such as premiums; in other circumstances, an award of one benefit may prevent a child or family accessing other types of support.
- Decisions relating to welfare benefits can be challenged through internal processes, such as revision or supersession, or through appeals to independent bodies, such as tribunals or courts.

Introduction

7.1   The fact that so many disabled children and their families face financial hardship (see paras 1.31–1.34 above) makes it essential that they are able to claim their full benefit entitlements. The assistance provided by a welfare benefits award can go some way towards mitigating the higher living expenses and lower earnings that are generally associated with caring for a disabled child and may also redress the social exclusion that families often feel. As a recent report shows,[1] an award of benefits 'can make the difference between a family getting by, and going under financially' and often results in a rise in self-esteem and social participation for both children and parents.

7.2   However, families face significant difficulties in gaining access to financial support for which they are eligible and to which they are (or may be) entitled. The benefits system is complex, reflecting many years of piecemeal reform. There are inadequate and insufficient take-up campaigns or sources of advice to inform families of their entitlements.[2] The embarrassment which families may feel about making a claim, the burden of the paperwork involved and the experiences of incompetence in the decision-making process have all been identified as barriers to seeking and obtaining full entitlements,[3] with particular difficulties found in relation to carers' access to payments.[4]

7.3   As a result, an awareness both of the existence of relevant benefits and of the particular tests for eligibility can empower the families of disabled children and disabled young people themselves in enforcing their welfare rights. Given the widespread inconsistency in decision-making by Department for Work and Pensions (DWP) officials, with over 20 per cent of awards increased on appeal,[5] an understanding of the principles governing entitlement and the procedure involved in claims is often vital to a successful claim.

7.4   Indeed, where accessible information sources have been set up, the effect is impressive. For example, in 2008 the London Borough of Camden set up a Welfare Rights Service closely linked to its 'DCatch' initiative which aims to improve daycare for disabled children. In its first year of operation, 61 families received advice and an additional 92 were provided with a more intensive casework service. That year, the service secured an additional £390,000 in previously unclaimed

---

1 G Preston, *Helter skelter: disabled children and the benefits system*, CASE Paper 92, Centre for the Analysis of Social Exclusion, London School of Economics, 2005 ('*Helter Skelter*'), p35.

2 G Preston, *Out of reach: benefits for disabled children*, Child Poverty Action Group and Contact a Family, 2006.

3 *Helter skelter*, pp18–26.

4 House of Commons Public Accounts Committee, *Supporting carers to care*, 42nd Report of Session 2008–09, HC 549, 8 September 2009.

5 DWP figures on appeals at http://research.dwp.gov.uk/asd/asd1/dla/dla_quarterly_statistics_feb05.asp.

allowances for the 92 households. On an ongoing basis, the extra gains for individual families' annual incomes range between £100 and £15,000 when weekly amounts of disability living allowance, carer's allowance, income support, tax credits (including the childcare element), housing benefit and council tax benefit are added together.[6]

7.5　　There are a large number of different benefits and tax credits within the welfare system, with a variety of bodies including the DWP, local authorities and Her Majesty's Revenue and Customs (HMRC) involved in managing different parts of the system. Each of the different types of benefit and tax credit is governed by a detailed set of rules of entitlement and procedure. It is not therefore possible here to provide information on all the benefits to which the families of disabled children may be entitled. Comprehensive and indepth guides to the benefits system can be found in the Child Poverty Action Group's *Welfare benefits and tax credits handbook 2010/2011*[7] and in the *Disability rights handbook*[8] published by Disability Alliance. The Decision Makers' Guide (DMG) produced by the DWP to provide guidance on benefits claims, and available online,[9] also contains detailed information on all aspects of welfare administered by the DWP.

7.6　　This chapter therefore outlines the key sources of financial support targeted at disabled children and their families, as well as more general considerations in relation to the procedure for claiming benefits and challenging welfare decisions. Special attention is given to disability living allowance, carer's allowance, community care grants, the Independent Living Fund and the various premiums which are available to the families of disabled children as a 'top up' to other benefits. These sources of support are principally those under the direction of the Pensions, Disability and Carers Service, an executive agency of the DWP. There will also be reference to the Family Fund, which, although provided by an independent charity, is a significant source of support and is funded by central government.

6　From personal correspondence with the authors, 6 July 2010.

7　Child Poverty Action Group, *Welfare benefits and tax credits handbook 2010/2011*, 2010.

8　Disability Alliance, *Disability rights handbook*, 35th edn, April 2010–April 2011.

9　See www.dwp.gov.uk/publications/specialist-guides/decision-makers-guide/.

Disability living allowance

Introduction

7.7   Disability living allowance (DLA) is one of the most important benefits for disabled children. Put simply, it is a benefit for people who need assistance with (1) looking after themselves and/or (2) getting around. DLA consists of two separate but interlinked elements: the 'care component' and 'mobility component'. Awards can be made to a claimant (here a disabled child) in respect of either one or both components. Each component is also payable at different weekly rates, judged according to the level of need. The care component comes at three levels: highest rate, middle rate and lowest rate; the mobility component is payable at higher and lower rates.

7.8   DLA is important not only because of the financial support it provides but also because receipt of DLA establishes a gateway (or, in the language used in the welfare rights field, a 'passport') to other benefits and entitlements, as will be discussed below. It is also important to note that awards of DLA do not absolve local authorities of their statutory duties to provide certain types of travel and care. For example, in assessing someone's ability to pay for transport services, any award of DLA mobility component should be disregarded.[10] Similarly, while receipt of DLA care component may be taken into account in relation to services provided by the local authority for the time of day for which the allowance is paid, a policy which treats DLA provided for day care as income in relation to night care is unlawful.[11]

7.9   The statutory provisions which govern DLA are sections 72–76 of the Social Security Contributions and Benefits Act (SSCBA) 1992. These contain the overarching conditions of entitlement for the allowance and certain supplementary provisions. Regulations[12] have also been made by the secretary of state, which flesh out the relevant legal tests and procedure applying to DLA. Finally, there is a wealth of case-law which interprets the complex conditions for eligibility set out in the legislation.

---

10 Social Security Contributions and Benefits Act (SSCBA) 1992 s73(14).
11 *R v Coventry CC ex p Carton* (2001) 4 CCLR 41. This case concerned four disabled adults, but the principle extends to disabled children.
12 Social Security (Disability Living Allowance) Regulations (SS(DLA) Regs) 1991 SI No 2890.

General eligibility requirements

7.10 Both the care and mobility components of DLA are available only to those who satisfy three general eligibility criteria.[13] First, the child must fulfil the 'residence' and 'presence' conditions, which require that he or she:

a) is 'ordinarily resident' in Great Britain;[14]
b) is present in Great Britain; and
c) was present in Great Britain for 26 weeks out of the past 12 months.

7.11 There is an exemption to the final condition for those who claim DLA on the ground of terminal illness and for children who are less than six months of age. Children of members of the armed forces serving abroad also qualify as being in Great Britain. It may also be possible in certain circumstances to argue that EU law allows a claimant who is an EU citizen or resident to claim DLA.[15]

7.12 Second, a child must not be 'subject to immigration control'. For benefits purposes, being subject to immigration control means that a person is not a national of a European Economic Area state and:

a) requires, but does not have, leave to enter or leave to remain in the UK;
b) has leave to enter or remain with a condition that no recourse to public funds can be made; or
c) has leave to enter or remain subject to a formal undertaking that no recourse to public funds will be made.

7.13 Third, if a child is in hospital, DLA will be paid only for the first 84 days he or she spends there (or 28 days where the child is aged 16 or over). If the child has two or more spells in hospital which are 28 days or less apart, then the total time spent in hospital will be added up to determine whether the allowance can be paid.[16] However, where the child is terminally ill, payment of DLA will continue for as long as he or she is not in an NHS or Defence Council hospital or similar institution, provided that the DWP has been notified.[17] Payment of the

---

13 SSCBA 1992 s71(6).
14 This, strictly speaking, excludes Northern Ireland and the Isle of Man, which administer their own system of benefits. However, legislation has provided for largely identical entitlements between these territories, so there should be no difference in payments between them.
15 See *Welfare benefits and tax credits handbook 2010/2011*, CPAG, 2010, chapter 60.
16 SS(DLA) Regs 1991 regs 8, 10, 12A and 12B.
17 SS(DLA) Regs 1991 reg 12B.

DLA mobility component can also continue where the recipient has a Motability agreement in operation (see below at para 7.55).

Care component

Eligibility requirements

7.14   In order to establish eligibility for the care component of DLA, a child needs to meet the tests for disability corresponding to one of the three rates. In this context, there are differences between the approach taken to children aged less than 16 and those of 16 and above, which arise because all younger children might be said to have care needs of some sort. Therefore, although many of the tests are common to both age groups, some are relevant to just the younger or older group.

7.15   The tests which are common to both age groups are as follows:[18]

- *Lowest rate*: The child is so severely disabled, physically or mentally, that he or she requires in connection with his or her bodily functions attention from another person for a significant portion of the day (whether during a single period or a number of periods).

- *Middle rate*: The child is so severely disabled physically or mentally that he or she requires:
  - frequent attention from another person throughout the day in connection with his or her bodily functions; or
  - continual supervision throughout the day in order to avoid substantial danger to him or herself or others; or
  - prolonged or repeated attention at night in connection with his or her bodily functions; or
  - another person to be awake for a prolonged period or at frequent intervals for the purpose of watching over him or her in order to avoid substantial danger to himself or herself or others.

- *Highest rate*: The child is:
  - terminally ill; or
  - so severely disabled physically or mentally that he or she requires:
    - frequent attention throughout the day in connection with his or her bodily functions or continual supervision

18   SSCBA 1992 s72(1)–(2) and (4)–(5).

throughout the day to avoid substantial danger to himself or herself or others; and

- prolonged or repeated attention in connection with his or her bodily functions at night, or another person to be awake for a prolonged period or at frequent intervals for the purpose of watching over him or her, in order to avoid substantial danger to himself or herself or others.

7.16 In addition, for children aged less than 16, one of two further tests also have to be passed to establish entitlement to any of the above rates[19] (although where a child under 16 satisfies the entitlement criteria for the middle rate care component because they are undergoing renal dialysis he or she does not need to meet either of these extra tests[20]):

a) the child's care needs relevant to the particular test are 'substantially in excess of the normal requirements' of persons of his or her age; or

b) the child has 'substantial requirements' of a kind which younger persons in normal physical and mental health may also have but which persons of his or her age and in normal physical and mental health would not have.

7.17 Finally, in relation to children aged 16 or over, a further (alternative) basis on which entitlement to the lowest rate can be established is where the child is so severely disabled physically or mentally that he or she cannot prepare a cooked main meal for him or herself if he or she has the ingredients.[21]

7.18 The time period throughout which the child must satisfy (or be likely to satisfy) the relevant condition(s) is nine months, made up of the following:

a) three months preceding the date on which the award would begin; and

b) six months following the date of the award.[22]

7.19 In determining whether the child has (or is likely to have) these needs throughout this nine-month period, a 'broad view' is appropriate: the decision-maker should not rule out a claim simply because the need

19 SSCBA 1992 s72(1A)(b), see para 7.32.
20 R(A) 1/93.
21 SSCBA 1992 s72(1)(a)(ii) and (1A)(a), see para 7.33.
22 SSCBA 1992 s72(2). If the child has a terminal condition and his or her death is expected within six months of the award, the award will be made if the child is likely to satisfy the conditions in the period leading up to his or her death.

has not arisen on every day but should simply apply his judgment to whether the needs existed 'throughout' the period.[23] Furthermore, it is possible to make a DLA claim, and receive a decision, up to three months in advance of the date on which the award would begin.[24]

7.20   Where a child is aged just under 16 at the date of claim, the claim is tested against the 'under 16' entitlement conditions for any period he remains under 16, and then against the '16 and over' conditions for the remainder of the six months.[25]

7.21   Given the relatively broad terms in which many of these conditions are expressed, a considerable amount of case-law has developed which applies them to particular facts. Significant interpretations given to particular phrases in the legislation by the tribunals and courts are discussed below.

'So severely disabled, physically or mentally'

7.22   To satisfy this part of the test, it is necessary to show that the child has a disability, which has been defined (apparently in ignorance of the social model of disability, see paras 1.5–1.7) as a 'functional deficiency'.[26] However, there is no need to have a particular medical diagnosis, although medical evidence is useful in supporting a claim. In relation to behavioural difficulties resulting in care needs, the question will be whether a child has the physical or mental ability to control the behaviour.[27] The word 'severely' in the legislation does not impose any additional requirement on the claimant; if there is a functional deficiency, physical or mental, which results in one of the disability tests being satisfied, then the severity condition is automatically met.[28]

'Requires'

7.23   For attention to be 'required', it will be necessary to show that it is 'reasonably required to enable the severely disabled person as far as possible to live a normal life'.[29] Therefore any service necessary for

---

23   *Moyna v Secretary of State for Work and Pensions* [2003] UKHL 44 at [19].
24   Social Security (Claims and Payments) Regulations (SS(CP) Regs) 1987 SI No 1968 reg 13A(1).
25   Welfare Reform Act 2007 ss52–53.
26   R(DLA) 3/06 at [42].
27   R(DLA) 3/06 at [40].
28   R(DLA) 10/02 at [29].
29   *Cockburn v Chief Adjudication Officer* [1997] 1 WLR 799 at page 814 per Lord Slynn.

the disabled child to participate in social activities will be included. It may be necessary to explain why any alternatives that avoid the need for such attention are not 'reasonable or practicable', taking account of the child's age and interests.[30]

'Attention in connection with bodily functions'

7.24 'Attention' means some kind of personal service of an active nature, performed in the presence of the disabled child.[31] It can be distinguished from 'supervision', which has a more passive meaning (see para 7.27 below). Attention may involve some degree of physical intimacy. 'Bodily functions' is a phrase to be interpreted broadly, to mean 'the normal actions of any organs or set of organs of the body', and therefore includes breathing, drinking, eating, going to the toilet, getting in and out of bed, hearing, walking, washing, seeing, sitting, waking, getting dressed and undressing.[32] It does not generally include other domestic tasks, such as cooking,[33] but if such a task is closely associated with a bodily function and performed as part of a continuous episode of attention in relation to that bodily function, the domestic task may then form part of the attention. Attention is given 'in connection with' any such function if 'it provides a substitute method of providing what the bodily function would provide if it were not totally or partially impaired'.[34]

'A significant portion of the day'

7.25 'Significant' here simply means not negligible or trivial.[35] An hour of attention may meet the test,[36] but the relevant time-scale may also vary from case to case according to the number of times attention has to be provided and how intense and important that attention is.[37]

---

30 *Cockburn v Chief Adjudication Officer* [1997] 1 WLR 799 at page 815 per Lord Slynn.
31 *Cockburn v Chief Adjudication Officer* [1997] 1 WLR 799 at page 808 per Lord Slynn.
32 *Cockburn v Chief Adjudication Officer* [1997] 1 WLR 799 at page 813 per Lord Slynn.
33 *In re Woodling* [1984] 1 WLR 348.
34 *Cockburn v Chief Adjudication Officer* [1997] 1 WLR 799 at page 808 per Lord Slynn.
35 DMG, para 61206.
36 CDLA/58/1993.
37 *Ramsden v Secretary of State for Work and Pensions* [2003] EWCA Civ 32.

'*Frequent attention throughout the day*'

7.26 For this condition to be satisfied, the need for attention must arise on several occasions (not just once or twice) during the course of the day (not just at the start and end of the day).[38] This test will be met if the disabled child has a range of needs which together call for frequent attention throughout the day.

'*Continual supervision ... in order to avoid substantial danger to him or herself or others*'

7.27 'Supervision' is, as stated above, different to 'attention'. It involves more passive involvement, such as being in the same room as a disabled child and being prepared to intervene if necessary.[39] To satisfy this test, four conditions must be met:[40]

a) the disability must be such as to give rise to a substantial danger to the disabled person or someone else;

b) the substantial danger must be one against which it is reasonable to guard, taking into account the likelihood of the danger occurring and the gravity of the consequences if it did;

c) there must be a need for supervision to ensure the danger is avoided, taking into account the availability of reasonable and practicable alternatives (see above, para 7.23); and

d) the supervision required must be continual.

'*Prolonged or repeated attention*'

7.28 'Prolonged' has been defined as 'some little time', with over 20 minutes considered 'prolonged' in the context of care.[41] 'Repeated' means twice or more.[42]

'*At frequent intervals*'

7.29 The attention in this context can be required in just one part of the night, not necessarily throughout.[43]

---

38 *R v National Insurance Commissioner ex p Secretary of State for Social Services* [1981] 1 WLR 1017.

39 R(A) 1/88.

40 R(A) 1/83 at [5].

41 R(A) 2/80.

42 DMG, para 61165.

43 DMG, para 61164.

'Watching over'

7.30 This phrase is to be given its ordinary meaning, and may not require as close an involvement as 'supervision'.[44]

'Terminally ill'

7.31 Being 'terminally ill' is defined as having a progressive disease from which death may reasonably be expected within six months of the date of the claim.[45] It is irrelevant that, by the time of the decision, a child has already lived for six months following diagnosis.[46] Any DLA claim that is made on the basis that the child is terminally ill must be made under the DLA 'special rules' and must therefore state that the claim is relying on these special rules.[47] In such cases, there is no need for the disabled child to satisfy the qualifying period rules generally applicable to claimants (see above).[48] The DLA Advisory Board has stated that an award of the DLA care component in accordance with these rules should normally be made for a fixed period of three years, and reconsidered at the end of that period,[49] unless the disabled person is already in receipt of the mobility component, in which case the care award will be made for the same period as the mobility award.[50]

The additional tests applying to children under 16

7.32 In relation to disabled children, all the tests referred to above require substantial additional needs 'outside the whole range of attention or supervision that would normally be required by a child of the same age who is not disabled'.[51] It is therefore the additional needs of the child, not the actual care given, which are key. These needs may come about by virtue of the extra time[52] or the 'quality or degree of attention or supervision' required.[53] A requirement to use particular medical or technical procedures may meet this test,[54] as might the

---

44 DMG, para 61161.
45 SSCBA 1992 s66(2)(a).
46 R(A) 1/94.
47 SSCBA 1992 s73(12).
48 SSCBA 1992 s72(5).
49 DMG, para 61503.
50 SSCBA 1992 s71(3).
51 DMG, para 61533.
52 DMG, para 61525.
53 CA/092/1992 at [5].
54 DMG, paras 61530–61531.

need for assistance at school, provided that this meets a need which comes within those defined in the legislation and is substantially in excess of that faced by other children of the same age.[55]

'The cooking test'

7.33　Only children aged 16 or over may qualify for the care component by satisfying this test. It is a hypothetical test, which is intended to evaluate a person's ability to perform everyday tasks, so it does not matter if the child does not in fact cook such meals. It requires a child to show that he or she is unable to prepare a main meal for one person freshly cooked on a traditional cooker. In determining whether the child has passed this test, the decision-maker should take 'a broad view' as to the child's cooking ability. It will not therefore necessarily be fatal to a claim if a child can pass the test on a few occasions over the nine-month qualifying period (see above).[56] A number of factors are relevant to the test. Both the child's physical abilities (such as gripping, lifting, bending and so on)[57] and mental abilities (such as the concentration and motivation required to plan and cook a meal)[58] may be taken into account.

Mobility component

Eligibility requirements

7.34　The general eligibility requirements applying to the care component (see above) apply also to the mobility component. In addition, a child must:

a)　be aged three years of age or over (for the higher rate); or five years of age or over (for the lower rate);[59]

b)　be able from time to time to benefit from enhanced facilities for locomotion (a broad approach should be taken to this requirement, which should be fulfilled if the child can show he or she enjoys, or receives some form of stimulation from, going outside);[60] and

c)　meet the 'higher rate' or 'lower rate' disability criteria (see below).

55　CDLA/3737/2002.

56　*Moyna v Secretary of State for Work and Pensions* [2003] UKHL 44.

57　R(DLA) 2/05 at [8].

58　CSDLA/80/1996 at [8].

59　A child can qualify for the mobility component during the three months leading up to his or her age of eligibility for the benefit: SSCBA 1992 s73(1A).

60　R(M) 2/83.

7.35 As with the care component, the disability criteria for the mobility component set a number of tests to determine whether the child's needs qualify him or her for the allowance and, if so, at what rate. The nine-month qualifying period for the mobility component is the same as for the care component (see above). Again, if a child is terminally ill and satisfies the conditions for entitlement to the mobility component, he or she does not need to satisfy the nine-month qualifying period. and, provided the child is likely to continue to satisfy the conditions for the rest of his or her life, the allowance is payable.[61]

7.36 The tests are as follows:

- For the lower rate:
  - the child is so severely disabled, physically or mentally, that, ignoring any ability to use familiar routes, he or she is unable to take advantage of his or her walking abilities outdoors without guidance or supervision from another person most of the time; and
  - (if the child is aged under 16) the child requires substantially more guidance or supervision than children of his or her age in normal physical or mental health, or children of the same age in normal physical health would not require such guidance or supervision.

- For the higher rate:
  - the child has a disability from a physical cause which means that he or she is unable or virtually unable to walk;
  - the child is both deaf and blind;
  - the child was born without feet, is a double amputee through or above the ankle or is otherwise without the whole of both legs as if they had been amputated through or above the ankle; or
  - the child is 'severely mentally impaired', has 'severe behavioural problems' and qualifies for the highest rate of DLA care component.[62]

7.37 Again, the wording of the legislation in relation to the entitlement to mobility component has received substantial interpretation in the case-law, which will be considered below.

'So severely disabled, physically or mentally'

7.38 This has the same meeting as in relation to the care component: see para 7.22.

---

61 SSCBA 1992 s73(12).
62 SSCBA 1992 s73(4A).

'Unable to take advantage of his/her walking abilities outdoors'

7.39 The use of this phrase in the legislation demonstrates that it is not the child's walking abilities which are the focus of entitlement to the lower rate, but his or her need for guidance or supervision to enable him or her to walk out of doors (in contrast to the higher rate tests, see below).[63]

'Guidance or supervision'

7.40 Any attention or supervision which forms part of the child's care component claim may be evidence in support of his or her mobility component claim, but there are differences to the two types of assistance. In relation to the mobility component, the guidance or support must in fact enable (and be necessary to enable) the child to walk out of doors.[64]

7.41 'Guidance' may involve physical leading or directing of the child, or be provided by suggestion and persuasion.[65] 'Supervision' can include monitoring a child's path in anticipation of some intervention to enable walking to continue or checking the route ahead for obstacles or dangers. Although no actual intervention may be required, it must be necessary for the helper to be prepared to intervene to allow the child to take advantage of the faculty of walking; his presence cannot simply be required for reassurance.[66] If the inability to walk out of doors is solely because of 'fear or anxiety' (and not because of a physical disability which makes the child unable to walk out of doors without guidance or supervision), there will be no entitlement unless the fear or anxiety amounts to a mental disability.[67]

7.42 In relation to the lower rate of the mobility component, any child aged under 16 must pass an additional test to establish either (1) that he or she requires substantially more guidance or supervision than children of his or her age in normal physical or mental health, or (2) children of the same age in normal physical health would not require such guidance or supervision. The decision-maker's interpretation of this test is analogous to the similar test applicable to the care component (see para 7.32).

---

63 DMG, para 61392.
64 R(DLA) 6/05.
65 R(DLA) 4/01.
66 CDLA/42/1994.
67 SS(DLA) Regs 1991 reg 12(7) and (8).

'Unable or virtually unable to walk'

7.43 This condition is met if the child's physical condition as a whole is such that (without having regard to circumstances to peculiar to the child as to the place of residence or as to the place of, or nature of, employment):[68]

- the child is unable to walk,
- the child's ability to walk out of doors is so limited, as regards the distance over which, the speed at which, the length of time for which or the manner in which the child can make progress on foot without severe discomfort, that she is virtually unable to walk, or
- the exertion required to walk would constitute a danger to the child's life or would be likely to lead to a serious deterioration in his or her health.

7.44 There are consequently a number of stages in fulfilling this condition. The first stage is that the child's physical condition as a whole must materially contribute to the inability or virtual inability to walk (even if other factors are also contributory).[69] As to the meaning of 'physical condition', any impediment which is entirely psychological or emotional in origin will not come within the definition. However, where behavioural problems resulting in an inability to walk are contributed to by a condition such as autism, Down's syndrome, William's syndrome or any other disability which has a chromosomal or physical origin, the test is likely to be met.[70] Furthermore, where a child with brain damage has behavioural problems which impact upon his or her ability to walk, the decision-maker should provide clear reasons if he or she finds that the behavioural problems are not caused by the brain damage.[71]

7.45 Next, the child must show that he or she suffers from an inability or virtual inability to walk. The former is established if a child is unable to move his or her body along by alternate, weightbearing steps.[72] If a child can or could walk regularly using an artificial walking aid or medication, they will not be treated as unable to walk, unless they lack both feet.[73] However, if a child makes progress by 'swinging through' on crutches, the child is not able to walk.[74]

---

68 SS(DLA) Regs 1991 reg 12(1)(a).
69 R(DLA) 4/06.
70 See R(M) 2/78 and R(M) 1/86.
71 CM/098/1989.
72 R(M) 2/89; CDLA/97/2001
73 SS(DLA) Regs 1991 reg 12(4)(a)–(b).
74 R(M) 2/89.

7.46   To be judged 'virtually' unable to walk, a child must be unable to walk 'to any appreciable extent or practically unable to walk'.[75] In making the assessment, the decision-maker must disregard any ability to walk while suffering severe discomfort.[76] The question must be approached by reference to the type of pavement normally found out of doors (not completely flat but also not exceptionally hazardous).[77] Finally, the decision-maker must assess the ability to walk in the light of the distance, manner, speed and time of the walking.[78]

7.47   The 'danger to life or serious deterioration in health' test relates only to the consequences of walking. Therefore, only where the effort of walking contributes to these outcomes is the test satisfied.[79] In order to establish a serious deterioration in health, the condition must worsen such that the child would never recover, would only recover after a significant period of time or could only recover after medical intervention.[80]

'Both deaf and blind'

7.48   A child will qualify under this ground if they are unable to walk without another person's assistance because the degree of disablement resulting from the loss of vision is 100 per cent, and the degree of disablement resulting from the loss of hearing is 80 per cent.[81]

'Severe mental impairment'

7.49   A child is severely mentally impaired if he or she has arrested development or incomplete physical development of the brain, which results in severe impairment of intelligence and social functioning.[82] Arrested development of the brain will be found where there is some defect in the operation of the brain, even if there is no ascertainable physical cause. Incomplete physical development results from a failure of the brain to grow properly. It is then necessary to show that one of these causes entails both severe mental impairment and severe impairment of social functioning. Where a child's IQ is below 55, his or her mental impairment is likely to be found to be severe,

---

75   R(M) 1/78 at [11]; R(M) 1/91 at [6].
76   SS(DLA) Regs 1991 reg 12(1)(a)(ii).
77   R(M) 1/91 at [8].
78   SS(DLA) Regs 1991 reg 12(1)(a)(ii).
79   R(M) 3/78.
80   R(M) 1/98.
81   SS(DLA) Regs 1991 reg 12(2)–(3).
82   SS(DLA) Regs 1991 reg 12(5).

but the IQ score is not itself definitive.[83] A lack of real-world intelligence or social capacity may themselves inform the intelligence
assessment[84] and the child may qualify if, for example, he or she has
no awareness of danger.[85]

Claiming DLA for disabled children

7.50   To make a claim, a parent or carer must complete a claim pack for
children, which is obtainable from the DWP Freephone Benefits
Enquiry Line (0800 243 355). It is of central importance when filling out this form to bear in mind the tests outlined above to which
the claim will be subjected, and particularly the need to show in certain contexts that the needs of a child under 16 are 'substantially in
excess' of those of other children of the same age. In support of a
claim, medical and school evidence and diary records can all be of
assistance. A child may exceptionally be asked to submit to a medical examination as part of the claim. If the child fails to attend the
examination without good reason, the claim will be refused.[86]

7.51   Where a child under 16 qualifies for DLA, the secretary of state
nominates an 'appointee', usually the child's mother or father or primary carer to receive and manage the funds on the child's behalf.[87]
This arrangement can also be made for older children who are unable
to manage the funds themselves. An award is usually paid directly
into the relevant bank account at four weekly intervals, although payments can be made more frequently. An award may be 'fixed-term'
or 'indefinite'. Where a recipient receives a fixed-term award of both
the care and mobility components, the length of the term for each
must be equal. Any change of circumstances which might affect an
award must be reported to the DWP, so that the amount of the award
can be appropriately increased or reduced.[88]

7.52   Where a child is given a fixed award, a claim can be made up to six
months before the expiry of the award for the award to be 'renewed'.[89]
This renewal claim is treated as a new claim as of the date on which
the old award finishes. However, any changed circumstances which

83 *Megarry v Chief Adjudication Officer* [1999] All ER (D) 1183.
84 *Megarry v Chief Adjudication Officer* [1999] All ER (D) 1183.
85 CDLA/3215/2001.
86 Social Security Act (SSA) 1998 s19.
87 Social Security (Claims and Payments) Regulations (SS(CP) Regs) 1987 SI No
    1968 reg 43.
88 SS(CP) Regs 1987 reg 32(1B).
89 SS(CP) Regs 1987 reg 13C.

may result in an increase or decrease of the award can mean that the old award is changed (upwards or downwards) through 'revision' or 'supersession' (see below, paras 7.120–131) before it expires. If a child's renewal claim is for the same level of award as previously received, there is no need to go through the three-month qualifying period (see above), but where the renewal award is different, this period will have to be completed.

Level of DLA awards

7.53   The current (July 2010) weekly rates of DLA awards are as follows:[90]

- Care component
  - Highest rate   £71.40
  - Middle rate   £47.80
  - Lowest rate   £18.95

- Mobility component
  - Higher rate   £49.85
  - Lower rate   £18.95

Effect on other benefits[91]

7.54   DLA income is not taxable and is not taken into account when calculating income for the purposes of tax credits or the means-tested benefits. A DLA award provided to a child will result in the provision of a disabled child premium (DCP) to top up certain benefits made to a person who is 'responsible' for that child, where the child lives in the recipient's 'household'. The benefits in relation to which DCP is available are: housing benefit (HB) and council tax benefit (CTB) and, in certain circumstances, income support (IS) and income-based jobseeker's allowance (JSA). If the child's DLA stops because he or she is admitted to hospital, the premium will continue.[92]

---

90   See http://www.direct.gov.uk/en/disabledpeople/financialsupport/dg_10011925.

91   For fuller details on the rules of entitlement to these other benefits, see *Welfare benefits and tax credits handbook 2010/2011*, CPAG, 2010.

92   Housing Benefit Regulations (HB Regs) 2006 SI No 213 Sch 3 para 16; Council Tax Benefit Regulations (CTB Regs) 2006 SI No 215 Sch 1 para 16; Income Support (General) Regulations (IS(G) Regs) 1987 SI No 1967 Sch 2 para 14; Jobseeker's Allowance Regulations (JSA Regs) 1996 SI No 207 Sch 1 para 16. The DCP is available in relation to an IS or income-based JSA claim only if a claim was made before 6 April 2004 and any dependent children were already included on that claim and no award of child tax credit has yet been made. In

7.55   The enhanced disability premium (EDP) is available where the child receives the highest rate of the care component, on the same principles as those applying to payment of DCP.[93]

7.56   Similarly, the calculation for the 'maximum child tax credit' in relation to childcare contains an additional 'disability element' where a DLA award is made to a child in a household where a person responsible for the child receives child tax credit.[94] An award of the highest rate care component to a child will result in a higher 'severe disability element' added to the 'maximum payments' available for childcare made under the tax credit system.[95]

7.57   Other forms of assistance which may follow a DLA award include payments under the social fund (see below, paras 7.75–7.94). Where a child receives the higher rate mobility component, his or her carer is likely to be exempt from vehicle excise duty (car tax) and to be entitled to a Blue Badge parking permit and participation in the Motability Scheme, which enables disabled people to exchange their mobility allowances to obtain a car, powered wheelchair or scooter. A child in receipt of the highest rate care component may also be able to access the Independent Living Fund to subsidise care provision (see below, paras 7.95–7.104).

Carer's allowance

Introduction

7.58   Carer's allowance (CA) is a benefit for those who care for a person (child or adult) who is 'severely disabled'.[96] The DWP describes CA as a 'contribution towards the income of carers who are unable to work full-time' rather than 'a wage for caring'.[97] However, the level of CA has been subjected to considerable criticism by carers' organisations

addition, if a child has over £3,000 capital, or if a child has been in hospital for more than 52 weeks, the DCP is not available for IS or income-based JSA (the child's capital does not affect the DCP for HB or CTB).

93   HB Regs 2006 Sch 3 para 15; CTB Regs 2006 Sch 1 para 15; IS(G) Regs 1987 Sch 2 para 13A; JSA Regs 1996 Sch 1 paras 15A and 201A.

94   Tax Credits Act 2002 s9; Child Tax Credit Regulations (CTC Regs) 2002 SI No 2007 reg 8(1)–(2).

95   CTC Regs 2002 reg 8(1) and (3).

96   SSCBA 1992 s70(1). Prior to 1 April 2003, CA was known as 'invalid care allowance'.

97   See House of Commons Public Accounts Committee, *Supporting carers to care*, 42nd Report of Session 2008–09, HC 549, 8 September 2009, p9 and Ev 10.

who assert that it is far too low to reflect the value of the care being provided.[98]

7.59　The law relating to CA can be found in statute (SSCBA 1992 s70), regulations (the Social Security (Invalid Care Allowance) Regulations (SS(ICA) Regs) 1976[99] and the case-law. The way in which CA interacts with other benefits is also governed by other pieces of legislation, as discussed below.

Eligibility

7.60　The conditions for CA eligibility are that a person:

a) is aged 16 or over;[100]

b) satisfies the residence conditions;[101]

c) is not subject to immigration control;[102]

d) is not in full-time education (21 hours or more of supervised study each week);[103]

e) does not earn more than £100 a week from employment;[104] and

f) for at least 35 hours a week, cares for a 'severely disabled person'.[105]

7.61　Both the legislation and case-law provide clarification as to the meaning of several of these criteria.

7.62　A 'severely disabled person' for CA purposes is defined as someone in receipt of the care component of DLA at the highest or middle rate.[106]

98 Carers UK, *Carers in crisis: a survey of carers' finances in 2008*, 2008.

99 SI No 409

100 SSCBA 1992 s70(3).

101 See para 7.10.

102 See para 7.12.

103 SS(ICA) Regs 1976 reg 5. Time spent receiving instruction or tuition, undertaking supervised study, an examination or practical work or taking part in any exercise, experiment or project as part of the curriculum does count as 'study' but time spent on meal breaks or unsupervised study does not.

104 SS(ICA) Regs 1976 reg 8. In relation to the earnings limit of £100 per week, this is calculated on the basis of net earnings after income tax, class 1 national insurance, and half of any contribution to a personal or occupational pension scheme.

105 SSCBA 1992 s70(1) and SS(ICA) Regs 1976 reg 4. There is no need for the carer to be related to, or to live with, the disabled person. A carer is eligible for CA if he cares for a person receiving attendance allowance or certain types of constant attendance allowance but as children are not eligible for these allowances, this eligibility condition is not discussed below.

106 SSCBA 1992 s70(2).

7.63   To qualify as a 'carer' under the legislation, a claimant must be 'regularly and substantially engaged in caring for that person'.[107] Regular and substantial care over the course of any particular week will be found where the claimant is likely to be 'engaged and regularly engaged for at least 35 hours a week'.[108] Although it is not necessary to provide care on every day of the week, the weekly test must be satisfied during each week for which CA is claimed; it is not possible to average out the amount of time spent caring over a number of weeks.[109] Furthermore, the calculation of time is based on the care given to any one severely disabled child; it is not possible to add together the time spent caring for two or more children to reach the 35 hour minimum.[110] Time spent preparing for the arrival of the disabled child, and clearing up after the visit can, however, be taken into account in calculating care time.[111]

7.64   Where two or more people satisfy the eligibility conditions in relation to any one severely disabled child on any particular day, only one person will be entitled to CA. The carers may jointly choose which of them should receive the CA. If they do not do so, the secretary of state can decide on the recipient.[112]

7.65   The legislation contains provision for ongoing entitlement to CA where a carer takes breaks from caring. CA will therefore continue even though the carer fails to satisfy the 35 hours a week condition in respect of a particular week if:

a) the carer has 'only temporarily' failed to satisfy the 35 hours a week condition; and

b) he or she has met the 35 hours a week minimum for at least 22 of the previous 26 weeks (or for at least 14 of the previous 26 weeks, if the carer or the severely disabled person was undergoing treatment in hospital as in-patient in hospital or 'similar institution', such as a care home or rehabilitation unit).[113]

7.66   Therefore, a carer can take four weeks of breaks over a 26-week period, or 12 weeks where the reason for the break is hospitalisation or similar institutionalisation. Any earnings of over £100 during such

---

107 SSCBA 1992 s70(1).
108 SS(ICA) Regs 1976 reg 4(1). For the purposes of CA, the week is measured from Sunday to the following Saturday: SSCBA 1992 s122.
109 R(G) 3/91.
110 SS(ICA) Regs 1976 reg 4(1A).
111 CG/6/1990.
112 SSCBA 1992 s70(7).
113 SS(ICA) Regs 1976 reg 4(1).

a break are disregarded for the purposes of the employment condition (see above, para 7.60). However, if the child's DLA stops, the CA will also stop. There is also provision for ongoing CA where the person being cared for dies. This entitlement continues for eight weeks following the death, provided that all of the other conditions apart from care remain satisfied.[114]

7.67   Until recently, it was possible in certain circumstances to claim an increase in CA where a carer had dependent children or for a spouse or civil partner or where another person cared for a child in respect of whom CA was given. However, these entitlements have been abolished: the dependent child increase on 6 April 2003 and the 'adult dependent' increase on 6 April 2010. Nevertheless, where a carer was entitled to, and had made a claim for, either of these increases as of the relevant date of abolition, he or she will remain entitled to them.

How to claim CA

7.68   In England, Wales and Scotland, it is possible to claim CA online through the CA e-service (see www.dwp.gov.uk/carersallowance/). Alternatively, it is possible to obtain a claim form through the Carer's Allowance Unit (tel: 0845 608 4321) or the Benefit Enquiry Line (0800 88 22 00). Forms can also be obtained from a Jobcentre Plus office, pension centre or downloaded online.[115] There is a shorter claim form for those in receipt of State Pension.[116]

7.69   It is possible for a claimant to claim up to three months in advance of the date on which his or her eligibility will be established. Any backdating is normally only possible for three months prior to the date on which the claim was received by the DWP. However, where the claim for CA is made within three months of the decision to award the DLA care component at the middle or highest rate to a disabled child, the CA award is backdated to the start of the week on which the DLA is first payable.[117]

---

114 SSCBA 1992 s70(1A).
115 See www.dwp.gov.uk/advisers/claimforms/ds7001_print.pdf.
116 See www.dwp.gov.uk/advisers/claimforms/ds700sp_print.pdf.
117 SS(CP) Regs 1987 reg 6.

Level of benefit

7.70 The weekly rate of CA, as of April 2010, is as follows:[118]

CA:	£53.10
[Adult dependant increase:	£31.70
Child dependant increase (first child):	£8.10
Child dependant increase (each subsequent child):	£11.35][119]

Effect of CA on other benefits

7.71 If a carer receives CA, his or her entitlement to other benefits may be affected. Establishing eligibility for CA may be sufficient to demonstrate entitlement to certain benefits, but receipt of CA may also result in non-eligibility for others. Key points to keep in mind in this respect are set out below.

7.72 If a carer is entitled to HB or CTB and is in receipt of CA, he or she is entitled to a carer premium to add to those benefits[120] and may also be able be entitled to disabled child premium or enhanced disability premium (see above, paras 7.54–7.55). In certain circumstances, these premiums may also be available to supplement any IS, income-based JSA or income-related employment and support allowance.[121]

7.73 However, a person in receipt of CA cannot usually receive one of the other benefits intended to compensate for inability to work.[122] Where someone is entitled to more than one of these benefits, a number of rules apply:[123]

a) a contributory benefit is paid in preference to a non-contributory benefit, topped up by the balance of any non-contributory benefit due;

b) weekly benefits are generally paid and topped up by the balance of any daily benefit; and

---

118 SSCBA 1992 Sch 4.
119 See para 7.67 above for the abolition of the dependency premiums for new CA claims.
120 HB Regs 2006 Sch 3 para 17; CTB Regs 2006 Sch 1 paras 8 and 17(3)–(4).
121 IS(G) Regs 1987 Sch 2 para 14ZA; JSA Regs 1996 Sch 1 paras 17 and 20J; Employment and Support Allowance Regulations (ESA Regs) 2008 SI No 794 Sch 4 para 8.
122 Including contribution-based JSA, incapacity benefit, contributory employment and support allowance, maternity allowance, retirement pension, widow's pension or bereavement allowance, widowed mother's or widowed parent's allowance, and severe disablement allowance.
123 Social Security (Overlapping Benefits) Regulations 1979.

c) the highest rate benefit is paid, unless the benefits are equal in amount, in which case only one is paid.

If, because of these rules, someone who qualifies for CA instead receives one of the other 'earnings replacement' benefits, that person is still categorised as 'entitled to' CA for the purposes of the premiums in the paragraph below.

7.74   CA is taxable.[124] It also counts as income for means-tested benefits, so receipt of CA may place a person outside eligibility for one of these benefits. In addition, if a claimant receives the carer premium for a disabled child who would be entitled to severe disability premium on their means-tested benefit, the child's entitlement to that premium is likely to be affected.[125] Given that the severe disability premium is worth more than the carer premium, it may be necessary for the disabled person in respect of whom CA is sought to state that he or she is aware of the carer's claim for this allowance and it may be worth considering not claiming the carer premium at all.

Discretionary payments: Social Fund (community care grants), Independent Living Fund and Family Fund

Social Fund (community care grants)

Introduction

7.75   Community care grants (CCGs) come under the umbrella of the Social Fund, which is a scheme intended to help people with needs which are difficult to meet from regular income.[126] This fund allows for payments to be made on either a 'regulated' or 'discretionary' basis. Regulated payments, which go towards certain maternity grants, funeral expenses, cold weather payments and winter fuel payments, are provided as of right once an applicant satisfies certain conditions. By contrast, discretionary payments are based on a more flexible approach in which decision-makers are not bound by any legal entitlements, but are guided by fixed principles in determining whether to provide support. Because the community care

---

124 Income Tax (Earning and Pensions) Act 2003 ss660, 661 and 676.
125 IS(G) Regs 1987 Sch 2 para 13; JSA Regs 1996 Sch 1 paras 15 and 20I; ESA Regs 2008 Sch 4 para 6; HB Regs 2006 Sch 3 para 14; CTB Regs 2006 Sch 1 para 14.
126 *The Social Fund Guide*, April 2010 ('the Guide'), Part 1, para 1.

discretionary grant goes towards needs which are of particular relevance to disabled children, this type of social fund payment is the focus of this section.

7.76 CCGs are not like conventional benefits. Their discretionary nature marks them out from the other types of support considered in this chapter. Furthermore, the governing legislation states that the local bodies which administer the payments on behalf of the DWP may take into account their own budgets in determining whether to provide support to any individual.[127]

7.77 The main legislation relevant to CCGs is sections 138–140 of SSCBA 1992. Section 138 divides up the fund between the 'regulated' and 'discretionary' payments, and categorises the discretionary payments into:

a) CCGs;
b) crisis loans; and
c) budgeting loans.

7.78 In relation to these discretionary payments, section 140 lays down a number of principles which the decision-maker should consider in assessing a claim:

a) the nature, extent and urgency of the need;
b) the existence of resources from which the need may be met;
c) the possibility that some other person or body may wholly or partly meet it;
d) any relevant allocation under section 168(1)–(4) of the Administration Act (this refers to the funding provided by central government to the Fund).

7.79 SSCBA 1992 s139 allows the secretary of state to make regulations governing more precisely the operation of the social fund and a number of such regulations have been made.[128] A number of legally binding directions have also been made by the secretary of state which go into further detail as to the basis on which payments will be made and the procedure to be followed. Finally, guidance, while not binding, has been published by the secretary of state to assist decision-makers. The most up-to-date consolidated version of these directions and guidance is contained in the *Social Fund Guide* (April 2010) ('the Guide').[129]

127 SSCBA 1992 s140(1)(e).
128 In relation to discretionary payments, the principal relevant regulations are: the Social Fund (Applications and Miscellaneous Provision) Regulations 2008, the Social Fund (Application for Review) Regulations (SF(AR) Regs)1988, and the Social Fund (Recovery by Deductions from Benefits) Regulations 1988.
129 See www.dwp.gov.uk/docs/social-fund-guide.pdf.

Where 'directions' are referred to below, these are contained in the Guide.

7.80   CCGs are intended to assist vulnerable people to live 'as independent a life as possible in the community'.[130] They are meant to 'complement' rather than replace the support or care duties of other bodies, such as local authorities, which have the lead role in delivering social care. As a result, the provision of a CCG is appropriate in certain well-defined circumstances:

a) to help people establish themselves in the community following a stay in institutional or residential care;
b) to help an applicant or a member of his or her family remain in the community rather than enter institutional or residential care;
c) to ease exceptional pressures on a family, that is in circumstances which put a family under greater pressure than might normally be associated with low income;
d) to go towards living expenses of a prisoner or young offender on leave where he or she will be visiting and under the care of a person in receipt of one of the qualifying benefits;
e) to help the applicant to set up home in the community as a part of a planned resettlement programme following a period during which he or she has been without a settled way of life; or
f) to help the applicant and/or other members of his or her family to visit a patient in hospital or residential care.[131]

7.81   In addition to the requirement to further one or more of these aims, a number of limitations apply, the key ones being:

a) The applicant must be in receipt of IS, income-based JSA, income-related employment and support allowance or pensions credit (unless he or she is due to leave institutional or residential care within six weeks of the date of the CCG application and he or she is likely to get one of these benefits when the applicant leaves).
b) The amount of any CCG will be reduced by the amount of any capital held by the applicant and his or her partner which exceeds £500 (or £1,000 if the applicant or partner is aged 60 or over). Certain types of capital, including any capital held by the applicant's children, will be disregarded.[132]
c) There are also specific exclusions defining what CCGs may not fund.[133] These include: telephone costs; expenses which the local

130 The Guide, Part 2, para 1.
131 Direction 4.
132 Direction 27.
133 Direction 29.

authority has a duty to meet; fuel costs; housing costs (except for minor repairs); council tax; and daily living expenses, except in relation to a prisoner or young offender on release on temporary licence.

7.82 In determining whether to grant the application, the decision-maker will have regard to the factors outlined in SSCBA 1992 s140 (see above), but may also apply the following ranking system:[134]

a) An application will have high priority where an award will have a substantial and immediate effect in resolving or improving the circumstances of the applicant and in meeting the CCG aims.
b) There will be a medium priority if an award will have a noticeable effect, although not substantial and immediate, in resolving or improving the applicant's circumstances and in meeting the CCG aims.
c) A low priority will be found if an award for the item requested will have only a minor effect in resolving or improving the applicant's circumstances.

7.83 Among the additional factors which may argue for a higher priority are where a person's ability to cope with independent living may be particularly difficult because of restricted mobility, learning difficulties, mental health problems, physical disability or mental or chronic physical illness.[135]

Amount of CCGs

7.84 The Guide states that, when there is sufficient priority for an award, the amount requested by the applicant for the item(s) should normally be granted, provided this amount is within a range of prices considered appropriate for an item of serviceable quality.[136] Exceptionally, where the CCG budget is under pressure, a lower amount may be awarded, but full reasons, including evidence of the budgetary difficulties, should be provided by the decision-maker.[137]

7.85 Awards cannot normally be made for less than £30. They are usually paid in cash to the applicant, although they may be exceptionally made direct to a supplier where there is firm evidence that the award may not be used for its intended purpose.[138]

134 The Guide, paras 349–351.
135 The Guide, para 353.
136 The Guide, para 368.
137 The Guide, paras 375–377.
138 The Guide, paras 319–320; SF(AR) Regs 1988 reg 2(3).

7.86   Awards are disregarded for tax purposes and in determining income for other means-tested benefits, and do not affect entitlement to non-means-tested benefits.

How to apply for a CCG

7.87   Applications for CCGs should be made on the approved form (the SF300), which is available from any DWP office or online, and submitted to the Jobcentre Plus office covering the applicant's area. Although supporting evidence is not required, it is likely to be helpful to show that you fall within one of the categories stipulated in the guidance.

7.88   It is not possible to apply for a CCG in respect of any item for which an applicant has already been accepted or refused within the past 28 days, unless there is a change of circumstances.[139]

Reviews

7.89   Although CCGs are discretionary, it is possible for challenges to be brought against decisions made in relation to grants, including the refusal of a CCG, the size of a CCG, the payment arrangements or the refusal to consider a repeat application. The initial route to challenge a CCG decision is through requesting a review by a reviewing officer.

7.90   A review of a decision must take place:

a) if an application for review is made (containing grounds for review and the signature of the applicant) within 28 days of issue of the decision (although this time limit may be extended for 'special reasons');[140] or

b) where the decision had been made in ignorance of, or based on a mistake as to, a material fact.[141]

7.91   A review of a decision may take place:

a) if the applicant misrepresented, or failed to disclose, any material fact[142] (in which case he or she may be liable to repay any overpayment); or

b) in such other circumstances as the reviewing officer thinks fit.[143]

139 Direction 7.
140 Social Services Act (SSA) 1998 s38(1)(a); SF(AR) Regs 1988 regs 2(2) and 2(4).
141 Direction 31.
142 SSA 1998 s38(1)(b).
143 SSA 1998 s38(1)(c).

7.92   In approaching a review, the officer must apply the legislation and guidance summarised above. In addition, he or she must consider whether:

a) the decision-maker applied the law correctly in arriving at his or her decision (in particular, that the decision is sustainable on the evidence; all relevant considerations and no irrelevant considerations were taken into account; and that the decision-maker interpreted the law correctly);

b) the decision-maker acted fairly and exercised his or her discretion to arrive at a conclusion that was reasonable in the circumstances – ie it was a decision that a reasonable decision-maker could have reached;

c) the required procedural steps have been followed and there has been no bias.[144]

7.93   Following a negative decision on review, an applicant may make a request for a further review to the social fund inspectors (SFIs), who work independently of the DWP, and who can confirm the reviewing officer's decision, substitute their own decision or refer the case back to a reviewing officer.[145]

7.94   This review must be requested in writing, containing grounds for review, direct to the SFI office in Birmingham within 28 days (although the 'special reasons' extension applies[146]) of the first-instance review decision. Following receipt of the review application, the SFI will write to set out the main issues and allow the applicant to provide further information within eight days. A decision in writing will then be reached, based on the same considerations as those binding the first-stage review (see above, para 7.92). This decision can itself be subject to a further request for review to the SFI or by judicial review in the High Court.

Independent Living Fund

Introduction

7.95   The Independent Living Fund (ILF) is an 'Executive Non-Departmental Public Body' of the DWP, which means that although it is funded by, and under the supervision of, the department it operates at an arm's length from it. The operation of the Fund is governed by the ILF (2006) Trust Deed ('the Trust Deed') and various agreements with the DWP.

144 Direction 39.
145 SF(AR) Regs 1988 reg 2(1)(b).
146 SF(AR) Regs 1988 reg 2(2)–(3).

7.96   The purpose of the ILF is to fund cash payments to assist certain severely disabled people to live independently.[147] It is available (subject to qualifying criteria) to disabled children aged 16 and 17. Like the parts of the social fund already discussed, it operates on a discretionary basis, so there is no entitlement to awards, although there are rules which govern the basis on which payments are made.

Eligibility for ILF funding

7.97   The pre-conditions which a child must satisfy in order to make an application are that the applicant:[148]

a) is 16 or over;
b) is present and ordinarily resident in the UK;
c) receives the higher rate care component of DLA;
d) has less than £23,000 in savings or capital;
e) receives at least £340 of support a week or £17,680 a year from the local authority for independent living (see paras 10.49–10.63 in relation to the transition to adult social care for disabled young people); and
f) contributes half of the DLA care component and (if he or she receives it) all the severe disability premium towards his or her care costs, which must not be provided by a relative living with the child.

7.98   In addition, the following individuals will be given priority in the distribution of payments under the Fund:[149]

a) those already receiving payments from the Fund; or
b) those normally in employment for at least 16 hours a week.

7.99   The priority criteria of at least 16 hours a week paid employment was introduced in 2010, and may unless relaxed severely limit the scope of eligible applicants, as well as discriminating against more disabled children. Due to the unprecedented number of applications in 2010, the ILF decided to accept no new claims until April 2011, a move which has called into question the future existence of the Fund.[150]

---

147 The Trust Deed, p3.
148 Part II of the First Schedule to the Trust Deed.
149 The Third Schedule to the Trust Deed.
150 See the ILF Equality Impact Assessment, March 2010 at www.ilf.org.uk/ reports/equality_schemes/equality_impact_assessment/index.html.

Applying for ILF funding

7.100　Application forms can be downloaded from the ILF website.[151] The ILF can also be contacted at 0845 601 8815 or 0115 945 0700. Completed application forms, and agreement forms should be sent to: The Independent Living Fund, Equinox House, Island Business Quarter, City Link, Nottingham NG2 4LA.

7.101　An application will be considered by an 'assessor', who must be a professionally registered social worker, occupational therapist or community nurse with knowledge and experience of establishing community care arrangements for disabled people. The assessor must assess the child's needs, following a visit, and apply the ILF criteria in deciding on the application.

Payments from the ILF

7.102　The amount awarded by the ILF is based on the cost of the care needed as well as the applicant's savings, income and certain other benefits and expenses, with the maximum available payment amounting to £475 per week.

7.103　Payments must be used to pay for support and services through the use of a care agency or a personal assistant to help with personal and domestic tasks including toileting, bathing, washing and dressing; eating and drinking, cooking, shopping and cleaning.[152] Awards cannot go towards care provided by a co-habiting partner or relative (including in-laws).[153]

Challenges to ILF decisions

7.104　Any decision or award made by the ILF can be challenged via a 'decision review' within four weeks of the decision date. The review must be requested in writing at the Nottingham address given above, and is considered by a Complaints and Review Manager who will aim to notify the applicant of the outcome of the review, with reasons, within three weeks.[154]

151　See www.ilf.org.uk/index.html.

152　The Second Schedule to the Trust Deed.

153　The Third Schedule to the Trust Deed.

154　See 'Your right to complain', Leaflet 19 at www.ilf.org.uk/cms_media/files/leaflet_19_revised.pdf.

Family Fund

Introduction

7.105　The Family Fund (FF) is the largest independent grant-giving organisation offering support to low-income families with a severely disabled child. Strictly speaking, the FF does not qualify as a benefit as, although it receives its funding from central government, it is a charity which operates independently of the state. Its website is at www.familyfund.org.uk.

7.106　　The FF considers applications for grants in relation to any item that might be of help to a severely disabled child and his or her family, and in particular items which are of special significance to disabled children or young people such as driving lessons or college equipment. Like the CCG and ILF, the FF functions on a discretionary basis, under a fixed budget and with no automatic entitlement to support. In addition, the FF does not provide funding in relation to goods or services which should be met or financed by a statutory agency.

Eligibility for FF

7.107　In order to qualify for an FF grant, an applicant must:
a) live in the United Kingdom, and have lived there for six months;
b) be permanently resident in the UK;
c) be the partner or carer of a severely disabled person aged 17 or under, who lives at home; and
d) have a household income of less than £25,000 (for England) or £27,000 (for Northern Ireland, Scotland or Wales).[155]

7.108　A child is 'severely disabled' and so potentially eligible for support from the FF where:
a) the child has additional complex needs or a serious or life threatening illness;
b) the child's additional needs impact on the family's choices and their opportunity to enjoy ordinary life and the degree of planning and support required to meet the child's needs is much greater than that usually required to meet the needs of children and young people;
c) the child requires a high level of support in three or more of the following areas: physical environment; education; communication; access to social activities; personal care, supervision and vigilance;

155　The discrepancy between the nations of the UK derives from the differing levels of funding received by the FF from each of these nation's administrations.

specialist resources, including information and communications technology; and medical or therapeutic treatment and condition management; and

d) the child's condition is long-term (that is, likely to last 12 months or more) or life limiting.

7.109 In calculating 'household income', the FF has introduced new rules as of 1 April 2010. For this purpose, the FF includes income from work, tax credits, occupational pensions, maintenance payments, any rental income, but not the DLA, attendance allowance or child benefits. The work income is assessed by reference to the net income (after income tax and national insurance). No account is taken of any savings which may be held by the family.

How to apply to the FF

7.110 A parent or guardian of a severely disabled child can apply for a grant by filling in an application form which can be requested by contacting the FF at info@familyfund.org.uk or by telephoning 0845 130 4542. Evidence of eligibility which will be required includes copies of recent payslips or HMRC income tax calculations, copies of any benefit award letters or bank statements and copies of a child's DLA award letter.

7.111 The FF states that it normally takes three or four months to arrive at a decision in relation to a complete application. Any appeal must be lodged within three months of the decision, by contacting the Applications Manager, Family Fund, 4 Alpha Court, Monks Cross Drive, York YO32 9WN or emailing info@familyfund.org.uk.

7.112 A subsequent grant application can usually only be made 12 months after the date of the last grant. This is the case even if an applicant is seeking support in relation to a different disabled child.

FF grants

7.113 FF awards can be made in a number of ways: via a payment card provided by the FF, in vouchers, direct from the supplier or through a payment made directly into a bank account. The FF also has relationships with particular suppliers in providing goods or services, such as Comet and the World of Appliances (for appliances), BSM (for driving lessons), Stone Computers (for computers) and Haven Holidays and Thomas Cook (for holidays).

7.114 Any grant must be used for the purpose specified in the award letter and receipts must be kept in case the FF undertakes an audit into any particular grant.

Challenging benefits decisions

Introduction

7.115   This section covers challenges to DLA, CA and other benefits decisions, but not to the CCG, ILF or FF, which are addressed in the relevant sections (above).

Making claims and challenges

7.116   Any parent of a child aged less than 18 who acts as his or her child's 'appointee' in bringing the claim will thereby have the same rights as the child if the child was acting on his or her own behalf in bringing any subsequent challenge to a decision. The three types of challenge which will be discussed below are 'revisions', 'supersessions' and 'appeals'.

Decisions

7.117   Any benefits decision ought to be made within the target time set by the DWP for the relevant benefit.[156] If there is delay in the processing of the claim, it may be possible to claim interim payments until the final decision is made,[157] to apply for a crisis loan from the social fund or in certain cases to apply for judicial review to the courts in relation to the decision-maker's delay.

7.118   The notification of the decision must also contain a notice of the claimant's right to appeal and to receive a written statement of the reasons for the decision if none was contained in the decision itself. The request for a written statement should be made within one month of the date of notification (although the statement may be provided beyond this one-month period, it may not then be possible to apply for revision or appeal in respect of the decision – see below).[158] In addition, where a claimant asks for an explanation, requests a written statement of reasons, makes an application for revision or appeals, and where the decision is not changed by revision or supersession

---

156 For DLA, the target time is 39 working days from the claim (or eight working days for 'special claims' in relation to terminal illness).

157 Social Security (Payments on Account, Overpayments and Recovery) Regulations 1988 SI No 664 reg 2.

158 Social Security and Child Support (Decisions and Appeals) Regulations (SSCS(DA) Regs) 1999 reg 28(1)(b)–(c).

(see below), an official from the DWP should contact him or her, usually by phone, to explain the decision.

7.119   Once the decision arrives, it is possible to request that minor errors be corrected by notifying the decision-maker. Any relevant time for the purposes of the time limits for other challenges (see below) will not start running until the corrected decision is notified.[159]

Revisions

7.120   A request for revision in accordance with the rules requires the decision-maker to reconsider a decision he or she has made and change it if appropriate. It is important to note that a revision can result in an outcome that is less favourable to the applicant than the first-instance decision originally made and that the decision-maker can consider matters other than those raised in the revision application.[160] In DLA cases, a decision-maker may consider a child's entitlement to the component which is not subject to appeal.

7.121   It is possible for a claimant (or, indeed, the DWP itself) to request a revision on any grounds (no grounds in fact need to be given by the requesting party[161]), provided that the request is received by the DWP with the time limits, which are as follows:[162]

a) within one calendar month of the notification of the original decision;

b) where a written statement of reasons is requested and is provided within the one-month period, within 14 days of expiry of the one-month period;

c) where a written statement is provided after the one-month period, within 14 days of notification of the written statement; or

d) within the appropriate period where a late application is accepted.

7.122   Where a late application for revision is made, the relevant decision must be identified, reasons for extending the time limits must be given and a final time limit of 13 months must be complied with. Where a written statement of reasons was supplied after the decision, the 13-month period is extended by 14 days if the statement arrived within a month of the decision, or if supplied later, by as many days

---

159 SSCS(DA) Regs 1999 reg 9A.
160 SSA 1998 ss9(2) and 10(2).
161 However, where a DLA decision is challenged on the ground that the person is terminally ill, the request for revision must include reference to this ground.
162 SSA 1998 ss8 and 10; SSCS(DA) Regs 1999 reg 3(1)(b).

as elapsed following the expiry of the one-month period).[163] An extension may only be accepted if:

a) it is reasonable to grant the application;
b) the application for revision has merit; and
c) special circumstances are relevant to the application and as a result of those special circumstances it was not practicable for the application to be made within the time limit.

7.123   The later an application is sent, the less likely an extension is. Furthermore, in deciding whether to grant an application, no account can be taken of a claim that the applicant or any person acting for him was unaware of or misunderstood the law applicable to his case; or that the Upper Tribunal or a court has taken a different view of the law from that previously understood and applied.[164]

7.124   When considering whether to revise a decision made within the time limits above, the decision-maker should generally re-take his decision for any reason he or she considers appropriate. These will include where the decision-maker:

a) reaches a different conclusion on the facts;
b) thinks the original decision was taken in the light of a mistaken view of the facts;
c) considers the original decision was based on an incorrect interpretation of the law;
d) considers the original decision was based on insufficient evidence; or
e) decides that there are new relevant facts which were not known at the time the decision was made.

7.125   In addition to the request for revision on any grounds, which are subject to the time limits above, there are certain grounds for revision which may be made at any time. These are that:

a) there has been an 'official error' by personnel at the DWP (this refers to a clear mistake of fact or law arising because an officer has failed to make a decision or take an administrative act that was required under social security legislation, which had a bearing on the final outcome);[165]
b) a decision was more favourable to the claimant than it should have been, because of the decision-maker's ignorance of or mistake as

---

163 SSCS(DA) Regs 1999 reg 4.
164 SSCS(DA) Regs 1999 reg 4(5)–(6).
165 SSCS(DA) Regs 1999 reg 3(5)(a).

to a material fact (although see below for different circumstances relating to disability determinations for DLA);[166] or

c) in relation to a disability determination for DLA which was more favourable to the claimant than it should have been, because of the decision-maker's ignorance of, or mistake as to, a material fact, a revision may take place at any time where the decision-maker is satisfied that when the original decision was made, the claimant knew or could reasonably have been expected to know that fact, and that it was relevant to the disability determination.[167]

7.126 A request should be sent to the office which made the original decision. Although not obligatory in relation to any benefits other than housing benefit and council tax benefit, it is good practice to make a written request for revision, explaining the grounds for revision and supplying relevant evidence. The decision-maker may seek further information to inform his or her decision on revision.

7.127 The decision-maker may decide that (1) there are no grounds for revision, (2) there are grounds for revision but that the original decision was correct or (3) the original decision should be changed. If a change is made, the revised decision usually has effect as of the date on which the original decision took effect,[168] however, where the revision itself results in a change to the date on which the original decision was effective, the new decision takes effect on the revised date.[169]

7.128 A challenge to a revision decision, or a refusal to revise, may be available through an appeal to the First-tier Tribunal (see below).

Supersessions

7.129 A supersession replaces a benefits decision (including those made by the First-tier Tribunal or Upper Tribunal) made at an earlier date. It is the appropriate course if (1) a claimant's circumstances have changed (or will change) following an earlier decision, and (2) an earlier decision was made as a result of ignorance of, or mistake about, material facts, or on the basis of an error of law (however, it is likely that in these circumstances a revision will in fact be carried out by the decision-maker).

7.130 A number of events may qualify as a change of circumstances, including a change in the law (although not a decision that the law has

---

166 SSCS(DA) Regs 1999 reg 3(5)(b).
167 SSCS(DA) Regs 1999 reg 3(5)(c).
168 SSA 1998 s9(3); SSCS(DA) Regs 1999 reg 5.
169 SSA 1998 s9(4).

been wrongly interpreted) and new medical evidence (although not a new medical opinion about pre-existing evidence). Where a claimant has been correctly refused benefit and his circumstances have since changed, supersession is not available; a fresh claim must instead be made.

7.131   A supersession can be applied for by notifying the decision-maker which took the decision under challenge. It is advisable to enclose any relevant decision with the notice of request for supersession.

7.132   There are detailed rules as to when the outcome of any supersession will take effect, depending on the nature of the challenge. Because these may result in less arrears accruing than following a successful revision, it may be advisable to pursue a revision, if both are available. Generally, the supersession takes effect as of the date of the supersession application (or if the decision-maker applied for the supersession, on the date of the decision).[170] However, there are exceptions, including the following:

a) If the supersession results in a more favourable rate of DLA for a child, the decision takes effect on the date the child became entitled to that rate, provided the DWP is notified within one month of the change (although this can be extended in certain circumstances).[171]

b) If the supersession results in a less favourable outcome, it will usually take effect on the date of the change of circumstances, except where the change relates to a change of circumstances in relation to a disability condition under DLA, in which case it takes effect on the date on which the DWP ought to have been informed about the change of circumstances (unless there was no duty to inform the DWP, in which case it takes effect on the day of the decision).[172]

Appeals

7.133   Most decisions of the DWP relevant to disabled children can be appealed to the First-tier Tribunal (Social Entitlement Chamber) (FTT), an independent tribunal which hears a range of appeals in relation to social security and child support, criminal injuries compensation

---

170 SSA 1998 s10(5).

171 SSCA(DA) Regs 1999 reg 7(9). The basis on which extensions can be sought is the same as that outlined more generally in relation to time limit extensions (see para 7.122 above). Following a successful out-of-time supersession, the decision takes effect as of the date on which the change of circumstances was notified to the decision-maker (for CA) or the date on which the supersession was applied for (for DLA).

172 SSCS(DA) Regs 1999 reg 7(2)(c) and 7A(1).

and asylum support. From here, there may be a further appeal to the Upper Tribunal (Administrative Appeals Chamber) (UT).[173]

7.134 Both the First-tier and Upper Tribunals are governed by rules of procedure.[174] These rules set out in some detail the powers of the respective tribunals, of which only some are outlined here.

7.135 Hearings of the FTT are usually presided over by a legally qualified judge, who sits with one or two other members who have medical or other professional expertise in the subject-matter of the dispute.[175] As with other forms of challenge, various procedural requirements apply to appeals to the FTT:

a) To lodge an appeal an appellant should complete and sign the appropriate appeal form (including the decision being appealed and the grounds on which it is being appealed), and send it to the office that made the decision.[176]

b) The form should be sent within the time limits (although the appeal may be considered outside the time limits if the decision-maker does not object or the FTT following an application by the appellant extends the time limit), which are:[177]

(i) within one month of the date of the decision; or

(ii) where a written statement of reasons was sent, either within one month and 14 days of the decision, or of the date of the written statement (whichever is the later).

7.136 Once the decision-maker receives the appeal papers, he or she will consider whether to revise the original decision. If a revised decision which is more advantageous to the appellant is made, the appeal lapses (even if the appellant does not obtain the outcome he or she wishes). If not, the decision-maker should forward the appeal to the FTT. The FTT will then send out further documents, asking about the nature of the appeal, whether an oral hearing or a decision based only the papers is requested and whether any witnesses will be called, or a representative will act, on the appellant's behalf.[178] The

---

173 Prior to 3 November 2008, the equivalent appeals lay to the social security appeals tribunals and the social security commissioners.

174 The Tribunal Procedure (First-tier Tribunal) (Social Entitlement Chamber) Rules (TP(FTT) Rules) 2008 and the Tribunal Procedure (Upper Tribunal) Rules (TP(UT) Rules) 2008.

175 Practice Statement, *Composition of tribunals in social security and child support cases in the social entitlement Chamber on or after 3 November 2008*, 30 October 2008.

176 SSCS(DA) Regs 1999 reg 33(2).

177 TP(FTT) Rules 2008 rr12 and 23(2) and Sch 1.

178 TP(FTT) Rules 2008 r24.

decision-maker will prepare a bundle of evidence and his or her writ-ten reasons for the hearing, but the appellant can, and should, send any documents, reports, statements and other evidence which he or she would like the tribunal to consider, within one month of receiving the decision-maker's bundle.[179]

7.137 Where a paper appeal takes place, the appellant will receive the FTT's decision in writing. If an oral hearing has been decided on, the FTT will send out a notification of the date and venue in advance. At the hearing, the decision-maker may be represented by a presenting officer and there may be expert witnesses who can give evidence on the case. The FTT procedure is relatively informal, but an appellant (and/or their representative) must be given a fair hearing and the chance to participate fully in the proceedings by setting out his or her case, as well as facing questions from the FTT Panel and the presenting officer.[180] The FTT is bound to consider issues raised in the appellant's grounds of appeal, and may (but does not have to) consider other relevant points. It is important that the FTT brings an independent eye to the decision-maker's evidence, and follows the relevant legal principles as set out in legislation, regulations, guid-ance and case-law.

7.138 The FTT's decision will usually be notified on the day of the hear-ing, with a decision notice provided in writing. The appellant also has a right to obtain a copy of the judge's record of proceedings and the FTT's statement of reasons, which sets out in more detail the basis for the decision: the former must be requested in writing within six months of the decision, and the latter within one month (although both periods can be extended).[181] It is advisable to have a copy of the statement of reasons in order to undertake any appeal to the UT (see below).

7.139 An FTT decision should be implemented by the DWP with im-mediate effect although an appeal to the UT may suspend the oper-ation of the decision. Where the decision was based on a procedural irregularity (such as where an appellant was not notified of a hearing) a decision can exceptionally be set aside following an application in writing within a month of the decision, with a new hearing subse-quently listed.[182] An FTT decision can also be superseded in the way outlined above, where the challenge is not based on an error of law.

179 TP(FTT) Rules 2008 r24(6)–(7).
180 TP(FTT) Rules 2008 r2.
181 TP(FTT) Rules 2008 r34.
182 TP(FTT) Rules 2008 r37.

7.140   Where there has been an error of law in the FTT's decision, either the appellant or the decision-maker can appeal to the UT.[183] Such errors could include misinterpreting the relevant law, denying a party a fair hearing during the proceedings, coming to a conclusion which is unsupported by the evidence, failing to give adequate reasons or making findings which no reasonable tribunal could have reached. The reason that the UT has jurisdiction only where there is an error of law is that its role is not to provide a full appeal of the FTT decision, but to review whether the approach of the FTT was in accordance with the law.

7.141   There is a two-stage process for any appeal to the UT. A appellant must first gain permission to appeal, and then undertake the appeal itself.[184] Permission is sought first from the FTT and then, if that fails, from the UT itself.[185] In considering whether to grant permission, the FTT must also consider whether to review its own decision. The permission application must take place within one month of receiving the written reasons for the decision or notice that an FTT decision was amended or corrected or that an application to set aside the decision failed (whichever is the latest).[186] The FTT or UT can, however, extend or shorten the time limit for appealing, although there is no guarantee that either will do so.[187] If permission from the FTT is refused, it may be sought from the UT by using the UT 1 (Social Entitlement) form, available from the Tribunals Service office, the Upper Tribunal Office or at www.osscsc.gov.uk.[188]

7.142   If the FTT grants permission to appeal, the notice of permission must be sent to the UT within a month of receipt along with the notice of appeal.[189] If it is the UT which has granted permission no action is required to initiate the appeal before the UT. The UT will set the appeal procedure running, with written submissions requested first from the decision-maker and then the appellant.[190] The substantive hearing may be dealt with in writing or orally, before a legally qualified judge. Before any oral hearing, the UT may request a written outline of the appellant's case, or 'skeleton argument', which should be submitted within the time-scale given by the tribunal. At

183 Tribunals, Courts and Enforcement Act (TCEA) 2007 s11.
184 TCEA 2007 s11(3).
185 TCEA 2007 s11(4)(a); TP(UT) Rules 2008 r21(2).
186 TP(FTT) Rules 2008 r38(3).
187 TP(FTT) Rules 2008 r5(3)(a).
188 TP(UT) Rules 2008 r21.
189 TP(UT) Rules 2008 r23.
190 TP(UT) Rules 2008 rr24 and 25.

the hearing, the UT will principally be concerned with legal issues rather than the merits of the case in determining whether the decision of the FTT acted lawfully. The decision-maker may have legal representation.

7.143　　The UT can uphold the FTT decision (where it believes the decision was lawful), 'remit' the case for a new decision by another FTT Panel (where it believes the decision was unlawful, but does not have enough evidence to make its own decision) or substitute its own decision (where it believes the decision was unlawful and it has enough evidence to make its own decision).[191] The decision may be given at the hearing itself or at a later stage in writing, with detailed reasons also following in writing.[192]

7.144　　As with the FTT decision, the UT decision may be set aside[193] or superseded. In addition, it may be possible to appeal the UT decision to the Court of Appeal[194] or apply for judicial review of the decision. Legal representation is likely to be needed for these purposes. Advice can be sought from solicitors' firms or law centres or from some of the organisations listed below.

Further sources of advice and support

7.145　As may be seen from the contents of this chapter, benefits law is extensive and complex, and the information set out above can only serve as an introduction to the subject. Further contact with some of the numerous bodies providing advocacy, advice and assistance in this field may be of help in relation to a claim for benefits or other financial support. Among these organisations are the following:

Disability Alliance

This organisation provides information on social security benefits, tax credits and social care to disabled people, their families, carers and professional advisers. For help or information go to www.disabilityalliance.org. Their postal address is Universal House, 88–94 Wentworth Street, London E1 7SA and telephone number is 020 7247 8759.

191　TCEA 2007 s12.
192　TP(UT) Rules 2008 r40.
193　TP(UT) Rules 2008 r43.
194　TCEA 2007 s13.

The Benefits Enquiry Line

This is a telephone helpline giving information on benefits for sick and disabled people, their representatives and carers, run by the DWP (in Northern Ireland, it is run by the Social Security Agency). The helpline also offers help filling out claim forms over the phone for applications for disability living allowance. In England, Wales and Scotland, the telephone number is 0800 88 22 00 (textphone: 0800 24 33 55). The Benefit Enquiry Line is open 8.30 am to 6.30 pm Monday to Friday and 9.00 am to 1.00 pm Saturday. In Northern Ireland, phone: 0800 220674.

The Citizens' Advice Bureau

There are about 3,300 CAB service outlets across the UK. To find your local one, check their website at www.citizensadvice.org.uk/.

Disability Law Service

This is a service providing legal advice to disabled people in the UK (although it only provides welfare advice to those within Greater London). Their phone number is 020 7791 9800 (Monday to Friday 10.00 am to 5 pm); fax: 020 7791 9802; e-mail: advice@dls.org.uk. Address: Disability Law Service, 39–45 Cavell Street, London E1 2BP.

Transition Information Network – www.transitioninfonetwork.org.uk

TIN is an alliance of organisations and individuals which provides advice and support for disabled young people making the transition to adulthood. Their website is www.transitioninfonetwork.org.uk and their address is Council for Disabled Children, 8 Wakley Street, London EC1V 7QE.

Dial UK – www.dialuk.info

This is a UK-wide network of local Disability Information and Advice Line services (DIALs), run by and for disabled people and providing information and advice on all aspects of living with a disability. Its website is www.dialuk.info.

7.146 Local welfare support units within local authorities may also be able to help disabled children and their families access welfare benefits. Legal assistance from a solicitors' firm may be advisable if a challenge is being considered. While paying a solicitor privately is likely to be expensive, it may be possible to be represented for free on the legal help scheme if the means test is passed.

Carers

Key points

- Carers who are the family or friends of disabled children ('carers') are entitled to separate carers' assessments – although in practice their needs are generally addressed during the disabled child's assessment.
- The purpose of a parent carer's assessment is (1) to help sustain their caring role (by ensuring that the local authority support provided to disabled child is adequate) and (2) to support parent carers to work or to access education, training or leisure facilities.
- A carer's assessment should provide an opportunity for a 'private discussion' in which carers can candidly express their views.
- When assessing the needs of a carer, care managers should not assume a willingness by the carer to continue caring, or continue to provide the same level of support.
- If the carer's assessment identifies a critical or substantial risk (for example, that the caring role may jeopardise continued involvement in employment or a significant relationship) then there is an obligation on the authority to take steps to prevent this risk occurring.
- The Childcare Act 2006 requires local authorities to take action to secure sufficient childcare services exist to meet the needs of parents of disabled children in their area.
- A range of carer specific employment protection rights exist, such as the right to take emergency and parental leave, to request flexible working arrangements and for carers not to be treated less favourably because of their caring responsibilities.
- Local authorities are empowered to provide a wide range of support services and equipment for carers.
- Where a parent carer is a disabled person, the statutory guidance advises that their community care assessment and care plan should provide for adequate supports in order to help them discharge their role as a parent.
- Although young carers are entitled to separate carers' assessments, in practice their needs are generally considered by way of a Children Act 1989 'child in need' assessment.
- The purpose of a young carer's assessment is to ensure that the young carer is not undertaking inappropriate caring roles.
- The young carer's assessment should ensure that the support provided to the disabled person is sufficient so as to avoid the need for a young person to have to provide such care.

Introduction[1]

8.1   Families and friends provide the vast majority of most disabled children's care, and it is well recognised that these caring roles can have adverse impacts in a range of areas (see paras 1.36–1.42 above). Throughout this chapter, we refer to the family and friends of disabled children who provide care to them as 'carers'. This definition excludes paid care workers. The evidence suggests, for instance, that carers lose an average of over £11,000 a year by taking on significant caring responsibilities;[2] that over half of all carers have a caring related health condition;[3] and that in consequence carers represent one of the UKs most socially excluded groups of people.[4] For parent carers the situation is no less bleak: a 2010 survey of 1,113 parent carers, found that due to financial difficulties, 23 per cent were going without heating, 14 per cent without food and 73 per cent without leisure and days out.[5]

8.2   Binding policy guidance[6] requires that when an assessment is being undertaken by children's services of a disabled child's needs (see paras 3.14–3.15) the views and attributes of all people providing care are taken into account. In addition, where a carer is providing – or intending to provide – 'a substantial amount of care on a regular basis', then the local authority must inform that person of their right to request a carer's assessment.[7]

8.3   Three Acts, all originating as Private Members Bills, have created the legal framework to protect carers' rights. These are the Carers (Recognition and Services) Act 1995, the Carers and Disabled Children Act 2000 and the Carers (Equal Opportunities) Act 2004 – abbreviated in this chapter to the CRSA 1995, the CDCA 2000 and the CEOA 2004 respectively. These Acts are primarily directed at those carers who are providing (or intending to provide) regular and

---

1   The material in this chapter draws heavily from L Clements, *Carers and their rights*, 3rd edn, Carers UK, 2009 ('Clements, 2009'), accessible at www.carersuk.org/Professionals/ResourcesandBriefings/Carersandtheirrights.

2   Carers UK, *Out of pocket: the financial impact of caring*, Carers UK, 2007.

3   Carers UK, *Missed opportunities: the impact of new rights for carers*, Carers UK, 2003.

4   Office of the Deputy Prime Minister, *Breaking the cycle: taking stock of progress and priorities for the future. A report by the Social Exclusion Unit*, 2004, para 6.17.

5   Contact a Family, *Counting the costs*, 2010.

6   Department of Health, *Framework for the assessment of children in need and their families*, 2000.

7   Carers (Recognition and Services) Act 1995 s1(2B) inserted by Carers (Equal Opportunities) Act 2004 s1.

substantial care (the meaning of 'regular' and 'substantial' is considered below).

8.4　It is not only people with parental responsibility for disabled children who provide regular and substantial care, and in consequence, are entitled to a separate carers' assessment. Many other friends and family members may provide this level of support, not least any of the disabled child's siblings. Carers who are under 18 years of age are generally referred to as 'young carers' and are considered separately below.

The duty to undertake a carer's assessment

8.5　A primary purpose of a carer's assessment is to ensure that the person's caring role does not become unsustainable. For this reason, the outcome of such an assessment will normally be action to ensure that the care services that the disabled child is receiving are sufficient to avoid this risk. If there is a risk of the caring role becoming unsustainable, then the local authority may have to provide additional support, for example services and/or equipment for the disabled child under the Chronically Sick and Disabled Persons Act 1970 or the Children Act 1989 (considered at paras 3.48–3.57 and 3.58–3.62 above) which thereby safeguard the wellbeing of the carer. Sometimes, however, the outcome which will ensure the carer's role is sustainable might be to give the carer a service and/or equipment in their own right: such 'carers' services' are considered separately below.

8.6　As noted in chapter 3 (para 3.14 above), assessments under the *Framework for the assessment of children in need and their families*[8] must be family centred and take full account of the capacities of those caring for the child. In addition, carers who are providing (or intending to provide) 'a substantial amount of care on a regular basis' have a right to request a 'carer's assessment'[9] under the CRSA 1995 s1(2). For people with parental responsibility for the child the right is duplicated by virtue of CDCA 2000 s6.

8　Department of Health, *Framework for the assessment of children in need and their families*, 2000; very similar guidance has been issued in Wales by the Welsh Assembly, *Framework for assessing children in need and their families*, 2001; Welsh Assembly, *Assessing children in need and their families: practice guidance*, 2001. although in this chapter, reference is made to the English guidance.

9　CRSA 1995 s1(2B) inserted by CEOA 2004 s1.

8.7 There is no statutory definition as to what constitutes 'regular' care or what amount of care is sufficiently 'substantial' to qualify a carer for the right to an assessment. The word 'regular' almost certainly adds little, since it connotes an activity that 'recurs at intervals' and does not mean 'frequent'. The conception of what is 'substantial' is, however, important and it is clear from the practice guidance issued under the various Carers Acts that the question is subjective: essentially 'what is the impact that the caring role is having on the person providing the care?' While this may be capable of being assessed in terms of the number of hours a carer is 'caring' – it will only be one test, since even a short period of care (particularly if it is arduous) may, for some people have a substantial impact on their well-being. Guidance to the CDCA 2000 states:[10]

> it is not only the time spent each week caring that has an impact on carers ... For some ... such as those caring for adults with severe mental health problems, caring can be a sporadic or cyclical responsibility. The carer may not be physically or practically caring at all at certain times, but still be anxious and stressed waiting for, or actively seeking to prevent, the next crisis. ... Any assessment of the carer's need for support has to look at the impact of the whole caring situation.

8.8 Since none of the Carers Acts include a requirement (found in social security law) that the care provided to the disabled child must be 'substantially in excess of the normal requirements of persons of his age'[11] it follows that virtually every parent of a disabled child is eligible for a separate carer's assessment.

8.9 In general, however, it should not be necessary for a parent carer to have a separate carer's assessment since a properly conducted assessment under the *Framework for the assessment of children in need and their families* should address all aspects of the parent carer's individual needs – for example, their need to work, to participate in training, education, leisure and other activities. Guidance issued by the Social Care Institute for Excellence for the CDCA 2000 and the CEOA 2004 advises (at para 71):[12]

10 Department of Health, *Carers and Disabled Children Act 2000: carers and people with parental responsibility for disabled children: practice guidance*, 2000, para 67; National Assembly for Wales *Guidance 2000 Act*, 2001, para 4.1.1.

11 Social Security Contributions and Benefits Act 1992 s72(6): see para 7.16.

12 This approach is recommended by the SCIE *Practice guide to the Carers (Equal Opportunities) Act 2004*, 2005, para 1. The guidance has the status of Department of Health practice guidance: see statement by Liam Byrne MP, Parliamentary Under Secretary of State for Care Services, *Hansard* 11 Jul 2005 col 722W.

the assessment should take account of the parent's ability to provide or continue to provide care for the child and consideration of whether they work, or undertake any education, training or leisure activity or wish to do so. This means that local authorities have a duty to ask carers about these activities and take their wishes into account when planning the care package.

8.10   However, if a local authority is failing to meet the obligations created by the Carers Acts in its assessments for disabled children (for example, it is failing to assess needs and put in place services to support carers who wish to remain in or return to work or want to take part in leisure, training or education activities) then the carer may have to insist on having a separate carer's assessment under the CRSA 1995 and CDCA 2000.

8.11   Furthermore, the right of a carer to a carer's assessment is not dependent upon the disabled child being assessed or entitled to services and/or equipment. Accordingly if a disabled child is being denied local authority support (or if there is delay in implementing any such support) a request for a separate carer's assessment by the family carer may also serve a useful purpose.

8.12   In such cases it will be maladministration for a local authority not to undertake a separate carer's assessment or to suggest that to do so is merely a 'goodwill gesture'.[13] *R (LH and MH) v Lambeth LBC*[14] illustrates the problems that can arise in this context. Although, in this case, the local authority accepted that the parent's mental and physical health was being adversely affected by her very substantial caring role, the care plan for her son omitted mention of how her needs would be addressed. The court declared that the local authority was in breach of its assessment obligations under the CA 1989 (to the child) and under the CRSA 1995 and the CDCA 2000 (to the mother).

8.13   Young carers may also face a similar problem in having their needs properly addressed. The 1995 and 2004 Acts apply to all carers, irrespective of their age, and so a young carer who is providing a substantial amount of care on a regular basis is, at law, entitled to a separate carer's assessment under the 1995 Act. In most cases, however, it will be more appropriate for their needs to be addressed under CA 1989[15] – ie by way of an assessment under the *Framework for the*

13   Public Service Ombudsman (Wales) Complaint No B2004/0707/S/370 against Swansea City Council, 22 February 2007, para 131.

14   [2006] EWHC 1190 (Admin).

15   SCIE, *Practice guide to the Carers (Equal Opportunities) Act 2004*, 2005.

assessment of children in need and their families. Legally, however, the young carer is entitled to have a separate carer's assessment, and this might be demanded if (again) an authority is failing to meet the obligations created by the Carers Acts in its assessments for the child as a child 'in need' (for example, it is failing to support a young carer who wishes to work or to take part in leisure, training or education activities).

The nature of a carer's assessment

8.14 Specific guidance has been issued in England and Wales as to how carers' assessments should be undertaken.[16]

8.15 Guidance on the CRSA 1995 ('the 1995 guidance') emphasises the importance of carers having the opportunity to have their assessments in the absence of the disabled person, so as to provide an 'opportunity for private discussion in which carers can candidly express their views'.[17] This should not be read as establishing a presumption that the interests of the carer and the person cared for will conflict, but simply as part of the need to recognise the dignity and autonomy of the carer as well as the disabled child being cared for.

8.16 The key objective of a carer's assessment is, as noted above, to ensure that the caring role does not become unsustainable. The English practice guidance[18] suggests that in determining what is 'sustainable' four dimensions of the carers' experience should be considered, namely:

- autonomy;
- health and safety;
- managing daily routines; and
- involvement.

8.17 In relation to the idea of 'autonomy', the guidance emphasises the importance of carers believing they have options/choices and are not

16 Department of Health, *Practitioners guide to carers' assessments under the Carers and Disabled Children Act 2000*, 2001 and Welsh Assembly, *Practitioners guide to carers' assessments*, 2001.

17 Department of Health, *Carers (Recognition and Services) Act 1995: practice guidance*, 1996, LAC (96)7, para 9.1 and, in Wales, as Welsh Office, *Carers (Recognition and Services) Act 1995 practice guidance*, 1996, WOC 16/96 and WHC (96)21.

18 Department of Health, *Carers and Disabled Children Act 2000: carers and people with parental responsibility for disabled children: practice guidance*, 2001, para 60.

trapped and isolated by their caring responsibilities. In this respect the 1995 guidance states:

> In assessing the carer's ability to care or continue to care, care managers should not assume a willingness by the carer to continue caring, or continue to provide the same level of support. They will wish to bear in mind the distinction between caring about someone and caring for them. Many carers continue to care deeply about a person even though their ability to care for them may change.

8.18   The domain of health and safety reflects its importance and the known impact of caring on the health and well-being of many parents of disabled children, see paras 1.40–1.47 above.

8.19   In relation to the carers' ability to 'manage daily routines' and their 'involvement', the guidance places particular emphasis on the impact that other responsibilities and aspirations may have on the well-being of the carer – for example, other caring responsibilities, the desire to participate in training, education and leisure activities and the need to maintain personal and social relationships. As we note in chapter 1 (paras 1.31–1.34 above) families caring for disabled children are more likely to experience significant poverty and other forms of deprivation, are likely to experience severe difficulties in maintaining employment and also have a higher incidence of lone parenthood. The likelihood of all of these known risks arising or being present should be considered during a carer's assessment.

The outcome of a carer's assessment

8.20   The purpose of a carer's assessment is to assess the risks of the caring role becoming unsustainable – and in this respect, practice guidance[19] requires social services departments to grade the 'extent of risk to the sustainability of the caring role' into one of four categories – namely 'critical, substantial, moderate and low'. These bands reflect those used in determining eligibility for adult social care generally.[20] The critical and substantial bands in the practice guidance are:

---

19 Department of Health, *Carers and Disabled Children Act 2000: carers and people with parental responsibility for disabled children: practice guidance*, 2001, para 70.

20 Department of Health, *Prioritising need in the context of putting people first: a whole system approach to eligibility for social care – guidance on eligibility criteria for adult social care, England 2010*, 2010.

Critical

- Critical risk to sustainability of the caring role arises when:
  - their life may be threatened;
  - major health problems have developed or will develop;
  - there is, or will be, an extensive loss of autonomy for the carer in decisions about the nature of tasks they will perform and how much time they will give to their caring role;
  - there is, or will be, an inability to look after their own domestic needs and other daily routines while sustaining their caring role;
  - involvement in employment or other responsibilities is, or will be, at risk;
  - many significant social support systems and relationships are, or will be, at risk.

Substantial

- Substantial risk to sustainability of the caring role arises when:
  - significant health problems have developed or will develop;
  - there is, or will be, some significant loss of autonomy for the carer in decisions about the nature of tasks they will perform and how much time they will give to their caring role;
  - there is, or will be, an inability to look after some of their own domestic needs and other daily routines while sustaining their caring role;
  - involvement in some significant aspects of employment or other responsibilities is, or will be, at risk;
  - some significant social support systems and relationships are, or will be, at risk.

8.21 If there is a critical or a substantial risk that a caring role will become unsustainable then there is almost certainly an obligation on the authority to take steps to ensure that this does not occur.[21] The nature of this obligation has been explained by the Commission for Social Care Inspection in the following terms:[22]

> there is a duty to address carers' eligible needs but discretion about whether to meet these through carers services or community care services – however, some practitioners appear to think [incorrectly] the discretion is about whether to help carers.

21 See, in this respect, SCIE, *Practice guide to the Carers (Equal Opportunities) Act 2004*, 2005, which (at p8) states that 'identification of a critical risk in a Carers' Act assessment triggers a local authority obligation to make an appropriate response to address this risk' and see also in this respect the comments made at chapter 3, para 3.46iv and v in relation to the duty to provide services to children in need.

22 Commission for Social Care Inspection, *Cutting the cake fairly: CSCI review of eligibility criteria for social care*, 2008, para 3.22.

8.22   To meet this duty, the local authority would be able to provide support services – for example, additional home and/or community based care and/or equipment for the disabled child (under the duties imposed by the Chronically Sick and Disabled Persons Act 1970 or the Children Act (CA) 1989 (see paras 3.48–3.57 and 3.58–3.62 above) which would of course indirectly support the carer. In the alternative, the authority may decide it is necessary to provide specific services or support to the carer, particularly if they have social care needs of their own.

Carers' support in employment, education, training and leisure activities

8.23   Carers have the right to have their employment, training, education and leisure aspirations addressed: it is no longer acceptable for a local authority to advise a parent that he or she should not expect to work, for example, because childcare is 'the responsibility of the parents, whether or not children have a disability'.[23] The practice guidance[24] states that all carers 'should be supported to stay in work or return to work where this is what they want' and:[25]

> People with parental responsibility for disabled children will also benefit from joining or re-joining the workforce. Such carers often face difficulties re-entering the workforce because of lack of suitable child-care services. Many parents of disabled children would like to return to work and, if they were able to do so, would benefit socially and emotionally as well as financially.

8.24   As has already been noted (see para 1.50 above) a problem faced by carers in their desire to work or participate in education or activities, is the lack of childcare facilities that have the capacity to meet their child's particular needs. Not infrequently the traditional services (such as day nurseries, after-school clubs and holiday play-schemes) do not have appropriate provision for disabled children. In relation to these difficulties, the legislation places specific and strategic obligations on local authorities.

---

23 Public Service Ombudsman (Wales) Complaint No B2004/0707/S/370 against Swansea City Council, 22 February 2007, para 78.

24 Department of Health *Carers and Disabled Children Act 2000: carers and people with parental responsibility for disabled children: practice guidance*, 2001, para 35.

25 Department of Health *Carers and Disabled Children Act 2000: carers and people with parental responsibility for disabled children: practice guidance*, 2001, para 36.

8.25   At the individual level, if an assessment identifies, for example, a risk to employment then this equates to a 'critical' risk (see para 8.20) and in consequence, is a situation that requires positive intervention by social services to address this risk. In addition, policy guidance issued by the Department of Health in 2005[26] stresses the duty on local authorities, during the assessment process, to ask carers about their wish to work, or undertake any education, training or leisure activities and to:

> take their wishes into account when planning the care package. For example, the package may provide the possibility of freeing some leisure time for the carer and for other children in the family through a structured playtime with the disabled child, while social services provides services to run the house. The local authority must take assessments carried out under section 6 of the 2000 Act into account when deciding what services, if any, to provide under section 17 of the Children Act 1989.

Childcare Act 2006

8.26   At the strategic level, the Childcare Act 2006 requires English and Welsh local authorities[27] to secure, 'so far as is reasonably practicable', sufficient childcare to meet the needs of parents of disabled children in their area who require childcare in order to work or to undertake training or education to prepare for work. In determining whether the provision of childcare is sufficient, councils must have regard to (among other things) the childcare needs of parents who are eligible for the childcare element of the working tax credit. The duty to secure sufficient childcare suitable for disabled children has been augmented in England[28] by significant central government investment under the Aiming High for Disabled Children programme.[29]

---

26 Department of Health *Carers and Disabled Children Act 2000 and Carers (Equal Opportunities) Act 2004: combined policy guidance*, 2005, para 71.

27 Childcare Act 2006 s6 (England) and s22 (Wales).

28 In Wales, guidance on the 2006 Act has been published as WAGC 013/2008 *Guidance to local authorities – Childcare Act 2006*, Guidance Circular No 008/2008.

29 HM Treasury/DfES, *Aiming high for disabled children*, 2007, para 4.32.

Carers' statutory employment rights

8.27   As noted in chapter 1 (see para 1.39) carers of disabled children experience considerable difficulties remaining in paid work, and specific
legislative provisions exist to address this problem. These employment rights are dealt with in detail by Clements[30] and in summary
comprise:

a) *Emergency leave employment rights*
   The right, under Employment Rights Act (ERA) 1996 s57A, of a
   carer to take unpaid time off work to care for a dependent where
   the need has arisen due to an unexpected or to a particularly pressing occurrence. In such situations the carer is required to notify
   the employer of the reason for the absence as soon as practicable
   and as to how long it is likely to last.

b) *Parental leave*
   Regulations[31] made pursuant to the ERA 1996 entitle parents who
   have worked for their employer for more than a year to take parental leave (generally unpaid) of up to 18 weeks for a disabled
   child (born after 14 December 1999) for whom disability living
   allowance (DLA) is paid or of up to 13 weeks for a child under five
   for whom no DLA is paid. The leave can be taken in periods of up
   to four weeks a year.

c) *Flexible working rights*
   ERA 1996 s80F[32] entitles parents of disabled children who have
   worked for their employer for at least 26 weeks to ask their employer to make changes to their working arrangements – ie to
   change the hours they work. Employers are only able to refuse
   such requests for specified reasons – generally by given a convincing reason why this would cause harm to their business. Regulations[33] detail the procedure for making the application and the
   consequences of so applying.

---

30 Clements, 2009. See fn 1.
31 Maternity and Parental Leave etc Regulations 1999 SI No 3312, Maternity and
    Parental Leave (Amendment) Regulations 2001 SI No 4010 and Maternity
    and Parental Leave etc and the Paternity and Adoption Leave (Amendment)
    Regulations 2008 SI No 1966.
32 Amended by Work and Families Act 2006 s12.
33 Flexible Working (Eligibility, Complaints and Remedies) Regulations 2002
    SI No 3236 as amended by Flexible Working (Eligibility, Complaints and
    Remedies) (Amendment) Regulations 2006 SI No 3314 and Flexible Working
    (Eligibility, Complaints and Remedies) (Amendment) Regulations 2007 SI No
    1184.

d) *Discriminatory treatment against carers*

In certain situations, treating parent carers less favourably because of their caring role can constitute what has come to be termed unlawful 'discrimination by association'. Such behaviour was held, by the European Court of Justice in *Coleman v Attridge Law*,[34] to be capable of contravening the EU Equal Treatment Framework Directive 2000/78/EC. In that case, the applicant claimed that she had been treated less favourably by her employers because of her caring responsibilities for her disabled son. In order to ensure that the judgment is properly reflected in UK law, section 13 of the Equality Act 2010 makes unlawful such associative discrimination – and this provision is considered at para 9.18 below.

Carers' services

8.28   As a matter of law, there is a distinction to be made between support services that are (1) provided directly to a carer and those that are (2) provided to a disabled child and which have a 'knock on' benefit to the carer. Respite or short break care, for example, is a service delivered to disabled children (eg in the form of a sitting service or a residential or temporary foster placement – see paras 3.50 and 3.59–3.62 above) which may benefit their carers by giving them a break from their caring role. At law the service is given to the disabled child (and in the above examples, it would be either under Chronically Sick and Disabled Persons Act 1970 s2 or the CA 1989) and so would be a disabled person's service.

8.29   There is no specific provision in any of the Carers Acts that empowers a local authority to provide services for carers of disabled children (unlike for carers of adults[35]). CA 1989 s17(3) provides, however, that any services that can be provided under this section may also be:

> provided for the family of a particular child in need or for any member of his family, if it is provided with a view to safeguarding or promoting the child's welfare.

8.30   Any service, equipment or payment that could sustain a family member's caring role would clearly come within CA 1989 s17(3). In relation

---

34 *Coleman v Attridge Law* (C-303/06) (2008) All ER (EC) 1105 ECJ (Grand Chamber): see para 9.4 below.

35 Carers and Disabled Children Act 2000 s2 – and for general analysis of this provision, see Clements, 2009, chapter 5, see fn 1.

to carers of adults, Clements[36] provides a lists of some of the supports that have been cited in official guidance that can fulfil this function, and these would all appear to be capable of being provided under CA 1989 s17(3). The list comprises:[37]

- trips (such as holidays or special events);
- driving lessons;
- travel assistance (including, for instance, help with taxi fares);
- training;
- laundry;
- gardening;
- help with housework;
- moving and handling classes;
- mobile phone;
- taxis to work to maximise the carer's time;
- a short holiday for the carer to enable them to have time to themselves;
- a computer for a carer who could not access computer services from a local library because he felt unable to leave the person he cared for;
- repairs/insurance costs for a car, where transport is crucial to the caring role;
- entry phone with audio/video system where the carer lives in a two-storey house and has mobility problems;
- £500 contribution to a flight for a grandmother to come from another country and care for a woman with MS – where the local homecare service could not deliver the necessary care.

Disabled parents

8.31   As noted in chapter 1 (para 1.40) it appears that a disproportionate number of disabled children have a disabled parent. The research evidence also strongly suggests that many such parents are dissatisfied with the way they are treated by the health and social care agencies.[38] In part, these difficulties appear to arise because the local authorities are unsure whether their adult or children's services should 'lead'

36 Clements, 2009. See fn 1.
37 Clements, 2009, para 5.25. See fn 1.
38 See, for instance, J Morris and M Wates, *SCIE Guide 19: Working together to support disabled parents*, SCIE, 2007 and R Olsen and H Tyers, *Think parent: supporting disabled adults as parents*, National Family and Parenting Institute, 2004.

in any given situation and which has budgetary responsibility. As a general rule the research and guidance concludes that the approach should be to 'think parent',[39] in the sense that if the parent's health and community care needs are recognised (one domain of which will be their need to discharge their parenting role) then this may address many of the child's specific care needs – particularly if the statutory agencies work collaboratively and make the most of their ability to respond flexibly.[40] However, 'thinking parent' should not minimise the duty to assess and meet the needs of the disabled child, as set out in chapter 3.

8.32 Department of Health[41] and National Assembly for Wales[42] guidance stresses that where a disabled child has a disabled parent, the family's needs which arise out of the parent's disability should in many cases be treated as an adult care services' responsibility and addressed in the context of the parent's community care assessment. The English 2010 policy guidance for example, states that:[43]

> in the course of assessing an individual's needs, councils should recognise that adults, who have parenting responsibilities for a child under 18 years, may require help with these responsibilities.

8.33 Practice guidance amplifies this advice, stating that although it will be a matter for professional judgment as to whether the CA 1989 or the adult community care assessment route should be chosen:[44]

> In exercising that judgement, professionals should bear in mind that the provision of services that assist disabled parents who need support in bringing up their children is often the most effective means of promoting the welfare of the children. Even though children may be well-cared for in domestic situation, an adult parent's well-being could be

---

39 R Olsen and H Tyers, *Think parent: supporting disabled adults as parents*, National Family and Parenting Institute, 2004.

40 R Olsen and H Tyers, *Think parent: supporting disabled adults as parents*, National Family and Parenting Institute, 2004.

41 Department of Health, *Prioritising need in the context of putting people first: a whole system approach to eligibility for social care. guidance on eligibility criteria for adult social care, England 2010*, 2010, para 26.

42 Welsh Assembly Government, *Creating a unified and fair system for assessing and managing care*, 2002, 09/2002 and 09A/2002, p65.

43 Department of Health, *Prioritising need in the context of putting people first: a whole system approach to eligibility for social care. guidance on eligibility criteria for adult social care, England 2010*, 2010, para 26.

44 Department of Health *Fair access to care services practice guidance*, 2003 Q4.2 (and see also Q.41). In Wales the relevant guidance is in Welsh Assembly Government *Creating a unified and fair system for assessing and managing care*, 2002, 09/2002 and 09A/2002, pp65–66.

undermined, and problems exacerbated, if s/he is not able to fulfil the parenting roles s/he aspires to. For this reason, 'parenting roles and responsibilities' fall into those elements of the eligibility framework ... dealing with family and other social roles and responsibilities.

Young carers

8.34   'Young carer' is the term that describes a person under the age of 18 who provides care for another person: either an adult or another child. Given the high support needs of some disabled children, not infrequently their siblings will be drawn into caring roles. Given the disproportionate number of disabled children who have a disabled parent, it may be that children in such cases may have to fulfil more than one caring role.

8.35   As noted above (see para 8.4) the CRSA 1995 covers carers of any age, and so young carers who are providing (or intending to provide) a substantial amount of care on a regular basis to a disabled sibling (or anyone else) are entitled to a separate carer's assessment under that Act.[45] It will generally (but not always) be appropriate for the young carer's needs to be assessed under the CA 1989[46] – ie by way of an assessment under the *Framework for the assessment of children in need and their families* (see paras 3.14–3.15).

8.36   Although the term 'young carers' appears in no legislation, the CA 1989 conception of a child 'in need' is of direct relevance to this group. As noted above (see para 3.5) section 17(1) of the CA 1989 places a duty on local authorities to safeguard and promote the welfare of such children. Many young carers will fit more than one category of children 'in need', as the definition[47] encompasses not only a disabled child but also any child who, without the provision of services by the local authority is either:

- unlikely to achieve or maintain, or to have the opportunity of achieving or maintaining, a reasonable standard of health or development; or
- whose health or development is likely to be significantly impaired, or further impaired.

---

45 The carer assessment (and services) rights under the Carers and Disabled Children Act 2000 are limited to carers aged 16 or over who are providing care for a person aged 18 or over.

46 SCIE, *Practice guide to the Carers (Equal Opportunities) Act 2004*, 2005.

47 CA 1989 s17(10).

8.37 Young carers who provide inappropriate amounts of care will, self evidently, be at risk of having their 'physical, intellectual, emotional, social or behavioural development'[48] impaired or indeed of actually suffering harm as a consequence. This point is underscored by the policy guidance to the CRSA 1995[49] which stated that 'many young carers with significant caring responsibilities should therefore be seen as children in need'.

Supporting young carers

8.38 Although the Carers Acts seek to promote the well-being of carers by seeking to help them access employment, education and recreational opportunities, they also seek to sustain the caring role. This is not the case, however, with young carers for whom the policy approach is to ensure that their ordinary childhood experiences are not diminished and their development is not impaired, by having to care for another. Such an aspiration is simply incompatible with the provision of substantial amounts of care to another family member.

8.39 If a child becomes a young carer, this is generally evidence of a care planning failure by the local authority – a failure to ensure that the disabled person's support services and equipment are sufficient to meet his or her needs without having to rely on the young carer. The *Framework for the assessment of children in need and their families* expresses this important difference by stressing the importance of local authorities taking steps to bring to an end the inappropriate caring in such cases – that (at para 3.62):

> Young carers should not be expected to carry inappropriate levels of caring which have an adverse impact on their development and life chances. It should not be assumed that children should take on similar levels of caring responsibilities as adults.

8.40 Many local authorities fund semi-independent (or at least 'arm's length') 'Young Carers Projects' which offer direct support and advice to the young people themselves, act as a conduit for supporting families in which there are young carers and also provide an opportunity for families to express the difficulties they are experiencing, without

48 The definition deriving from CA 1989 s17(11).
49 Department of Health, *Carers (Recognition and Services) Act 1995: practice guidance*, 1996, LAC (96)7, para 14 and in Wales as Welsh Office, *Carers (Recognition and Services) Act 1995 practice guidance*, 1996, WOC 16/96 and WHC (96)21, para 14 – both citing guidance issued by the Social Services Inspectorate, namely Guidance letter CI (95)12, Annex A, para 1.1.

the immediate worry that this might lead, as some fear, to intervention by the local authorities 'child protection' agencies.[50] While young carers' projects continue to be a respected resource for many young people, there has been an increasing recognition that they should not be the only service for young carers and their families. For a number of years, it has been accepted as best practice that provision to safeguard young carers and meet their needs should be embedded into local planning for all children and their families.[51]

Conclusion

8.41   As has just been stated, the object of services for young carers should be to bring their caring role to an end. This is a fundamentally different objective than for adult carers, where the objective is generally to help sustain the caring role. However, it must be borne in mind that all carers (child or adult) have a right to refuse to care. The often unseen work done by carers is all too easily taken for granted and authorities may find that a failure to meet their obligations to adult carers at an early stage may be a false economy if they are left to meet the full care needs of a disabled child when their friends and family feel no longer able to carry on caring.

---

50   See, for example, J Frank, *Making it work: good practice with young carers and their families*, The Children's Society and the Princess Royal Trust for Carers, 2002 and J Frank and J McLarnon, *Young carers and their families: key principles of practice. Supportive practice guidance for those working directly with, or commissioning services for young carers and their families*, The Children's Society, 2008.

51   See, for example, Princess Royal Trust for Carers and The Children's Society, *A guide to including young carers and their families in your local Children and Young People's Plan*, 2009 and Princess Royal Trust for Carers, *Delivering Every Child Matters for young carers*, 2006.

CHAPTER 9

Equality and non-discrimination

continued

Key points

- Disabled children have had the benefit of protection from discrimination under the Disability Discrimination Act (DDA) 1995 for the past 15 years.
- Despite this, disabled children remain routinely excluded and treated less favourably than others in many areas of public life.
- The Equality Act (EA) 2010 comes into force from October 2010 and replaces the DDA 1995 and other previous equality legislation.
- The EA 2010 outlaws a wide range of discriminatory treatment, alongside harassment and victimisation.
- Discrimination will also generally include a failure to make reasonable adjustments so that disabled children are not placed at a substantial disadvantage compared with non-disabled children.
- As well as discrimination against disabled children, family and friends of disabled children will be protected from 'discrimination by association'.
- The new duties will cover every area of public life, including schools and service providers.
- The prohibition of discrimination is supported by a powerful single equality duty and a general power to take 'positive action' to support the achievement of equality.
- Enforcement action in relation to most of the duties under the EA 2010 can be taken in the county court. However, breaches of the schools duties must be dealt with by the First-tier Tribunal or by an exclusion or admission appeals panel.

Introduction

9.1   Disabled children in England and Wales have had formal legal protection against discrimination since the enactment of the Disability Discrimination Act (DDA) 1995. However, disabled children still experience routine exclusion from many parts of public life – whether through being denied access to school trips on alleged health and safety grounds or being told that a playground doesn't have equipment that they are able to use. The vision of ordinary lives for disabled children enshrined in the Children Act 1989 (see chapter 3) requires disabled children to be able to access every opportunity available to non-disabled children. This chapter is about the legislation which seeks to ensure that this happens – previously the DDA 1995, but now the Equality Act (EA) 2010. Any reference in this chapter to a section or schedule is, unless the context shows otherwise, a reference to a section in or schedule to the EA 2010.

9.2   This book is being published at a watershed moment for equalities law in the UK. On 8 April 2010, the EA 2010 received royal assent after completing its passage through parliament. The EA 2010 came into force in October 2010, when this book published. The Equality and Human Rights Commission (EHRC)[1] states that the purpose of the EA 2010 is to produce a 'modern, single legal framework, providing clearer, streamlined law that is more effective at tackling disadvantage and discrimination'.[2] However, in many respects the EA 2010 codifies and builds on rather than replacing previous legislation, most importantly here the DDA 1995 and its amendments (collectively 'the DDA scheme'). This chapter therefore focuses on the provisions of the EA 2010 and its related codes of practice and guidance but also draws out the key themes of the previous DDA scheme and some of the judgments made under it.

The DDA scheme and transition to the Equality Act 2010

9.3   Protection from discrimination against disabled children in relation to their disabilities was first introduced by the DDA 1995 and then extended by the Special Educational Needs and Disability Act (SENDA) 2001 and the Disability Discrimination Act (DDA) 2005. The DDA scheme followed earlier legislation prohibiting discrimination on the grounds of sex[3] and race.[4] Under the DDA scheme, disabled people (including disabled children) were protected from a number of different forms of discrimination in a wide range of contexts, for example, in the provision of goods and services, education, performance of public authority functions and so on.

9.4   The provisions of the DDA scheme (and now the EA 2010) must also be understood in the light of European law on non-discrimination. This was made clearly apparent by the judgment of the Grand Chamber

---

1   Created by the Equality Act 2006 and replacing (among other bodies) the Disability Rights Commission.

2   See www.equalityhumanrights.com/legislative-framework/equality-bill/.

3   Sex Discrimination Act 1972.

4   Race Relations Act 1976.

of the European Court of Justice (ECJ) in *Coleman v Attridge Law*.[5] The case examined how a European Framework Directive[6] which required member states to introduce measures to combat discrimination on various grounds (including disability), should be interpreted. The ECJ held that the directive prohibited discrimination against persons *associated with* a disabled person (in Sharon Coleman's case, as a parent of a disabled child). In particular, the ECJ held[7] that:

> Where it is established that the ... harassment which is suffered by an employee who is not himself disabled is related to the disability of his child, whose care is provided primarily by that employee, such conduct is contrary to the prohibition of harassment laid down by [the Framework Directive].

9.5   The judgment of the ECJ in *Coleman v Attridge Law* has been reflected in the EA 2010: see para 9.18. The EA 2010 must also be interpreted in the context of the Human Rights Act 1998 and the European Convention on Human Rights (ECHR) since a breach of the provisions of the EA 2010 may also constitute a violation of ECHR article 14 (the prohibition of certain forms of discrimination).

The Equality Act 2010

Introduction

9.6   The EA 2010 extends protection from discrimination to people with what are termed 'protected characteristics' in almost every area of life. The Act has two main purposes – to harmonise discrimination law, and to strengthen the law to support progress on equality.[8] The principle of equality underpinning the EA 2010 'is intended to promote and protect the dignity of all persons in society'.[9] The policy of the Act is therefore to promote equality in every area and as such any exceptions to the duties it imposes are to be interpreted restrictively.[10]

9.7   Despite its intention being to clarify and streamline equalities legislation, the EA 2010 is 251 pages long and contains 218 sections and 28 schedules. Moreover, the meaning of its provisions must be

---

5   (C 223/08) [2008] ECR I-5603.
6   Directive 2000/78.
7   [2008] ECR I-5603 at [63]; ruling at [2].
8   Explanatory Notes to the EA 2010 at [10].
9   Part 3 Code of Practice, p13.
10 Part 3 Code of Practice, 15.5.

interpreted in light of both the court's decisions in relation to its predecessor legislation (in this context the DDA scheme) and the statutory codes of practice which the EHRC will produce in time for it to come into force. The EHRC has consulted on draft statutory codes of practice for employment, equal pay and services and, most relevant here, public functions and associations ('the Part 3 Code of Practice').[11] The EHRC has also consulted on draft non-statutory guidance in the areas of employment, services, public functions and associations ('the Services and Public Functions Guidance'), and education ('the Education Guidance').[12] References in this chapter are to the draft codes and guidance.

9.8   This chapter considers the provisions of the EA 2010 and the codes of practice and guidance of most relevance to disabled children and their families – namely the sections that relate to 'prohibited conduct' (Part 2, Chapter 2), services and public function (Part 3), education (Part 6) and 'advancement of equality' (Part 11). It also covers the issue of enforcement (Part 9). While other areas such as associations (Part 7)[13] and transport (Part 12) may well be of great importance to some disabled children, the aspects of the EA 2010 listed above are those which should make a difference to the lives of *all* disabled children. For reasons of space, consideration of the public sector duty regarding socio-economic inequalities in EA 2010 s1 has also been omitted, notwithstanding that in the longer term it is possible that the creation of this duty may come to be seen as a pivotal development.[14]

11 The purpose of the codes of practice is 'to provide a detailed explanation of the Act and to apply legal concepts in the Act to everyday situations where services are provided': Part 3 Code of Practice, p9.

12 References to the guidance are references to the guidance aimed at individuals rather than to the parallel provider guidance. Non-statutory guidance from the EHRC is not intended to act as an aid to a court or tribunal in the interpretation of the EA 2010, but the guidance is 'aligned' with the codes of practice and should therefore assist individuals and organisations to achieve compliance with the Act: Services and Public Functions Guidance, pp10–11.

13 Discrimination by organisations such as the Scouts or the Guides is covered by the provisions of the EA 2010 in relation to associations: Part 3 Code of Practice, 13.7.

14 The duty in section 1 requires that when government departments, local authorities, health bodies and other similar public bodies are making decisions 'of a strategic nature' they must have 'due regard to the desirability of exercising them in a way that is designed to reduce the inequalities of outcome which result from socio-economic disadvantage'. Although this may be a largely aspirational obligation, it has the capacity to be of considerable importance, not least given the disproportionate numbers of disabled children and their families who live in poverty (see paras 1.31–1.34).

Disability – protected characteristic

9.9   Section 4 of the EA 2010 specifies that disability is a 'protected characteristic' for the purposes of the Act.[15] The definition of 'disability'
is provided in section 6(1), which states:

> A person (P) has a disability if –
> (a) P has a physical or mental impairment,[16] and
> (b) the impairment has a substantial and long-term adverse effect on
>   P's ability to carry out normal day-to-day activities.

9.10   This definition is materially the same as the definition in DDA 1995
s1. It is deliberately a broad definition, and there is no need for a
medical diagnosis – what matters is the effect of an impairment, not
its cause.[17] The elements of the definition are fleshed out by Schedule
1, which:

a) provides for regulations to specify conditions which do or do not
   fall within the definition of 'impairment';
b) states that an impairment is 'long-term' if it has lasted for 12
   months or is likely to last for 12 months;
c) states that a severe disfigurement is to be treated as an impairment having 'a substantial adverse effect on the ability of the person concerned to carry out normal day-to-day activities';
d) clarifies that an impairment has a 'substantial adverse effect' if
   it is being treated and but for that treatment it would have that
   effect;
e) specifies that cancer, HIV infection and multiple sclerosis are all
   disabilities within the meaning of section 6 (so that a child diagnosed with any of these conditions does not need to fulfil any of
   the other elements of the section 6 test);[18]
f) states that a person with a progressive condition meets the 'substantial adverse effect' test if the condition is likely to result in
   such an effect in future, even if it does not at the relevant time.[19]

---

15 Age, gender reassignment, marriage and civil partnership, pregnancy and
maternity, race, religion or belief, sex and sexual orientation.
16 Which includes a sensory impairment: Part 3 Code of Practice, 2.7.
17 Part 3 Code of Practice, Appendix 1, p282. Likewise, determination of whether
a person is 'disabled' no longer requires specific consideration of the eight
capacities, such as mobility or speech, hearing or eyesight, listed in the DDA
1995.
18 Schedule 1 para 6.
19 Schedule 1 para 8. Regulations may specify what constitutes a progressive
condition: para 8(3).

9.11   The schedule further provides a power[20] for regulations to specify certain symptoms or presentations ('effects of a prescribed description') which may or may not amount to 'substantial adverse effects' within the meaning of section 6. A further power is given to make regulations which can provide for 'persons of prescribed descriptions' to be treated as having disabilities. This will allow the secretary of state to add diseases and conditions to the list of those which automatically constitute disabilities for the purposes of the Act.

9.12   The secretary of state may also issue guidance in relation to the definition of disability.[21] Guidance under the DDA scheme was previously issued by the Disability Rights Commission[22] and pointed towards a generous approach to the definition of disability.[23] It is likely that any new guidance will take the same line.

9.13   The Part 3 Code of Practice makes clear that the status of being 'non-disabled' is not a protected characteristic. This 'assymetrical protection' stems from 'the need to prohibit the historic discrimination against disabled people'.[24] As a result, it will always be lawful under the EA 2010 for a service provider to treat a disabled person more favourably than they treat a non-disabled person.[25]

'Prohibited conduct'

Discrimination

9.14   The EA 2010 effectively outlaws certain forms of behaviour, in so far as they are directed against disabled children and others with 'protected characteristics'. The Act refers to these forms of behaviour as 'prohibited conduct', which is generically known as 'discrimination', and consists of (so far as material to disabled children):

20   Schedule 1 para 4.
21   Section 6(5); Sch 1 Pt 2 paras 10–16.
22   Disability Rights Commission, *Guidance on matters to be taken into account in determining questions relating to the definition of disability*, 2006. The DRC guidance was non-statutory other than that under DDA 1995 s3(3) a tribunal or court had to take it into account when determining whether a person was disabled. The DRC guidance stated that 'In the vast majority of cases there is unlikely to be any doubt whether or not a person has or has had a disability'.
23   For example, the statement at A7 that 'It may not always be possible, nor is it necessary, to categorise a condition as either a physical or a mental impairment'.
24   Part 3 Code of Practice, 2.12.
25   Part 3 Code of Practice, 5.56.

a) *direct discrimination* (section 13);
b) *combined discrimination* in relation to two or more protected characteristics (section 14);
c) *discrimination arising from disability* (section 15); and
d) *indirect discrimination* (section 19).[26]

9.15 A failure to comply with a duty to make reasonable adjustments also constitutes discrimination: see paras 9.32–9.35. Each of the forms of discrimination is considered below.

9.16 *Direct discrimination*, the most obvious form of discrimination, is prohibited by section 13. In the context of disability, direct discrimination takes place when a decision is taken concerning a disabled person which is based on prejudicial or stereotypical assumptions concerning disability generally, or the specific disability in question. As a general rule,[27] direct discrimination is simply unlawful and incapable of 'justification' – although in relation to employment alone, there is a limited exception for 'genuine occupational requirements': thus, for instance, it would not be unlawful to limit applications for the post of the Archbishop of Canterbury only to Christians.

9.17 The Part 3 Code of Practice suggests that 'being denied a choice or excluded from an opportunity is likely to be less favourable treatment'.[28] As both of these are routine features of the lives of disabled children, the EA 2010 has the potential in this respect to require significant changes in the practice of service providers, public authorities and others.

9.18 Direct discrimination can arise when a person is treated less favourably as a result of their association with a disabled child – for instance a parent denied a business loan simply because he lived with a disabled child. In Sharon Coleman's case (see para 9.4) she argued that her employer made it difficult for her to get time off work to care for her disabled son, whereas it placed no similar restrictions on other employees who took time off for other reasons.[29] What matters is that the less favourable treatment occurred because of the

26 Collectively defined as 'disability discrimination': see section 25(2). The EA 2010 also prohibits instructing, causing or inducing someone to discriminate against, harass or victimise a disabled person and knowingly helping someone discriminate against, harass or victimise another person.
27 For the specific statutory exceptions, see section 191 and Schedule 22 and also note para 10.51.
28 Part 3 Code of Practice, 5.6. The example given to illustrate this in the code is a pub which allows a child with cerebral palsy to drink in its beer garden but not in its family room.
29 Part 3 Code of Practice, 5.16 and 5.20–21.

child's disability; ie 'but for' the child's disability the treatment would not have occurred.

9.19 *'Combined discrimination'*, prohibited by section 14, takes place when a person is treated less favourably because of a combination of two protected characteristics – for instance, disability and sexual orientation.[30] So for example, a claim for combined discrimination may arise where disabled girls are treated less favourably than disabled boys – or vice versa.

9.20 Where a person has two or more disabilities, they can only ever amount to one characteristic for the purposes of a combined discrimination claim. A person who is treated less favourably because of two disabilities would, however, be able to bring claims for direct discrimination because of each disability separately.[31]

9.21 For combined discrimination, the comparator (the hypothetical person with whom a comparison is made to work out whether there has been discrimination) is a person who has neither of the protected characteristics in the relevant combination.[32] So in the case of a disabled girl who felt she had been treated less favourably by reason of both her gender and her disability, the comparator would be a non-disabled boy.

9.22 A claim for combined discrimination cannot be made in relation to disability discrimination in schools.[33]

9.23 *'Discrimination arising from disability'*, prohibited by section 15, is the government's response to an unexpected 2008 judgment of the House of Lords in the case referred to as *Malcolm*.[34] Prior to this decision, 'less favourable treatment' under the DDA scheme was assessed by comparing the treatment of the disabled person with the treatment of a hypothetical non-disabled person who did not display

---

30 It is important to note that age is not a protected characteristic in relation to the provision of services or public functions when a person is under 18 (section 28(1)(a)) and is not a protected characteristic at all in relation to schools (section 84). A claim for 'combined discrimination' cannot therefore be brought against a service provider for combined discrimination against a disabled child in relation to their status as a child as well as in relation to their disability.

31 Part 3 Code of Practice, 5.35.

32 Part 3 Code of Practice, 5.43.

33 Section 14(5), which specifies that no such claim can be made in education cases where a claim of direct discrimination in relation to disability (contrary to section 13) could be brought to the First-tier Tribunal.

34 *Lewisham LBC v Malcolm (Equality and Human Rights Commission intervening)* [2008] 1 AC 1399. This was a case decided in the housing context but in general, the courts have subsequently applied this approach to all the 'less favourable treatment' provisions of the DDA scheme.

the same characteristics as the disabled person. A well-known example of this approach involved a child with autism who misbehaved in a dinner queue, hit a teacher and was excluded as a result. Under the pre-*Malcolm* approach, this could amount to less favourable treatment if it could be shown that the child's behaviour was a function of his autism and that a non-disabled child would not have misbehaved in the same situation.

9.24   Following *Malcolm*, the comparator for 'less favourable treatment' became a non-disabled person with the same characteristics, or who behaved in the same way, as the disabled person. So in the example above, so long as a non-disabled child would have been excluded for misbehaving in the dinner queue, it would not have been less favourable treatment to exclude the disabled child (albeit that in such a case there would have been a requirement to make reasonable adjustments, see paras 9.32–9.35).

9.25   Section 15 attempts to resolve this problem by 're-establishing an appropriate balance between enabling a disabled person to make out a case of experiencing a detriment which arises because of his or her disability, and providing an opportunity for an employer or other person to defend the treatment'.[35] It removes the need for any comparator[36] and specifies instead that a person discriminates against a disabled person if he or she:

- treats him or her unfavourably[37] 'because of something arising 'in consequence of' his or her disability;[38] and
- cannot show that the treatment is 'a proportionate means of achieving a legitimate aim'.[39]

35 Explanatory Notes to the EA 2010 at [70].

36 Part 3 Code of Practice, 7.6.

37 Meaning that the disabled person is put at a disadvantage: Part 3 Code of Practice, 7.7.

38 Meaning 'anything which is the result, effect or outcome of a disabled person's disability': Part 3 Code of Practice, 7.8.

39 Section 15(1)(a) and (b). The Part 3 Code of Practice, 6.2 refers to this as 'objective justification'. The term 'legitimate aim' is not defined in the EA 2010, but the Part 3 Code of Practice, 6.19 states that a legitimate aim 'must be legal, must not be discriminatory in itself, and it must represent a real, objective consideration'. A service provider who is simply aiming to reduce costs or improve competitiveness 'cannot expect to satisfy the test': Part 3 Code of Practice, 6.20. 'Proportionate' is also not defined in the EA 2010 but for treatment to be proportionate it must be necessary: Part 3 Code of Practice, 6.20. Again, financial considerations alone cannot render treatment proportionate: Part 3 Code of Practice, 6.24. See Lester, Pannick and Herberg, *Human rights law and practice*, 3rd edn, LexisNexis, 2009, 4.8 for detailed discussion of the concept of proportionality in relation to ECHR article 8.

9.26   So unlike direct discrimination, discrimination arising from disability can be justified, if it is a proportionate means of achieving a legitimate aim. Furthermore, no discrimination contrary to section 15 occurs if the person did not know, and could not reasonably have been expected to know, that the disabled person 'had the disability'.[40] However, a person relying on this defence must have done all they could reasonably be expected to do to find out if the person has a disability.[41] This is particularly the case where the individual has an ongoing relationship with the disabled person.[42]

9.27   Where a person is treated less favourably because of something arising 'in consequence of' his disability, the onus will generally be on the person responsible for the treatment, to show that what was done was a proportionate means of achieving a legitimate aim. In the 'dinner queue' example above, the 'legitimate aim' might be the protection of the health and safety of teachers and other people in the queue – and a proportionate response would be implementation of 'reasonable adjustments' – for example, staff training concerning autistic spectrum disorders and strategies to avoid such difficulties as well as training for the pupil about behaviour in such social situations, such as queuing.[43] In such cases a failure to make a relevant reasonable adjustment is likely to make it 'very difficult' for an individual to show that any potentially discriminatory treatment was a proportionate means of achieving a legitimate aim.[44]

9.28   The Part 3 Code of Practice gives the following as an example of discrimination arising from disability:

> A mother seeks admission to a privately run nursery for her son who has Hirschprung's disease, which means that he does not have full bowel control. The nursery says that they cannot admit her son because he is not toilet trained and all the children at the nursery are. The refusal to admit the boy is not because of his disability itself; but he is experiencing detrimental treatment as a consequence of his disability.[45]

---

40   Section 15(2); the phrasing suggests that there has to be knowledge of the *specific* person's disability, not merely that they are 'disabled'.

41   Part 3 Code of Practice, 7.10.

42   Part 3 Code of Practice, 7.11.

43   See Teacher Training Resource Bank, *Removing barriers for disabled pupils – Session Five – Less favourable treatment: examples from DRC code of practice, with trainer's notes Handout 9* at http://www.ttrb.ac.uk/.

44   Part 3 Code of Practice, 7.15; the code also makes the point that unlawful discrimination may still arise even if a reasonable adjustment has been made, if the adjustment is unrelated to the treatment complained of.

45   Part 3 Code of Practice, 7.3.

9.29 The final type of discrimination likely to be relevant to disabled children is *indirect discrimination*, contrary to section 19. The extension of the prohibition on indirect discrimination to disability is new and follows the *Malcolm* judgment (see paras 9.23–9.24).[46] The indirect discrimination provisions aim to address forms of discrimination which, while they do not explicitly entail or propose different treatment, in practice disadvantage people with particular protected characteristics.[47] Indirect discrimination occurs if a person applies a 'provision, criterion or practice' which is discriminatory in relation to (in this case) a person's disability.[48] A four-stage test is set out[49] to determine whether a particular 'provision, criterion or practice' is discriminatory in relation to a disabled child:

- it applies, or would apply, to people who are not disabled;
- it puts, or would put, disabled people 'at a particular disadvantage'[50] when compared with non-disabled people;
- it puts, or would put, the individual disabled child at that disadvantage; and
- the person applying or operating the provision, criterion or practice cannot show it to be a proportionate means of achieving a legitimate aim.[51]

9.30 The Part 3 Code of Practice suggests[52] that it is 'unlikely' that the protected characteristic in a claim of indirect discrimination will be taken to be disability in general, but rather the individual's specific disability. It may therefore be that if an individual with a visual impairment claims to have been indirectly discriminated against, the appropriate comparator would be a person without any visual impairment, rather than a non-disabled person.

9.31 Because a failure to make reasonable adjustments will also amount to discrimination (see below), it may be that the indirect discrimination provisions of the EA 2010 add little to the protection afforded

---

46 Explanatory Notes to the EA 2010 at [81].

47 Part 3 Code of Practice, 4.4.

48 Section 19(1). The terms 'provision, criterion or practice' overlap and should be 'construed widely so as to include, for example, any (formal or informal) policies, rules, practices, arrangements, criteria, prerequisites, qualifications or provisions': Part 3 Code of Practice, 6.3. The terms also cover proposals and one-off discretionary decisions: Part 3 Code of Practice, 6.4.

49 Section 19(2).

50 Section 19(2)(b).

51 See fn 39 above for discussion of the concepts of 'proportionate' and 'legitimate aim'.

52 At 6.9.

to disabled children. However, given the systemic discrimination against disabled people still present in our society there appears to be little harm in taking a 'belt and braces' approach to outlawing all forms of discrimination.

Reasonable adjustments

9.32   The EA 2010 protects disabled people from discriminatory treatment in specified areas by the imposition of a duty to make reasonable adjustments in their favour.[53] This duty was also central to the DDA scheme and remains a 'cornerstone' of the EA 2010.[54] The duty is anticipatory,[55] continuing and evolving[56] and reflects the policy of the Act, which is to 'provide access to a service as close as it is reasonably possible to get to the standard normally offered to the public at large'.[57]

9.33   There are three elements to the reasonable adjustment duty:[58]

- a requirement, where a *provision, criterion or practice* puts a disabled person at a substantial disadvantage[59] in comparison with persons who are not disabled, to take such steps as is reasonable to avoid the disadvantage;[60]
- a requirement, where a *physical feature* puts a disabled person at a substantial disadvantage in comparison with persons who are not disabled, to take such steps as is reasonable to avoid the disadvantage;[61] and

---

53 The generic elements of which are set out at sections 20–22.

54 Part 3 Code of Practice, 8.3.

55 Part 3 Code of Practice, 8.16–8.19.

56 Part 3 Code of Practice, 8.25. By 'continuing and evolving' the code of practice means that the duty does not simply apply on a one-off basis, but that the need to make further or different adjustments must be continually monitored by the person or body subject to the duty. The duty is 'not something that needs simply to be considered once and then forgotten': Education Guidance, p39.

57 Part 3 Code of Practice, 8.4.

58 Section 20(2).

59 Meaning more than minor or trivial: Part 3 Code of Practice, 8.27. Whether disadvantage is substantial is measured by comparison with what the position would be if the disabled person in question did not have a disability: Part 3 Code of Practice, 8.28. It is more likely to be reasonable for a service provider with substantial financial resources to have to make an adjustment with a significant cost than for a service provider with fewer resources: Part 3 Code of Practice, 8.32.

60 Section 20(3). See the Part 3 Code of Practice, 8.31 for steps which it may be reasonable for an individual to take to avoid substantial disadvantage.

61 Section 20(4). This potentially includes removing the feature, altering it or providing a reasonable means of avoiding it: section 20(9). The duty applies to

- a requirement, where a disabled person would, but for the provision of an auxiliary aid, be put at a substantial disadvantage in comparison with persons who are not disabled, to take such steps as is reasonable to *provide the auxiliary aid*[62] *or service.*[63]

9.34　The reasonable adjustment duty therefore obliges a person subject to it both to make physical and practice adjustments and to provide auxiliary aids, to the extent necessary to avoid substantial disadvantage to disabled people. A further specific aspect of the duty is to provide information in accessible formats.[64] Disabled people may not be compelled to meet the costs of compliance with the duty.[65] The content of the duty in specific areas is governed by schedules to the Act as set out in section 20(13), the most relevant here being services and public functions (Schedule 2) and education (Schedule 13).

9.35　A failure to comply with any of the three aspects of the duty set out above is a breach of the duty[66] and constitutes discrimination.[67] The detail of how the reasonable adjustments duty will operate will be set out in regulations.[68]

Harassment and victimisation

9.36　Finally, Part 2 of the EA 2010 outlaws two specific forms of discrimination, harassment and victimisation. Harassment occurs in two circumstances potentially relevant to disabled children:

- a person engages in 'unwanted conduct'[69] related to a child's disability and the conduct has the purpose of violating the child's

---

physical features in the broadest sense, including 'any other physical element or quality': section 20(10). An extensive but non-exhaustive list of physical features is provided by the Part 3 Code of Practice, 8.64–8.65.

62　Section 20(6).

63　Services are included within this aspect of the duty by section 20(11). An auxiliary aid or service is 'is anything which provides additional support or assistance to a disabled person': Part 3 Code of Practice, 8.52.

64　Section 20(6).

65　Section 20(7).

66　Section 21(1).

67　Section 21(2).

68　To be made in accordance with section 22.

69　Unwanted conduct can include any kind of behaviour, including spoken or written words or abuse, imagery, graffiti, physical gestures, facial expressions, mimicry, jokes, pranks, acts affecting a person's surroundings or other physical behaviour: Part 3 Code of Practice, 9.3.

dignity or 'creating an intimidating, hostile, degrading, humiliating or offensive environment';[70] or

- the conduct is as above but is of a 'sexual nature'.[71]

Whether the conduct has the necessary purpose should be judged in all the circumstances, including the perceptions of the disabled child.[72]

9.37   Victimisation occurs if a person is subjected 'to a detriment' because he or she does, or it is believed that he or she has done or may do, a 'protected act'.[73] The 'protected acts' are, in essence, any act done in relation to the EA 2010, including bringing a claim that there has been disability discrimination.[74] A person can be unlawfully victimised, even though he or she does not have the 'protected characteristic'. Accordingly a mother of a disabled child could make such a claim if she were told that she would be refused a carer's service (see paras 8.28–8.30) if she complained about the disability discrimination she believed to be taking place in a respite care centre.

Services and public functions

Provision of services

9.38   Service providers[75] are prohibited from discriminating against disabled children and others with protected characteristics. The code of practice states that:

> Part 3 is based on the principle that people with the protected characteristics defined in the Act should not be discriminated against when using any service provided publicly or privately, whether that service is for payment or not.[76]

---

70 Section 26(1).
71 Section 26(2).
72 Section 26(4).
73 Section 27(1).
74 Section 27(2).
75 A 'service provider' is a person concerned with the provision of a service to the public, whether for payment or not: section 29(1). The term encompasses those providing goods and facilities as well as services: section 31(2). It also includes services provided in the exercise of a public function: section 31(3). An extensive but non-exhaustive list of service providers is given in the Part 3 Code of Practice, 11.3. The Education Guidance clarifies (at p132) that the service provider duties apply to early years providers such as private day nurseries, childminders, accredited childminder networks, pre-schools and playgroups and Sure Start children's centres.
76 Part 3 Code of Practice, p7.

9.39 The EA 2010 does not distinguish between service providers of different types or size; the same duties apply to all service providers, although the Part 3 Code of Practice recognises that the way the duties are put into practice may vary between service providers – for example, what might be a reasonable adjustment for a large and well-resourced service provider to make might not be the same for one that is small and poorly resourced.[77]

9.40 In particular, service providers must not:

- discriminate against a disabled child who requires[78] their service by not providing that service[79] (see paras 9.14–9.15 for the meaning of 'discriminate');
- discriminate against a disabled child while providing them with a service by providing it on worse terms than offered to others, terminating the service or 'subjecting [the child] to any other detriment';[80]
- harass a disabled child who requires or is receiving their service[81] (see para 9.36 for the meaning of 'harassment'); or
- victimise a disabled child by not providing the service or providing it on worse terms[82] (see para 9.37 for the meaning of 'victimisation').

9.41 Service providers are also subject to the duty to make reasonable adjustments:[83] see paras 9.32–9.35. The Part 3 Code of Practice suggests that service providers are not expected to anticipate the needs of every individual who may wish to use their services, but to consider what reasonable steps may be required to overcome barriers faced by persons with particular kinds of disability – the examples given being visual impairments or mobility impairments.[84] This of course begs the question as to whether it would be 'reasonable' for a service provider not to anticipate the need to make adjustments to ensure access for persons with other types of disability. The code of practice does

---

77 Part 3 Code of Practice, p14 – and in this context see also para 8.30 where such factors are further considered.
78 'Requiring' a service also means 'seeking to obtain or use the service': section 31(6).
79 Section 29(1). 'Not providing the service' also means providing a poorer quality of service or providing it on less favourable terms or in a less favourable manner than it is generally offered to the public: section 31(7).
80 Section 29(2).
81 Section 29(3).
82 Section 29(4) and (5).
83 Section 29(7)(a).
84 Part 3 Code of Practice, 8.22.

suggest that once a service provider becomes aware of the requirements of a particular disabled person it may be reasonable for them
to take a particular step to meet their individual needs.[85] See paras
9.48–9.51 for more on the duty to make reasonable adjustments in
relation to service providers.

9.42   Service providers also need to take active steps to ensure that discrimination is not occurring in the provision of their services.[86] This
is particularly so as a service provider will be liable for unlawful acts
committed by their employees unless they have taken reasonable
steps to prevent such acts.[87] Service providers are advised by the Part
3 Code of Practice to take a number of steps to ensure compliance
with their duties, including establishing a policy to ensure equality of
access to their services and communicating this policy effectively to
their staff.[88]

9.43   The draft non-statutory guidance concerning services and public functions (see para 9.7) contains a specific chapter (chapter 11)
concerning the provision of health and social care services, both of
particular relevance to disabled children. The guidance advises that
the standard of care that should be expected from EA 2010 compliant
providers would include:

> Staff providing care to you, whether in your home or another setting,
> should be respectful, treat you with dignity and maintain appropriate
> levels of confidentiality. This doesn't just include health professionals
> – it includes everyone who is involved with you, from reception staff
> to care assistants and from ambulance workers to consultants.[89]

Performance of public functions

9.44   In addition to duties on service providers, Part 3 of the EA 2010 puts
duties on persons performing public functions. Together, these duties
mean that every action (or inaction) of a public authority and the exercise of every public function (even if not related to the provision of
services) is covered by the EA 2010 – unless specifically excluded.[90]

---

85 Part 3 Code of Practice, 8.24.
86 Part 3 Code of Practice, 4.10.
87 Part 3 Code of Practice, 3.10.
88 Part 3 Code of Practice, 4.11.
89 Services and Public Functions Guidance, p204.
90 Section 29(6). The public functions provisions are residual and apply only
    where other provisions of the EA 2010 do not: Part 3 Code of Practice, 12.2. See
    also Part 3 Code of Practice, 12.20.

9.45   The term 'public function' has the same meaning in the EA 2010 as the phrase 'function of a public nature' within the Human Rights Act 1998.[91] An example given in the Part 3 Code of Practice of a public function which is not a service is law enforcement[92] but it will also apply to many public functions relevant to disabled children, for instance the education functions of a local authority. The duty applies primarily to 'policy' functions such as the setting of budgets and the determination of entitlements to benefits and services[93] as decisions on individual cases are likely to be covered by the service provision duties.

9.46   In practice, the duties under the EA 2010 imposed on persons exercising public functions and those providing a service are 'essentially the same'.[94] The duty in relation to public functions is, however, more clearly expressed: a person carrying out a public function must not 'do anything that constitutes discrimination, harassment or victimisation'.[95] Persons carrying out a public function also owe the reasonable adjustment duty.[96]

9.47   The leading case on the duty prohibiting discrimination by public authorities under the DDA scheme[97] is *R (Lunt and another) v Liverpool CC*.[98] The case involved an application by a vehicle developer for approval of a specific type of taxi in Liverpool. The local authority's refusal was challenged successfully on the ground that the council had failed to take into account a class of wheelchair users with wheelchairs of a certain length and that this failure amounted to unjustified discrimination. The approach taken in *Lunt* was followed by the court in *R (Gill) v Secretary of State for Justice*,[99] where a prisoner had

---

91 Section 31(4). This term has been the subject of significant judicial consideration within the Human Rights Act scheme. Although it should be given a broad interpretation, there will be occasions where it will not be obvious if a body is providing a function of a public nature – for instance, a private company carrying out a function under contract from a local authority. See Lester, Pannick and Herberg, *Human rights law and practice*, 3rd edn, LexisNexis, 2009, 2.6.3. The Part 3 Code of Practice states (at p8) that: '"Public functions" ... are often carried out under a statutory power or duty, such as policing, licensing or determining the framework for benefit entitlement.'

92 Part 3 Code of Practice, 12.3.

93 Part 3 Code of Practice, 12.3.

94 Part 3 Code of Practice, 12.7.

95 Section 29(6).

96 Section 29(7)(b).

97 DDA 1995 s21B.

98 [2009] EWHC 2356 (Admin).

99 [2010] EWHC 364 (Admin).

been prevented from accessing offending behaviour programmes in prison because of his learning disability. The court held that the secretary of state had unlawfully breached the duty on public authorities under the DDA scheme and had discriminated against the prisoner by failing to provide programmes which were accessible to him.[100] The approach of the court in *Lunt* and *Gill* should inform the way the public functions duties under the EA 2010 are understood in relation to disabled people.

Reasonable adjustments – service providers and public functions

9.48   The operation of the duty to make reasonable adjustments on service providers and persons carrying out a public function is governed by Schedule 2.[101] The schedule specifies that all three aspects of the reasonable adjustment duty apply:[102] see paras 9.32–9.35. In addition to the duty to help disabled persons avoid any disadvantage they might face, service providers and persons carrying out a public function have an additional duty to 'adopt a reasonable alternative method of providing the service or exercising the function'.[103]

9.49   The meaning of 'substantial disadvantage'[104] in relation to the exercise of a public function is either being placed at a substantial disadvantage in relation to a potential benefit or suffering an 'unreasonably adverse experience' when being subjected to a 'detriment'.[105]

9.50   To ensure compliance with the reasonable adjustment duty, the Part 3 Code of Practice recommends:

- regular reviews of whether services are accessible to disabled people;
- access audits, carried out by suitably qualified persons; and
- regular training to staff relevant to the adjustments made.[106]

9.51   Schedule 2 contains an important exception to the reasonable adjustment duty on service providers. The duty does not require a service

---

100   [2010] EWHC 364 (Admin) at [80].
101   Schedule 2 para 1 states that the schedule applies where a duty to make reasonable adjustments is imposed by this Part of the Act.
102   Schedule 2 para 2(1).
103   Schedule 2 para 2(3)(b).
104   See para 9.33 and fn 59 above.
105   Schedule 2 para 2(5).
106   Part 3 Code of Practice, 4.12. The code goes on to suggest at 4.13 that small businesses and other small organisations may find a less formal approach sufficient.

provider to take any step which would 'fundamentally alter' the nature of the service or of the trade or profession of the service provider.[107] The use of the phrase 'fundamentally alter' indicates that this is a high threshold which is not intended to be a general 'get out clause' to prevent service providers from making reasonable adjustments in favour of disabled children and others with protected characteristics. A more straightforward exception is also established in relation to persons carrying out a public function, who are not required by the duty to take a step which they have no power at law to take.[108]

Exceptions

9.52 Schedule 3 exempts from the duties on service providers and persons carrying out public functions:

- parliament;[109]
- the preparation or consideration of legislation in the UK Parliament or the devolved Scottish Parliament and Welsh Assembly;[110]
- judicial functions;[111]
- a decision not to commence or continue criminal proceedings;[112]
- the armed forces;[113]
- the security services;[114]
- specified immigration decisions;[115] and
- transport by air[116] or by land other than in specified vehicles.[117]

9.53 Of greater relevance to disabled children, the duty does not require a local education authority to remove or alter physical features[118] (see paras 9.56–9.65 for the duties on schools and local education authorities). There is also no duty on a person who takes a disabled child into their home and treats that child as a member of their family.[119] Insurance businesses do not breach the service provider duty if they

---

107 Schedule 2 para 2(7).
108 Schedule 2 para 8.
109 Schedule 3 para 1.
110 Schedule 3 para 2.
111 Schedule 3 para 3(1)(a).
112 Schedule 3 para 3(1)(c).
113 Schedule 3 para 4.
114 Schedule 3 para 5.
115 Schedule 3 para 16.
116 Schedule 3 para 33.
117 Schedule 3 para 34.
118 Schedule 3 para 10.
119 Schedule 3 para 15.

reasonably take into account relevant information in relation to the assessment of risk for a disabled child.[120]

9.54   Other than the above specified exceptions, the duties apply to all service providers and all those carrying out a public function. The EA 2010 thereby obliges a wide range of public and private individuals and organisations to consider their policies, procedures and practices to ensure that they are avoiding discrimination and making necessary reasonable adjustments.

Education

9.55   The Education Guidance notes that 'major inequalities remain for certain groups which prevent some individuals from making the most of their abilities and talents and achieving their full potential'.[121] This is certainly the case for disabled pupils (see in this context paras 1.58–1.63 and chapter 4, where the duties in relation to children with special educational needs (SEN) are discussed). In one early DDA case,[122] a disabled child was excluded from his school's nativity play, prevented from making a Christmas card to take home, was not invited to the school disco and was left out of a school trip and a class photograph. The school was ordered to apologise, to revise its policies for disabled pupils and for recruiting staff and the governing body and staff also had to attend disability equality training. While it is hoped that such blatant examples of discrimination will be rare, the equality duties on education providers and in particular on schools remain of central importance to the life chances of disabled children.

Schools and LEAs

9.56   Chapter 1 of Part 6 of the EA 2010 is concerned with education provided by schools[123] (and local education authorities (LEAs) in the

---

120 Schedule 3 para 21.
121 Education Guidance, p60.
122 Personal correspondence with the authors, 25 July 2010.
123 Meaning schools maintained by the local education authority and independent schools, both special and mainstream: section 85(7). Where schools are providing a non-educational service, for example through renting their premises to a community group, they are covered by the provisions of Part 3 of the EA 2010 in relation to service providers: Part 3 Code of Practice, 11.8.

context of accessibility strategies see 9.60–9.61). Chapter 2 of Part 6 deals with further and higher education.

9.57 The responsible body[124] for a school must not discriminate against a disabled child in relation to admissions,[125] exclusions[126] or the provision of education in the school[127] (see paras 9.14–9.15 for the meaning of 'discrimination') and must not harass[128] or victimise[129] a pupil or prospective pupil (see paras 9.36–9.37 for the meaning of 'harassment' and 'victimisation'). This effectively prohibits[130] discrimination in relation to all aspects of school life and obliges the authorities regularly to review their practices, policies and procedures.[131]

9.58 Although the responsible bodies for schools are also under the duty to make reasonable adjustments[132] (see paras 9.32–9.35) this is limited to the requirement to make adjustments to provisions, criteria or practices and to provide auxiliary aids and services[133] – the latter being an important development from the DDA scheme. The duty to make reasonable adjustments to physical features does not apply to schools as this is covered by school accessibility plans (see para 9.62). The reasonable adjustment duty applies in relation to

---

124 Meaning the local authority or governing body of a maintained school and the proprietor of an independent school.

125 Section 85(1). Although the use of admissions criteria is permitted, schools must ensure that the criteria they use does not discriminate, either directly or indirectly, against anyone with a protected characteristic, and indirect discrimination may occur if admissions criteria exclude a greater proportion of (for example) disabled children: Education Guidance, p69.

126 Section 85(2)(e). The Education Guidance reiterates (at p80) the requirement in the English and Welsh School Exclusions Guidance that 'pupils should only be excluded from school as a last resort': see chapter 4, paras 4.114–4.123 for more on school exclusions.

127 Section 85(2)(a).

128 Section 85(3).

129 Section 85(4) and (5). Disabled children are also protected from victimisation as a result of the conduct of their parents: section 86.

130 The prohibitions do not apply to anything done in relation to the content of the school curriculum: section 89. This ensures that the Act does not inhibit the ability of schools to include a full range of issues, ideas and materials in their syllabus and to expose pupils to thoughts and ideas of all kinds. The way in which the curriculum is taught is, however, covered by the reference to education in section 85(2)(a), so as to ensure issues are taught in a way which does not subject pupils to discrimination: Explanatory Notes to the EA 2010 at [306].

131 Education Guidance, p76.

132 Section 85(6).

133 Schedule 13 para 2(2).

disabled pupils generally, not just those already at the school.[134] The Education Guidance states that 'disabled people are a diverse group with different requirements that schools need to consider strategically' in achieving compliance with the reasonable adjustments duty.[135] A key reasonable adjustment will often be to avoid operating blanket policies – such as a policy that pupils must wear a certain type of trousers when those trousers exacerbated a child's eczema, or a policy that any pupil swearing at a teacher will be excluded when a pupil in the school has difficulties with social communication and expressing his emotions.[136] In meeting the reasonable adjustment duty, responsible bodies must have regard to the Education Code of Practice, once issued.[137]

9.59   A maintained school governing body or an independent special school proprietor in England can be given directions by the secretary of state[138] if it fails to comply with one of the duties imposed on it by the EA 2010.[139]

Accessibility strategies and plans

9.60   Two schedules apply in relation to schools. The first, Schedule 10, deals with accessibility for disabled pupils.[140] Under this schedule, local authorities must prepare an accessibility strategy for their maintained schools[141] which sets out a plan for:

- increasing the extent to which disabled pupils can 'participate in the schools' curriculum';[142]
- improving the physical environment of the school for the purpose of increasing access for disabled children;[143] and
- improving the delivery of information for disabled pupils.[144]

---

134 Schedule 13 para 2(3)(b).
135 Education Guidance, p38.
136 Both examples of education cases brought under the DDA scheme: personal correspondence with the authors, 25 July 2010.
137 Schedule 13 para 7 – at the time this book went to press (July 2010) the code had not been published.
138 Under Education Act 1996 ss496–497.
139 Section 87.
140 Both current and prospective pupils: Schedule 10 para 6(4).
141 Schedule 10 para 1. Such strategies are already required to be in place under the DDA. Maintained schools are those included within the definition in the School Standards and Framework Act 1998: Schedule 10 para 6(7).
142 Schedule 10 para 2(a).
143 Schedule 10 para 1(2)(b).
144 Schedule 10 para 1(2)(c) and(3).

9.61   The accessibility strategy must be in writing,[145] must be kept under review[146] and must be implemented.[147] Adequate resources must be allocated for implementing the strategy[148] and the authority must have regard to any guidance which may be issued by the secretary of state.[149] It is highly likely that the strategy will need to cover staff training, the importance of which in achieving compliance with the EA 2010 cannot be overestimated.[150]

9.62   At the school level (including independent schools), the responsible body must prepare an accessibility plan.[151] Each school's plan must cover the same matters as an accessibility strategy[152] (see above) and the responsible body is subject to the same procedural requirements as a local authority – producing the plan in writing, keeping it under review and implementing it.[153] Again, adequate resources must be allocated to the implementation of the plan.[154] Importantly, any inspection of the school can review the performance of the responsible body in preparing and implementing its accessibility plan.[155] This gives the duty teeth, as any failure to produce a plan or any seriously inadequate plan is likely to be criticised in inspection reports.

9.63   Schedule 10 creates a power for the secretary of state or the Welsh ministers to give a direction to a responsible body of a school if it has failed to discharge the duty to produce an accessibility plan, is acting unreasonably (for instance, by producing an obviously deficient plan) or if it has failed to comply with a tribunal order in relation to disability discrimination.[156] This power arises whether or not a complaint has been made,[157] enabling the minister to require a school to stop

145 Schedule 10 para 1(4).
146 Schedule 10 para 1(5).
147 Schedule 10 para 1(6).
148 Schedule 10 para 2(1)(a). The precise duty is to 'have regard to the need to allocate adequate resources for implementing the strategy'.
149 Schedule 10 para 2(1)(b) and (2)–(3).
150 Education Guidance, p77.
151 Schedule 10 para 3(1).
152 Schedule 10 para 3(2)–(3).
153 Schedule 10 para 3(4)–(6).
154 Schedule 10 para 4(1).
155 Schedule 10 para 3(7)–(8). In England, equality and diversity are now a 'limiting judgement' in Ofsted inspections. This means that if equality measures are not being implemented effectively this will restrict the overall inspection grade: Education Guidance, p77.
156 Schedule 10 para 5(5).
157 Schedule 10 para 5(1).

a discriminatory practice or policy.[158] The power is, however, subject to either a complaint having been made to a local commissioner,[159] or the minister considering that such a complaint could have been made.[160]

Exceptions – selection

9.64 The second schedule relevant to schools is Schedule 11, which sets out the exceptions to duties imposed on schools by the EA 2010. Part 3 of this schedule deals with the disability-related exception regarding 'permitted forms of selection'.[161] Selection permitted for maintained schools is that specified in the School Standards and Framework Act 1998.[162] Permitted selection for independent schools is defined as:

> Arrangements which provide for some or all of [a school's] pupils to be selected by reference to general or special ability or aptitude, with a view to admitting only pupils of high ability or aptitude.[163]

9.65 Taken together, these exceptions significantly weaken the duty on schools not to discriminate against disabled pupils in relation to admissions.

Further and higher education

9.66 The relevant provisions of the EA 2010 in relation to further and higher education are considered at paras 10.43–10.48.

General qualifications bodies

9.67 The EA 2010 imposes specific duties on qualifications bodies[164] responsible for public examinations not to discriminate against disabled children and others with protected characteristics. The primary

---

158 Explanatory Notes to the EA 2010 at [303].
159 Under Chapter 2 of Part 10 of the Apprenticeships, Skills, Children and Learning Act 2009, which governs parental complaints about governing bodies.
160 Schedule 10 para 5(7). A direction can also be made if the local commissioner has made a recommendation following an investigation and the responsible body has not complied with the recommendation: Schedule 10 para 5(8).
161 Schedule 11 para 8(1).
162 Sections 99 and 104; Schedule 11 para 8(2)(a) and (b).
163 Schedule 11, para 8(2)(c).
164 A qualifications body is an authority or body which can confer a relevant qualification: section 97(2). A 'relevant qualification' is any qualification which may be prescribed by the secretary of state or the Welsh ministers: section 97(3). Responsible bodies of schools are not qualifications bodies (section

duty on such bodies is not to discriminate against disabled children in their arrangements for deciding 'upon whom to confer a relevant qualification',[165] in setting the terms on which qualifications will be awarded[166] or by not awarding a qualification[167] (see paras 9.14–9.15 for the meaning of 'discrimination'). Furthermore, once a qualification has been awarded, a body must not discriminate against a disabled child by withdrawing the qualification,[168] varying the terms on which it is held[169] or subjecting the child to any other detriment.[170]

9.68   Qualifications bodies are also prohibited from harassing[171] or victimising[172] a disabled child (see paras 9.36 and 9.37 respectively for the meaning of the terms 'harassment' and 'victimisation').

9.69   Qualifications bodies owe the duty to make reasonable adjustments for disabled children.[173] However, the appropriate regulator may (subject to consultation[174]) specify aspects of the body's functions to which the duty does not apply.[175] The Explanatory Notes to the EA 2010[176] suggest that 'it could be specified that the requirement to achieve a particular mark to gain a particular qualification is not subject to reasonable adjustments' or that giving an exemption from a part of an exam would not be a reasonable adjustment.[177] An example given in the Explanatory Notes of a reasonable adjustment by a qualifications body is as follows:

> A visually impaired candidate is granted a modified paper (enlarged font) by a qualifications body in order that she can read her English GCSE exam.[178]

97(4)(a)) so any in-school examinations will not be covered by this duty, but will be covered by the schools duties.

165 Section 96(1)(a).
166 Section 96(1)(b).
167 Section 96(1)(c).
168 Section 96(2)(a).
169 Section 96(2)(b).
170 Section 96(2)(c).
171 Section 96(3).
172 Section 96(4) and (5).
173 Section 96(6).
174 Section 96(9)(a).
175 Section 96(7).
176 Explanatory Notes at [327].
177 The exemption under the DDA scheme in relation to 'competence standards' has been abolished given the what constituted such a standard: Explanatory Notes at [328].
178 Explanatory Notes at [328].

9.70   In deciding whether to exclude certain functions from the reasonable adjustments duty, the regulator must have regard to the need to:

- minimise the extent to which disabled persons are disadvantaged in attaining the qualification because of their disabilities;[179]
- ensure that the qualification gives a reliable indication of the knowledge, skills and understanding of a person upon whom it is conferred;[180] and
- maintain public confidence in the qualification.[181]

9.71   Arguably, the inclusion of the 'public confidence' factor in the consideration of whether to exempt a qualification body's function from the reasonable adjustments duty puts too great an emphasis on the 'standards' agenda and means insufficient weight will be given to the first criterion – the need to minimise the disadvantages faced by disabled people taking public examinations.

9.72   In achieving compliance with the reasonable adjustment duty, qualifications bodies must have regard to the Education Code of Practice, once issued.[182] The Education Guidance states that qualifications bodies 'should be able to respond quickly to individual requests for particular adjustments' and requires that 'each case should be determined on its own merits, not by following a blanket policy'.[183]

Advancement of equality

Public sector equality duty

9.73   Part 11 of the EA 2010 imposes a general public sector equality duty, replacing the previous public sector duties for the individual equality strands.[184] The existing duty in DDA 1995 s49A is scheduled to remain in force until the single equality duty comes into force in April 2011.[185] The single equality duty gives public bodies legal

---

179   Section 96(8)(a).
180   Section 96(8)(b).
181   Section 96(8)(c).
182   Schedule 13 para 7 – at the time this book went to press (July 2010) the code had not been published.
183   Education Guidance, p115.
184   In relation to disability, DDA 1995 s49A, inserted by the DDA 2005. This section also replaces the Race Relations Act 1976 s71 and the Sex Discrimination Act 1975 s76A.
185   See (for example) the Education Guidance, p61.

responsibilities to demonstrate that they are taking action on equality in policy-making, the delivery of services and public sector employment.[186] The single equality duty is similar in 'spirit and intention'[187] to the pre-existing duties, but is structured differently in some important specific respects.

9.74 In relation to disabled children, the duty on public authorities[188] is to have due regard to the need to:

- eliminate discrimination, harassment, victimisation and any other conduct that is prohibited under the Act;[189]
- advance equality of opportunity between disabled children and others;[190] and
- foster good relations between disabled children and others.[191]

9.75 The 'equality of opportunity' limb of the duty in relation to disabled children requires particular regard to the following needs:

- removing or minimising disadvantages 'suffered' by disabled children that are connected to their disability;[192]
- taking steps to meet the needs of disabled children that are different from non-disabled children;[193] and
- encouraging disabled children to participate in public life.[194]

9.76 The 'foster good relations' limb of the duty requires particular regard to the need to:

- tackle prejudice;[195] and
- promote understanding.[196]

---

186 Education Guidance, p62.
187 Education Guidance, p62.
188 'Public authorities' are defined in Schedule 19 (brought into effect through section 150). They include central government departments, health bodies, local government organisations and governing bodies of maintained schools. Further public authorities may be specified by the secretary of state or the Welsh ministers (section 151) subject to consultation and consent (section 152).
189 Section 149(1)(a).
190 Section 149(1)(b).
191 Section 149(1)(c).
192 Section 149(3)(a).
193 Section 149(3)(b). This includes steps to take account of a disabled child's disabilities: section 149(4).
194 Section 149(3)(c).
195 Section 149(5)(a).
196 Section 149(5)(b).

9.77　Any person who is not a public authority but who exercises public functions[197] (eg, a private company providing public services on a contracted-out basis) must also have due regard to these matters in the exercise of their public functions.[198]

9.78　Compliance with the public sector equality duty may involve treating disabled children more favourably than others, so long as to do so would not contravene the EA 2010 in some other way.[199]

9.79　Regulations may be made to impose specific duties on public authorities for the purpose of enabling better performance by the authority of its general public sector equality duty.[200] This could replicate the duty under the previous DDA scheme on public authorities to prepare disability equality schemes.

9.80　The public sector equality duty does not apply to the provision of education in schools in relation to the protected characteristic of age – but does apply to schools in relation to disability.[201] Further exemptions from the duty include the courts[202] and parliament.[203]

9.81　A breach of the public sector equality duty does not create an individual cause of action.[204] However, such breaches can be scrutinised by the High Court on an application for judicial review.[205] The courts have given significant consideration to the disability equality duty under section 49A DDA 1995.[206] Given the similarities between the section 49A duty and the single equality duty under the EA 2010, it is likely that these judgments will continue to be relevant in the interpretation of the new duty – and as set out above, the section 49A duty remains in force until April 2011.

197　A 'public function' is a function of a public nature for the purposes of the Human Rights Act 1998: section 150(5). See fn 91 above for more on the definition of a 'function of a public nature'.

198　Section 149(2).

199　Section 149(6).

200　Section 153.

201　Schedule 18 para 1(1).

202　Schedule 18 para 3.

203　Schedule 18 para 4.

204　Section 156, meaning that an individual may not go to a court or tribunal and seek redress in their individual case for an alleged breach of the duty, other than by way of judicial review (see above).

205　See the Part 3 Code of Practice, 16.34–16.39 for more on the use of judicial review to remedy breaches of the EA 2010.

206　The DDA 1995 s49A duty is also helpfully explained in 'The Duty to Promote Disability Equality: Statutory Code of Practice', the code of practice produced by the Disability Rights Commission.

9.82 Some key themes can be drawn out from the most important disability equality cases:

a) The duty applies to decision-making in relation to individual cases as much as it does to 'policy' decisions, both being an aspect of carrying out a local authority's functions: see *R (JL) v Islington LBC*[207] and *R (AM) v Birmingham CC.*[208]

b) 'Due' regard, as opposed to a duty merely to 'have regard', requires 'specific regard, by way of conscious approach, to the statutory criteria': see *R (Sanders) v Harlow DC.*[209]

c) The duty has to be considered rigorously, with an open mind and in substance, when the relevant decision is taken: *R (Brown) v Secretary of State for Work and Pensions.*[210]

d) There should be some form of 'audit trail' or documentation to show that the duty was given due consideration at the appropriate time: *R (JL) v Islington LBC.*[211]

e) Active steps are required to be taken to promote equality of opportunity when relevant decisions are made: *R(E) v Governing Body of the Jews Free School* (Administrative Court).[212]

9.83 To achieve compliance with the DDA 1995 s49A duty (and looking ahead, to comply with the single equality duty), a public authority must not only give it due regard in all future decision-making but must also take action to address the shortcomings of past decisions which have failed to have regard to disability equality.[213] The DDA scheme and the EA 2010 both impose a continuing duty to prioritise

---

207 [2009] EWHC 458 (Admin) per Black J at [114].

208 (2009) 12 CCLR 407 per Cranston J at [25], citing with approval the Disability Rights Commission Code of Practice, 2.42: 'when preparing individual community care plans, a local authority should have due regard to the need to promote disability equality. Disability equality is of particular relevance in this context.'

209 [2009] EWHC 559 (Admin) per Davis J at [84].

210 [2008] EWHC 3158 (Admin) at [92].

211 [2009] EWHC 458 at [121].

212 [2008] ELR 445 per Munby J at [213] (in the context of the equivalent provision in the Race Relations Act 1976), stating: 'proper compliance ... requires that appropriate consideration has been given to the need to achieve statutory goals whose achievement will almost inevitably, give the words "eliminate" and "promote", involve the taking of active steps'.

213 Disability Equality Code of Practice, 2.38. The code makes specific reference to 'closing the gaps in service or employment outcomes, so that, for example, disabled and non-disabled people express the same level of satisfaction with their social housing, or achieve a more equal pattern of educational attainment'.

reviews of functions which are most relevant to disabled people.[214] The duty may require an authority to consider whether additional, targeted services are required in order to deliver an equal outcome for disabled and non-disabled people.[215]

9.84   The central importance of the equality duties has been recognised by the courts:

> An important reason why the laws of discrimination have moved from derision to acceptance to respect over the last three decades has been the recognition of the importance not only of respecting rights but also of doing so visibly and clearly by recording the fact.[216]

9.85   Although the courts have found compliance with the substance if not the form of the duties in several cases,[217] there have also been notable cases where the disability equality duty has been found to have been breached. In *R (JL) v Islington LBC*,[218] for example, the local authority's decision to halve the number of care hours allocated to an autistic child (JL) was held to have been made without regard for the duty because the decision diminished JL's equality of opportunity[219] and there was no evidence that a proper impact assessment had been carried out to see the likely affects that the proposals would have on disabled children.[220] Furthermore, in *R (Boyejo) v Barnet LBC*,[221] a case concerning a decision to cease to provide on-site services for sheltered housing residents, a failure to bring the DDA 1995 s49A duty to the attention of decision-makers amounted to an unlawful failure to have due regard to the duty.[222]

Positive action

9.86   The EA 2010 creates a further power to secure the advancement of equality through taking 'positive action'. There is no definition of what constitutes 'positive action' in the EA 2010. The Explanatory

---

214 Disability Equality Code of Practice, 2.39.
215 Disability Equality Code of Practice, 2.39.
216 *R (Chavda and others) v Harrow LBC* [2007] EWHC 3064 (Admin) at [40].
217 See, for example, the Court of Appeal decision upholding the first instance decision in *R (Domb) v Hammersmith and Fulham LBC* [2009] LGR 843.
218 [2009] EWHC 458 (Admin); (2009) 12 CCLR 322.
219 [2009] EWHC 458 (Admin); (2009) 12 CCLR 322 at [117].
220 [2009] EWHC 458 (Admin); (2009) 12 CCLR 322 at [121].
221 [2009] EWHC 3261 (Admin); (2010) 13 CCLR 72.
222 [2009] EWHC 3261 (Admin); (2010) 13 CCLR 72 at [58].

Notes to the EA 2010 suggest that it will allow measures to be targeted at particular groups, including training to enable them to gain employment, or health services to address their needs.[223]

9.87 The power to take positive action arises in relation to disabled children if a person reasonably thinks that:

- disabled children suffer a disadvantage in relation to their disabilities;[224]
- disabled children have needs which are different to non-disabled children;[225] or
- participation in an activity by disabled children is disproportionately low.[226]

9.88 The EA 2010 further specifies that positive action is permitted if it is a proportionate means of achieving one of the following aims:

- enabling or encouraging disabled children to overcome or minimise their disadvantages;[227]
- meeting disabled children's needs;[228] or
- enabling or encouraging disabled children to participate in activities where their participation is disproportionately low.[229]

9.89 However, the positive action power does not create a power for a person to do anything which is prohibited under any other Act.[230] Further actions which do not fall within the scope of the duty may be specified by regulations.[231]

9.90 Subject to any qualifications imposed by regulations, the positive action power is extremely broad and should mean that significantly greater thought is given by everyone in public life to the ways in which disabled children can be supported to overcome the disadvantages they face, both as a result of their impairments and as a result of socially constructed barriers to them leading ordinary lives.

223 Explanatory Notes to the EA 2010 at [519].
224 Section 158(1)(a).
225 Section 158(1)(b).
226 Section 158(1)(c).
227 Section 158(2)(a).
228 Section 158(2)(b).
229 Section 158(2)(c).
230 Section 158(6).
231 Section 158(3).

Enforcement

9.91   Section 113(1) of the EA 2010 specifies that proceedings relating to a breach of one of the duties in the Act must be brought in accordance with Part 9, 'Enforcement'. A key exception to this, however, is that a claim for judicial review is not prevented, albeit that in relation to most of the EA 2010 the specific enforcement route would provide an alternative remedy which would effectively bar an application for judicial review[232] (see paras 2.38–2.40).

9.92   Under Part 9, claims for breach of duties by service providers or public authorities must be brought in the county court.[233] Claims for breaches of the education duties must also generally be brought in the county court; however, this does not apply where the claim may be brought to the First-tier Tribunal or the Special Educational Needs Tribunal for Wales.[234] This includes any claim that a responsible body of a school has breached its duties to a child, when the appeal right to the tribunal is conferred on the child's parents.[235] Admissions and exclusions appeals are also excluded from the jurisdiction of the county court and must be heard by the relevant appeal panel.[236] However, claims of breaches of the education duties against a local authority must be brought in the county court under the service provision duties or public function duties: see paras 9.38–9.54.

County court – time limits

9.93   Any claim to the county court must be made within six months of the date of the act complained of, or within any other period as the court thinks just and equitable.[237] Where conduct extends over a period,

---

232 Section 113(3)(a). An obvious exception to this is the public sector equality duty, which is only enforceable through an application for judicial review: see para 9.81.

233 Section 114(1)(a).

234 Section 114(3), read with section 116(1).

235 Schedule 17 para 3.

236 Schedule 17 paras 13 and 14.

237 Section 118(1). The wording of the EA 2010 suggests that this could conceivably be shorter than six months, but the Part 3 Code of Practice, 16.10 states that this means 'such *longer* period as the court thinks is just and equitable' (emphasis added). The date when time stops running is the date the claim form is issued: Part 3 Code of Practice, 16.12. The court should exercise this discretion having regard to all the circumstances, including the prejudice each party would suffer as a result of the decision: Part 3 Code of Practice, 16.20.

time only starts to run when the period ends.[238] In any complaint in relation to a failure to act, time starts to run when the negative decision was taken.[239] The limitation period is extended to nine months if the matter is referred for conciliation by the Equality and Human Rights Commission.[240]

County court – remedies

9.94 The county court has available to it all the remedies open to the High Court to grant either on a claim in tort or in an application for judicial review.[241] In practice, this means that the court can make a declaration that the EA 2010 has been breached, grant a mandatory order requiring a party to comply with its duties under the Act or award damages. The ability of the court to award damages for injury to feelings (whether alone or in conjunction with another award) is expressly stated.[242] The court may also award aggravated and/or exemplary damages when the person committing the unlawful act has behaved in a high-handed, malicious, insulting or oppressive manner.[243]

Tribunal appeals

9.95 Claims of disability discrimination by schools must be made to the First-tier Tribunal (Special Educational Needs and Disability) or, in Wales, the Special Educational Needs Tribunal for Wales (see paras 4.131–4.140 for the tribunal in the context of SEN appeals). Claims to the English tribunal are governed by the tribunal procedural rules.[244] Claims to the Welsh tribunal will be governed by regulations to be

238 Section 118(6)(a). This would also encompass a 'continuing state of affairs', for instance a series of connected acts by different persons employed by the same service provider: Part 3 Code of Practice, 16.18.

239 Section 118(6)(b). In the absence of evidence to the contrary, a failure to act will be 'decided' when a person does something inconsistent with taking the action or on the expiry of the period when a person might reasonably have been expected to do the act: section 118(7).

240 Section 118(4): see the Equality Act 2006 s27 for the conciliation arrangements.

241 Section 119(2). Damages should not, however, be awarded for breaches of section 19 (indirect discrimination) unless the court has first considered whether to make any other dispersal, unless the court is satisfied that the discrimination was intentional: section 119(5) and (6).

242 Section 119(4).

243 Part 3 Code of Practice, 16.55–16.56.

244 The Tribunal Procedure (First-tier Tribunal) (Health, Education and Social Care Chambers) Rules 2008 SI No 2699.

made by the Welsh ministers.[245] The limitation period for a tribunal claim in both England and Wales is six months from the date of the act or conduct complained of,[246] although this is extended to nine months where a request for conciliation is made to the EHRC.[247] The tribunal has discretion to consider a claim that is out of time.[248]

9.96   If a breach of duty is identified, the tribunal may make any order that it sees fit to make,[249] other than awarding financial compensation or damages.[250] The tribunal should in particular look to 'obviate' or reduce the adverse effect on the disabled child of any discriminatory treatment in deciding how to exercise its discretion to make any order it thinks fit.[251]

School admissions and exclusions appeals

9.97   As set out above (see paras 4.108 and 4.120), claims of disability discrimination in relation to school admissions and *permanent* exclusions must be dealt with by the relevant appeal panel.[252] The panel hearing the claim of disability discrimination has the powers given to it by the relevant appeal arrangements.[253] Disability discrimination claims in relation to fixed-term exclusions continue to be dealt with by the tribunal under its general jurisdiction to consider claims of disability discrimination in relation to the education of pupils at school.

Burden of proof and general procedural matters

9.98   The EA 2010 establishes a specific burden of proof for cases alleging breaches of its provisions. If there are facts from which the court or

---

245 Schedule 17 para 6(2). Paragraph 6(3) sets out the matters which may be prescribed by the regulations.

246 Schedule 17 para 4(1). The same provisions apply as in the county court in relation to conduct extending over a period and failures to act: see para 9.93.

247 Schedule 17 para 4(2).

248 Schedule 17 para 4(3). The Education Guidance suggests (at p122) that it will be 'very unusual' for the tribunal to exercise its discretion to hear claims out of time.

249 Schedule 17 para 5(2).

250 Schedule 17 para 5(3)(b).

251 Schedule 17 para 5(3)(a).

252 See Schedule 17 para 13(2) in relation to admissions decisions and para 14(2) in relation to exclusion decisions.

253 Schedule 17 para 13(3) and (4) in relation to admissions appeals and para 14(3) and (4) in relation to exclusion appeals.

tribunal could decide, in the absence of any other explanation, that a person contravened the provision concerned, the court or tribunal must hold that the contravention occurred.[254] A court or tribunal can look at circumstantial evidence (which may include events before and after the alleged unlawful act) to help establish the basic facts.[255] However, a court or tribunal must not make this finding of a breach of the EA 2010 if the person can show that they did not contravene the provision.[256] Thus, once a person has established facts from which a court could conclude that there has been an act of unlawful discrimination, harassment or victimisation, the burden of proof shifts to the respondent. To defend a claim successfully, the alleged discriminator will have to prove, on the balance of probabilities, that they did not unlawfully discriminate, harass, victimise or fail to make reasonable adjustments.[257]

9.99   In relation to the need for individuals alleging breaches of the Act to be able to obtain relevant information, the EA 2010 requires the relevant minister to prescribe forms through which questions can be put to the alleged discriminator.[258] Any questions and answers are admissible as evidence in proceedings, whether or not in the prescribed form.[259] A court or tribunal can draw adverse inferences from any failure to answer a relevant question posed, or from an 'evasive or equivocal' answer.[260]

9.100   Where a claim involves an allegation of breach of the duty to make reasonable adjustments, whether an adjustment is 'reasonable' is an objective question for the court or tribunal to determine.[261]

---

254 Section 136(2). This includes the First-tier Tribunal and the Special Educational Needs Tribunal for Wales: section 136(6)(d) and (e).
255 Part 3 Code of Practice, 16.25.
256 Section 136(3).
257 Part 3 Code of Practice, 16.26.
258 Section 138(2).
259 Section 138(3).
260 Section 138(4), subject to the qualifications to this set out in section 138(5).
261 Part 3 Code of Practice, 8.34.

CHAPTER 10

Transition to adulthood

Key points

- The process of transition to adulthood involves changes in both the law and service provision for disabled young people.
- This process can be managed very badly and transition to adult services has been described as a 'cliff edge' or 'black hole'.
- There is no reason in law why this should be the case; the fundamental duties for disabled young people as adults remain to assess their needs and provide services to meet their needs.
- A whole range of government guidance requires a multi-agency approach to effective transition planning for disabled young people.
- Unless there has been significant social care or health input in the life of a disabled young person, education should generally take the lead in transition planning.
- The education duties are to produce a transition plan following the annual review of a child's statement of special educational needs (SEN) at 14 and to carry out a learning difficulty assessment in the child's last year at school.
- Providers of further and higher education have duties not to discriminate against disabled young people.
- Disabled young people can continue to receive social care services under Chronically Sick and Disabled Persons Act (CSDPA) 1970 s2. However, the statutory basis for other social care services, for example residential care, may change at 18. Eligibility for adult social care services should be determined after assessment, which should take into account the results of any assessments carried out when the young person was a child.
- Disabled young people who are accommodated by local authorities as children are entitled to a personal adviser and pathway plan under the leaving care legislation.
- The fundamental duties on health bodies remain the same when a disabled child becomes a disabled adult. However, the move from paediatric to adult services can be extremely disruptive and must be properly planned. Government guidance expects a health transition plan to be developed for every disabled young person with health needs.
- The approach to NHS 'continuing care' for disabled young people with complex health needs changes when they reach 18 and there are duties to ensure that this particularly vital transition is managed properly.

> • The Mental Capacity Act 2005 applies in almost all respects to 16- and 17-year-olds. It is essential that the capacity to make each individual decision of disabled young people is properly assessed and that if decisions have to be taken on their behalf they are made in the young person's best interests.

Introduction

10.1 This chapter deals with the law relating to disabled people as they move into adulthood. This process is frequently referred to simply as 'transition'. It is often an extremely difficult time for disabled people and their families, as all too frequently the services and supports they may have fought for as children fall away while adult services are not ready to step in: see paras 1.72–1.75 for more on disabled young people's experiences at this life stage. However, as disabled young people move into adulthood the fundamental duties owed to them by public bodies remain the same – to assess their needs and to use person-centred planning to secure mainstream and specialist services and support that meet these needs.

10.2 At the point of transition to adulthood, legal and organisational arrangements change, new information needs to be accessed and new plans have to be made.[1] System failures in this important stage contribute to negative outcomes and poor quality of life for disabled young people.[2] The report from the parliamentary hearings which informed the 'Aiming High for Disabled Children' review described transition to adulthood as 'the black hole', meaning 'a time when young people have few options, become more isolated and families experience a drop in levels of support'.[3] This language was echoed in a 2007 report from the (then) social care inspectorate, which described the transition process for some disabled young people as a 'nightmare'.[4] Although self-assessment evidence from the Transition Support Programme (see below) suggests that local areas in England

1 J Read, L Clements and D Reubain, *Disabled children and the law – research and good practice*, Jessica Kingsley Publishers, 2006, p166.
2 J Read, L Clements and D Reubain, *Disabled children and the law – research and good practice*, Jessica Kingsley Publishers, 2006, pp168–171.
3 *Report of the Parliamentary Hearings on Services for Disabled Children*, 2006, p53.
4 Commission for Social Care Inspection (CSCI), *Growing up matters: better transition planning for young people with complex needs*, 2007.

have recognised the need to improve transition processes, the experiences of transition to adulthood for many individual young people remain unacceptable.

10.3   This chapter sets out the law in the three key service areas affecting disabled young people – education, social care and health. It further shows how the assessment and planning duties at transition to adulthood should result in the young person's housing needs being met and their potential to work and make a positive contribution to society fulfilled to the maximum possible extent. It also summarises the provisions of the Mental Capacity Act 2005 which govern decisions made about disabled young people who lack capacity to take these decisions for themselves.

10.4   This chapter makes many references to court and ombudsman findings concerning serious management failings by health and social care authorities of the transitional process. Such failings cause significant and sometimes long-term hardship to disabled young people and their families. Frequently the disabled young person is vulnerable and the harm is to their emotional well-being and education/social development,[5] although on occasions it is even more profound, as was the finding of the ombudsmen in a complaint concerning 'Mr W'. In this sad and extreme case, the local government ombudsman[6] found that arrangements by the local authority for this young man's transition into adult accommodation fell significantly below a reasonable standard: indeed Mr W died after a period of deteriorating health, including admission to hospital.

10.5   The failure of local authorities and health bodies to ensure continuity of care for disabled people moving into adulthood is not a new concern. The problem is primarily organisational, in that at this stage the people responsible for the care planning and commissioning arrangements for the young person generally change: from children's services to adult services; from paediatric services to general adult healthcare, and so on. The creation of separate social services departments in England for children and adults by the Children Act (CA) 2004 has almost certainly exacerbated this profound and long

---

5   As was the case, for example, in a case summarised in Local Government Ombudsman, digest of cases 2007/8, H1, which concerned a young person who had been accommodated by a local authority in a series of inappropriate residential placements for almost two years and in respect of which the ombudsman recommended a compensation payment of over £12,000.

6   Local Government Ombudsman and Parliamentary and Health Service Ombudsman, *Six lives: the provision of public services to people with learning disabilities* HC 203–201, TSO, 2009, p64.

standing problem.[7] This danger was acknowledged by the statutory guidance concerning the role of directors of adult social services[8] which (as noted below, para 10.52) requires that they, together with their opposite number in children's services, have in place 'adequate arrangements' to ensure 'continuity of care for young disabled people throughout their transition to becoming adults'.

10.6   Disabled Persons (Services, Consultation and Representation) Act (DPSCRA) 1986 ss5 and 6 endeavours to address the problem of transition to adulthood, in relation to disabled children for whom there is a statement of special educational needs (SEN) (see paras 4.45–4.60). Section 5 of the 1986 Act requires that when the child is 14 the relevant social services officer be contacted with a view to a social care assessment of the young person's needs being undertaken – so that services are in place when educational provision ceases. This statutory obligation, which is considered at para 10.22, appears to be more honoured in the breach than by compliance.

10.7   While a period of up to four years to plan for a young person's transition into adulthood might appear a generous timescale, experience suggests that transition planning too often remains poor. Not untypically, councils simply fail to comply with their statutory responsibilities and even when the transition process is instigated, it is frequently characterised by delay, officer turnover, a lack of incisive action, broken undertakings, ignored complaints and a persistent failure to locate suitable placements (which may require a very specific and costly package of care) during which the authority loses the ability to look at the 'whole child' and his or her spectrum of needs – and becomes particularly insensitive to the impact these failures are having on the family carers.[9]

10.8   The basic duty owed to disabled young people in transition, across all service areas, is that the responsible statutory body must assess their needs and put in place a plan to ensure that those needs are met. Whatever the type of assessment, it is crucial that the young person and her or his family are made aware of its purpose, how it will

---

7   See, for example, L Clements, 'Respite and short break care and disabled children' (2008) 18 *Seen & Heard*, pp23–31.

8   Department of Health, *Guidance on the Statutory Chief Officer Post of Director of Adult Social Services issued under s7(1) Local Authority Social Services Act 1970*, 2006.

9   There are abundant local government ombudsmen reports which highlight failures of this kind – but for a not untypical example, see the report on an investigation into complaint 08/001/991 against the Isle of Wight Council, 4 June 2009.

be conducted and, most importantly, the nature of the decisions that rest on it. In addition, professionals should adopt a 'person-centred planning' approach:[10] giving disabled young people every opportunity to take decisions about their lives with the necessary support. The previous government in England stated its commitment to 'supporting local authorities and partner agencies develop a person centred approach to the statutory transition planning process'[11] and there is no reason to think the coalition government will take a different view. An overall policy objective for young people with learning disabilities remains to give them greater choice and control over their lives through support to develop person-centred plans.[12]

10.9   Alongside the availability of appropriate provision, a successful transition to adulthood for a disabled young person will almost always depend upon proper planning in which the needs, preferences and wishes of the young person and their parents should be central: not least because this a legal obligation – CA 1989 ss1(3) and 17(4A). All too often, it appears that this fundamental prerequisite is overlooked: in a 2008 Report,[13] for example, the local government ombudsman found maladministration through a failure to communicate with and consult a young person who was moved to a residential educational placement, seemingly with almost no reference to his wishes and feelings. The courts have also considered similar failures. *R (CD) v Anglesey CC*[14] concerned a 15-year-old disabled person for whom the local authority's transition care plan was 'substantially contrary' to her wishes and feelings. In a damning judgment the court castigated the local authority for its failures, observing:

> Of course a 15-year-old who does not suffer substantial disabilities and who is directed to stay at a location to which she or he has strong objection can, as is the frequent experience of the Division, vote with her or his feet. C can do no such thing; but it would, for obvious reasons, be wrong to pay any less respect to her wishes and feelings in consequence.

10 Department of Health, *National service framework for children, young people and maternity services: standard 8,* 2004, p38; Department of Health, *Valuing people: a new strategy for learning disability for the 21st century: towards person centred approaches,* 2002.

11 HM Government, *Valuing people now: a new three-year strategy for people with learning disabilities,* 2009, 3.33.

12 HM Government, *Valuing people now: a new three-year strategy for people with learning disabilities,* 2009, p52.

13 Local Government Ombudsman, digest of cases 2008/9, Case L3: in a similar vein, see also Local Government Ombudsman, digest of cases 2007/8, Case H4.

14 [2004] EWHC 1635 (Admin); (2004) 7 CCLR 589 at [61].

10.10 Young people in transition and their families should not feel that they have to limit their ambitions. The National Service Framework for Children (England) describes the main focus of transition planning as 'the fulfilment of the hopes, dreams and potential of the disabled young person, in particular to maximise education, training and employment opportunities, to enjoy social relationships and to live independently'.[15] *Valuing people now*, the updated learning disability strategy for England, notes that 'work defines us ... [but] because so few people with learning disabilities do work, there is no expectation from others that they can, and consequently little is done to offer them the opportunity'.[16] Transition planning should therefore focus on realistic but ambitious plans for disabled young people in adulthood. For example, *Valuing people now* states that planning for employment should be a 'key objective in person centred plans, including person centred transition plans'.[17] In recent years, post-school education policy has emphasised the need to develop and fund provision which offers disabled young people increased opportunities in the labour market.[18] In relation to leisure opportunities, local authorities in England have a duty[19] to take reasonable steps to secure leisure activities for young people in their area, including disabled young people up to the age of 25.

10.11 Proper transition planning involves a process that takes time, skill and sensitivity and works to avoid common pitfalls. For example, if the planning starts too late, there is a danger that those involved will simply go through the motions, that young people and their parents will not participate fully and that only limited options will be on offer that do not reflect the range of outcomes which young people might wish to aim for. While people may feel protected by formal procedures, they may also find them inhibiting when it comes to

15 Department of Health, *National service framework for children, young people and maternity services: core standards*, 2004, standard 8, p38.

16 The Department for Education is currently (July 2010) running a campaign called 'Aspirations for Life' as part of the Valuing Employment Now strategy to raise aspirations and expectations for children and young people with learning disabilities, with a particular focus on employment. See www.aspirationsforlife. org.

17 HM Government, *Valuing people now: a new three-year strategy for people with learning disabilities*, 2009, 3.29.

18 See, for example, Learning and Skills Council for England, *Learning for living and work: improving education and training opportunities for people with learning difficulties and/or disabilities*, 2006.

19 Education Act 1996 s507B, inserted by Education and Inspections Act 2006 s6(1).

expressing their opinions and aspirations. Some may find it difficult if policy and practice appear to privilege cultural norms that are not their own.[20] Some young people may require forms of communication other than speech and may be prevented from participating if this is not fully acknowledged.[21] In what is an essentially personal process, concerns, tensions and differences of view may emerge between family members.

10.12   All these issues need to be addressed for transition planning to succeed in its object of promoting fulfilling lives for disabled young people. Above all, regardless of the formal legal obligations on individual services which are set out below, multi-agency co-operation is essential if satisfactory outcomes are to be achieved for disabled young people.[22] For disabled young people as for their non-disabled peers, autonomy and independence should increase as they reach adulthood, though the meaning and expression of independence and autonomy will differ considerably between individuals.[23]

10.13   The vital importance of a successful transition to adulthood for disabled young people has long been recognised in government policy publications and guidance.[24] Much of this guidance is contained in subject specific documents – such as the SEN Code of Practice and the Valuing People Guidance, which are considered further below. However, as a result of the 'Aiming High for Disabled Children' review, a transition support programme[25] was established in England to promote good transition practice across all areas of relevance

---

20 L Jones, K Atkin and W Ahmad, 'Supporting Asian deaf young people and their families: the role of professionals and services', (2001) 16 *Disability and Society*, pp51–70.

21 P Rabiee, P Sloper and B Beresford, 'Desired outcomes for children and young people with complex health care needs and children who do not use speech for communication', (2005) 135 *Health and Social Care in the Community*, pp478–487. See also (undated) guidance published by the Council for Disabled Children and Participation Works, *How to involve children and young people with communication impairments in decision-making*, available from www. participationworks.org.uk.

22 B. Beresford, 'On the road to nowhere? Young disabled people and transition', (2004) 306 *Child: Care, Health and Development*, pp581–587. See also SEN CoP, 9:59.

23 J Read, L Clements and D Reubain, *Disabled children and the law – research and good practice*, Jessica Kingsley Publishers, 2006, ch 7.

24 See, for example, Prime Minister's Strategy Unit, *Improving the life chances of disabled people*, 2005 and Department for Children Schools and Families/ Department of Health, *A transition guide for all services: key information for professionals about the transition process for disabled young people*, 2007.

25 See www.transitionsupportprogramme.org.uk/.

to disabled young people as they journey through this phase of their lives. As part of the transition support programme every local area in England has drawn up a transition development plan, setting out how they will use the additional funding received from government for this work. In addition, again in England, *A transition guide for all services*[26] explains how all relevant services should work together with a young person to identify how they can best support that person to achieve their desired outcomes. Particular emphasis is placed on the need for strategic transition protocols[27] and local transition pathways in every local area. *Transition: moving on well*[28] sets out good practice for health professionals and their partners in transition planning for young people with complex health needs or disabilities. Government guidance repeatedly calls for all transition planning for young people to take full account of the approaches set out in these documents.[29] In Wales no overarching guidance on managing transitions exists, although brief mention is made in the social services assessment guidance[30] and as part of a broad policy initiative for all disabled children and young people pilot transition programmes have been established (overseen by the Care Co-ordination Network UK (CCNUK)) with a view to formulating best practice in this area.[31]

10.14　The role of services and the law that governs them is to support the fulfilment of independent adult lives to the maximum possible extent for every individual disabled young person. Addressing the fragmentation of services at transition to adulthood can be a key role for a young person's key worker or lead professional (see paras

26　Department for Children, Schools and Families/Department of Health, *A transition guide for all services: key information for professionals about the transition process for disabled young people*, 2007 (*'A transition guide for all services'*).

27　See National Transition Support Team, *'How to' guide: How to develop a transition protocol*, NCB, 2009, available at www.transitionsupportprogramme. org.uk/PDF/How_to_develop_a_protocol.pdf.

28　Department for Children, Schools and Families/Department of Health, *Transition: moving on well – a good practice guide for health professionals and their partners on transition planning for young people with complex health needs or a disability*, 2008 (*'Transition: moving on well'*).

29　See, for example, Department of Health, *The National framework for NHS continuing healthcare and NHS-funded nursing care*, 2009, para 120.

30　Welsh Assembly Government, *Creating a unified and fair system for assessing and managing care* NAfWC 09/2002 and 09A/2002 (2002), p65.

31　Welsh Assembly Government, *Written statement: a progress update on the Welsh Assembly Government's policy agenda for disabled children and young people*, 2009, and see also a basic guide for young people focussed on disabled young people with a statement of SEN: WAG, *My life, my way: a young persons guide to transition*, 2009.

3.10–3.12) or their personal adviser if the young person is eligible for 'leaving care' services: see para 10.70. Since 2004, the *National service framework* in England has required that a multi-agency transition group is in place, with specific arrangements made for managing the transition of those with high levels of need, those in residential schools/living away from home, looked after young people leaving care, and those with rare conditions.[32] The English guidance, *A transition guide for all services,*[33] stresses the critical importance of multi-agency working at both an individual and strategic level:

> The emergence of children's trust working models, co-located services, the participation of families and the promotion of joint working are all having a positive impact on the range of services available to support disabled young people, and are contributing to improved outcomes for individuals.[34]

10.15   Proper multi-agency working must engage both children's and adult services, for instance the children's trust and the learning disability partnership board, and may involve the creation of a dedicated 'transition team' working across children's and adult services. However, even if these structures are not in place in the relevant local area, there remains a key obligation to work on a multi-agency basis at the level of the individual young person, as set out below.

Education

10.16   If there is not substantial health or social care involvement in the life of a disabled young person, then education should be the lead agency with responsibility for ensuring a smooth transition to adult life for that young person. In relation to that transition, a positive outcome for many disabled young people will be the provision for them of appropriate education or training opportunities beyond the minimum school leaving age (currently 16).[35]

---

32   DfES/Department of Health, *National service framework for children, young people and maternity services: standard 8: disabled children and young people and those with complex health needs,* 2004, ch 7.

33   *A transition guide for all services.*

34   *A transition guide for all services,* p26.

35   At the time of writing (July 2010) the raising of the 'participation age' for education and training to 18 under the Education and Skills Act 2008 is not yet in force and it is unclear whether the coalition government intends to bring it into force. Even if no further legislation is passed, the secretary of state may delay until June 2015 before bringing these provisions into force: Education and Skills Act 2008 s173(10).

10.17   The two main education duties to support successful transition to adulthood for disabled young people are the transition planning duties from age 14 set out in the SEN Code of Practice and the duties to carry out a learning difficulty assessment in the young person's last year at school. The first of these duties is about proper planning for positive futures for disabled young people after school. The second is about ensuring that the young person's educational and related care needs are met after they finish compulsory education. These duties are considered in some detail in turn below. This section also considers the duties on further education providers under the Equality Act 2010.

10.18   Where a young person has a statement of SEN, this statement continues to have legal force while that young person remains in school or until such time as the local education authority (LEA) determines to 'cease to maintain' it (see paras 4.100–4.106). If a young person moves into further education their statement cannot move with them and their learning difficulty assessment and plan (see below) will be the critical document setting out the support they can expect to receive.

SEN transition planning

10.19   For children with statements of SEN (see paras 4.45–4.60) the Year 9 annual review (when the child is 14) should be extended to plan for the child's transition from school. This review is of critical importance and should be attended by the Connexions service[36] and a representative of adult social services, if the child is likely to need adult social care support.

10.20   Vital as the Year 9 transition review is, it is too often mishandled and at times appears to be almost completely ignored. A common problem is the failure of social services and/or the NHS to participate in the process, despite being sent notification of the review. This failure is not infrequently due to the relevant officers, on receiving the papers, checking to see if the child is receiving care or other support from their department. If there is no involvement or knowledge of the child, then no action is taken. It is important therefore, that in appropriate cases, before the review meeting takes place these agencies have it impressed upon them the importance of their attendance

---

36 A national service working through local Connexions services bringing together all the key youth support services and providing advice and information; www.connexions-direct.com. Under the Education and Skills Act 2008, funding and responsibility for delivering the Connexions service now rests with LEAs.

and the need (in the case of social services) for a core assessment to be undertaken (see para 3.15) as part of the transitional planning process. A failure to do this was held to be maladministration by the local government ombudsman in a 2006 complaint.[37] In that case, not only did social services fail to attend the annual review at 14, but the review did not happen until the disabled person was 15 and then even the education department failed to participate.

10.21 It is not unknown for the education and social services/children's services sections within the local authority to be unco-operative with each other. A 2009 local government ombudsman report[38] referred to just such a situation and also drew attention to a social services misconception of its relevance to the Year 9 review. In that case, although the parent contacted the social services department at the suggestion of the education department, it was 'unwilling to engage with her' because of 'differences' between the two departments – a point found 'unacceptable' by the ombudsman. The social services section then declined to get involved because the young person's needs were not sufficient to meet its eligibility criteria (para 52). However, the ombudsman considered that this decision was due to the authority's failure to appreciate the very considerable support the young person was receiving from his educational placement and that once this support was no longer available his needs would have become 'more manifest'. It followed that the council's failure to engage appropriately at the Year 9 review constituted maladministration.

10.22 The Year 9 transition review should lead to the production of a *transition plan* which should be reviewed at each subsequent annual review. Although education has the lead responsibility, transition planning must be a multi-agency process, with regulations requiring that social services departments and other agencies should contribute to the transition plan.[39] In particular, under Disabled Persons (Services, Consultation and Representation) Act 1986 s5, the LEA must seek information from adult social services during the transition planning process as to whether a young person is likely to

37 Report on an investigation into complaint 05/B/00611 against Northamptonshire County Council, 30 November 2006. Although the ombudsman was uncertain as to the extent of an injustice that the child had suffered in this case, he recommended compensation be paid of over £5,000.

38 Report on an investigation into complaint no CC 3/B/16496 against Warwick County Council, 26 September 2005.

39 Education (Special Educational Needs) (England) (Consolidation) Regulations 2001 SI No 3455 reg 21; Education (Special Educational Needs) (Wales) Regulations 2001 SI No 152 (W20) reg 21; SEN CoP, 9:58–9:60.

require adult social services assistance.[40] Health bodies should also ensure that their adult NHS continuing healthcare unit is appropriately represented at all transition planning meetings relating to disabled young people whose needs suggest that there may be potential eligibility for adult NHS continuing healthcare funding (see paras 10.82–10.83).[41]

10.23 The transition plan should be developed in a person-centred way ensuring that young people and their families are involved in the process.[42] Young people may need the support of an advocate to make sure their views and aspirations are heard and shape the transition plan. When completed, the transition plan should 'draw together information from a range of individuals within and beyond school in order to plan coherently for the young person's transition to adult life'.[43] When first drawn up in Year 9, the plan should cover both ongoing school provision and plans for post-school arrangements. The SEN Code of Practice requires adherence to the following principles, stating that transition plans should be:

- participative;
- holistic;
- supporting;
- evolving;
- inclusive; and
- collaborative.[44]

10.24 The delivery of the transition plan is the responsibility of Connexions and the Connexions personal adviser should co-ordinate its delivery.[45] The views of the young person should be sought and recorded in preparing the plan and in its delivery.[46]

10.25 Failures to undertake proper transition planning for young people with special educational needs will constitute maladministration: as was held to be the case in a 2003 local government ombudsman report[47] where a young person was left without any education for a year

---

40 SEN CoP, 9:58.
41 Department of Health, *National framework for NHS continuing healthcare and NHS-funded nursing care*, 2009, para 121.
42 Department of Health, *Person centred planning: advice for using person-centred thinking, planning and reviews in schools and transition*, 2010.
43 SEN CoP, 9:51.
44 SEN CoP, 9:52.
45 SEN CoP, 9:53.
46 SEN CoP, 9:55.
47 Report 03/B/16496–7, Reported in the Local Government Ombudsman *Digest of Cases 2005/6*, A13 – compensation of £5,000 was recommended in this case.

due to 'a series of administrative failings' which resulted in his SEN statement lapsing because of differences about his post-16 education.

10.26　While the formal transition planning obligations only apply to those young people with statements of SEN, schools are required to ensure that young people with SEN but without a statement receive 'appropriate advice and guidance' on their post-school options.[48] The Connexions service has the responsibility for providing support to all young people with SEN (indeed all young people generally). The main way in which young people without statements of SEN can access additional support as they move into further education is through a learning difficulty assessment and resulting action plan: see paras 10.30–10.39.

Post-school provision for young people with SEN

10.27　The law in relation to the provision of education to young people with learning difficulties[49] aged 16–25 was substantially amended by the Apprenticeship, Skills, Children and Learning Act (ASCLA) 2009 and there remains confusion as to how this new system will operate – or even if it will be retained by the new coalition government in England.[50] The ASCLA 2009 inserted a new section (s15ZA) into the Education Act 1996 which places the duty on local authorities in England to secure enough suitable education and training to meet the reasonable needs of these young people. Under the ASCLA 2009, local authorities will be responsible for all learners aged 19–25 who have a learning difficulty assessment (see paras 10.30–10.39) regardless of where it is decided that their assessed needs should be met (for example, local further education sector college or specialist further education college).

10.28　The 2009 Act's transfer of responsibility to local authorities for planning, commissioning and funding education and training for young people with a learning difficulty aged 16–25 is intended to establish a single point of accountability.[51] The still-more-ambitious

48　SEN CoP, 9:65.

49　As defined in Education Act 1996 s15ZA.

50　As this book went to press, the Department for Business, Innovation and Skills launched a new consultation on significant amendments to the further education funding system: BIS, *A simplified further education and skills funding system and methodology: consultation document*, July 2010. See also BIS, *Skills for sustainable growth: consultation on the future direction of skills policy*, July 2010.

51　Department for Children, Schools and Families, *Supporting young people with learning difficulties to participate and progress – incorporating guidance on learning difficulty assessments*, 2010 ('*Learning difficulty assessment guidance*'), 1.2.

policy intention is to create a 'seamless system for identifying needs for all learners aged 0–25 years with Special Education Needs'.[52] Local authorities have been 'strongly recommended' to review their processes to identify the young people for whom they are now required to assume responsibility.[53] However, the experience of the authors is that at present there is significant confusion 'on the ground' as to how the new system is to work, with reports that some local authorities are requiring the outcome of learning difficulty assessments (see paras 10.30–10.39) to be tailored to avoid potential liability for expensive placements. This runs contrary to the whole intention of ASCLA 2009 to secure appropriate education for disabled young people with the minimum of disruption and should be strongly challenged, whether through a complaint or, where the situation is sufficiently urgent, through judicial review proceedings.

10.29   In relation to commissioning post-16 provision, the guidance[54] states as follows:

> A local authority's strategic planning for the learning needs of its residents will take account of the learning requirements for learners with a statement of SEN or with learning difficulties and/or disabilities as for all other learners for whom it has a funding responsibility. Local authorities will take account of the breadth and scale of provision available locally, regionally and nationally when considering how best to meet their duties for these individual learners in an appropriate and cost effective way. Local authorities should not seek to replicate a resource locally to meet all learner requirements which exist or emerge this will not necessarily be in the learner's best interests, nor will it be cost effective or demonstrate value for money.

Learning difficulty assessments

10.30   The legal mechanism to ensure that disabled young people have their educational and related care needs met after they finish compulsory education is a 'learning difficulty assessment'.[55] Learning difficulty assessments should be the 'culmination of careful planning, starting at least at 14, placing the learner at the centre' and setting them 'on a pathway to a positive outcome, and wherever possible/appropriate leading to employment'.[56]

---

52 *Learning difficulty assessment guidance*, 2.2.
53 *Learning difficulty assessment guidance*, 1.14.
54 *Learning difficulty assessment guidance*, 1.18.
55 Education Act 1996 s13(5) defines a learning difficulty assessment as an assessment under Learning and Skills Act 2000 s139A or s140.
56 *Learning difficulty assessment guidance*, 1.10.

10.31   Young people with statements of SEN *must* have a learning difficulty assessment in their last year of school: Learning and Skills Act 2000 s139A[57] (England) and s140 (Wales). Learning difficulty assessments *may* also be carried out in the final year of school for young people with SEN but without statements. Where a young person does not have a statement of SEN, local authorities must have a transparent process setting out the circumstances in which they will use their power to assess.[58] Furthermore, the guidance suggests that the power to assess should be exercised when:

a) a young person has needs which are 'very unclear or very complex';

b) there has been a major change in circumstance that has affected needs;

c) specific highly specialist support may be required;

d) a young person will, in the view of the special educational needs co-ordinator (SENCO – see para 4.23) or others, struggle to access post-16 learning without support over and above that usually offered within the college;

e) a young person will find significant difficulty in coping with the transition to a different learning environment; or

f) a young person has needs equivalent to those requiring statementing but has not been formally assessed.[59]

10.32   Learning difficulty assessments should always be undertaken by the person who is best placed to identify and make judgments about the needs a learner is likely to have when he or she undertakes further education, training or higher education.[60] Assessors[61] should be qualified to NVQ Level 4 and should have received specific training in relation to the needs of disabled young people, being more than basic disability awareness training.[62] All learning difficulty assessments should be person-centred[63] and must take account of the young person's views and wishes.[64] The assessor should work closely with the young person,

---

57 Inserted by Education and Skills Act 2008 s80.
58 *Learning difficulty assessment guidance*, 3.4.
59 *Learning difficulty assessment guidance*, 1.7 and 1.9.
60 *Learning difficulty assessment guidance*, 3.10.
61 Assessors should be independent of any provider both locally and nationally; *Learning difficulty assessment guidance*, 3.10. Other than this stipulation, it is for a local authority to decide which professionals should be assessors.
62 *Learning difficulty assessment guidance*, 3.12–3.13.
63 *Learning difficulty assessment guidance*, 3.17–3.22.
64 *Learning difficulty assessment guidance*, 3.23–3.27.

the young person's parents and/or carers and other professionals to ensure the assessment of their educational and training needs and the provision needed to meet them is evidence based and valid.[65] Learning difficulty assessments should be holistic and multi-agency, linking into other assessment processes as required.[66] An extensive list of professionals who may be expected to contribute to a learning difficulty assessment is given in the statutory guidance at 3.39.

10.33   Where a young person is attending a residential school, the 'home' local authority should complete the learning difficulty assessment, seeking support from the 'host' local authority (in whose area the school is located) as required.[67]

10.34   Learning difficulty assessments should result in a written report of the person's educational and training needs and the provision required to meet them, known as an 'action plan'.[68] In *Alloway v Bromley*,[69] a case concerning the previous duty to carry out assessments in England under the Learning and Skills Act 2000 s140, the court held that provision identified as capable of meeting assessed needs had to be 'actually and practically available'. Assessments and resulting action plans should clearly identify the young person's needs and set out 'appropriate provision that can actually and realistically be provided to meet them'.[70]

10.35   Furthermore, the placement recommended as capable of delivering the required provision must be named in the assessment.[71] In *R (P) v Windsor and Maidenhead RBC and another*[72] the mother of a young person, who had been educated according to particular educational principles, wanted this type of education to continue after he reached 16 and proposed that he should attend a residential college that she considered suitable. The defendant local authority proposed one of its own secondary schools – although it stipulated that if the Learning and Skills Council[73] (LSC) was prepared to

---

65 *Learning difficulty assessment guidance*, 3.11.

66 *Learning difficulty assessment guidance*, 3.36.

67 *Learning difficulty assessment guidance*, 3.40. Further information on which authority has the responsibility for carrying out learning difficulty assessments in complex cases is given in part 3 of the annex to the guidance.

68 Learning and Skills Act 2000 s139B(3).

69 [2008] EWHC 2499 (Admin).

70 *Alloway v Bromley LBC* [2008] EWHC 2499 (Admin); *Learning difficulty assessment guidance*, 3.6.

71 *R (P) v Windsor and Maidenhead RBC* [2010] EWHC 1408 (Admin).

72 [2010] EWHC 1408 (Admin).

73 The body with the relevant funding prior to ASCLA 2009.

provide the funding, then it was happy for him to attend the residential college. The LSC ultimately refused funding and the mother sought judicial review of the learning difficulties assessment that had been completed by Connexions for the authority. The application succeeded because the local authority, by failing (a) to recommend a particular placement in the statement and (b) to consider the competing merits of the two potential options, had left the reader of the assessment 'in the dark' about what provision the young person needed – ie whether he should attend a school or further education college. The court further suggested (at [60]) that learning difficulty assessments should also consider an individual's care needs if they were closely linked to his or her educational and training needs.

10.36   Having determined that a young person requires a learning difficulty assessment 'a local authority must continue to support the young person through to positive outcomes up to the age of 25'.[74] Periodic reviews (at intervals of no more than two years) should take place while the young person is in education or training until they reach 25.[75]

10.37   For the majority of young people who have additional needs, education and training provision will be delivered in a mainstream setting, usually their local further education sector college.[76] Where assessment suggests that a young person's needs are such that they can only be met by an independent specialist provider, the intention is that local authorities will negotiate the funding of this placement with the Young People's Learning Agency (YPLA). Where a young person requires residential college provision, this can be arranged by local authorities under ASCLA 2009 s46. The residential element of a young person's provision may also be part-funded through adult social care funding, as part of their personal budget. Local authorities also have duties to secure transport provision to colleges and other further education provision.[77]

10.38   While funding for a period of further education or training can be of a great benefit in a young person's transitional arrangements, it

---

74 *Learning difficulty assessment guidance*, 1.8. Local authorities in England must secure sufficient suitable education and training (Education Act 1996 s15ZA) and work experience (Education Act 1996 s560A) for young people with learning difficulty assessments up to the age of 25.

75 *Learning difficulty assessment guidance*, Annex, 6.1.

76 Young People's Learning Agency, *Placement information – learners with learning difficulties and/or disabilities at independent specialist providers*, 2010, para 7.

77 Education Act 1996 s509AA and s508F–G. See *Learning difficulty assessment guidance*, 1.26–1.32.

can only be one part of a longer-term plan. All too often such a place-ment results in the young person's needs being neglected, or being given less priority by the local authority; a case of 'out of sight, out of mind'. A complaint considered by the local government ombudsman illustrates this situation.[78] It concerned a young disabled adult who had been living at a centre partly funded by the Learning Skills Coun-cil with the aim that this would provide a transition to her perma-nent adult placement. When this transition arrangement finished, the council offered only one choice of a permanent placement – at an adult centre, which the family (and indeed the adult centre itself) considered unsuitable. Although the family explained their reasons for rejecting the proposal the council failed to respond – effectively washing its hands of responsibility, albeit it subsequently made fur-ther placement suggestions, none of which, however, were able to provide the necessary care. The ombudsman was highly critical of the council's delay, its flawed community care assessment and care planning processes and its failure to engage in meaningful discus-sions with the family – who had been required to provide care for their adult daughter in consequence. Since her care needs at a suit-able adult centre would have cost the council about £1,000 per week, the ombudsman recommended a compensation payment be made to the parents of £1,000 per week for every week they had to care for their daughter as a consequence of the council's maladministration (a period of two years).

10.39   The Getting a Life[79] project has found that aspirations are often far too low for young people with learning difficulties, and that post-16 assessments too often focus on what young people cannot do rath-er than on what they can do. Young people with learning difficulties and/or disabilities are twice as likely to be not in education, employ-ment or training (NEET) as those without.[80] The stated intention of the reforms introduced by the ASCLA 2009 is to end these negative assumptions and outcomes and ensure that local authorities concen-trate on the core purpose of their duties – to help disabled young people achieve ordinary independent lives. Where a young person

---

78 Report on an investigation into complaint no 05/C/11921 against Trafford Metropolitan Borough Council 2007. See also complaint no 07 A 11108 against Surrey County Council, 11 November 2008, where the a similar delay occurred after the disabled young person was placed in further education college – in this case, delays with adaptations to her parents' home.

79 See www.gettingalife.org.uk.

80 *Learning difficulty assessment guidance*, 2.10.

or their parent is dissatisfied with a learning difficulty assessment, the local authority must have in place an effective complaints process through which such grievances can be addressed and hopefully resolved.[81] Guidance published by the Young People's Learning Agency (YPLA) states that a review panel process will be put in place at a future date to provide another level of scrutiny of local authority decision-making.[82] In the absence of effective local redress, young people and parents can complain to the local government ombudsman or (if the situation is sufficiently urgent) make an application for judicial review to the High Court (see paras 2.38–2.40).

Disabled student allowances

10.40   Disabled student allowances (DSAs) are grants to help meet the extra course costs students in higher education can face as a direct result of a disability, ongoing health condition, mental health condition or specific learning difficulty.[83] DSAs can be used to meet a wide range of additional disability-related costs, including:

- specialist equipment needed for studying – for example, computer software;
- non-medical helpers, such as a note-taker or reader;
- extra travel costs resulting from a student's disability; and
- other costs – for example, tapes or Braille paper.[84]

10.41   The amount of support available through a DSA is dependent on the extent of the person's needs, not their financial circumstances. As at July 2010 the maximum general allowance was £1,724 a year for full-time students and £1,293 a year for part-time students. Substantial specific amounts are also available in respect of the provision of specialist equipment and the funding of a non-medical helper[85] to support the student.[86]

---

81 *Learning difficulty assessment guidance*, 3.45–3.48.

82 YPLA, *Placement information – learners with learning difficulties and/or disabilities at independent specialist providers*, 2010, paras 45–47.

83 See www.direct.gov.uk/dsas.

84 See www.direct.gov.uk/dsas.

85 Readers, sign-language interpreters, notetakers and other non-medical assistants.

86 Applications should be made to local authorities using the form DSA1 (disabled students' allowance form), which can be downloaded from the www. direct.gov.uk site in England and at the www.studentfinancewales.co.uk site in Wales.

10.42　It is important to note that the availability of financial support through DSAs does not absolve higher education providers of their responsibilities under the Equality Act 2010, and in particular their duties to make reasonable adjustments to ensure equality of access for disabled people – see below.

Equality Act 2010 – further and higher education

10.43　The duties imposed on schools and LEAs by the Equality Act (EA) 2010 are considered in chapter 9. This section considers the equality duties which are specific to providers of further and higher education. These provisions are set out in EA 2010 Part 6 Chapter 2.

10.44　In relation to admissions, a responsible body[87] of a further or higher education institution must not discriminate[88] against a disabled young person:

- in the arrangements it makes for deciding who is offered admission as a student;
- as to the terms on which it offers to admit the person as a student; or
- by not admitting the person as a student.[89]

10.45　Furthermore, responsible bodies must not discriminate against a disabled person in respect of the provision of education within the institution,[90] by excluding the disabled person[91] or in the way qualifications are offered.[92] Harassment[93] and victimisation[94] by responsible bodies are also prohibited.[95]

10.46　Finally, the responsible bodies of further education and higher education institutions owe the duty to make reasonable adjustments in favour of current or prospective disabled students.[96] All aspects of the duty apply – for example, the obligation to make appropriate changes to their provisions, criteria and/or practices; to provide auxiliary aids and services and to adapt physical features. See paras

---

87　Governing bodies or boards of management: EA 2010 s91(12).
88　See paras 9.14–9.15 for the meaning of 'discrimination'.
89　EA 2010 s91(1).
90　EA 2010 s91(2)(a).
91　EA 2010 s91(2)(e).
92　EA 2010 s91(3).
93　EA 2010 s91(5).
94　EA 2010 s91(6)–(8).
95　See paras 9.36–9.37 for the meaning of 'harassment' and 'victimisation'.
96　EA 2010 s91(9). See paras 9.32–9.35 for the duty to make reasonable adjustments under the EA 2010.

9.32–9.35 for more on the reasonable adjustment duties. In this context, it should also be noted that the social services authority also have responsibilities to under the Chronically Sick and Disabled Persons Act 1970 s2 to deliver services to meet the assessed community care needs of disabled young people – considered at para 10.50 and generally at paras 3.48–3.57.

10.47   The duties itemised above also apply to local authorities and school governing bodies in relation to courses of further education for which they are the responsible body[97] and to providers of recreational or training facilities.[98] All these duties are explained in more detail in the Equality and Human Rights Commission's (EHRC's) guidance on education.[99]

10.48   Taken together, these duties require providers of further and higher education to adapt their provision to the greatest possible extent to enable disabled people to access its benefits. If the EA 2010 has its intended effect, a far greater supply of further and higher education placements should be available to disabled young people in future than are presently available. Individuals with grievances in relation to breaches of the further and higher education duties under the EA 2010 can bring county court proceedings to seek remedies including damages: see paras 9.91–9.94.

Social care

10.49   Far too many disabled young people currently experience a disrupted transition from children to adult social care services. Half the councils responding to a 2007 survey by the Commission for Social Care Inspection reported that young people's care packages changed at, or after, transition to adulthood and that this generally represented a significant reduction in services.[100] The local government ombudsman has repeatedly expressed concern about failures in transition planning and the severe shortfalls in provision at this crucial stage. The ombudsman has in particular emphasised the duty to continue

97   EA 2010 s92.
98   EA 2010 s93.
99   EHRC, *What the Equality Act 2010 means for you in education: a guide for students, pupils and parents*, 2010, chs 4 and 5.
100 CSCI, *Growing up matters: Better transition planning for young people with complex needs*, 2007.

to meet assessed needs and not to 'use available services as a starting point and just fit people into them'.[101]

10.50 There is no reason in law why disabled young people's social care transition should be so disrupted, since (as detailed in chapter 3) most services are provided to disabled children under CSDPA 1970 s2 which applies to both children and adults. While it is the case that in general services for children under the CA 1989 cease to be available once a person turns 18 (but see paras 10.64–10.76 in relation to young people leaving care) the relevant residential care obligations are mirrored by those in the equivalent adult care statute – the National Assistance Act 1948 Part III.

10.51 To facilitate a seamless transition, local authorities have a clear obligation under the Children Acts and other statutes[102] to make sure that their children's services and adult services departments are co-operating to anticipate the transition of young disabled people. If effective assessments have been carried out when the young person is a child (see paras 3.13–3.24), the outcomes of these assessments in the forms of records and care plans can be adopted to form the basis of adult assessment and planning. If there has been no assessment or only inadequate assessments when a young person is a child, adult services will need to carry out a full assessment under the NHS and Community Care Act 1990 s47. In either event, it will almost always be necessary to determine whether the young person is eligible for adult community care services using the approach prescribed by the statutory guidance.[103]

10.52 There is also a clear expectation that adult social services departments will engage effectively in transition planning for disabled young people. The statutory guidance on the role of director of adult social services requires that 'adequate arrangements' are in place 'to ensure all young people with long-term social care needs have been assessed and, where eligible, receive a service which meets their needs throughout their transition to becoming adults'.[104] To deliver

---

101 Complaint no 03/C/16371 against Stockton-on-Tees BC, 18 January 2005.

102 For example, the Disabled Persons (Services, Consultation and Representation) Act 1986 ss5–6 in relation to children aged over 14 with statements of SEN (see chapter 4).

103 Department of Health, *Prioritising need in the context of putting people first: a whole system approach to eligibility for social care – guidance on eligibility criteria for adult social care in England*, 2010 ('Prioritising Need Guidance') and in Wales, Welsh Assembly Government *Creating a unified and fair system for assessing and managing care*, NAfWC 09/2002 and 09A/2002, 2002.

104 Department of Health, *Guidance on the Statutory Chief Officer Post of Director of Adult Social Services*, 2006, para 27.

on this expectation, many local areas have set up transition teams – either 'actual', multi-disciplinary teams based together, usually either in children's services or adult social care, or 'virtual' teams which meet regularly and have effective systems for communicating between agencies.

10.53   Because young people with learning disabilities are often particularly disadvantaged in transition to adulthood, the *Valuing People* white paper called for person-centred transition planning for these young people to be a priority.[105] The English guidance on adult eligibility criteria[106] states further (at [135]) that:

> Councils should have in place arrangements to ensure that young people with social care needs have every opportunity to lead as independent a life as possible and that they are not disadvantaged by the move from children's to adult services.

10.54   In similar terms the equivalent guidance in Wales advises that:[107]

> Services provided should aim to continue to achieve similar outcomes in relation to promoting their independence and quality of life. Arrangements should be put in place to make this transition as seamless as possible and to ensure consistency and fairness in dealing with the needs of these individuals.

10.55   Despite the abundant guidance in this area, the evidence suggests that all too often local authorities fail properly to manage complex social care transitions. Typically the problem stems from local authorities resource difficulties (both financial and personnel) and inflexible bureaucratic arrangements. Two local government ombudsman investigations illustrate these difficulties. A 2005 report[108] concerned a care plan that had identified a number of suitable placements for a young person as part of his transition from his residential college. The authority's care purchasing panel refused to fund any of the proposed placements and instead determined that he should move to a council-run facility with significantly lower costs. The young person's behaviour deteriorated rapidly at this facility such that he had

---

105   *Valuing people: a new strategy for learning disability for the 21st century*, Circular HSC 2001/016: LAC(2001)23, para 3.38. Person-centred approaches to transition planning are also required by the DfES/Department of Health, *National service framework for children, young people and maternity services: standard 8: disabled children and young people and those with complex health needs*, 2004, ch 7.

106   Prioritising Need Guidance.

107   Welsh Assembly Government, *Creating a unified and fair system for assessing and managing care*, NAfWC 09/2002 and 09A/2002, 2002, Annex 1 p65.

108   Complaint no 04/A/10159 against Southend on Sea BC, 1 September 2005.

to be moved again to a secure psychiatric unit where he was sedated for eight months. Once at the unit, which was run by the NHS, the authority withdrew all its funding. In finding maladministration (and recommending compensation of £35,000) the ombudsman held that the placement in the council-run facility 'flew in the face of the assessment'.

10.56 A 2003 ombudsman report[109] concerned a young person due to leave college, for whom his parents had identified a suitable independent residential placement which the social worker agreed met his needs. Although the council was aware that there was considerable demand for this placement and a quick funding decision was needed, it required the funding request to be put to a series of 'panels' – with the consequence that the placement was delayed by two years. The ombudsman again found maladministration (and recommended similar levels of compensation). In his opinion, once a need such as this had been identified it had to be met (regardless of resources) and it 'was unacceptable for it not to have made specific budgetary provision that would enable it to respond more quickly once a placement was offered'.

10.57 Where a disabled young person is receiving social care services prior to the age of 18, the statutory basis for this service may change on their 18th birthday. An obvious example of this is residential accommodation, whether or not made in the form of residential short breaks. While a young person is aged under 18, this provision will be made under CA 1989 s17, s20(1) or s20(4) (see chapter 3). From the young person's 18th birthday, the provision will generally be made under the National Assistance Act 1948 s21. It is, however, essential to note that there is no reason that this change in the legal basis of the provision should make *any* practical difference to the service being provided – so long as the service continues to meet the young person's assessed needs. If a new placement is required at transition to adulthood, funding decisions to enable such a placement to be made should be taken as quickly as possible and a failure to do so (as noted above) may constitute maladministration.

---

109 Complaint no 00/B/18600 against East Sussex CC, 29 January 2003. See also the not dissimilar report on complaint no 02/C/17068 against Bolton MBC, 30 November 2004, where the ombudsman found that the service user was not in any way properly prepared for his return to the community on leaving school and that 'there is overwhelming evidence that' the council's reluctance to fund the parents' preferred option was because of the impact this would have 'on the Social Services agency budget'.

10.58   The law relating to the provision of social care services to disabled adults is reviewed comprehensively by Clements and Thompson[110] and there is insufficient space in this book to go into the detail of this substantial subject. Clements and Thompson also review the important housing obligations owed to disabled adults.[111]

10.59   However, it is essential to bear in mind the vital importance of adult community care assessment and care planning duties in achieving the adult lives that disabled young people want. Whether a young person is planning to live at home with his or her parents or wants an alternative (such as one of the various supported living arrangements or residential care), adult social care services should facilitate this choice if the young person meets their eligibility criteria. Neither living in a family home nor living in a residential care setting should preclude a young person receiving services and support which meet their assessed needs and promote their autonomy and independence.

10.60   A 2008 local government ombudsman report[112] illustrates the problems that can arise where a disabled young person and her family seek a transitional plan that will enable her to live in the family home. In this case, although the young person was in a good quality residential placement and college, she and her parents wanted her to live at the family home – subject to adaptations being undertaken to make it suitable. The local authority failed to progress these adaptations (and the associated disabled facilities grant – see paras 6.16–6.44) with the necessary expedition – such that the ombudsman considered that the young person spent at least two-and-a-half years in residential care unnecessarily. The ombudsman also considered that this delay engaged the young person's rights under article 8 of the European Convention on Human Rights, and in his opinion:

> The greater a person's disability, the greater is the need to give proper and timely consideration to that person's basic rights and, what concerns me most, the values and principles underlying those rights – such as dignity, equality, fairness and respect.

110   L Clements and P Thompson, *Community care and the law*, 4th edn, LAG, 2007 ('Clements and Thompson'). The Law Commission is currently undertaking a major review of adult social care law which may result in new legislation in both England and Wales from 2011. See Law Commission, *Consultation Paper No 192 – Adult Social Care* (2010), www.lawcom.gov.uk/adult_social_care.htm.

111   Clements and Thompson, chapter 15.

112   Report on an investigation into complaint no 07 A 11108 against Surrey County Council, 11 November 2008.

Carers

10.61 Whether disabled young people remain with their families or progress towards living separately, it is important that the rights of family carers are not neglected. Although there is no legal obligation on parents to provide or continue to provide care for their adult children (see para 8.17) many continue to offer a great deal of support to their disabled sons and daughters as they become young adults. Local authorities are under a statutory duty, when the young person is being assessed for adult care services, to offer many such family carers the right to a separate assessment. This should address the level of support that they are willing to offer, any plans they may have in relation to work, leisure, education or training as well as any ways that the caring role impacts on their health and well-being (see paras 8.5–8.19 for more on carers' assessments).

Personalisation

10.62 In adult social care as in children's services, the move towards personalisation appears to be resulting in some local authorities ignoring their assessment and care planning duties. It is critically important that disabled young people do not simply accept whatever personal budget may be calculated through a resource allocation system (RAS – see para 3.70) but demand a proper assessment of their needs and a care plan to show how their eligible needs will be met, whether by a direct payment, through a nominal personal budget or through the provision of direct services. Any attempt to determine a personal budget prior to the assessment of a young person's needs will be unlawful.

Supporting people

10.63 Where disabled young people are living independently, the costs of housing support services may be met through the 'Supporting People' programme.[113] The availability or otherwise of 'Supporting People' funding does not affect the duty on adult social services departments to meet the eligible assessed needs of disabled young people. However, Supporting People funding can be used to provide 'a greater breadth of housing related solutions in any given case',[114] for instance funding a warden service in a sheltered housing scheme rather than

113 Clements and Thompson, paras 15.96–15.111.
114 Clements and Thompson, para 15.97.

providing a home help service or funding residential care – if this meets the young person's needs and accords with the young person's wishes and feelings.

Duties to disabled young people 'leaving care'

10.64   As detailed in chapter 3 (para 3.84), where a disabled child is accommodated under the CA 1989 s20 the child becomes a 'looked after' child. The child is then entitled to the same protection and support as a child who is in the local authority's care under a care order or otherwise – as some disabled children will be. Disabled young people who are looked after have the same entitlements when leaving care as other looked after young people.[115]

10.65   In recognition of the poor outcomes for children looked after by local authorities, the Children (Leaving Care) Act (CLCA) 2000 introduced significant new duties into the CA 1989, requiring local authorities to continue to support these young people into adulthood. These duties are clarified by regulations and guidance issued by the Department of Health.[116] This guidance is binding 'policy' guidance issued under Local Authority Social Services Act 1970 s7 (see para 2.25) and states that the purpose of the leaving care provisions is 'to improve the life chances of young people living in and leaving local authority care' and that its main aims are:

> to delay young people's discharge from care until they are prepared and ready to leave; to improve the assessment, preparation and planning for leaving care; to provide better personal support for young people after leaving care; and to improve the financial arrangements for care leavers.

10.66   The general duty on local authorities in relation to children leaving care is to 'advise, assist and befriend [such a child] with a view to promoting his welfare when they have ceased to look after him'.[117] However, the CLCA 2000 also inserts a range of specific duties and powers into the CA 1989 in relation to young people leaving care.

---

115 Department of Education/Department of Health, *National service framework for children, young people and maternity services: standard 8: disabled children and young people and those with complex health needs*, 2004, 7.2.

116 Department of Health, *Children (Leaving Care) Act 2000 Regulations and Guidance* ('Leaving Care Guidance') 2000. The National Assembly for Wales has produced separate regulations (Children (Leaving Care) (Wales) Regulations 2001 SI No 2189 (W151)) and guidance.

117 CA 1989 Sch 2 para 19A.

These duties and powers generally apply until a young person reaches 21. As an exception to this, help given to meet expenses concerned with education or training may continue to the young person's 24th birthday[118] or, in the case of a former relevant child (see para 10.69 c)), to the end of an agreed programme of education or training as set out in their pathway plan.[119]

10.67 The leaving care duties apply to the following groups of young people:

a) *Eligible children* – children aged 16 and 17 who have been looked after for at least 13 weeks since the age of 14 and who remain looked after.[120]

b) *Relevant children* – children aged 16 and 17 who were looked after for at least 13 weeks since the age of 14, were looked after at some time while 16 or 17 but have stopped being looked after.[121]

c) *Former relevant children* – a young person aged 18–21 who was either an eligible or relevant child.[122] Importantly, if a former relevant child's pathway plan (see para 10.71) sets out a programme of education or training extending beyond his or her 21st birthday, he or she remains a relevant child until that programme is completed.[123]

10.68 To become an eligible or relevant child, the child must have been accommodated by the local authority and therefore 'looked after' (see para 3.84) for at least 13 weeks since the age of 14. Importantly in relation to disabled children, short-term periods of respite care should be ignored for the purposes of calculating whether 13 weeks have been reached.[124]

10.69 The CLCA 2000 imposes different duties on local authorities in respect of eligible, relevant and former relevant children. These are:

118 CA 1989 s24B(3).

119 CA 1989 s23C(7).

120 CA 1989 Sch 2 para 19B(2) and the Children (Leaving Care) (England) Regulations 2001 SI No 2874 ('Leaving Care (England) Regs') reg 3; Children (Leaving Care) (Wales) Regulations 2001 SI No 2189 ('Leaving Care (Wales) Regs') reg 3.

121 CA 1989 s23A(2) and the Leaving Care (England) Regs reg 4; Leaving Care (Wales) Regs reg 4.

122 CA 1989 s23C(1).

123 CA 1989 s23C(7).

124 Leaving Care (England) Regs regs 3(3) and 4(3); Leaving Care (Wales) Regs, reg 3(2) and 4(2A). The Leaving Care Guidance explains (at 2.12) that this is because 'The 2000 Act is intended to help those children and young people who depend on the council in place of family'.

a) Eligible children – in addition to all the provisions of the looked-after system (see paras 3.84–3.87), an eligible child is entitled to a needs assessment leading to a pathway plan[125] and to have a personal adviser[126] (see below).

b) Relevant children are also entitled to a pathway plan[127] and personal adviser.[128] In addition, relevant children must be supported and maintained by the local authority, unless they are satisfied that the child's welfare does not require such support and maintenance.[129] In particular, local authorities must provide assistance (including cash if required) in order to meet a relevant child's needs in relation to education, training or employment as provided for in his or her pathway plan.[130] If a local authority has lost touch with a relevant child, they must take reasonable steps to re-establish contact.[131]

c) Former relevant children – local authorities must continue to appoint a personal adviser for a former relevant child and keep his or her pathway plan under review.[132] Furthermore, authorities must provide former relevant children with assistance with employment and education and training.[133] They must also provide other assistance 'to the extent that [the former relevant child's] welfare requires it'.[134] Local authorities must take reasonable steps to keep in touch with former relevant children, whether or not the young person remains in their area, and to re-establish contact if they lose touch.[135]

10.70   Eligible, relevant and former relevant children are therefore all entitled to both personal advisers and pathway plans. Personal advisers must be appointed by the local authority to support and befriend the young person. The functions of the personal adviser are specified by the regulations[136] and include providing advice and support, co-ordinating

---

125 CA 1989 Sch 2 para 19B(4).
126 CA 1989 Sch 2 para 19C.
127 CA 1989 s23B(3).
128 CA 1989 s23B(2).
129 CA 1989 s23B(8).
130 Leaving Care (England) Regs reg 11; Leaving Care (Wales) Regs reg 11.
131 CA 1989 s23B(11).
132 CA 1989 s23C(3).
133 CA 1989 s23C(4)(a) and (b).
134 CA 1989 s23C(4)(c).
135 CA 1989 s23C(2).
136 Leaving Care (England) Regs reg 12; Leaving Care (Wales) Regs reg 12.

the provision of services and participating in pathway planning and reviews. However, the personal adviser must not themselves develop the pathway plan[137] or carry out the review, albeit that particularly in relation to reviews they may play a very active role.[138] Young people should be given a choice of personal adviser.[139] It is expected that the same personal adviser will remain with the young person once he or she becomes a former relevant child (see above, para 10.69 c)).[140]

10.71   Pathway plans must set out the result of the needs assessment which must be completed within three months of a young person's 16th birthday.[141] The assessment must address a wide range of issues, including the young person's health and development, need for education, training and employment, financial needs and care and support needs.[142] The assessment can be carried out at the same time as an assessment under any other Act.[143] The young person must be properly involved in the assessment.[144]

10.72   Pathway plans should be produced 'as soon as possible' after the assessment is completed.[145] They should cover all the issues identified in the assessment.[146] The Leaving Care Guidance states that young people will be 'central to drawing up their own plan, setting out their own goals and identifying with their personal adviser how the local authority will help them'. The guidance specifically states that pathway plans should ensure that disabled young people obtain access to mainstream healthcare services as well as to any specialist service related to their impairment.[147] Pathway plans should contain contingency plans[148] to address potential difficulties and should be

---

137 *R (J) v Caerphilly CBC* [2005] EWHC 586 (Admin), [2005] 2 FCR 153.
138 *R (A) v Lambeth LBC* [2010] EWHC 1652.
139 Leaving Care Guidance, 6.14.
140 Leaving Care Guidance, 7.9.
141 Leaving Care Guidance, 5.7.
142 Leaving Care (England) Regs reg 7(4); Leaving Care (Wales) Regs reg 7(4).
143 CA 1989 s23B(4). See Leaving Care Guidance, Figure 1, p39 for the relationship between assessments under the *Framework for the assessment of children in need and their families* (para 3.14) and leaving care assessments and pathway planning.
144 Leaving Care Guidance, 5.5.
145 Leaving Care Guidance, 5.17.
146 The full list of issues which must be covered by a pathway plan is set out Leaving Care (England) Regs and the Leaving Care (Wales) Regs.
147 Leaving Care Guidance, 5.44.
148 Leaving Care Guidance, 5.45–5.47.

reviewed every six months[149] to check that the goals and milestones are still right for the young person and that they are being met.[150]

10.73   In *R (J) v Caerphilly CBC*[151] Munby J (as he then was) considered the assessments and pathway planning produced in relation to a relevant child with complex needs and a history of offending behaviour. The local authority's efforts were all declared to be unlawful, as none of the versions of the plan produced amounted to a 'detailed operational plan' clarifying who would do what and by when to help J (judgment at [45]–[46]). Munby J held that one of the 'telling indicators' of the plan's inadequacy was the failure to identify specialist support for J – a relevant factor in pathway planning for many disabled young people (judgment at [41]). Munby J further emphasised the need to involve the young person in the planning process, even if they are 'unco-operative' (judgment at [56]).

10.74   Following assessment and pathway planning, the Leaving Care Guidance mandates that the support provided to young people leaving care should be, broadly, the support that a good parent might be expected to give.[152] It further provides that all young people should be central to discussions about their future.[153] The guidance contains specific mandatory provisions in relation to disabled young people. For example, at 3.45, the guidance states that 'advice on disability benefits should be available as a priority' for young disabled care leavers. Furthermore, the guidance contains a section of principles in relation to disabled care leavers, which essentially requires their additional needs to be addressed by the care leaving process.[154] Local authorities are reminded of their duties under education and social care legislation to meet the needs of disabled care leavers in a holistic way.

10.75   Specific and substantial as are the duties on local authorities in such cases, the evidence suggests that the failures highlighted by the *Caerphilly* judgment (above) are not isolated. While a number of the young people to whom these duties are owed may be unco-operative this was not considered an adequate excuse for failure in the *Caerphilly* judgment. A 2009 local government ombudsman report[155] also

---

149 Leaving Care (England) Regs reg 7(9); Leaving Care (Wales) Regs reg 9.
150 Leaving Care Guidance, 5.53.
151 [2005] EWHC 586 (Admin), [2005] 2 FCR 153.
152 Leaving Care Guidance, 4.3.
153 Leaving Care Guidance, 4.4.
154 Leaving Care Guidance, 4.16–4.30.
155 Report on an investigation into complaint no 08 013 283 against Lambeth LBC, 18 May 2009.

concerned a young man who was at times unco-operative and who had been in local authority care since the age of 13, and for whom therefore the CLCA 2000 duties were engaged. Sadly his pathway plans were materially defective and agreed action was not followed through; his personal adviser failed to provide appropriate support and assistance and when he went on sick leave, he was not replaced. During this period the young man endeavoured to sustain his place on a university course and in his lodgings – although ultimately his lack of support led him to leave the course and to be threatened with eviction for rent arrears. The ombudsman identified multiple maladministration in the way that this case had been handled, and observed (para 54):

> In its corporate parenting role the Council should persevere in keep-ing in touch with the young person. ... In this case I consider that the Council had to take account of the effects of Mr Smith's bouts of depression and to make sure that relevant details of his vulnerability and background were known to those who were working with him ... That made it all the more important for the Council to put effective mechanisms in place to prevent a recurrence of past failures. It did not do so and that was further maladministration by the Council.

10.76 It is therefore obvious that the leaving care scheme offers valuable services and supports to young people who have been accommodated by local authorities. This is a primary reason why it is so important to establish under which statutory provision a disabled child who lives away from her family home is being accommodated. If a child is not in local authority care, it will only be if the accommodation is being provided under one of the duties or powers contained in CA 1989 s20 (see para 3.78) that they will benefit from the leaving care provisions.

Health

10.77 Although some paediatric services for disabled children may be far from perfect, young people with significant health needs too fre-quently find that the health services they require as adults are unco-ordinated or simply not available. As with social care, there is no good reason in law for this to be so, as the duties under the NHS Acts remain fundamentally the same for children and adults (see paras 5.16–5.18). However, a genuine difficulty is created by the fact that many therapeutic interventions, particularly speech and language therapy, are delivered to disabled children through their statements of SEN (see chapter 4) and so adult health services will need to take on an additional responsibility for meeting the young person's therapeutic needs.

10.78　Given the potential disruptions in young people's healthcare, the Children Act guidance stresses the 'crucial' role of GPs through their knowledge of the whole family and their ability to monitor the individual young person's health and well-being.[156] The focus of the Children Act guidance is on ensuring that as far as possible disabled young people are not accommodated in hospital on a long-stay basis.

10.79　Since 2004, the National Service Framework in England has required that health services develop appropriate adolescent/young persons services with a view to enabling smooth transition to comprehensive adult multi-disciplinary care.[157]

10.80　The good practice guidance for health services in England on transition to adulthood emphasises the importance of a health transition plan.[158] The guidance is clear that a health transition plan should be 'an integral part of the broader transition plan', linked closely to plans held by education and social care.[159] The health plan should be developed by the young person alongside a multi-disciplinary team (including the GP), supported by the most relevant health professional who can review it regularly with them.[160] Planning should start at the latest when the child is 13.[161] An example of a health transition planning tool is given at Annex B in the guidance. Similarly, *Valuing people*[162] stressed the need for all young people with learning disabilities approaching the end of their secondary schooling to have a health action plan. These are completed with young people by a range of staff, most commonly a community nurse or a school nurse.

10.81　Health services provided for disabled young people must be suitable for their needs. One parent told the parliamentary hearings on services for disabled children that their son had been offered short

---

156　Children Act 1989 Guidance and Regulations, Vol 6, *Children with disabilities*, HMSO, para 16.11.

157　DfES/Department of Health, *National service framework for children, young people and maternity services: standard 8: disabled children and young people and those with complex health needs*, 2004, ch 7.

158　*Transition: moving on well.*

159　*Transition: moving on well*, pp10–11.

160　*Transition: moving on well*, p11.

161　*Transition: moving on well*, p11.

162　*Valuing people: a new strategy for learning disability for the 21st century*, Circular HSC 2001/016: LAC(2001)23, para 6.15.

break care in a respite unit with adults aged over 70.[163] This is clearly unacceptable and such an approach is likely to contravene a young person's rights to private life in relation to their personal and psychological integrity: see para 2.5.

Continuing care

10.82 Where a disabled young person has a significant level of health needs, responsibility for meeting those needs rests with the responsible health body under the children's continuing care provisions: see paras 5.53–5.64. There is an even clearer responsibility on health bodies to take responsibility for *all* the health and social care needs of disabled adults with substantial health needs. The framework for continuing care in England is set by the National Framework for Continuing Care, revised in July 2009 and supplemented by practice guidance published in April 2010.[164] A very similar framework exists in Wales.[165] The national framework introduced a single approach to determining eligibility for continuing care in England. In short, where an adult's primary need is a health need, they are eligible for NHS continuing healthcare.[166]

10.83 Young people receiving children's continuing care will need to be re-assessed against the adult continuing care framework at the age of 17 to ensure an effective adult care package is commissioned in time for the young person's 18th birthday.[167] In preparation for this, children's continuing care teams should notify adult teams that a child is receiving continuing care at their 14th birthday.[168] A formal referral to the adult NHS continuing healthcare team at the relevant health body should follow at age 16.[169] There should be consistency in the young person's care package, which should not change simply because of the move from children's to adult services or because of a switch in the organisation with commissioning or funding responsibilities.[170]

---

163 *Parliamentary hearings on services for disabled children – full report*, p60.

164 Department of Health, *NHS continuing healthcare practice guidance*, 2010.

165 Welsh Assembly Government *Continuing NHS healthcare: the national framework for implementation in Wales*, Welsh Assembly Government Circular 015/2010, 2010.

166 Department of Health, *National framework for NHS continuing healthcare and NHS-funded nursing care*, 2009 ('Continuing Care Framework'), para 25.

167 Continuing Care Framework, para 125.

168 Continuing Care Framework, para 123.

169 Continuing Care Framework, para 124.

170 Continuing Care Framework, para 130.

Palliative care

10.84 Young people with life-limiting and life-threatening conditions will have additional support needs at transition to adulthood. As young people with life-limiting conditions are now surviving much longer, this has become an important issue. Recent guidance[171] published through the transition support programme summarises the difficulties faced by these young people in transition to adulthood and suggests good practice ways in which these difficulties can be addressed.

Mental health

10.85 The law in relation to meeting the mental health needs of disabled young people is covered extensively in chapter 5, see paras 5.65–5.82. Given the high incidence of mental ill-health among disabled young people, particularly those with learning disabilities, it is essential that child and adolescent mental health services (CAMHS) and adult mental health services engage effectively in transition planning, at an individual and strategic level.[172]

Multi-agency disputes

10.86 Problematical as it is for many disabled young people to sustain adequate social care support during their transition into adulthood, these difficulties are frequently compounded if there is (or is thought to be) NHS responsibility for some or all of the package. In such cases the usual difficulties can be exacerbated as disabled young person and their families find themselves caught in the paralysing cross fire of an inter-authority funding dispute. In this respect, a complaint considered by the Public Services Ombudsman for Wales[173] in 2008 is not untypical:

171 National Transition Support Team, *'How to' guide: moving on to adult care services – young people with life-limiting and life-threatening conditions*, NCB, 2009, available at www.transitionsupportprogramme.org.uk/pdf/ACT.pdf. See also ACT, *Transition care pathway: a framework for the development of integrated multi-agency care pathways for young people with life-threatening and life-limiting conditions*, 2007.

172 See National Transition Support Team, *'How to' guide: How to support young people with learning disabilities and mental health issues*, NCB, 2009, available at www.transitionsupportprogramme.org.uk/pdf/HowTo_FPLD.pdf.

173 Report by the Public Services Ombudsman for Wales on an investigation into a complaint against Torfaen Local Health Board Gwent Healthcare NHS Trust and Torfaen County Borough Council, 24 February 2008, Report Reference Numbers 1712/200701931, 1712/200701932 and 1712/200702681.

it contains elements of delay, officers leaving their post, disputes over funding and parents being required to make 'snap' decisions about fundamental matters, without having the relevant information.

10.87   The complaint concerned a young person with learning disabilities and extreme challenging behaviour who, when aged 14, was assessed by the local authority as in need (when he left school) of 2:1 support in a community environment. A year later, when aged 15, a transition worker from the council met with the parents and discussed various options – however, nothing came of this and the transition worker left and was not replaced. Three years later (when he became 18) no firm plans had been made and the parents were told that they had to make a quick decision as a potential placement had become available; however, they were unable to act on this, in part because they were unable to visit the placement, due to their son being ill. At this time the council had formed the view that the young man ought to be funded by the NHS under its continuing healthcare responsibilities – and as a consequence, in the opinion of the ombudsman, there was a 'jockeying for position' between these two bodies over who was to be responsible. The ombudsman held that the failure of the local authority's transitional planning constituted maladministration as did its failure – and that of the NHS bodies – to co-operate (see in this respect paras 5.10–5.15). A consequence of the failure had been that the young man had been cared for over 15 months by his parents in their home with little support. The ombudsman considered that the agencies had thereby profited (because they had avoided funding an expensive package during this time). The ombudsman recommended that an award be paid of £25,000 (£20,000 from the local health board and £5,000 from the council) and that this be placed in trust for the young man, with terms of the trust being agreed with his parents. This case illustrates the imperative for local agencies to meet the needs of disabled young people first, resolving any disputes which may arise as to which agency should take sole or lead funding responsibility only once needs have been met.

Mental capacity

10.88   Issues relating to the capacity of disabled children to consent to decisions taken on their behalf have been discussed in chapters 1 (paras 1.21–1.23) and 5 (paras 5.83–5.89). However, it is essential to note that when a young person reaches 16, the vast majority of the provisions of the Mental Capacity Act (MCA) 2005 apply in the same way as if the young person were an adult.[174]

10.89   The provisions of the MCA 2005 are, in some respects, complex although the statutory code of practice[175] ('the MCA Code') is an excellent and accessible guide to the relevant law and practice. The Act details the key legal principles, provisions and mechanisms that apply to the determination of whether or not a person has mental capacity to make a decision, and as to what can/should happen if they are adjudged to lack the requisite capacity. The Act applies to persons aged 16 or more.

10.90   The Act adopts a 'matter specific' approach to capacity[176] which is 'time- and situation-specific'[177] and does not allow a person to be written off as generally 'incapacitated'. A person may therefore have capacity to make a decision about one matter (for example, who they would like to see) but not another (how to invest the large legacy they have just inherited). The Act provides a four-point test for deciding whether or not a person has capacity to make a particular decision: it provides that a person will lack capacity only if it can be shown that he or she is unable to do any of the following:[178]

a) to understand the information relevant to the decision;
b) to retain that information;
c) to use or weigh that information as part of the process of making the decision; or
d) to communicate his or her decision (whether by talking, using sign language or any other means).

10.91   All those concerned with young people who may lack capacity must have regard to the principles set out in MCA 2005 s1, including the presumption that all persons have capacity to make decisions, unless it is shown that they lack it in any specific situation; that no one is to be treated as unable to make a decision unless 'all practicable steps' have been taken to help them do so, without success; and the requirement that if a person is adjudged to lack the requisite capacity, that

---

174 Certain statutory limitations apply in relation to 16- to 17-year-olds: for example, they are not able to make a lasting power of attorney (MCA 2005 s9(2)), an advance decision to refuse treatment (MCA 2005 s24(1)) or a will (MCA 2005 s18(2)).

175 Department for Constitutional Affairs, *Mental Capacity Act 2005 Code of Practice*, TSO, 2007.

176 MCA 2005 s2(1).

177 A Weereratne and others, *The Mental Capacity Act 2005: personal welfare decisions*, LexisNexis, 2008, para 2.23.

178 MCA 2005 s3(1).

any substitute decision must be made in their 'best interests'. The Act provides (at section 4) a checklist of the factors that should be considered when determining what is in a person's 'best interests'. The MCA Code contains a specific chapter (chapter 12) on the application of the Act to children and young people, which includes advice on such best interests determinations (para 12.18).

10.92　　A key area of contention in relation to the MCA 2005 has been the provisions in relation to 'deprivations of liberty': if there is any concern as to whether a disabled young person is being deprived of their liberty, careful regard should be had to the specific code of practice[179] concerning the deprivation of liberty safeguards[180] (and see also paras 3.94–3.96).

---

179 Department of Health, *Mental Capacity Act 2005: deprivation of liberty safeguards – Code of Practice to supplement the main Mental Capacity Act 2005 Code of Practice*, 2008.

180 These safeguards were introduced into the Mental Capacity Act 2005 by the Mental Health Act 2007. The safeguards provide a framework for approving the deprivation of liberty for people who lack the capacity to consent to treatment or care in either a hospital or care home that, in their own best interests, can only be provided in circumstances that amount to a deprivation of liberty.

APPENDICES

Legislation[1]

CARERS AND DISABLED CHILDREN ACT 2000

Right of carers to assessment

1 (1) If an individual aged 16 or over ('the carer')–

  (a) provides or intends to provide a substantial amount of care on a regular basis for another individual aged 18 or over ('the person cared for'); and

  (b) asks a local authority to carry out an assessment of his ability to provide and to continue to provide care for the person cared for,

  the local authority must carry out such an assessment if it is satisfied that the person cared for is someone for whom it may provide or arrange for the provision of community care services.

  (2) For the purposes of such an assessment, the local authority may take into account, so far as it considers it to be material, an assessment under section 1(1) of the Carers (Recognition and Services) Act 1995.

  (3) Subsection (1) does not apply if the individual provides or will provide the care in question–

  (a) by virtue of a contract of employment or other contract with any person; or

  (b) as a volunteer for a voluntary organisation.

  (3A) An assessment under subsection (1) must include consideration of whether the carer–

  (a) works or wishes to work,

  (b) is undertaking, or wishes to undertake, education, training or any leisure activity.

  (4) The Secretary of State (or, in relation to Wales, the National Assembly for Wales) may give directions as to the manner in which an assessment under subsection (1) is to be carried out or the form it is to take.

  (5) Subject to any such directions, it is to be carried out in such manner, and is to take such form, as the local authority considers appropriate.

  (6) In this section, 'voluntary organisation' has the same meaning as in the National Assistance Act 1948.

Services for carers

2 (1) The local authority must consider the assessment and decide–

  (a) whether the carer has needs in relation to the care which he provides or intends to provide;

  (b) if so, whether they could be satisfied (wholly or partly) by services which the local authority may provide; and

  (c) if they could be so satisfied, whether or not to provide services to the carer.

  (2) The services referred to are any services which–

  (a) the local authority sees fit to provide; and

  (b) will in the local authority's view help the carer care for the person cared for,

  and may take the form of physical help or other forms of support.

  (3) A service, although provided to the carer–

  (a) may take the form of a service delivered to the person cared for if it is one which, if provided to him instead of to the carer, could fall within community care services and they both agree it is to be so delivered; but

  (b) if a service is delivered to the person cared for it may not, except in prescribed circumstances, include anything of an intimate nature.

(4) Regulations may make provision about what is, or is not, of an intimate nature for the purposes of subsection (3).

Assessments and services for both carer and person cared for

4 (1) In section 1 of the Carers (Recognition and Services) Act 1995 (which provides for carers to be assessed as to their ability to care in connection with an assessment of the needs of the individual cared for), after subsection (2) insert–

'(2A) For the purposes of an assessment under subsection (1) or (2), the local authority may take into account, so far as it considers it to be material, an assessment under section 1 or 6 of the Carers and Disabled Children Act 2000.'

(2) Subsection (4) applies if the local authority–
  (a) is either providing services under this Act to the carer, or is providing community care services to or in respect of the person cared for (but not both); and
  (b) proposes to provide another service to (or in respect of) the one who is not receiving any such service,
  and the new service, or any service already being provided, is one which could be provided either under this Act, or by way of community care services.

(3) Subsection (4) also applies if–
  (a) the local authority is not providing services to the carer (under this Act) or to the person cared for (by way of community care services), but proposes to provide services to each of them following an assessment under section 1 and under section 47 of the National Health Service and Community Care Act 1990; or
  (b) the local authority is providing services both to the carer (under this Act) and to the person cared for (by way of community care services), and proposes to provide to either of them a new service,
  and (in a paragraph (a) case) any of the services, or (in a paragraph (b) case) the new service, is one which could be provided either under this Act, or by way of community care services.

(4) In the case of each such service, the local authority must decide whether the service is, or is in future, to be provided under this Act, or by way of community care services (and hence whether it is, or is in future, to be provided to the carer, or to the person cared for).

(5) The local authority's decision under subsection (4) is to be made without regard to the means of the carer or of the person cared for.

Assessments: persons with parental responsibility for disabled children

6 (1) If a person with parental responsibility for a disabled child–
  (a) provides or intends to provide a substantial amount of care on a regular basis for the child; and
  (b) asks a local authority to carry out an assessment of his ability to provide and to continue to provide care for the child,
  the local authority must carry out such an assessment if it is satisfied that the child and his family are persons for whom it may provide or arrange for the provision of services under section 17 of the Children Act 1989 ('the 1989 Act').

(2) For the purposes of such an assessment, the local authority may take into account, so far as it considers it to be material, an assessment under section 1(2) of the Carers (Recognition and Services) Act 1995.

(2A) An assessment under subsection (1) must include consideration of whether the person with parental responsibility for the child–

    (a) works or wishes to work,

    (b) is undertaking, or wishes to undertake, education, training or any leisure activity.

(3) The Secretary of State (or, in relation to Wales, the National Assembly for Wales) may give directions as to the manner in which an assessment under subsection (1) is to be carried out or the form it is to take.

(4) Subject to any such directions, it is to be carried out in such manner, and is to take such form, as the local authority considers appropriate.

(5) The local authority must take the assessment into account when deciding what, if any, services to provide under section 17 of the 1989 Act.

(6) Terms used in this section have the same meaning as in Part III of the 1989 Act.

CARERS (RECOGNITION AND SERVICES) ACT 1995

Assessment of ability of carers to provide care: England and Wales

1(1) Subject to subsection (3) below, in any case where–

    (a) a local authority carry out an assessment under section 47(1)(a) of the National Health Service and Community Care Act 1990 of the needs of a person ('the relevant person') for community care services, and

    (b) an individual ('the carer') provides or intends to provide a substantial amount of care on a regular basis for the relevant person,

the carer may request the local authority, before they make their decision as to whether the needs of the relevant person call for the provision of any services, to carry out an assessment of his ability to provide and to continue to provide care for the relevant person; and if he makes such a request, the local authority shall carry out such an assessment and shall take into account the results of that assessment in making that decision.

(2) Subject to subsection (3) below, in any case where–

    (a) a local authority assess the needs of a disabled child for the purposes of Part III of the Children Act 1989 or section 2 of the Chronically Sick and Disabled Persons Act 1970, and

    (b) an individual ('the carer') provides or intends to provide a substantial amount of care on a regular basis for the disabled child,

the carer may request the local authority, before they make their decision as to whether the needs of the disabled child call for the provision of any services, to carry out an assessment of his ability to provide and to continue to provide care for the disabled child; and if he makes such a request, the local authority shall carry out such an assessment and shall take into account the results of that assessment in making that decision.

(2A) For the purposes of an assessment under subsection (1) or (2), the local authority may take into account, so far as it considers it to be material, an assessment under section 1 or 6 of the Carers and Disabled Children Act 2000.

(2B) In any case where–

    (a) a local authority are carrying out an assessment mentioned in paragraph (a) of either subsection (1) or subsection (2) above in relation to the relevant person or (as the case may be) a disabled child, and

    (b) it appears to the local authority that an individual may be entitled to request (but has not requested) an assessment under the subsection in question of his ability to provide and to continue to provide care for the relevant person or the disabled child,

the local authority must inform the individual that he may be so entitled before they make their decision as to the needs of the relevant person or the disabled child.

(2C) An assessment under subsection (1) or (2) above must include consideration of whether the carer–

    (a) works or wishes to work,

    (b) is undertaking, or wishes to undertake, education, training or any leisure activity.

(3) No request may be made under subsection (1) or (2) above by an individual who provides or will provide the care in question–

    (a) by virtue of a contract of employment or other contract with any person; or

    (b) as a volunteer for a voluntary organisation.

(4) The Secretary of State may give directions as to the manner in which an assessment under subsection (1) or (2) above is to be carried out or the form it is to take but, subject to any such directions, it shall be carried out in such manner and take such form as the local authority consider appropriate.

(5) Section 8 of the Disabled Persons (Services, Consultation and Representation) Act 1986 (duty of local authority to take into account ability of carers) shall not apply in any case where–

(a) an assessment is made under subsection (1) above in respect of an individual who provides the care in question for a disabled person; or

(b) an assessment is made under subsection (2) above.

(6) In this section–

'community care services' has the meaning given by section 46(3) of the National Health Service and Community Care Act 1990;

'child' means a person under the age of eighteen;

'disabled child' means a child who is disabled within the meaning of Part III of the Children Act 1989;

'disabled person' means a person to whom section 29 of the National Assistance Act 1948 applies;

'local authority' has the meaning given by section 46(3) of the National Health Service and Community Care Act 1990; and

'voluntary organisation' has the same meaning as in the National Assistance Act 1948.

(7) ...

Assessment of ability of carers to provide care: Scotland

2   ...

Isles of Scilly

3(1) The Secretary of State may by order provide that section 1 shall apply, with such modifications (if any) as may be specified in the order, as if the Council of the Isles of Scilly were a local authority within the meaning of that section.

(2) The power of the Secretary of State to make an order under this section shall be exercisable by statutory instrument; and a statutory instrument containing such an order shall be subject to annulment in pursuance of a resolution of either House of Parliament.

Financial provision

4   There shall be paid out of money provided by Parliament any increase attributable to this Act in the sums payable out of money so provided under any other enactment.

Short title, commencement and extent

5(1) This Act may be cited as the Carers (Recognition and Services) Act 1995.

(2) This Act shall come into force on 1st April 1996.

(3) Sections 1 and 3 do not extend to Scotland.

(4) Section 2 does not extend to England and Wales.

(5) This Act does not extend to Northern Ireland.

CHILDREN ACT 1989

Part III: Local Authority Support for Children and Families

Provision of services for children and their families

Provision of services for children in need, their families and others

17 (1) It shall be the general duty of every local authority (in addition to the other duties imposed on them by this Part)–

(a) to safeguard and promote the welfare of children within their area who are in need; and

(b) so far as is consistent with that duty, to promote the upbringing of such children by their families,

by providing a range and level of services appropriate to those children's needs.

(2) For the purpose principally of facilitating the discharge of their general duty under this section, every local authority shall have the specific duties and powers set out in Part I of Schedule 2.

(3) Any service provided by an authority in the exercise of functions conferred on them by this section may be provided for the family of a particular child in need or for any member of his family, if it is provided with a view to safeguarding or promoting the child's welfare.

(4) The appropriate national authority may by order amend any provision of Part I of Schedule 2 or add any further duty or power to those for the time being mentioned there.

(4A) Before determining what (if any) services to provide for a particular child in need in the exercise of functions conferred on them by this section, a local authority shall, so far as is reasonably practicable and consistent with the child's welfare–

(a) ascertain the child's wishes and feelings regarding the provision of those services; and

(b) give due consideration (having regard to his age and understanding) to such wishes and feelings of the child as they have been able to ascertain.

(5) Every local authority–

(a) shall facilitate the provision by others (including in particular voluntary organisations) of services *which it is a function*[2] of the authority to provide by virtue of this section, or section 18, 20, *22A to 22C*,[3] 23B to 23D, 24A or 24B; and

(b) may make such arrangements as they see fit for any person to act on their behalf in the provision of any such service.

(6) The services provided by a local authority in the exercise of functions conferred on them by this section may include providing accommodation and giving assistance in kind, [or in exceptional circumstances'][4] in cash.

(7) Assistance may be unconditional or subject to conditions as to the repayment of the assistance or of its value (in whole or in part).

---

2 Inserted by Children and Young Persons Act (CYPA) 2008. See CYPA 2008 s44(3), (4), (5)(a) for date in force.

3 Inserted by CYPA 2008. See CYPA 2008 s44(3), (4), (5)(a) for date in force

4 Words in square brackets repealed by CYPA 2008 from date to be appointed: see CYPA 2008 s44(3), (4), (5)(a).

(8) Before giving any assistance or imposing any conditions, a local authority shall have regard to the means of the child concerned and of each of his parents.

(9) No person shall be liable to make any repayment of assistance or of its value at any time when he is in receipt [of income support under Part VII of the Social Security Contributions and Benefits Act 1992],[5] of any element of child tax credit other than the family element, of working tax credit, of an income-based jobseeker's allowance or of an income-related employment and support allowance.

(10) For the purposes of this Part a child shall be taken to be in need if–
   (a) he is unlikely to achieve or maintain, or to have the opportunity of achieving or maintaining, a reasonable standard of health or development without the provision for him of services by a local authority under this Part;
   (b) his health or development is likely to be significantly impaired, or further impaired, without the provision for him of such services; or
   (c) he is disabled,
   and 'family', in relation to such a child, includes any person who has parental responsibility for the child and any other person with whom he has been living.

(11) For the purposes of this Part, a child is disabled if he is blind, deaf or dumb or suffers from mental disorder of any kind or is substantially and permanently handicapped by illness, injury or congenital deformity or such other disability as may be prescribed; and in this Part–
   'development' means physical, intellectual, emotional, social or behavioural development; and
   'health' means physical or mental health.

(12) The Treasury may by regulations prescribe circumstances in which a person is to be treated for the purposes of this Part (or for such of those purposes as are prescribed) as in receipt of any element of child tax credit other than the family element or of working tax credit.

Direct payments

17A(1) The appropriate national authority may by regulations make provision for and in connection with requiring or authorising the responsible authority in the case of a person of a prescribed description who falls within subsection (2) to make, with that person's consent, such payments to him as they may determine in accordance with the regulations in respect of his securing the provision of the service mentioned in that subsection.

(2) A person falls within this subsection if he is–
   (a) a person with parental responsibility for a disabled child,
   (b) a disabled person with parental responsibility for a child, or
   (c) a disabled child aged 16 or 17,
   and a local authority ('the responsible authority') have decided for the purposes of section 17 that the child's needs (or, if he is such a disabled child, his needs) call for the provision by them of a service in exercise of functions conferred on them under that section.

(3) Subsections (3) to (5) and (7) of section 57 of the 2001 Act shall apply, with any necessary modifications, in relation to regulations under this section as they apply in relation to regulations under that section.

5 Repealed by Welfare Reform Act (WRA) 2009 from a date to be appointed: see WRA 2009 ss9, 61(3), (4).

(3A) The modifications mentioned in subsection (3) include, in particular, the omission of the provisions inserted into section 57 of the 2001 Act by the Health and Social Care Act 2008.[6]

(4) Regulations under this section shall provide that, where payments are made under the regulations to a person falling within subsection (5)–

  (a) the payments shall be made at the rate mentioned in subsection (4)(a) of section 57 of the 2001 Act (as applied by subsection (3)); and

  (b) subsection (4)(b) of that section shall not apply.

(5) A person falls within this subsection if he is–

  (a) a person falling within subsection (2)(a) or (b) and the child in question is aged 16 or 17, or

  (b) a person who is in receipt [of income support under Part 7 of the Social Security Contributions and Benefits Act 1992][7], of any element of child tax credit other than the family element, of working tax credit, of an income-based jobseeker's allowance or of an income-related employment and support allowance.

(6) In this section–

  'the 2001 Act' means the Health and Social Care Act 2001;

  'disabled' in relation to an adult has the same meaning as that given by section 17(11) in relation to a child;

  'prescribed' means specified in or determined in accordance with regulations under this section (and has the same meaning in the provisions of the 2001 Act mentioned in subsection (3) as they apply by virtue of that subsection).

Provision of accommodation for children

Provision of accommodation for children: general

20 (1) Every local authority shall provide accommodation for any child in need within their area who appears to them to require accommodation as a result of–

  (a) there being no person who has parental responsibility for him;

  (b) his being lost or having been abandoned; or

  (c) the person who has been caring for him being prevented (whether or not permanently, and for whatever reason) from providing him with suitable accommodation or care.

(2) Where a local authority provide accommodation under subsection (1) for a child who is ordinarily resident in the area of another local authority, that other local authority may take over the provision of accommodation for the child within–

  (a) three months of being notified in writing that the child is being provided with accommodation; or

  (b) such other longer period as may be prescribed.

(3) Every local authority shall provide accommodation for any child in need within their area who has reached the age of sixteen and whose welfare the authority consider is likely to be seriously prejudiced if they do not provide him with accommodation.

---

6 Subs (3A) inserted by the Health and Social Care Act 2008. Not yet in force: see Health and Social Care Act 2008 s170(3).

7 Words in square brackets repealed by WRA 2009. Not yet in force: see WRA 2009 ss9, 61(3), (4).

(4) A local authority may provide accommodation for any child within their area (even though a person who has parental responsibility for him is able to provide him with accommodation) if they consider that to do so would safeguard or promote the child's welfare.

(5) A local authority may provide accommodation for any person who has reached the age of sixteen but is under twenty-one in any community home which takes children who have reached the age of sixteen if they consider that to do so would safeguard or promote his welfare.

(6) Before providing accommodation under this section, a local authority shall, so far as is reasonably practicable and consistent with the child's welfare–
   (a) ascertain the child's wishes and feelings regarding the provision of accommodation; and
   (b) give due consideration (having regard to his age and understanding) to such wishes and feelings of the child as they have been able to ascertain.

(7) A local authority may not provide accommodation under this section for any child if any person who–
   (a) has parental responsibility for him; and
   (b) is willing and able to–
      (i) provide accommodation for him; or
      (ii) arrange for accommodation to be provided for him,
   objects.

(8) Any person who has parental responsibility for a child may at any time remove the child from accommodation provided by or on behalf of the local authority under this section.

(9) Subsections (7) and (8) do not apply while any person–
   (a) in whose favour a residence order is in force with respect to the child;
   (aa) who is a special guardian of the child; or
   (b) who has care of the child by virtue of an order made in the exercise of the High Court's inherent jurisdiction with respect to children,
   agrees to the child being looked after in accommodation provided by or on behalf of the local authority.

(10) Where there is more than one such person as is mentioned in subsection (9), all of them must agree.

(11) Subsections (7) and (8) do not apply where a child who has reached the age of sixteen agrees to being provided with accommodation under this section.

SCHEDULE 2

Local Authority Support for Children and Families

Sections 17, 23, 29

Part I: Provision of services for families

Identification of children in need and provision of information

1 (1) Every local authority shall take reasonable steps to identify the extent to which there are children in need within their area.

(2) Every local authority shall–
   (a) publish information–
      (i) about services provided by them under sections 17, 18, 20, 23B to 23D, 24A and 24B; and

(ii) where they consider it appropriate, about the provision by others (including, in particular, voluntary organisations) of services which the authority have power to provide under those sections; and

(b) take such steps as are reasonably practicable to ensure that those who might benefit from the services receive the information relevant to them.

1A ...

Maintenance of a register of disabled children

2 (1) Every local authority shall open and maintain a register of disabled children within their area.

(2) The register may be kept by means of a computer.

Assessment of children's needs

3 Where it appears to a local authority that a child within their area is in need, the authority may assess his needs for the purposes of this Act at the same time as any assessment of his needs is made under–

(a) the Chronically Sick and Disabled Persons Act 1970;

(b) Part IV of the Education Act 1996;

(c) the Disabled Persons (Services, Consultation and Representation) Act 1986; or

(d) any other enactment.

Prevention of neglect and abuse

4 (1) Every local authority shall take reasonable steps, through the provision of services under Part III of this Act, to prevent children within their area suffering ill-treatment or neglect.

(2) Where a local authority believe that a child who is at any time within their area–

(a) is likely to suffer harm; but

(b) lives or proposes to live in the area of another local authority

they shall inform that other local authority.

(3) When informing that other local authority they shall specify–

(a) the harm that they believe he is likely to suffer; and

(b) (if they can) where the child lives or proposes to live.

Provision of accommodation in order to protect child

5(1) Where–

(a) it appears to a local authority that a child who is living on particular premises is suffering, or is likely to suffer, ill treatment at the hands of another person who is living on those premises; and

(b) that other person proposes to move from the premises,

the authority may assist that other person to obtain alternative accommodation.

(2) Assistance given under this paragraph may be in cash.

(3) Subsections (7) to (9) of section 17 shall apply in relation to assistance given under this paragraph as they apply in relation to assistance given under that section.

Provision for disabled children[8]

6 (1) Every local authority shall provide services designed–

    (a) to minimise the effect on disabled children within their area of their disabilities; and

    (b) to give such children the opportunity to lead lives which are as normal as possible; and

    (c) to assist individuals who provide care for such children to continue to do so, or to do so more effectively, by giving them breaks from caring.

  (2) The duty imposed by sub-paragraph (1)(c) shall be performed in accordance with regulations made by the appropriate national authority.

Provision to reduce need for care proceedings etc

7 Every local authority shall take reasonable steps designed–

    (a) to reduce the need to bring–

        (i) proceedings for care or supervision orders with respect to children within their area;

        (ii) criminal proceedings against such children;

        (iii) any family or other proceedings with respect to such children which might lead to them being placed in the authority's care; or

        (iv) proceedings under the inherent jurisdiction of the High Court with respect to children;

    (b) to encourage children within their area not to commit criminal offences; and

    (c) to avoid the need for children within their area to be placed in secure accommodation.

Provision for children living with their families

8 Every local authority shall make such provision as they consider appropriate for the following services to be available with respect to children in need within their area while they are living with their families–

    (a) advice, guidance and counselling;

    (b) occupational, social, cultural, or recreational activities;

    (c) home help (which may include laundry facilities);

    (d) facilities for, or assistance with, travelling to and from home for the purpose of taking advantage of any other service provided under this Act or of any similar service;

    (e) assistance to enable the child concerned and his family to have a holiday.

Provision for accommodated children[9]

8A(1) Every local authority shall make provision for such services as they consider appropriate to be available with respect to accommodated children.

  (2) 'Accommodated children' are those children in respect of whose accommodation the local authority have been notified under section 85 or 86.

  (3) The services shall be provided with a view to promoting contact between each accommodated child and that child's family.

  (4) The services may, in particular, include–

    (a) advice, guidance and counselling;

---

8   Para 6 has been amended by CYPA 2008. Check CYPA 2008 s44(3), (4), (5)(a) for when in force.

9   Para 8A inserted by CYPA 2008 s19. Not yet in force: see CYPA s44(3), (4), (5)(a).

(b) services necessary to enable the child to visit, or to be visited by, members of the family;

(c) assistance to enable the child and members of the family to have a holiday together.

(5) Nothing in this paragraph affects the duty imposed by paragraph 10.

Family centres

9 (1) Every local authority shall provide such family centres as they consider appropriate in relation to children within their area.

(2) 'Family centre' means a centre at which any of the persons mentioned in subparagraph (3) may–

(a) attend for occupational, social, cultural or recreational activities;

(b) attend for advice, guidance or counselling; or

(c) be provided with accommodation while he is receiving advice, guidance or counselling.

(3) The persons are–

(a) a child;

(b) his parents;

(c) any person who is not a parent of his but who has parental responsibility for him;

(d) any other person who is looking after him.

Maintenance of the family home

10   Every local authority shall take such steps as are reasonably practicable, where any child within their area who is in need and whom they are not looking after is living apart from his family–

(a) to enable him to live with his family; or

(b) to promote contact between him and his family,

if, in their opinion, it is necessary to do so in order to safeguard or promote his welfare.

Duty to consider racial groups to which children in need belong

11   Every local authority shall, in making any arrangements–

(a) for the provision of day care within their area; or

(b) designed to encourage persons to act as local authority foster parents,

have regard to the different racial groups to which children within their area who are in need belong.

Part II: Children looked after by local authorities

Regulations as to conditions under which child in care is allowed to live with parent, etc

12A   Regulations under section 22C may, in particular, impose requirements on a local authority as to–

(a) the making of any decision by a local authority to allow a child in their care to live with any person falling within section 22C(3) (including requirements as to those who must be consulted before the decision is made and those who must be notified when it has been made);

(b) the supervision or medical examination of the child concerned;

(c) the removal of the child, in such circumstances as may be prescribed, from the care of the person with whom the child has been allowed to live;

(d) the records to be kept by local authorities.

Regulations as to placements of a kind specified in section 22C(6)(d)

12B   Regulations under section 22C as to placements of the kind specified in section 22C(6)(d) may, in particular, make provision as to–
(a) the persons to be notified of any proposed arrangements;
(b) the opportunities such persons are to have to make representations in relation to the arrangements proposed;
(c) the persons to be notified of any proposed changes in arrangements;
(d) the records to be kept by local authorities;
(e) the supervision by local authorities of any arrangements made.

Placements out of area

12C   Regulations under section 22C may, in particular, impose requirements which a local authority must comply with–
(a) before a child looked after by them is provided with accommodation at a place outside the area of the authority; or
(b) if the child's welfare requires the immediate provision of such accommodation, within such period of the accommodation being provided as may be prescribed.

Avoidance of disruption in education

12D(1)   Regulations under section 22C may, in particular, impose requirements which a local authority must comply with before making any decision concerning a child's placement if he is in the fourth key stage.
(2) A child is 'in the fourth key stage' if he is a pupil in the fourth key stage for the purposes of Part 6 or 7 of the Education 2002 (see section 82 and 103 of that Act).

Regulations as to placing of children with local authority foster parents

12E   Regulations under section 22C may, in particular, make provision–
(a) with regard to the welfare of children placed with local authority foster parents;
(b) as to the arrangements to be made by local authorities in connection with the health and education of such children;
(c) as to the records to be kept by local authorities;
(d) for securing that where possible the local authority foster parent with whom a child is to be placed is–
(i) of the same religious persuasion as the child; or
(ii) gives an undertaking that the child will be brought up in that religious persuasion;
(e) for securing the children placed with local authority foster parents, and the premises in which they are accommodated, will be supervised and inspected by a local authority and that the children will be removed from those premises if their welfare appears to require it.

12F(1)   Regulations under section 22C may, in particular, also make provision–
(a) for securing that a child is not placed with a local authority foster parent unless that person is for the time being approved as a local authority foster parent by such local authority as may be prescribed;
(b) establishing a procedure under which any person in respect of whom a qualifying determination has been made may apply to the appropriate

national authority for a review of that determination by a panel constituted by that national authority.

(2) A determination is a qualifying determination if–

    (a) it relates to the issue of whether a person should be approved, or should continue to be approved, as a local authority foster parent; and

    (b) it is of a prescribed description.

(3) Regulations made by virtue of sub-paragraph (1)(b) may include provision as to–

    (a) the duties and powers of a panel;

    (b) the administration and procedures of a panel;

    (c) the appointment of members of a panel (including the number, or any limit on the number, of members who may be appointed and any conditions for appointment);

    (d) the payment of fees to members of a panel;

    (e) the duties of any person in connection with a review conducted under the regulations;

    (f) the monitoring of any such reviews.

(4) Regulations made by virtue of sub-paragraph (3)(e) may impose a duty to pay to the appropriate national authority such sum as that national authority may determine; but such a duty may not be imposed upon a person who has applied for a review of a qualifying determination.

(5) The appropriate national authority must secure that, taking one financial year with another, the aggregate of the sums which become payable to it under regulations made by virtue of sub-paragraph (4) does not exceed the cost to it of performing its independent review functions.

(6) The appropriate national authority may make an arrangement with an organisation under which independent review functions are performed by the organisation on the national authority's behalf.

(7) If the appropriate national authority makes such an arrangement with an organisation, the organisation is to perform its functions under the arrangement in accordance with any general or special directions given by that national authority.

(8) The arrangement may include provision for payments to be made to the organisation by the appropriate national authority.

(9) Payments made by the appropriate national authority in accordance with such provision shall be taken into account in determining (for the purpose of sub-paragraph (5)) the cost to that national authority of performing its independent review functions.

(10) Where the Welsh Ministers are the appropriate national authority, sub-paragraphs (6) and (8) also apply as if references to an organisation included references to the Secretary of State.

(11) In this paragraph–

'financial year' means a period of twelve months ending with 31st March;

'independent review function' means a function conferred or imposed on a national authority by regulations made by virtue of sub-paragraph (1)(b);

'organisation' includes a public body and a private or voluntary organisation.

12G Regulations under section 22C may, in particular, also make provision as to the circumstances in which local authorities may make arrangements for duties imposed on them by the regulations to be discharged on their behalf.

Promotion and maintenance of contact between child and family

15 (1) Where a child is being looked after by a local authority, the authority shall, unless it is not reasonably practicable or consistent with his welfare, endeavour to promote contact between the child and–

(a) his parents;

(b) any person who is not a parent of his but who has parental responsibility for him; and

(c) any relative, friend or other person connected with him.

(2) Where a child is being looked after by a local authority–

(a) the authority shall take such steps as are reasonably practicable to secure that–

(i) his parents; and

(ii) any person who is not a parent of his but who has parental responsibility for him,

are kept informed of where he is being accommodated; and

(b) every such person shall secure that the authority are kept informed of his or her address.

(3) Where a local authority ('the receiving authority') take over the provision of accommodation for a child from another local authority ('the transferring authority') under section 20(2)–

(a) the receiving authority shall (where reasonably practicable) inform–

(i) the child's parents; and

(ii) any person who is not a parent of his but who has parental responsibility for him;

(b) sub-paragraph (2)(a) shall apply to the transferring authority, as well as the receiving authority, until at least one such person has been informed of the change; and

(c) sub-paragraph (2)(b) shall not require any person to inform the receiving authority of his address until he has been so informed.

(4) Nothing in this paragraph requires a local authority to inform any person of the whereabouts of a child if–

(a) the child is in the care of the authority; and

(b) the authority has reasonable cause to believe that informing the person would prejudice the child's welfare.

(5) Any person who fails (without reasonable excuse) to comply with sub-paragraph (2)(b) shall be guilty of an offence and liable on summary conviction to a fine not exceeding level 2 on the standard scale.

(6) It shall be a defence in any proceedings under sub-paragraph (5) to prove that the defendant was residing at the same address as another person who was the child's parent or had parental responsibility for the child and had reasonable cause to believe that the other person had informed the appropriate authority that both of them were residing at that address.

Visits to or by children: expenses

16 (1) This paragraph applies where–

(a) a child is being looked after by a local authority; and

(b) the conditions mentioned in sub-paragraph (3) are satisfied.

(2) The authority may–

(a) make payments to–

  (i) a parent of the child;
  (ii) any person who is not a parent of his but who has parental responsibility for him; or
  (iii) any relative, friend or other person connected with him,
  in respect of travelling, subsistence or other expenses incurred by that person in visiting the child; or
  (b) make payments to the child, or to any person on his behalf, in respect of travelling, subsistence or other expenses incurred by or on behalf of the child in his visiting–
  (i) a parent of his;
  (ii) any person who is not a parent of his but who has parental responsibility for him; or
  (iii) any relative, friend or other person connected with him.
(3) The conditions are that–
  (a) it appears to the authority that the visit in question could not otherwise be made without undue financial hardship; and
  (b) the circumstances warrant the making of the payments.

Appointment of visitor for child who is not being visited[10]
17 (1) Where it appears to a local authority in relation to any child that they are looking after that–
  (a) communication between the child and–
  (i) a parent of his, or
  (ii) any person who is not a parent of his but who has parental responsibility for him,
  has been infrequent; or
  (b) he has not visited or been visited by (or lived with) any such person during the preceding twelve months,
  and that it would be in the child's best interests for an independent person to be appointed to be his visitor for the purposes of this paragraph, they shall appoint such a visitor.
(2) A person so appointed shall–
  (a) have the duty of visiting, advising and befriending the child; and
  (b) be entitled to recover from the authority who appointed him any reasonable expenses incurred by him for the purposes of his functions under this paragraph.
(3) A person's appointment as a visitor in pursuance of this paragraph shall be determined if–
  (a) he gives notice in writing to the authority who appointed him that he resigns the appointment; or
  (b) the authority give him notice in writing that they have terminated it.
(4) The determination of such an appointment shall not prejudice any duty under this paragraph to make a further appointment.
(5) Where a local authority propose to appoint a visitor for a child under this paragraph, the appointment shall not be made if–
  (a) the child objects to it; and

---

10 Para 17 has been repealed by CYPA 2008: see CYPA 2008 s44(3), (4), (5)(a) for when in force.

(b) the authority are satisfied that he has sufficient understanding to make an informed decision.

(6) Where a visitor has been appointed for a child under this paragraph, the local authority shall determine the appointment if–

(a) the child objects to its continuing; and

(b) the authority are satisfied that he has sufficient understanding to make an informed decision.

(7) The appropriate national authority may make regulations as to the circumstances in which a person appointed as a visitor under this paragraph is to be regarded as independent of the local authority appointing him.

Power to guarantee apprenticeship deeds etc

18 (1) While a child is being looked after by a local authority, or is a person qualifying for advice and assistance, the authority may undertake any obligation by way of guarantee under any deed of apprenticeship or articles of clerkship which he enters into.

(2) Where a local authority have undertaken any such obligation under any deed or articles they may at any time (whether or not they are still looking after the person concerned) undertake the like obligation under any supplemental deed or articles.

Arrangements to assist children to live abroad

19 (1) A local authority may only arrange for, or assist in arranging for, any child in their care to live outside England and Wales with the approval of the court.

(2) A local authority may, with the approval of every person who has parental responsibility for the child arrange for, or assist in arranging for, any other child looked after by them to live outside England and Wales.

(3) The court shall not give its approval under sub-paragraph (1) unless it is satisfied that–

(a) living outside England and Wales would be in the child's best interests;

(b) suitable arrangements have been, or will be, made for his reception and welfare in the country in which he will live;

(c) the child has consented to living in that country; and

(d) every person who has parental responsibility for the child has consented to his living in that country.

(4) Where the court is satisfied that the child does not have sufficient understanding to give or withhold his consent, it may disregard sub-paragraph (3)(c) and give its approval if the child is to live in the country concerned with a parent, guardian, special guardian, or other suitable person.

(5) Where a person whose consent is required by sub-paragraph (3)(d) fails to give his consent, the court may disregard that provision and give its approval if it is satisfied that that person–

(a) cannot be found;

(b) is incapable of consenting; or

(c) is withholding his consent unreasonably.

(6) Section 85 of the Adoption and Children Act 2002 (which imposes restrictions on taking children out of the United Kingdom) shall not apply in the case of any child who is to live outside England and Wales with the approval of the court given under this paragraph.

(7) Where a court decides to give its approval under this paragraph it may order that its decision is not to have effect during the appeal period.

(8) In sub-paragraph (7) 'the appeal period' means–

(a) where an appeal is made against the decision, the period between the making of the decision and the determination of the appeal; and

(b) otherwise, the period during which an appeal may be made against the decision.

(9) This paragraph does not apply to a local authority placing a child for adoption with prospective adopters.

Preparation for ceasing to be looked after

19A It is the duty of the local authority looking after a child to advise, assist and befriend him with a view to promoting his welfare when they have ceased to look after him.

19B(1) A local authority shall have the following additional functions in relation to an eligible child whom they are looking after.

(2) In sub-paragraph (1) 'eligible child' means, subject to sub-paragraph (3), a child who–

(a) is aged sixteen or seventeen; and

(b) has been looked after by a local authority for a prescribed period, or periods amounting in all to a prescribed period, which began after he reached a prescribed age and ended after he reached the age of sixteen.

(3) The appropriate national authority may prescribe–

(a) additional categories of eligible children; and

(b) categories of children who are not to be eligible children despite falling within sub-paragraph (2).

(4) For each eligible child, the local authority shall carry out an assessment of his needs with a view to determining what advice, assistance and support it would be appropriate for them to provide him under this Act–

(a) while they are still looking after him; and

(b) after they cease to look after him,

and shall then prepare a pathway plan for him.

(5) The local authority shall keep the pathway plan under regular review.

(6) Any such review may be carried out at the same time as a review of the child's case carried out by virtue of section 26.

(7) The appropriate national authority may by regulations make provision as to assessments for the purposes of sub-paragraph (4).

(8) The regulations may in particular provide for the matters set out in section 23B(6).

Personal advisers

19C A local authority shall arrange for each child whom they are looking after who is an eligible child for the purposes of paragraph 19B to have a personal adviser.

Death of children being looked after by local authorities

20 (1) If a child who is being looked after by a local authority dies, the authority–

(a) shall notify the appropriate national authority and (in the case of a local authority in England) Her Majesty's Chief Inspector of Education, Children's Services and Skills;

(b) shall, so far as is reasonably practicable, notify the child's parents and every person who is not a parent of his but who has parental responsibility for him;

(c) may, with the consent (so far as it is reasonably practicable to obtain it) of every person who has parental responsibility for the child, arrange for the child's body to be buried or cremated; and

(d) may, if the conditions mentioned in sub-paragraph (2) are satisfied, make payments to any person who has parental responsibility for the child, or any relative, friend or other person connected with the child, in respect of travelling, subsistence or other expenses incurred by that person in attending the child's funeral.

(2) The conditions are that–

(a) it appears to the authority that the person concerned could not otherwise attend the child's funeral without undue financial hardship; and

(b) that the circumstances warrant the making of the payments.

(3) Sub-paragraph (1) does not authorise cremation where it does not accord with the practice of the child's religious persuasion.

(4) Where a local authority have exercised their power under sub-paragraph (1)(c) with respect to a child who was under sixteen when he died, they may recover from any parent of the child any expenses incurred by them.

(5) Any sums so recoverable shall, without prejudice to any other method of recovery, be recoverable summarily as a civil debt.

(6) Nothing in this paragraph affects any enactment regulating or authorising the burial, cremation or anatomical examination of the body of a deceased person.

Part III: Contributions towards maintenance of children looked after by local authorities

Liability to contribute

21 (1) Where a local authority are looking after a child (other than in the cases mentioned in sub-paragraph (7)) they shall consider whether they should recover contributions towards the child's maintenance from any person liable to contribute ('a contributor').

(2) An authority may only recover contributions from a contributor if they consider it reasonable to do so.

(3) The persons liable to contribute are–

(a) where the child is under sixteen, each of his parents;

(b) where he has reached the age of sixteen, the child himself.

(4) A parent is not liable to contribute during any period when he is in receipt [of income support under Part VII of the Social Security Contributions and Benefits Act 1992],[11] of any element of child tax credit other than the family element, of working tax credit, of an income-based jobseeker's allowance or of an income-related employment and support allowance.

(5) A person is not liable to contribute towards the maintenance of a child in the care of a local authority in respect of any period during which the child is *liv-*

---

11 Words in square brackets repealed by WRA 2009: see WRA ss9, 61(3), (4) for when in force.

ing with, under arrangements made by the authority in accordance with section 22C,[12] a parent of his.

(6) A contributor is not obliged to make any contribution towards a child's maintenance except as agreed or determined in accordance with this Part of this Schedule.

(7) The cases are where the child is looked after by a local authority under–
   (a) section 21;
   (b) an interim care order;
   (c) section 92 of the Powers of Criminal Courts (Sentencing) Act 2000.

Agreed contributions

22 (1) Contributions towards a child's maintenance may only be recovered if the local authority have served a notice ('a contribution notice') on the contributor specifying–
   (a) the weekly sum which they consider that he should contribute; and
   (b) arrangements for payment.

(2) The contribution notice must be in writing and dated.

(3) Arrangements for payment shall, in particular, include–
   (a) the date on which liability to contribute begins (which must not be earlier than the date of the notice);
   (b) the date on which liability under the notice will end (if the child has not before that date ceased to be looked after by the authority); and
   (c) the date on which the first payment is to be made.

(4) The authority may specify in a contribution notice a weekly sum which is a standard contribution determined by them for all children looked after by them.

(5) The authority may not specify in a contribution notice a weekly sum greater than that which they consider–
   (a) they would normally be prepared to pay if they had placed a similar child with local authority foster parents; and
   (b) it is reasonably practicable for the contributor to pay (having regard to his means).

(6) An authority may at any time withdraw a contribution notice (without prejudice to their power to serve another).

(7) Where the authority and the contributor agree–
   (a) the sum which the contributor is to contribute; and
   (b) arrangements for payment,
   (whether as specified in the contribution notice or otherwise)
   and the contributor notifies the authority in writing that he so agrees, the authority may recover summarily as a civil debt any contribution which is overdue and unpaid.

(8) A contributor may, by serving a notice in writing on the authority, withdraw his agreement in relation to any period of liability falling after the date of service of the notice.

(9) Sub-paragraph (7) is without prejudice to any other method of recovery.

---

12 Words in italics inserted by CYPA 2008: see CYPA 2008 s44(3), (4), (5)(a) for when in force.

Contribution orders

23 (1) Where a contributor has been served with a contribution notice and has–

(a) failed to reach any agreement with the local authority as mentioned in paragraph 22(7) within the period of one month beginning with the day on which the contribution notice was served; or

(b) served a notice under paragraph 22(8) withdrawing his agreement,

the authority may apply to the court for an order under this paragraph.

(2) On such an application the court may make an order ('a contribution order') requiring the contributor to contribute a weekly sum towards the child's maintenance in accordance with arrangements for payment specified by the court.

(3) A contribution order–

(a) shall not specify a weekly sum greater than that specified in the contribution notice; and

(b) shall be made with due regard to the contributor's means.

(4) A contribution order shall not–

(a) take effect before the date specified in the contribution notice; or

(b) have effect while the contributor is not liable to contribute (by virtue of paragraph 21); or

(c) remain in force after the child has ceased to be looked after by the authority who obtained the order.

(5) An authority may not apply to the court under sub-paragraph (1) in relation to a contribution notice which they have withdrawn.

(6) Where–

(a) a contribution order is in force;

(b) the authority serve another contribution notice; and

(c) the contributor and the authority reach an agreement under paragraph 22(7) in respect of that other contribution notice,

the effect of the agreement shall be to discharge the order from the date on which it is agreed that the agreement shall take effect.

(7) Where an agreement is reached under sub-paragraph (6) the authority shall notify the court–

(a) of the agreement; and

(b) of the date on which it took effect.

(8) A contribution order may be varied or revoked on the application of the contributor or the authority.

(9) In proceedings for the variation of a contribution order, the authority shall specify–

(a) the weekly sum which, having regard to paragraph 22, they propose that the contributor should contribute under the order as varied; and

(b) the proposed arrangements for payment.

(10) Where a contribution order is varied, the order–

(a) shall not specify a weekly sum greater than that specified by the authority in the proceedings for variation; and

(b) shall be made with due regard to the contributor's means.

(11) An appeal shall lie in accordance with rules of court from any order made under this paragraph.

Enforcement of contribution orders etc

24 (1) A contribution order made by a magistrates' court shall be enforceable as a magistrates' court maintenance order (within the meaning of section 150(1) of the Magistrates' Courts Act 1980).

(2) Where a contributor has agreed, or has been ordered, to make contributions to a local authority, any other local authority within whose area the contributor is for the time being living may–

(a) at the request of the local authority who served the contributions notice; and

(b) subject to agreement as to any sum to be deducted in respect of services rendered,

collect from the contributor any contributions due on behalf of the authority who served the notice.

(3) In sub-paragraph (2) the reference to any other local authority includes a reference to–

(a) a local authority within the meaning of section 1(2) of the Social Work (Scotland) Act 1968; and

(b) a Health and Social Services Board established under Article 16 of the Health and Personal Social Services (Northern Ireland) Order 1972.

(4) The power to collect sums under sub-paragraph (2) includes the power to–

(a) receive and give a discharge for any contributions due; and

(b) (if necessary) enforce payment of any contributions,

even though those contributions may have fallen due at a time when the contributor was living elsewhere.

(5) Any contribution collected under sub-paragraph (2) shall be paid (subject to any agreed deduction) to the local authority who served the contribution notice.

(6) In any proceedings under this paragraph, a document which purports to be–

(a) a copy of an order made by a court under or by virtue of paragraph 23; and

(b) certified as a true copy by the designated officer for the court,

shall be evidence of the order.

(7) In any proceedings under this paragraph, a certificate which–

(a) purports to be signed by the clerk or some other duly authorised officer of the local authority who obtained the contribution order; and

(b) states that any sum due to the authority under the order is overdue and unpaid,

shall be evidence that the sum is overdue and unpaid.

Regulations

25 The appropriate national authority may make regulations–

(a) as to the considerations which a local authority must take into account in deciding–

(i) whether it is reasonable to recover contributions; and

(ii) what the arrangements for payment should be;

(b) as to the procedures a local authority must follow in reaching agreements with–

(i) contributors (under paragraphs 22 and 23); and

(ii) any other local authority (under paragraph 23).

CHRONICALLY SICK AND DISABLED PERSONS ACT 1970

Provision of welfare services

2 (1) Where a local authority having functions under section 29 of the National Assistance Act 1948 are satisfied in the case of any person to whom that section applies who is ordinarily resident in their area that it is necessary in order to meet the needs of that person for that authority to make arrangements for all or any of the following matters, namely–

(a) the provision of practical assistance for that person in his home;

(b) the provision for that person of, or assistance to that person in obtaining, wireless, television, library or similar recreational facilities;

(c) the provision for that person of lectures, games, outings or other recreational facilities outside his home or assistance to that person in taking advantage of educational facilities available to him;

(d) the provision for that person of facilities for, or assistance in, travelling to and from his home for the purpose of participating in any services provided under arrangements made by the authority under the said section 29 or, with the approval of the authority, in any services provided otherwise than as aforesaid which are similar to services which could be provided under such arrangements;

(e) the provision of assistance for that person in arranging for the carrying out of any works of adaptation in his home or the provision of any additional facilities designed to secure his greater safety, comfort or convenience;

(f) facilitating the taking of holidays by that person, whether at holiday homes or otherwise and whether provided under arrangements made by the authority or otherwise;

(g) the provision of meals for that person whether in his home or elsewhere;

(h) the provision for that person of, or assistance to that person in obtaining, a telephone and any special equipment necessary to enable him to use a telephone,

then, subject to the provisions of section 7(1) of the Local Authority Social Services Act 1970 (which requires local authorities in the exercise of certain functions, including functions under the said section 29, to act under the general guidance of the Secretary of State and to the provisions of section 7A of that Act (which requires local authorities to exercise their social services functions in accordance with directions given by the Secretary of State, it shall be the duty of that authority to make those arrangements in exercise of their functions under the said section 29.

(1A) Subsections (3) to (5) of section 32 of the National Assistance Act 1948 (which relate to the determination of any question arising under Part 3 of that Act as to a person's ordinary residence) apply in relation to any question arising under this section as to a person's ordinary residence as they apply in relation to such a question arising under Part 3 of that Act.

(2) [Repealed]

Application of Act to authorities having functions under the Children Act 1989

28A This Act applies with respect to disabled children in relation to whom a local authority have functions under Part III of the Children Act 1989 as it applies in relation to persons to whom section 29 of the National Assistance Act 1948 applies.

EDUCATION ACT 1996

Education in accordance with parental wishes

Pupils to be educated in accordance with parents' wishes

9   In exercising or performing all their respective powers and duties under the Education Acts, the Secretary of State and local authorities shall have regard to the general principle that pupils are to be educated in accordance with the wishes of their parents, so far as that is compatible with the provision of efficient instruction and training and the avoidance of unreasonable public expenditure.

Exceptional provision of education in pupil referral units or elsewhere

19(1) Each local authority shall make arrangements for the provision of suitable education at school or otherwise than at school for those children of compulsory school age who, by reason of illness, exclusion from school or otherwise, may not for any period receive suitable education unless such arrangements are made for them.

(1A) In relation to England, subsection (1) does not apply in the case of a child–

(a) who will cease to be of compulsory school age within the next six weeks, and

(b) does not have any relevant examinations to complete.

In paragraph (b) 'relevant examinations' means any public examinations or other assessments for which the child has been entered.[13]

(2) Any school established (whether before or after the commencement of this Act) and maintained by a local authority which–

(a) is specially organised to provide education for [such children] *children falling within subsection (1)*,[14] and

(b) is not a county school or a special school,

shall be known as a 'pupil referral unit'.

(2A) Subsection (2) does not apply in relation to schools in England.

(2B) Any school established in England (whether before or after the commencement of this Act) and maintained by a local authority which–

(a) is specially organised to provide education for [such children] *children falling within subsection (1)*,[15] and

(b) is not a community or foundation school, a community or foundation special school, or a maintained nursery school,

shall be known as a 'pupil referral unit'.]

(3) A local authority may secure the provision of boarding accommodation at any pupil referral unit.

[(3A) In relation to England, the duty imposed by subsection (1) includes, except in prescribed cases, a duty to make arrangements for the provision of suitable full-time education at school or otherwise than at school for–

(a) children of compulsory school age who have been permanently excluded

---

13 Subsection 1A added by Children, Schools and Families Act (CSFA) 2010. Not yet in force: see CSFA 2010 s29(5).

14 Words in square brackets repealed and words in italics substituted by CSFA 2010. Not yet in force: see CSFA 2010 s29(5).

15 Words in square brackets repealed and words in italics substituted by CSFA 2010. Not yet in force: see CSFA 2010 s29(5).

on disciplinary grounds from relevant schools or pupil referral units, and have not subsequently been admitted to schools other than pupil referral units, and

(b) children of compulsory school age who are excluded for a fixed period on disciplinary grounds from any pupil referral unit maintained by the authority.]¹⁶

(3A) In relation to England, the education to be provided for a child in pursuance of arrangements made by a local authority under subsection (1) shall be–
(a) full-time education, or
(b) in the case of a child within subsection (3AA), education on such part-time basis as the authority consider to be in the child's best interests.

*(3AA) A child is within this subsection if the local authority consider that, for reasons which relate to the physical or mental health of the child, it would not be in the child's best interests for full-time education to be provided for the child.*¹⁷

(3B) [The education referred to in subsection (3A)] *Regulations may provide that the education to be provided for a child in pursuance of arrangements made by a local authority in England under subsection (1) must be provided from a day that, in relation to the pupil concerned, is determined in accordance with* [regulations] *the regulations.*¹⁸

(4) A local authority may make arrangements for the provision of suitable education otherwise than at school for those young persons who, by reason of illness, exclusion from school or otherwise, may not for any period receive suitable education unless such arrangements are made for them.

(4A) In determining what arrangements to make under subsection (1) or (4) in the case of any child or young person a local authority shall have regard to any guidance given from time to time by the Secretary of State.

(5) Any child for whom education is provided otherwise than at school in pursuance of this section, and any young person for whom full-time education is so provided in pursuance of this section, shall be treated for the purposes of this Act as a pupil.

(6) In this section–
['relevant school' means–
(a) a maintained school,
(b) an Academy,
(c) a city technology college, or
(d) a city college for the technology of the arts;]¹⁹
'suitable education', in relation to a child or young person, means efficient education suitable to his age, ability and aptitude and to any special educational needs he may have [(and 'suitable full-time education' is to be read accordingly)].²⁰

(7) Schedule 1 has effect in relation to pupil referral units.

16 Subsection 3A (in square brackets) substituted by subss3A and 3AA below by CSFA 2010. Not yet in force: see CSFA 2010 s29(5).
17 Subsections 3A and 3AA inserted by CSFA 2010. Not yet in force: see CSFA 2010 s29(5).
18 Words in square brackets repealed and substituted by words in italics by CSFA 2010 from a date to be appointed.
19 Words in square brackets repealed by CSFA 2010 from a date to be appointed.
20 Words in square brackets repealed by CSFA 2010 from a date to be appointed.

Part IV: Special Educational Needs
Chapter I: Children with Special Educational Needs

Introductory

Meaning of 'special educational needs' and 'special educational provision' etc

312 (1) A child has 'special educational needs' for the purposes of this Act if he has a learning difficulty which calls for special educational provision to be made for him.

(2) Subject to subsections (3) and (3A) a child has a 'learning difficulty' for the purposes of this Act if–

(a) he has a significantly greater difficulty in learning than the majority of children of his age,

(b) he has a disability which either prevents or hinders him from making use of educational facilities of a kind generally provided for children of his age in schools within the area of the local authority, or

(c) he is under compulsory school age and is, or would be if special educational provision were not made for him, likely to fall within paragraph (a) or (b) when of that age.

(3) A child is not to be taken as having a learning difficulty solely because the language (or form of the language) in which he is, or will be, taught is different from a language (or form of a language) which has at any time been spoken in his home.

(3A) Subsection (2) does not apply–

(a) for the purposes of sections 15ZA, 15A, 15B and 507B, or

(b) for the purposes of sections 18A and 562H (except for the purpose of determining, for the purposes of those sections, whether a child has special educational needs).

(4) In this Act 'special educational provision' means–

(a) in relation to a child who has attained the age of two, educational provision which is additional to, or otherwise different from, the educational provision made generally for children of his age in schools maintained by the local authority (other than special schools), and

(b) in relation to a child under that age, educational provision of any kind.

(5) In this Part–

'child' includes any person who has not attained the age of 19 and is a registered pupil at a school;

'maintained school' means any community, foundation or voluntary school or any community or foundation special school not established in a hospital.

Code of Practice

Code of Practice

313 (1) The Secretary of State shall issue, and may from time to time revise, a code of practice giving practical guidance in respect of the discharge by local authorities and the governing bodies of maintained schools and maintained nursery schools of their functions under this Part.

(2) It shall be the duty of–

(a) local authorities, and such governing bodies, exercising functions under this Part, and

(b) any other person exercising any function for the purpose of the discharge by local authorities, and such governing bodies, of functions under this Part, to have regard to the provisions of the code.

(3) On any appeal under this Part to the Tribunal, the Tribunal shall have regard to any provision of the code which appears to the Tribunal to be relevant to any question arising on the appeal.

(4) The Secretary of State shall publish the code as for the time being in force.

(5) In this Chapter[21] 'the Tribunal', in relation to an appeal, means–

(a) where the local authority concerned is in England, the First-tier Tribunal,

(b) where the local authority concerned is in Wales, the Special Educational Needs Tribunal for Wales.

Duty to educate children with special educational needs in mainstream schools

316 (1) This section applies to a child with special educational needs who should be educated in a school.

(2) If no statement is maintained under section 324 for the child, he must be educated in a mainstream school.

(3) If a statement is maintained under section 324 for the child, he must be educated in a mainstream school unless that is incompatible with–

(a) the wishes of his parent, or

(b) the provision of efficient education for other children.

(4) In this section and section 316A 'mainstream school' means any school other than–

(a) a special school, or

(b) an independent school which is not–

(i) a city technology college,

(ii) a city college for the technology of the arts, or

(iii) an Academy.

Education otherwise than in mainstream schools

316 (1) Section 316 does not prevent a child from being educated in–

(a) an independent school which is not a mainstream school, or

(b) a school approved under section 342,

if the cost is met otherwise than by a local authority.

(2) Section 316(2) does not require a child to be educated in a mainstream school during any period in which–

(a) he is admitted to a special school for the purposes of an assessment under section 323 of his educational needs and his admission to that school is with the agreement of–

(i) the local authority,

(ii) the head teacher of the school or, if the school is in Wales, its governing body,

(iii) his parent, and

(iv) any person whose advice is to be sought in accordance with regulations made under paragraph 2 of Schedule 26;

(b) he remains admitted to a special school, in prescribed circumstances, following an assessment under section 323 at that school;

21 'Chapter' inserted by Education and Skills Act (ESA) 2008: see ESA 2008 s173(4) for when in force.

    (c) he is admitted to a special school, following a change in his circumstances, with the agreement of–
        (i) the local authority,
        (ii) the head teacher of the school or, if the school is in Wales, its governing body, and
        (iii) his parent;
    (d) he is admitted to a community or foundation special school which is established in a hospital.
  (3) Section 316 does not affect the operation of–
    (a) section 348, or
    (b) paragraph 3 of Schedule 27.
  (4) If a local authority decide–
    (a) to make a statement for a child under section 324, but
    (b) not to name in the statement the school for which a parent has expressed a preference under paragraph 3 of Schedule 27,
    they shall, in making the statement, comply with section 316(3).
  (5) A local authority may, in relation to their mainstream schools taken as a whole, rely on the exception in section 316(3)(b) only if they show that there are no reasonable steps that they could take to prevent the incompatibility.
  (6) An authority in relation to a particular mainstream school may rely on the exception in section 316(3)(b) only if it shows that there are no reasonable steps that it or another authority in relation to the school could take to prevent the incompatibility.
  (7) The exception in section 316(3)(b) does not permit a governing body to fail to comply with the duty imposed by section 324(5)(b).
  (8) An authority must have regard to guidance about section 316 and this section issued–
    (a) for England, by the Secretary of State,
    (b) for Wales, by the National Assembly for Wales.
  (9) That guidance shall, in particular, relate to steps which may, or may not, be regarded as reasonable for the purposes of subsections (5) and (6).
  (10) 'Prescribed', in relation to Wales, means prescribed in regulations made by the National Assembly for Wales.
  (11) 'Authority'–
    (a) in relation to a maintained school [or maintained nursery school], means each of the following–
        (i) the local authority,
        (ii) the school's governing body, and
    (b) in relation to a pupil referral unit, means the local authority.

Duties of governing body or local authority in relation to pupils with special educational needs

317 (1) The governing body of a community, foundation or voluntary school or a maintained nursery school shall–
    (a) use their best endeavours, in exercising their functions in relation to the school, to secure that, if any registered pupil has special educational needs, the special educational provision which his learning difficulty calls for is made,
    (b) secure that, where the responsible person has been informed by the local

authority that a registered pupil has special educational needs, those needs are made known to all who are likely to teach him, and

(c) secure that the teachers in the school are aware of the importance of identifying, and providing for, those registered pupils who have special educational needs.

(2) In subsection (1)(b) 'the responsible person' means the head teacher or the appropriate governor (that is, the chairman of the governing body or, where the governing body have designated another governor for the purposes of this subsection, that other governor).

(3) To the extent that it appears necessary or desirable for the purpose of co-ordinating provision for children with special educational needs–

(a) the governing bodies of community, foundation and voluntary schools and maintained nursery schools shall, in exercising functions relating to the provision for such children, consult the local authority ... and the governing bodies of other such schools,

(b) [Repealed.]

(3A) The governing body of a community, foundation or voluntary school or a maintained nursery school shall designate a member of the staff at the school (to be known as the 'special educational needs co-ordinator') as having responsibility for co-ordinating the provision for pupils with special educational needs.

(3B) Regulations may–

(a) require the governing bodies of schools falling within subsection (3A) to ensure that special educational needs co-ordinators have prescribed qualifications or prescribed experience (or both), and

(b) confer on the governing bodies of those schools other functions relating to special educational needs co-ordinators.

(4) Where a child who has special educational needs is being educated in a community, foundation or voluntary school or a maintained nursery school, those concerned with making special educational provision for the child shall secure, so far as is reasonably practicable and is compatible with–

(a) the child receiving the special educational provision which his learning difficulty calls for,

(b) the provision of efficient education for the children with whom he will be educated, and

(c) the efficient use of resources,

that the child engages in the activities of the school together with children who do not have special educational needs.

(5) The governing body of a community, foundation or voluntary school, a maintained nursery school, or a community or foundation special school shall–

(a) in the case of a school in England, prepare a report containing special needs information, and

(b) in the case of a school in Wales, include special needs information in the report prepared under section 30(1) of the Education Act 2002 (governors' report).

(6) In subsection (5) 'special needs information' means–

(a) such information as may be prescribed about the implementation of the governing body's policy for pupils with special educational needs, and

(b) information as to–

(i) the arrangements for the admission of disabled persons as pupils at the school,

    (ii) the steps taken to prevent disabled pupils from being treated less favourably than other pupils,

    (iii) the facilities provided to assist access to the school by disabled pupils, and

    (iv) the plan prepared by the governing body under section 28D of the Disability Discrimination Act 1995 ('the 1995 Act').

(6A) In subsection (6)(b) 'disabled person' means a person who is a disabled person for the purposes of the 1995 Act; and section 28Q of the 1995 Act (interpretation) applies for the purposes of subsection (6)(b) as it applies for the purposes of Chapter 1 of Part 4 of that Act.

Duty to inform parent where special educational provision made

317A(1)This section applies if–

    (a) a child for whom no statement is maintained under section 324 is a registered pupil at–

       (i) a community, foundation or voluntary school or a maintained nursery school, or

       (ii) a pupil referral unit,

    (b) special educational provision is made for him at the school because it is considered that he has special educational needs, and

    (c) his parent has not previously been informed under this section of special educational provision made for him at the school.

  (2) If the school is a pupil referral unit, the local authority must secure that the head teacher informs the child's parent that special educational provision is being made for him at the school because it is considered that he has special educational needs.

  (3) In any other case, the governing body must inform the child's parent that special educational provision is being made for him there because it is considered that he has special educational needs.

Special educational provision otherwise than in schools

319 (1) Where a local authority are satisfied that it would be inappropriate for–

    (a) the special educational provision which a learning difficulty of a child in their area calls for, or

    (b) any part of any such provision,

to be made in a school, they may arrange for the provision (or, as the case may be, for that part of it) to be made otherwise than in a school.

  (2) Before making an arrangement under this section, a local authority shall consult the child's parent.

Identification and assessment of children with special educational needs

321 General duty of local authority towards children for whom they are responsible

321 (1) A local authority shall exercise their powers with a view to securing that, of the children for whom they are responsible, they identify those to whom subsection (2) below applies.

  (2) This subsection applies to a child if–

    (a) he has special educational needs, and

    (b) it is necessary for the authority to determine the special educational provision which any learning difficulty he may have calls for.

(3) For the purposes of this Part a local authority are responsible for a child if he is in their area and–

   (a) he is a registered pupil at a maintained school or maintained nursery school,

   (b) education is provided for him at a school which is not a maintained school or maintained nursery school but is so provided at the expense of the authority,

   (c) he does not come within paragraph (a) or (b) above but is a registered pupil at a school and has been brought to the authority's attention as having (or probably having) special educational needs, or

   (d) he is not a registered pupil at a school but is not under the age of two or over compulsory school age and has been brought to their attention as having (or probably having) special educational needs.

Assessment of educational needs

323 (1) Where a local authority are of the opinion that a child for whom they are responsible falls, or probably falls, within subsection (2), they shall serve a notice on the child's parent informing him–

   (a) that they are considering whether to make an assessment of the child's educational needs,

   (b) of the procedure to be followed in making the assessment,

   (c) of the name of the officer of the authority from whom further information may be obtained, and

   (d) of the parent's right to make representations, and submit written evidence, to the authority within such period (which must not be less than 29 days beginning with the date on which the notice is served) as may be specified in the notice.

(2) A child falls within this subsection if–

   (a) he has special educational needs, and

   (b) it is necessary for the authority to determine the special educational provision which any learning difficulty he may have calls for.

(3) Where–

   (a) a local authority have served a notice under subsection (1) and the period specified in the notice in accordance with subsection (1)(d) has expired, and

   (b) the authority remain of the opinion, after taking into account any representations made and any evidence submitted to them in response to the notice, that the child falls, or probably falls, within subsection (2),

they shall make an assessment of his educational needs.

(4) Where a local authority decide to make an assessment under this section, they shall give notice in writing to the child's parent of that decision and of their reasons for making it.

(5) Schedule 26 has effect in relation to the making of assessments under this section.

(6) Where, at any time after serving a notice under subsection (1), a local authority decide not to assess the educational needs of the child concerned they shall give notice in writing to the child's parent of their decision.

Statement of special educational needs

324 (1) If, in the light of an assessment under section 323 of any child's educational needs and of any representations made by the child's parent in pursuance

of Schedule 27, it is necessary for the local authority to determine the special educational provision which any learning difficulty he may have calls for, the authority shall make and maintain a statement of his special educational needs.

(2) The statement shall be in such form and contain such information as may be prescribed.

(3) In particular, the statement shall–
   (a) give details of the authority's assessment of the child's special educational needs, and
   (b) specify the special educational provision to be made for the purpose of meeting those needs, including the particulars required by subsection (4).

(4) The statement shall–
   (a) specify the type of school or other institution which the local authority consider would be appropriate for the child,
   (b) if they are not required under Schedule 27 to specify the name of any school in the statement, specify the name of any school or institution (whether in the United Kingdom or elsewhere) which they consider would be appropriate for the child and should be specified in the statement, and
   (c) specify any provision for the child for which they make arrangements under section 319 and which they consider should be specified in the statement.

(4A) Subsection (4)(b) does not require the name of a school or institution to be specified if the child's parent has made suitable arrangements for the special educational provision specified in the statement to be made for the child.

(5) Where a local authority maintain a statement under this section, then–
   (a) unless the child's parent has made suitable arrangements, the authority–
      (i) shall arrange that the special educational provision specified in the statement is made for the child, and
      (ii) may arrange that any non-educational provision specified in the statement is made for him in such manner as they consider appropriate, and
   (b) if the name of a maintained school or maintained nursery school is specified in the statement, the governing body of the school shall admit the child to the school.

(5A) Subsection (5)(b) has effect regardless of any duty imposed on the governing body of a school by section 1(6) of the School Standards and Framework Act 1998.

(6) Subsection (5)(b) does not affect any power to exclude from a school a pupil who is already a registered pupil there.

(7) Schedule 27 has effect in relation to the making and maintenance of statements under this section.

Appeal against decision not to make statement

325 (1) If, after making an assessment under section 323 of the educational needs of any child for whom no statement is maintained under section 324, the local authority do not propose to make such a statement, they shall give notice in writing of their decision to the child's parent.

(2) In such a case, the child's parent may appeal to the Tribunal against the decision.

(2A) A notice under subsection (1) must inform the parent of the right of appeal under subsection (2) and contain such other information as may be prescribed.

(2B) Regulations may provide that where a local authority are under a duty under this section to serve any notice, the duty must be performed within the prescribed period.

(3) On an appeal under this section, the Tribunal may–
   (a) dismiss the appeal,
   (b) order the local authority to make and maintain such a statement, or
   (c) remit the case to the authority for them to reconsider whether, having regard to any observations made by the Tribunal, it is necessary for the authority to determine the special educational provision which any learning difficulty the child may have calls for.

Appeal against contents of statement

326 (1) The parent of a child for whom a local education authority maintain a statement under section 324 may appeal to the Tribunal–
   (a) when the statement is first made,
   (b) if an amendment is made to the statement, or
   (c) if, after conducting an assessment under section 323, the local education authority determine not to amend the statement.

(1A) An appeal under this section may be against any of the following–
   (a) the description in the statement of the local education authority's assessment of the child's special educational needs,
   (b) the special educational provision specified in the statement (including the name of a school so specified),
   (c) if no school is specified in the statement, that fact.

(2) Subsection (1)(b) does not apply where the amendment is made in pursuance of–
   (a) paragraph 8 (change of named school) or 11(3)(b) (amendment ordered by Tribunal) of Schedule 27, or
   (b) directions under section 442 (revocation of school attendance order); and subsection (1)(c) does not apply to a determination made following the service of notice under paragraph 2A (amendment by LEA) of Schedule 27 of a proposal to amend the statement.

(3) On an appeal under this section, the Tribunal may–
   (a) dismiss the appeal,
   (b) order the authority to amend the statement, so far as it describes the authority's assessment of the child's special educational needs or specifies the special educational provision, and make such other consequential amendments to the statement as the Tribunal think fit, or
   (c) order the authority to cease to maintain the statement.

(4) On an appeal under this section the Tribunal shall not order the local education authority to specify the name of any school in the statement (either in substitution for an existing name or in a case where no school is named) unless–
   (a) the parent has expressed a preference for the school in pursuance of arrangements under paragraph 3 (choice of school) of Schedule 27, or

(b) in the proceedings the parent, the local education authority, or both have proposed the school, or[22]

(c) *in the case of proceedings relating to a statement maintained by a local educa-tion authority in Wales only, the child has proposed the school in the proceed-ings (whether or not the parent, the local education authority or both have also proposed the school).*[23]

(5) Before determining any appeal under this section the Tribunal may, with the agreement of the parties, correct any deficiency in the statement.

Reviews of educational needs

328 (1) Regulations may prescribe the frequency with which assessments under sec-tion 323 are to be repeated in respect of children for whom statements are maintained under section 324.

(2) Where—

(a) the parent of a child for whom a statement is maintained under section 324 asks the local education authority to arrange for an assessment to be made in respect of the child under section 323,

(b) no such assessment has been made within the period of six months end-ing with the date on which the request is made, and

(c) it is necessary for the authority to make a further assessment under sec-tion 323,

the authority shall comply with the request.

(3) If in any case where subsection (2)(a) and (b) applies the authority determine not to comply with the request—

(a) they shall give notice in writing of that fact to the child's parent, and

(b) the parent may appeal to the Tribunal against the determination.

(3A) A notice under subsection(3)(a) must inform the parent of the right of appeal under subsection (3)(b) and contain such other information as may be prescribed.

(3B) Regulations may provide that where a local education authority are under a duty under this section to serve any notice, the duty must be performed within the prescribed period.

(4) On an appeal under subsection (3) the Tribunal may—

(a) dismiss the appeal, or

(b) order the authority to arrange for an assessment to be made in respect of the child under section 323.

(5) A statement under section 324 shall be reviewed by the local education authority—

(a) on the making of an assessment in respect of the child concerned under section 323,

(aa) where the child concerned—

(i) has been subject to a detention order, and

(ii) immediately before release was detained in relevant youth accommodation,

on the child's release from detention, and

22 Words in italics inserted by Education (Wales) Measure 2009. Not yet in force: see Education (Wales) Measure 2009 s26(3).

23 Para 4(c) inserted by Education (Wales) Measure 2009. Not yet in force: see Education (Wales) Measure 2009 s26(3).

(b) in any event, within the period of 12 months beginning with the making of the statement or, as the case may be, with the previous review.

(6) Regulations may make provision–

   (a) as to the manner in which reviews of such statements are to be conducted,

   (b) as to the participation in such reviews of such persons as may be pre-scribed, and

   (c) in connection with such other matters relating to such reviews as the Sec-retary of State considers appropriate.

Appeal against determination of local authority in England not to amend statement following review

328A(1)*This section applies where a local authority in England–*

   (a) conduct a review of a statement in accordance with section 328(5)(b), and

   (b) determine not to amend the statement.

   (2) The authority shall give written notice of the determination and of their reasons for making it to the parent of the child concerned.

   (3) The parent may appeal to the Tribunal.

   (4) Subsections (1A), (3), (4) and (5) of section 326 apply to an appeal under this section as they apply to an appeal under that section, but with the omission of subsection (3)(c).

   (5) A notice under subsection (2) must inform the parent of the right of appeal and of the period within which the right may be exercised.

   (6) A notice under subsection (2) must be given to the parent within the period of seven days beginning with the day on which the determination is made.[24]

Assessment of educational needs at request of child's parent

329(1)Where–

   (a) the parent of a child for whom a local education authority are responsi-ble but for whom no statement is maintained under section 324 asks the authority to arrange for an assessment to be made in respect of the child under section 323,

   (b) no such assessment has been made within the period of six months end-ing with the date on which the request is made, and

   (c) it is necessary for the authority to make an assessment under that section,

   the authority shall comply with the request.

(2) If in any case where subsection (1)(a) and (b) applies the authority determine not to comply with the request–

   (a) they shall give notice in writing of that fact to the child's parent, and

   (b) the parent may appeal to the Tribunal against the determination.

(2A) A notice under subsection (2)(a) must inform the parent of the right of appeal under subsection (2)(b) and contain such other information as may be prescribed.

(3) On an appeal under subsection (2) the Tribunal may–

   (a) dismiss the appeal, or

   (b) order the authority to arrange for an assessment to be made in respect of the child under section 323.

---

24 Section 328A inserted by CSFA 2010. See CSFA 2010 s29(5) for when in force.

Review or assessment of educational needs at request of responsible body

329A(1) This section applies if–

    (a) a child is a registered pupil at a relevant school (whether or not he is a child in respect of whom a statement is maintained under section 324),

    (b) the responsible body asks the local education authority to arrange for an assessment to be made in respect of him under section 323, and

    (c) no such assessment has been made within the period of six months ending with the date on which the request is made.

(2) If it is necessary for the authority to make an assessment or further assessment under section 323, they must comply with the request.

(3) Before deciding whether to comply with the request, the authority must serve on the child's parent a notice informing him–

    (a) that they are considering whether to make an assessment of the child's educational needs,

    (b) of the procedure to be followed in making the assessment,

    (c) of the name of their officer from whom further information may be obtained, and

    (d) of the parent's right to make representations, and submit written evidence, to them before the end of the period specified in the notice ('the specified period').

(4) The specified period must not be less than 29 days beginning with the date on which the notice is served.

(5) The authority may not decide whether to comply with the request until the specified period has expired.

(6) The authority must take into account any representations made, and any evidence submitted, to them in response to the notice.

(7) If, as a result of this section, a local education authority decide to make an assessment under section 323, they must give written notice to the child's parent and to the responsible body which made the request, of the decision and of their reasons for making it.

(8) If, after serving a notice under subsection (3), the authority decide not to assess the educational needs of the child–

    (a) they must give written notice of the decision and of their reasons for making it to his parent and to the responsible body which made the request, and

    (b) the parent may appeal to the Tribunal against the decision.

(9) A notice given under subsection (8)(a) to the child's parent must–

    (a) inform the parent of his right to appeal, and

    (b) contain such other information (if any) as may be prescribed.

(10) On an appeal under subsection (8) the Tribunal may–

    (a) dismiss it, or

    (b) order the authority to arrange for an assessment to be made in respect of the child under section 323.

(11) This section applies to a child for whom relevant early years education is provided as it applies to a child who is a registered pupil at a relevant school.

(12) 'Relevant school' means–

    (a) a maintained school,

    (b) a maintained nursery school,

(c) a pupil referral unit,

(d) an independent school,

(e) a school approved under section 342.

(13) 'The responsible body' means–

(a) in relation to a pupil referral unit, the head teacher,

(b) in relation to any other relevant school, the proprietor or head teacher, and

(c) in relation to a provider of relevant nursery early years education, the person or body of persons responsible for the management of the provision of that nursery early years education.

(14) 'Relevant early years education'–

(a) in relation to England, has the same meaning as it has (in relation to England) in section 123 of the School Standards and Framework Act 1998 except that it does not include early years education provided by a local education authority at a maintained nursery school for a pupil at the school;

(b) in relation to Wales, has the same meaning as it has (in relation to Wales) in section 123 of the School Standards and Framework Act 1998 except that it does not include early years education provided by a local education authority at a maintained nursery school.

(15) 'Prescribed', in relation to Wales, means prescribed in regulations made by the National Asembly for Wales.

Assessment of educational needs of children under two

331 (1) Where a local education authority are of the opinion that a child in their area who is under the age of two falls, or probably falls, within subsection (2)–

(a) they may, with the consent of his parent, make an assessment of the child's educational needs, and

(b) they shall make such an assessment if requested to do so by his parent.

(2) A child falls within this subsection if–

(a) he has special educational needs, and

(b) it is necessary for the authority to determine the special educational provision which any learning difficulty he may have calls for.

(3) An assessment under this section shall be made in such manner as the authority consider appropriate.

(4) After making an assessment under this section, the authority–

(a) may make a statement of the child's special educational needs, and

(b) may maintain that statement,

in such manner as they consider appropriate.

SCHEDULE 26

Making of Assessments under Section 323

Section 323

Introductory

1   In this Schedule 'assessment' means an assessment of a child's educational needs under section 323.

Medical and other advice

2(1) Regulations shall make provision as to the advice which a local authority are to seek in making assessments.

(2) Without prejudice to the generality of sub-paragraph (1), the regulations shall require the authority, except in such circumstances as may be prescribed, to seek medical, psychological and educational advice and such other advice as may be prescribed.

Manner, and timing, of assessments, etc

3 (1) Regulations may make provision–

(a) as to the manner in which assessments are to be conducted,

(b) requiring the local authority, where, after conducting an assessment under section 323 of the educational needs of a child for whom a statement is maintained under section 324, they determine not to amend the statement, to serve on the parent of the child a notice giving the prescribed information, and

(c) in connection with such other matters relating to the making of assessments as the Secretary of State considers appropriate.

(2) Sub-paragraph (1)(b) does not apply to a determination made following the service of notice under paragraph 2A of Schedule 27 (amendment of statement by local authority) of a proposal to amend the statement.

(3) Regulations may provide–

(a) that where a local authority are under a duty under section 323, 329 or 329A, or under regulations under sub-paragraph (1)(b), to serve any notice, the duty must be performed within the prescribed period,

(b) that where a local authority have served a notice under section 323(1) or 329A(3) on a child's parent, they must decide within the prescribed period whether or not to make an assessment of the child's educational needs,

(c) that where a request has been made to a local authority under section 329(1), they must decide within the prescribed period whether or not to comply with the request, and

(d) that where a local authority are under a duty to make an assessment, the duty must be performed within the prescribed period.

(4) Provision made under sub-paragraph (3)–

(a) may be subject to prescribed exceptions, and

(b) does not relieve the authority of the duty to serve a notice, or make a decision or assessment, which has not been served or made within the prescribed period.

Attendance at examinations

4 (1) Where a local authority are considering whether to make an assessment, they may serve a notice on the parent of the child concerned requiring the child's attendance for examination in accordance with the provisions of the notice.

(2) The parent of a child examined under this paragraph may be present at the examination if he so desires.

(3) A notice under this paragraph shall–

(a) state the purpose of the examination,

(b) state the time and place at which the examination will be held,

(c) name an officer of the authority from whom further information may be obtained,

(d) inform the parent that he may submit such information to the authority as he may wish, and

(e) inform the parent of his right to be present at the examination.

Offence

5 (1) Any parent who fails without reasonable excuse to comply with any requirements of a notice served on him under paragraph 4 commits an offence if
the notice relates to a child who is not over compulsory school age at the time
stated in it as the time for holding the examination.

(2) A person guilty of an offence under this paragraph is liable on summary conviction to a fine not exceeding level 2 on the standard scale.

SCHEDULE 27

Making and Maintenance of Statements under Section 324

Section 324

Introductory

1 In this Schedule–

'amendment notice' has the meaning given in paragraph 2A,

'statement' means a statement under section 324,

'periodic review' means a review conducted in accordance with section
328(5)(b), and

're-assessment review' means a review conducted in accordance with section
328(5)(a).

Copy of proposed statement

2(1) Before making a statement, a local authority shall serve on the parent of the
child concerned a copy of the proposed statement.

(2) But that is subject to sub-paragraphs (3) and (4).

(3) The copy of the proposed statement shall not specify any prescribed matter.

(4) The copy of the proposed statement shall not specify any matter in pursuance
of section 324(4).

Amendments to a statement

2A(1) A local authority shall not amend a statement except–

(a) in compliance with an order of the Tribunal,

(b) as directed by the Secretary of State under section 442(4), or

(c) in accordance with the procedure laid down in this Schedule.

(2) If, following a re-assessment review, a local authority propose to amend a
statement, they shall serve on the parent of the child concerned a copy of the
proposed amended statement.

(3) Sub-paragraphs (3) and (4) of paragraph 2 apply to a copy of a proposed
amended statement served under sub-paragraph (2) as they apply to a copy of
a proposed statement served under paragraph 2(1).

(4) If, following a periodic review, a local authority propose to amend a statement,
they shall serve on the parent of the child concerned–

(a) a copy of the existing statement, and

(b) an amendment notice.

(5) If, at any other time, a local authority propose to amend a statement, they shall
proceed as if the proposed amendment were an amendment proposed after a
periodic review.

(6) An amendment notice is a notice in writing giving details of the amendments
to the statement proposed by the authority.

Provision of additional information

2B(1) Sub-paragraph (2) applies when a local authority serve on a parent–

    (a) a copy of a proposed statement under paragraph 2,

    (b) a copy of a proposed amended statement under paragraph 2A, or

    (c) an amendment notice under paragraph 2A.

  (2) The local authority shall also serve on the parent a written notice explaining (to the extent that they are applicable)–

    (a) the arrangements under paragraph 3,

    (b) the effect of paragraph 4, and

    (c) the right to appeal under section 326.

  (3) A notice under sub-paragraph (2) must contain such other information as may be prescribed.

Choice of school

3(1) Every local authority shall make arrangements for enabling a parent–

    (a) on whom a copy of a proposed statement has been served under paragraph 2,

    (b) on whom a copy of a proposed amended statement has been served under paragraph 2A, or

    (c) on whom an amendment notice has been served under paragraph 2A which contains a proposed amendment about–

      (i) the type or name of a school or institution, or

      (ii) the provision made for the child concerned under arrangements made under section 319,

to be specified in the statement,

to express a preference as to the maintained school at which he wishes education to be provided for his child and to give reasons for his preference.

  (2) Any such preference must be expressed or made within the period of 15 days beginning–

    (a) with the date on which the written notice mentioned in paragraph 2B was served on the parent, or

    (b) if a meeting has (or meetings have) been arranged under paragraph 4(1)(b) or (2), with the date fixed for that meeting (or the last of those meetings).

  (3) Where a local authority make a statement in a case where the parent of the child concerned has expressed a preference in pursuance of such arrangements as to the school at which he wishes education to be provided for his child, they shall specify the name of that school in the statement unless–

    (a) the school is unsuitable to the child's age, ability or aptitude or to his special educational needs, or

    (b) the attendance of the child at the school would be incompatible with the provision of efficient education for the children with whom he would be educated or the efficient use of resources.

  (4) [Repealed.]

Consultation on specifying name of school in statement

3A(1) Sub-paragraph (2) applies if a local authority are considering–

    (a) specifying the name of a maintained school or maintained nursery school in a statement, or

    (b) amending a statement–

(i) if no school was specified in the statement before the amendment, so that a maintained school or maintained nursery school will be specified in it,

(ii) if a school was specified in the statement before the amendment, so that a different school, which is a maintained school or maintained nursery school, will be specified in it.

(2) The local authority shall–

(a) serve a copy of the proposed statement or amended statement, or of the existing statement and of the amendment notice, on each affected body, and

(b) consult each affected body.

(3) 'Affected body' means–

(a) the governing body of any school which the local authority are considering specifying; and

(b) if a school which the local authority are considering specifying is maintained by another local authority, that authority.

Representations

4(1) A parent on whom a copy of a proposed statement has been served under paragraph 2, or on whom a proposed amended statement or an amendment notice has been served under paragraph 2A, may–

(a) make representations (or further representations) to the local authority about the content of the proposed statement or the statement as it will have effect if amended in the way proposed by the authority, and

(b) require the authority to arrange a meeting between him and an officer of the authority at which the proposed statement or the statement as it will have effect if amended in the way proposed by the authority can be discussed.

(2) Where a parent, having attended a meeting arranged by a local authority under sub-paragraph (1)(b) in relation to–

(c) a proposed statement, or

(d) an amendment proposed following a re-assessment review,

disagrees with any part of the assessment in question, he may require the authority to arrange such meeting or meetings as they consider will enable him to discuss the relevant advice with the appropriate person or persons.

(3) In this paragraph–

'relevant advice' means such of the advice given to the authority in connection with the assessment as they consider to be relevant to that part of the assessment with which the parent disagrees, and

'appropriate person' means the person who gave the relevant advice or any other person who, in the opinion of the authority, is the appropriate person to discuss it with the parent.

(4) Any representations under sub-paragraph (1)(a) must be made within the period of 15 days beginning–

(a) with the date on which the written notice mentioned in paragraph 2B was served on the parent, or

(b) if a meeting has (or meetings have) been arranged under sub-paragraph (1)(b) or (2), with the date fixed for that meeting (or the last of those meetings).

(5) A requirement under sub-paragraph (1)(b) must be made within the period

of 15 days beginning with the date on which the written notice mentioned in paragraph 2B was served on the parent.

(6) A requirement under sub-paragraph (2) must be made within the period of 15 days beginning with the date fixed for the meeting arranged under sub-paragraph (1)(b).

Making the statement

5(1) Where representations are made to a local authority under paragraph 4(1)(a), the authority shall not make or amend the statement until they have considered the representations and the period or the last of the periods allowed by paragraph 4 for making requirements or further representations has expired.

(2) If a local authority make a statement, it may be in the form originally proposed (except as to the matters required to be excluded from the copy of the proposed statement) or in a form modified in the light of the representations.

(2A) If a local authority amend a statement following service of a proposed amended statement under paragraph 2A, the amended statement made may be in the form proposed or in a form modified in the light of the representations.

(2B) If a local authority amend a statement following service of an amendment notice, the amendments may be those proposed in the notice or amendments modified in the light of the representations.

(3) Regulations may provide that, where a local authority are under a duty (subject to compliance with the preceding requirements of this Schedule) to make a statement, the duty to make the statement, or any step required to be taken for or in connection with the performance of the duty or the maintenance of the statement (including any step in relation to the amendment of the statement) must, subject to prescribed exceptions, be performed within the prescribed period.]

(4) Such provision shall not relieve the authority of the duty to make a statement, or take any step, which has not been performed or taken within that period.

Service of statement

6(1) Where a local authority make or amend a statement they shall serve a copy of the statement, or the amended statement, on the parent of the child concerned.

(2) They shall, at the same time, give the parent written notice of his right to appeal under section 326(1) against–
  (a) the description in the statement of the authority's assessment of the child's special educational needs,
  (b) the special educational provision specified in the statement (including the name of a school specified in the statement), or
  (c) if no school is named in the statement, that fact.

(3) A notice under sub-paragraph (2) must contain such other information as may be prescribed.

Keeping, disclosure and transfer of statements

7(1) Regulations may make provision as to the keeping and disclosure of statements.

(2) Regulations may make provision, where a local authority become responsible for a child for whom a statement is maintained by another authority, for the

transfer of the statement to them and for Part IV to have effect as if the duty to maintain the transferred statement were their duty.

Change of named school

8 (1) Sub-paragraph (2) applies where–
- (a) the parent of a child for whom a statement is maintained which specifies the name of a school or institution asks the local authority to substitute for that name the name of a maintained school or maintained nursery school specified by the parent, and
- (b) the request is not made less than 12 months after–
  - (i) an earlier request under this paragraph,
  - (ii) the service of a copy of the statement or amended statement under paragraph 6,
  - (iii) [Repealed.]
  - (iv) if there is an appeal to the Tribunal under section 326 or this paragraph, the date when the appeal is concluded,

  whichever is the later.

(2) The local authority shall comply with the request unless–
- (a) the school is unsuitable to the child's age, ability or aptitude or to his special educational needs, or
- (b) the attendance of the child at the school would be incompatible with the provision of efficient education for the children with whom he would be educated or the efficient use of resources.

(3) Where the local authority determine not to comply with the request–
- (a) they shall give notice in writing of that fact to the parent of the child, and
- (b) the parent of the child may appeal to the Tribunal against the determination.

(3A) A notice under sub-paragraph (3)(a) must inform the parent of the right of appeal under sub-paragraph (3)(b) and contain such other information as may be prescribed.

(4) On the appeal the Tribunal may–
- (a) dismiss the appeal, or
- (b) order the local authority to substitute for the name of the school or other institution specified in the statement the name of the school specified by the parent.

(5) Regulations may provide that, where a local authority are under a duty to comply with a request under this paragraph, the duty must, subject to prescribed exceptions, be performed within the prescribed period.

(6) Such provision shall not relieve the authority of the duty to comply with such a request which has not been complied with within that period.

Procedure for amending or ceasing to maintain a statement

9(1) A local authority may not cease to maintain, a statement except in accordance with paragraph 11.

(2) Sub-paragraph (1) does not apply where the local authority–
- (a) cease to maintain a statement for a child who has ceased to be a child for whom they are responsible, or
- (b) [Repealed.]

(c) are ordered to cease to maintain a statement under section 326(3)(c),

(d) [Repealed.]

10 [Repealed.]

11 (1) A local authority may cease to maintain a statement only if it is no longer necessary to maintain it.

(2) Where the local authority determine to cease to maintain a statement–

(a) they shall give notice in writing of that fact to the parent of the child, and

(b) the parent of the child may appeal to the Tribunal against the determination.

(2A) A notice under sub-paragraph (2)(a) must inform the parent of the right of appeal under sub-paragraph (2)(b) and contain such other information as may be prescribed.

(2B) Where the local authority determine to cease to maintain a statement following a periodic review or a re-assessment review, regulations may provide that a notice under sub-paragraph (2)(a) must be given within the prescribed period beginning with the date of the review.

(3) On an appeal under this paragraph the Tribunal may–

(a) dismiss the appeal, or

(b) order the local authority to continue to maintain the statement in its existing form or with such amendments of–

(i) the description in the statement of the authority's assessment of the child's special educational needs, or

(ii) the special educational provision specified in the statement,

and such other consequential amendments, as the Tribunal may determine.

(4) Except where there is an appeal to the Tribunal under this paragraph, a local authority may only cease to maintain a statement under this paragraph within the prescribed period beginning with the service of the notice under sub-paragraph (2).

(5) A local authority may not, under this paragraph, cease to maintain a statement if–

(a) there has been an appeal under this paragraph against the authority's determination to cease to maintain the statement, and

(b) the appeal has not been determined by the Tribunal or withdrawn.

EQUALITY ACT 2010
Part 2: Equality: Key Concepts
Chapter 1: Protected Characteristics
The protected characteristics

4 The following characteristics are protected characteristics–
   age;
   disability;
   gender reassignment;
   marriage and civil partnership;
   pregnancy and maternity;
   race;
   religion or belief;
   sex;
   sexual orientation.

Disability

6(1) A person (P) has a disability if–
   (a) P has a physical or mental impairment, and
   (b) the impairment has a substantial and long-term adverse effect on P's ability to carry out normal day-to-day activities.
(2) A reference to a disabled person is a reference to a person who has a disability.
(3) In relation to the protected characteristic of disability–
   (a) a reference to a person who has a particular protected characteristic is a reference to a person who has a particular disability;
   (b) a reference to persons who share a protected characteristic is a reference to persons who have the same disability.
(4) This Act (except Part 12 and section 190) applies in relation to a person who has had a disability as it applies in relation to a person who has the disability; accordingly (except in that Part and that section)–
   (a) a reference (however expressed) to a person who has a disability includes a reference to a person who has had the disability, and
   (b) a reference (however expressed) to a person who does not have a disability includes a reference to a person who has not had the disability.
(5) A Minister of the Crown may issue guidance about matters to be taken into account in deciding any question for the purposes of subsection (1).
(6) Schedule 1 (disability: supplementary provision) has effect.

Chapter 2: Prohibited Conduct
Discrimination

Direct discrimination

13(1) A person (A) discriminates against another (B) if, because of a protected characteristic, A treats B less favourably than A treats or would treat others.
(2) If the protected characteristic is age, A does not discriminate against B if A can show A's treatment of B to be a proportionate means of achieving a legitimate aim.
(3) If the protected characteristic is disability, and B is not a disabled person, A does not discriminate against B only because A treats or would treat disabled persons more favourably than A treats B.

(4) If the protected characteristic is marriage and civil partnership, this section applies to a contravention of Part 5 (work) only if the treatment is because it is B who is married or a civil partner.

(5) If the protected characteristic is race, less favourable treatment includes segregating B from others.

(6) If the protected characteristic is sex–

   (a) less favourable treatment of a woman includes less favourable treatment of her because she is breast-feeding;

   (b) in a case where B is a man, no account is to be taken of special treatment afforded to a woman in connection with pregnancy or childbirth.

(7) Subsection (6)(a) does not apply for the purposes of Part 5 (work).

(8) This section is subject to sections 17(6) and 18(7).

Combined discrimination: dual characteristics

14(1) A person (A) discriminates against another (B) if, because of a combination of two relevant protected characteristics, A treats B less favourably than A treats or would treat a person who does not share either of those characteristics.

(2) The relevant protected characteristics are–

   (a) age;

   (b) disability;

   (c) gender reassignment;

   (d) race

   (e) religion or belief;

   (f) sex;

   (g) sexual orientation.

(3) For the purposes of establishing a contravention of this Act by virtue of subsection (1), B need not show that A's treatment of B is direct discrimination because of each of the characteristics in the combination (taken separately).

(4) But B cannot establish a contravention of this Act by virtue of subsection (1) if, in reliance on another provision of this Act or any other enactment, A shows that A's treatment of B is not direct discrimination because of either or both of the characteristics in the combination.

(5) Subsection (1) does not apply to a combination of characteristics that includes disability in circumstances where, if a claim of direct discrimination because of disability were to be brought, it would come within section 116 (special educational needs).

(6) A Minister of the Crown may by order amend this section so as to–

   (a) make further provision about circumstances in which B can, or in which B cannot, establish a contravention of this Act by virtue of subsection (1);

   (b) specify other circumstances in which subsection (1) does not apply.

(7) The references to direct discrimination are to a contravention of this Act by virtue of section 13.

Discrimination arising from disability

15(1) A person (A) discriminates against a disabled person (B) if–

   (a) A treats B unfavourably because of something arising in consequence of B's disability, and

   (b) A cannot show that the treatment is a proportionate means of achieving a legitimate aim.

(2) Subsection (1) does not apply if A shows that A did not know, and could not reasonably have been expected to know, that B had the disability.

Indirect discrimination

19(1) A person (A) discriminates against another (B) if A applies to B a provision, criterion or practice which is discriminatory in relation to a relevant protected characteristic of B's.

(2) For the purposes of subsection (1), a provision, criterion or practice is discriminatory in relation to a relevant protected characteristic of B's if–

(a) A applies, or would apply, it to persons with whom B does not share the characteristic,

(b) it puts, or would put, persons with whom B shares the characteristic at a particular disadvantage when compared with persons with whom B does not share it,

(c) it puts, or would put, B at that disadvantage, and

(d) A cannot show it to be a proportionate means of achieving a legitimate aim.

(3) The relevant protected characteristics are–

age;
disability;
gender reassignment;
marriage and civil partnership;
race;
religion or belief;
sex;
sexual orientation.

Adjustments for disabled persons

Duty to make adjustments

20(1) Where this Act imposes a duty to make reasonable adjustments on a person, this section, sections 21 and 22 and the applicable Schedule apply; and for those purposes, a person on whom the duty is imposed is referred to as A.

(2) The duty comprises the following three requirements.

(3) The first requirement is a requirement, where a provision, criterion or practice of A's puts a disabled person at a substantial disadvantage in relation to a relevant matter in comparison with persons who are not disabled, to take such steps as it is reasonable to have to take to avoid the disadvantage.

(4) The second requirement is a requirement, where a physical feature puts a disabled person at a substantial disadvantage in relation to a relevant matter in comparison with persons who are not disabled, to take such steps as it is reasonable to have to take to avoid the disadvantage.

(5) The third requirement is a requirement, where a disabled person would, but for the provision of an auxiliary aid, be put at a substantial disadvantage in relation to a relevant matter in comparison with persons who are not disabled, to take such steps as it is reasonable to have to take to provide the auxiliary aid.

(6) Where the first or third requirement relates to the provision of information, the steps which it is reasonable for A to have to take include steps for ensuring that in the circumstances concerned the information is provided in an accessible format.

(7) A person (A) who is subject to a duty to make reasonable adjustments is not (subject to express provision to the contrary) entitled to require a disabled person, in relation to whom A is required to comply with the duty, to pay to any extent A's costs of complying with the duty.

(8) A reference in section 21 or 22 or an applicable Schedule to the first, second or third requirement is to be construed in accordance with this section.

(9) In relation to the second requirement, a reference in this section or an applicable Schedule to avoiding a substantial disadvantage includes a reference to—

(a) removing the physical feature in question,

(b) altering it, or

(c) providing a reasonable means of avoiding it.

(10) A reference in this section, section 21 or 22 or an applicable Schedule (apart from paragraphs 2 to 4 of Schedule 4) to a physical feature is a reference to—

(a) a feature arising from the design or construction of a building,

(b) a feature of an approach to, exit from or access to a building,

(c) a fixture or fitting, or furniture, furnishings, materials, equipment or other chattels, in or on premises, or

(d) any other physical element or quality.

(11) A reference in this section, section 21 or 22 or an applicable Schedule to an auxiliary aid includes a reference to an auxiliary service.

(12) A reference in this section or an applicable Schedule to chattels is to be read, in relation to Scotland, as a reference to moveable property.

(13) The applicable Schedule is, in relation to the Part of this Act specified in the first column of the Table, the Schedule specified in the second column.

Part of this Act	Applicable Schedule
Part 3 (services and public functions)	Schedule 2
Part 4 (premises)	Schedule 4
Part 5 (work)	Schedule 8
Part 6 (education)	Schedule 13
Part 7 (associations)	Schedule 15
Each of the Parts mentioned above	Schedule 21

Failure to comply with duty

21(1) A failure to comply with the first, second or third requirement is a failure to comply with a duty to make reasonable adjustments.

(2) A discriminates against a disabled person if A fails to comply with that duty in relation to that person.

(3) A provision of an applicable Schedule which imposes a duty to comply with the first, second or third requirement applies only for the purpose of establishing whether A has contravened this Act by virtue of subsection (2); a failure to comply is, accordingly, not actionable by virtue of another provision of this Act or otherwise.

Regulations

22(1) Regulations may prescribe–
   (a) matters to be taken into account in deciding whether it is reasonable for A to take a step for the purposes of a prescribed provision of an applicable Schedule;
   (b) descriptions of persons to whom the first, second or third requirement does not apply.

(2) Regulations may make provision as to–
   (a) circumstances in which it is, or in which it is not, reasonable for a person of a prescribed description to have to take steps of a prescribed description;
   (b) what is, or what is not, a provision, criterion or practice;
   (c) things which are, or which are not, to be treated as physical features;
   (d) things which are, or which are not, to be treated as alterations of physical features;
   (e) things which are, or which are not, to be treated as auxiliary aids.

(3) Provision made by virtue of this section may amend an applicable Schedule.

Part 11: Advancement of Equality

Chapter 1: Public Sector Equality Duty

Public sector equality duty

149 (1) A public authority must, in the exercise of its functions, have due regard to the need to–
   (a) eliminate discrimination, harassment, victimisation and any other conduct that is prohibited by or under this Act;
   (b) advance equality of opportunity between persons who share a relevant protected characteristic and persons who do not share it;
   (c) foster good relations between persons who share a relevant protected characteristic and persons who do not share it.

(2) A person who is not a public authority but who exercises public functions must, in the exercise of those functions, have due regard to the matters mentioned in subsection (1).

(3) Having due regard to the need to advance equality of opportunity between persons who share a relevant protected characteristic and persons who do not share it involves having due regard, in particular, to the need to–
   (a) remove or minimise disadvantages suffered by persons who share a relevant protected characteristic that are connected to that characteristic;
   (b) take steps to meet the needs of persons who share a relevant protected characteristic that are different from the needs of persons who do not share it;
   (c) encourage persons who share a relevant protected characteristic to participate in public life or in any other activity in which participation by such persons is disproportionately low.

(4) The steps involved in meeting the needs of disabled persons that are different from the needs of persons who are not disabled include, in particular, steps to take account of disabled persons' disabilities.

(5) Having due regard to the need to foster good relations between persons who share a relevant protected characteristic and persons who do not share it involves having due regard, in particular, to the need to–

    (a) tackle prejudice, and

    (b) promote understanding.

(6) Compliance with the duties in this section may involve treating some persons more favourably than others; but that is not to be taken as permitting conduct that would otherwise be prohibited by or under this Act.

(7) The relevant protected characteristics are–

> age;
> disability;
> gender reassignment;
> pregnancy and maternity;
> race;
> religion or belief;
> sex;
> sexual orientation.

(8) A reference to conduct that is prohibited by or under this Act includes a reference to–

    (a) a breach of an equality clause or rule;

    (b) a breach of a non-discrimination rule.

(9) Schedule 18 (exceptions) has effect.

Chapter 2: Positive Action

Positive action: general

158 (1) This section applies if a person (P) reasonably thinks that–

    (a) persons who share a protected characteristic suffer a disadvantage connected to the characteristic,

    (b) persons who share a protected characteristic have needs that are different from the needs of persons who do not share it, or

    (c) participation in an activity by persons who share a protected characteristic is disproportionately low.

(2) This Act does not prohibit P from taking any action which is a proportionate means of achieving the aim of–

    (a) enabling or encouraging persons who share the protected characteristic to overcome or minimise that disadvantage,

    (b) meeting those needs, or

    (c) enabling or encouraging persons who share the protected characteristic to participate in that activity.

(3) Regulations may specify action, or descriptions of action, to which subsection (2) does not apply.

(4) This section does not apply to–

    (a) action within section 159(3), or

    (b) anything that is permitted by virtue of section 104.

(5) If section 104(7) is repealed by virtue of section 105, this section will not apply to anything that would have been so permitted but for the repeal.

(6) This section does not enable P to do anything that is prohibited by or under an enactment other than this Act.

SCHEDULE 1
Disability: Supplementary Provision

Section 6

Part 1: Determination of Disability

Impairment

1   Regulations may make provision for a condition of a prescribed description to be, or not to be, an impairment.

Long-term effects

2 (1) The effect of an impairment is long-term if–
   (a) it has lasted for at least 12 months,
   (b) it is likely to last for at least 12 months, or
   (c) it is likely to last for the rest of the life of the person affected.
   (2) If an impairment ceases to have a substantial adverse effect on a person's ability to carry out normal day-to-day activities, it is to be treated as continuing to have that effect if that effect is likely to recur.
   (3) For the purposes of sub-paragraph (2), the likelihood of an effect recurring is to be disregarded in such circumstances as may be prescribed.
   (4) Regulations may prescribe circumstances in which, despite sub-paragraph (1), an effect is to be treated as being, or as not being, long-term.

Severe disfigurement

3 (1) An impairment which consists of a severe disfigurement is to be treated as having a substantial adverse effect on the ability of the person concerned to carry out normal day-to-day activities.
   (2) Regulations may provide that in prescribed circumstances a severe disfigurement is not to be treated as having that effect.
   (3) The regulations may, in particular, make provision in relation to deliberately acquired disfigurement.

Substantial adverse effects

4   Regulations may make provision for an effect of a prescribed description on the ability of a person to carry out normal day-to-day activities to be treated as being, or as not being, a substantial adverse effect.

Effect of medical treatment

5 (1) An impairment is to be treated as having a substantial adverse effect on the ability of the person concerned to carry out normal day-to-day activities if–
   (a) measures are being taken to treat or correct it, and
   (b) but for that, it would be likely to have that effect.
   (2) 'Measures' includes, in particular, medical treatment and the use of a prosthesis or other aid.
   (3) Sub-paragraph (1) does not apply–
   (a) in relation to the impairment of a person's sight, to the extent that the impairment is, in the person's case, correctable by spectacles or contact lenses or in such other ways as may be prescribed;
   (b) in relation to such other impairments as may be prescribed, in such circumstances as are prescribed.

Certain medical conditions

6 (1) Cancer, HIV infection and multiple sclerosis are each a disability.

(2) HIV infection is infection by a virus capable of causing the Acquired Immune Deficiency Syndrome.

Deemed disability

7 (1) Regulations may provide for persons of prescribed descriptions to be treated as having disabilities.

(2) The regulations may prescribe circumstances in which a person who has a disability is to be treated as no longer having the disability.

(3) This paragraph does not affect the other provisions of this Schedule.

Progressive conditions

8 (1) This paragraph applies to a person (P) if–

(a) P has a progressive condition,

(b) as a result of that condition P has an impairment which has (or had) an effect on P's ability to carry out normal day-to-day activities, but

(c) the effect is not (or was not) a substantial adverse effect.

(2) P is to be taken to have an impairment which has a substantial adverse effect if the condition is likely to result in P having such an impairment.

(3) Regulations may make provision for a condition of a prescribed description to be treated as being, or as not being, progressive.

Past disabilities

9 (1) A question as to whether a person had a disability at a particular time ('the relevant time') is to be determined, for the purposes of section 6, as if the provisions of, or made under, this Act were in force when the act complained of was done had been in force at the relevant time.

(2) The relevant time may be a time before the coming into force of the provision of this Act to which the question relates.

Part 2: Guidance

Preliminary

10 This Part of this Schedule applies in relation to guidance referred to in section 6(5).

Examples

11 The guidance may give examples of–

(a) effects which it would, or would not, be reasonable, in relation to particular activities, to regard as substantial adverse effects;

(b) substantial adverse effects which it would, or would not, be reasonable to regard as long-term.

Adjudicating bodies

12 (1) In determining whether a person is a disabled person, an adjudicating body must take account of such guidance as it thinks is relevant.

(2) An adjudicating body is–

(a) a court;

(b) a tribunal;

(c) a person (other than a court or tribunal) who may decide a claim relating to a contravention of Part 6 (education).

Representations

13   Before issuing the guidance, the Minister must–

(a) publish a draft of it;

(b) consider any representations made to the Minister about the draft;

(c) make such modifications as the Minister thinks appropriate in the light of the representations.

Parliamentary procedure

14 (1) If the Minister decides to proceed with proposed guidance, a draft of it must be laid before Parliament.

(2) If, before the end of the 40-day period, either House resolves not to approve the draft, the Minister must take no further steps in relation to the proposed guidance.

(3) If no such resolution is made before the end of that period, the Minister must issue the guidance in the form of the draft.

(4) Sub-paragraph (2) does not prevent a new draft of proposed guidance being laid before Parliament.

(5) The 40-day period–

(a) begins on the date on which the draft is laid before both Houses (or, if laid before each House on a different date, on the later date);

(b) does not include a period during which Parliament is prorogued or dissolved;

(c) does not include a period during which both Houses are adjourned for more than 4 days.

Commencement

15   The guidance comes into force on the day appointed by order by the Minister.

Revision and revocation

16 (1) The Minister may–

(a) revise the whole or part of guidance and re-issue it;

(b) by order revoke guidance.

(2) A reference to guidance includes a reference to guidance which has been revised and re-issued.

HOUSING GRANTS, CONSTRUCTION AND REGENERATION ACT 1996

Grants: certificate required in case of owner's application

21(1) A local housing authority shall not entertain an owner's application for a grant unless it is accompanied by an owner's certificate in respect of the dwelling to which the application relates or, in the case of a common parts application, in respect of each flat in the building occupied or proposed to be occupied by a disabled occupant.

(2) An 'owner's certificate', for the purposes of an application for a grant, certifies that the applicant–

(a) has or proposes to acquire a qualifying owner's interest, and

(b) intends that the disabled occupant will live in the dwelling or flat as his only or main residence throughout the grant condition period or for such shorter period as his health and other relevant circumstances permit.

Grants: certificates required in case of tenant's application

22(1) A local housing authority shall not entertain a tenant's application for a grant unless it is accompanied by a tenant's certificate.

(2) A 'tenant's certificate', for the purposes of an application for a grant, certifies–

(a) that the application is a tenant's application, and

(b) that the applicant intends that he (if he is the disabled occupant) or the disabled occupant will live in the dwelling or flat as his only or main residence throughout the grant condition period or for such shorter period as his health and other relevant circumstances permit.

(3) Except where the authority consider it unreasonable in the circumstances to require such a certificate, they shall not entertain a tenant's application for a grant unless it is also accompanied by an owner's certificate from the person who at the time of the application is the landlord under the tenancy.

Certificates required in case of occupier's application

22A(1) A local housing authority shall not entertain an occupier's application for a grant unless it is accompanied by an occupier's certificate.

(2) An 'occupier's certificate', for the purposes of an application for a grant, certifies–

(a) that the application is an occupier's application, and

(b) that the applicant intends that he (if he is the disabled occupant) or the disabled occupant will live in the qualifying houseboat or caravan (as the case may be) as his only or main residence throughout the grant condition period or for such shorter period as his health and other relevant circumstances permit.

(3) Except where the authority consider it unreasonable in the circumstances to require such a certificate, they shall not entertain an occupier's application for a grant unless it is also accompanied by a consent certificate from each person (other than the applicant) who at the time of the application–

(a) is entitled to possession of the premises at which the qualifying houseboat is moored or, as the case may be, the land on which the caravan is stationed; or

(b) is entitled to dispose of the qualifying houseboat or, as the case may be, the caravan.

(4) A 'consent certificate', for the purposes of subsection (3), certifies that the person by whom the certificate is given consents to the carrying out of the relevant works.

Grants: purposes for which grant must or may be given

23(1) The purposes for which an application for a grant must be approved, subject to the provisions of this Chapter, are the following–

(a) facilitating access by the disabled occupant to and from–
  (i) the dwelling, qualifying houseboat or caravan, or
  (ii) the building in which the dwelling or, as the case may be, flat is situated;

(b) making–
  (i) the dwelling, qualifying houseboat or caravan, or
  (ii) the building,
  safe for the disabled occupant and other persons residing with him;

(c) facilitating access by the disabled occupant to a room used or usable as the principal family room;

(d) facilitating access by the disabled occupant to, or providing for the disabled occupant, a room used or usable for sleeping;

(e) facilitating access by the disabled occupant to, or providing for the disabled occupant, a room in which there is a lavatory, or facilitating the use by the disabled occupant of such a facility;

(f) facilitating access by the disabled occupant to, or providing for the disabled occupant, a room in which there is a bath or shower (or both), or facilitating the use by the disabled occupant of such a facility;

(g) facilitating access by the disabled occupant to, or providing for the disabled occupant, a room in which there is a washhand basin, or facilitating the use by the disabled occupant of such a facility;

(h) facilitating the preparation and cooking of food by the disabled occupant;

(i) improving any heating system in the dwelling, qualifying houseboat or caravan to meet the needs of the disabled occupant or, if there is no existing heating system there or any such system is unsuitable for use by the disabled occupant, providing a heating system suitable to meet his needs;

(j) facilitating the use by the disabled occupant of a source of power, light or heat by altering the position of one or more means of access to or control of that source or by providing additional means of control;

(k) facilitating access and movement by the disabled occupant around the dwelling, qualifying houseboat or caravan in order to enable him to care for a person who is normally resident there and is in need of such care;

(l) such other purposes as may be specified by order of the Secretary of State.

(2) [Repealed.]

(3) If in the opinion of the local housing authority the relevant works are more or less extensive than is necessary to achieve any of the purposes set out in subsection (1), they may, with the consent of the applicant, treat the application as varied so that the relevant works are limited to or, as the case may be, include such works as seem to the authority to be necessary for that purpose.

Grants: approval of application

24(1) The local housing authority shall approve an application for a grant for purposes within section 23(1), subject to the following provisions.

(2) Where an authority entertain an owner's application for a grant made by a person who proposes to acquire a qualifying owner's interest, they shall not approve the application until they are satisfied that he has done so.

(3) A local housing authority shall not approve an application for a grant unless they are satisfied–

(a) that the relevant works are necessary and appropriate to meet the needs of the disabled occupant, and

(b) that it is reasonable and practicable to carry out the relevant works having regard to the age and condition of–

(i) the dwelling, qualifying houseboat or caravan, or

(ii) the building.

In considering the matters mentioned in paragraph (a) a local housing authority which is not itself a social services authority shall consult the social services authority.

(4) [Repealed.]

(5) A local housing authority shall not approve a common parts application for a grant unless they are satisfied that the applicant has a power or is under a duty to carry out the relevant works.

Delayed payment of mandatory grant

36(1) The local housing authority may approve an application for a grant on terms that payment of the grant, or part of it, will not be made before a date specified in the notification of their decision on the application.

(2) That date shall not be more than twelve months, or such other period as may be specified by order of the Secretary of State, after the date of the application.

LOCAL AUTHORITY SOCIAL SERVICES ACT 1970

Local authorities to exercise social services functions under guidance of Secretary of State

7(1) Local authorities shall, in the exercise of their social services functions, including the exercise of any discretion conferred by any relevant enactment, act under the general guidance of the Secretary of State.

(2) [Repealed.]

(3) [Repealed.]

International conventions

UN CONVENTION ON THE RIGHTS OF THE CHILD

Article 2

1. States Parties shall respect and ensure the rights set forth in the present Convention to each child within their jurisdiction without discrimination of any kind, irrespective of the child's or his or her parent's or legal guardian's race, colour, sex, language, religion, political or other opinion, national, ethnic or social origin, property, disability, birth or other status.
2. States Parties shall take all appropriate measures to ensure that the child is protected against all forms of discrimination or punishment on the basis of the status, activities, expressed opinions, or beliefs of the child's parents, legal guardians, or family members.

Article 3

1. In all actions concerning children, whether undertaken by public or private social welfare institutions, courts of law, administrative authorities or legislative bodies, the best interests of the child shall be a primary consideration.
2. States Parties undertake to ensure the child such protection and care as is necessary for his or her well-being, taking into account the rights and duties of his or her parents, legal guardians, or other individuals legally responsible for him or her, and, to this end, shall take all appropriate legislative and administrative measures.
3. States Parties shall ensure that the institutions, services and facilities responsible for the care or protection of children shall conform with the standards established by competent authorities, particularly in the areas of safety, health, in the number and suitability of their staff, as well as competent supervision.

Article 4

States Parties shall undertake all appropriate legislative, administrative, and other measures for the implementation of the rights recognized in the present Convention. With regard to economic, social and cultural rights, States Parties shall undertake such measures to the maximum extent of their available resources and, where needed, within the framework of international co-operation.

Article 12

1. States Parties shall assure to the child who is capable of forming his or her own views the right to express those views freely in all matters affecting the child, the views of the child being given due weight in accordance with the age and maturity of the child.
2. For this purpose, the child shall in particular be provided the opportunity to be heard in any judicial and administrative proceedings affecting the child, either directly, or through a representative or an appropriate body, in a manner consistent with the procedural rules of national law.

Article 23

1. States Parties recognize that a mentally or physically disabled child should enjoy a full and decent life, in conditions which ensure dignity, promote self-reliance and facilitate the child's active participation in the community.
2. States Parties recognize the right of the disabled child to special care and shall encourage and ensure the extension, subject to available resources, to the eli-

gible child and those responsible for his or her care, of assistance for which application is made and which is appropriate to the child's condition and to the circumstances of the parents or others caring for the child.

3. Recognizing the special needs of a disabled child, assistance extended in accordance with paragraph 2 of the present article shall be provided free of charge, whenever possible, taking into account the financial resources of the parents or others caring for the child, and shall be designed to ensure that the disabled child has effective access to and receives education, training, health care services, rehabilitation services, preparation for employment and recreation opportunities in a manner conducive to the child's achieving the fullest possible social integration and individual development, including his or her cultural and spiritual development

4. States Parties shall promote, in the spirit of international cooperation, the exchange of appropriate information in the field of preventive health care and of medical, psychological and functional treatment of disabled children, including dissemination of and access to information concerning methods of rehabilitation, education and vocational services, with the aim of enabling States Parties to improve their capabilities and skills and to widen their experience in these areas. In this regard, particular account shall be taken of the needs of developing countries.

Article 24

1. States Parties recognize the right of the child to the enjoyment of the highest attainable standard of health and to facilities for the treatment of illness and rehabilitation of health. States Parties shall strive to ensure that no child is deprived of his or her right of access to such health care services.

2. States Parties shall pursue full implementation of this right and, in particular, shall take appropriate measures:
   (a) To diminish infant and child mortality;
   (b) To ensure the provision of necessary medical assistance and health care to all children with emphasis on the development of primary health care;
   (c) To combat disease and malnutrition, including within the framework of primary health care, through, inter alia, the application of readily available technology and through the provision of adequate nutritious foods and clean drinking-water, taking into consideration the dangers and risks of environmental pollution;
   (d) To ensure appropriate pre-natal and post-natal health care for mothers;
   (e) To ensure that all segments of society, in particular parents and children, are informed, have access to education and are supported in the use of basic knowledge of child health and nutrition, the advantages of breastfeeding, hygiene and environmental sanitation and the prevention of accidents;
   (f) To develop preventive health care, guidance for parents and family planning education and services.

3. States Parties shall take all effective and appropriate measures with a view to abolishing traditional practices prejudicial to the health of children.

4. States Parties undertake to promote and encourage international co-operation with a view to achieving progressively the full realization of the right recognized in the present article. In this regard, particular account shall be taken of the needs of developing countries.

UN CONVENTION ON THE RIGHTS OF PERSONS WITH DISABILITIES

Article 3 – General principles
The principles of the present Convention shall be:
a. Respect for inherent dignity, individual autonomy including the freedom to make one's own choices, and independence of persons;
b. Non-discrimination;
c. Full and effective participation and inclusion in society;
d. Respect for difference and acceptance of persons with disabilities as part of human diversity and humanity;
e. Equality of opportunity;
f. Accessibility;
g. Equality between men and women;
h. Respect for the evolving capacities of children with disabilities and respect for the right of children with disabilities to preserve their identities.

Article 7 – Children with disabilities
1. States Parties shall take all necessary measures to ensure the full enjoyment by children with disabilities of all human rights and fundamental freedoms on an equal basis with other children.
2. In all actions concerning children with disabilities, the best interests of the child shall be a primary consideration.
3. States Parties shall ensure that children with disabilities have the right to express their views freely on all matters affecting them, their views being given due weight in accordance with their age and maturity, on an equal basis with other children, and to be provided with disability and age-appropriate assistance to realize that right.

Article 9 – Accessibility
1. To enable persons with disabilities to live independently and participate fully in all aspects of life, States Parties shall take appropriate measures to ensure to persons with disabilities access, on an equal basis with others, to the physical environment, to transportation, to information and communications, including information and communications technologies and systems, and to other facilities and services open or provided to the public, both in urban and in rural areas. These measures, which shall include the identification and elimination of obstacles and barriers to accessibility, shall apply to, inter alia:
   a. Buildings, roads, transportation and other indoor and outdoor facilities, including schools, housing, medical facilities and workplaces;
   b. Information, communications and other services, including electronic services and emergency services.
2. States Parties shall also take appropriate measures to:
   a. Develop, promulgate and monitor the implementation of minimum standards and guidelines for the accessibility of facilities and services open or provided to the public;
   b. Ensure that private entities that offer facilities and services which are open or provided to the public take into account all aspects of accessibility for persons with disabilities;

c. Provide training for stakeholders on accessibility issues facing persons with disabilities;

d. Provide in buildings and other facilities open to the public signage in Braille and in easy to read and understand forms;

e. Provide forms of live assistance and intermediaries, including guides, readers and professional sign language interpreters, to facilitate accessibility to buildings and other facilities open to the public;

f. Promote other appropriate forms of assistance and support to persons with disabilities to ensure their access to information;

g. Promote access for persons with disabilities to new information and communications technologies and systems, including the Internet;

h. Promote the design, development, production and distribution of accessible information and communications technologies and systems at an early stage, so that these technologies and systems become accessible at minimum cost.

Article 19 – Living independently and being included in the community

States Parties to this Convention recognize the equal right of all persons with disabilities to live in the community, with choices equal to others, and shall take effective and appropriate measures to facilitate full enjoyment by persons with disabilities of this right and their full inclusion and participation in the community, including by ensuring that:

a. Persons with disabilities have the opportunity to choose their place of residence and where and with whom they live on an equal basis with others and are not obliged to live in a particular living arrangement;

b. Persons with disabilities have access to a range of in-home, residential and other community support services, including personal assistance necessary to support living and inclusion in the community, and to prevent isolation or segregation from the community;

c. Community services and facilities for the general population are available on an equal basis to persons with disabilities and are responsive to their needs.

Article 23 – Respect for home and the family

1. States Parties shall take effective and appropriate measures to eliminate discrimination against persons with disabilities in all matters relating to marriage, family, parenthood and relationships, on an equal basis with others, so as to ensure that:

a. The right of all persons with disabilities who are of marriageable age to marry and to found a family on the basis of free and full consent of the intending spouses is recognized;

b. The rights of persons with disabilities to decide freely and responsibly on the number and spacing of their children and to have access to age-appropriate information, reproductive and family planning education are recognized, and the means necessary to enable them to exercise these rights are provided;

c. Persons with disabilities, including children, retain their fertility on an equal basis with others.

2. States Parties shall ensure the rights and responsibilities of persons with disabilities, with regard to guardianship, wardship, trusteeship, adoption of

children or similar institutions, where these concepts exist in national legislation; in all cases the best interests of the child shall be paramount. States Parties shall render appropriate assistance to persons with disabilities in the performance of their child-rearing responsibilities.

3. States Parties shall ensure that children with disabilities have equal rights with respect to family life. With a view to realizing these rights, and to prevent concealment, abandonment, neglect and segregation of children with disabilities, States Parties shall undertake to provide early and comprehensive information, services and support to children with disabilities and their families.

4. States Parties shall ensure that a child shall not be separated from his or her parents against their will, except when competent authorities subject to judicial review determine, in accordance with applicable law and procedures, that such separation is necessary for the best interests of the child. In no case shall a child be separated from parents on the basis of a disability of either the child or one or both of the parents.

5. States Parties shall, where the immediate family is unable to care for a child with disabilities, undertake every effort to provide alternative care within the wider family, and failing that, within the community in a family setting.

Article 24 – Education

1. States Parties recognize the right of persons with disabilities to education. With a view to realizing this right without discrimination and on the basis of equal opportunity, States Parties shall ensure an inclusive education system at all levels and life long learning directed to:

   a. The full development of human potential and sense of dignity and self-worth, and the strengthening of respect for human rights, fundamental freedoms and human diversity;

   b. The development by persons with disabilities of their personality, talents and creativity, as well as their mental and physical abilities, to their fullest potential;

   c. Enabling persons with disabilities to participate effectively in a free society.

2. In realizing this right, States Parties shall ensure that:

   a. Persons with disabilities are not excluded from the general education system on the basis of disability, and that children with disabilities are not excluded from free and compulsory primary education, or from secondary education, on the basis of disability;

   b. Persons with disabilities can access an inclusive, quality and free primary education and secondary education on an equal basis with others in the communities in which they live;

   c. Reasonable accommodation of the individual's requirements is provided;

   d. Persons with disabilities receive the support required, within the general education system, to facilitate their effective education;

   e. Effective individualized support measures are provided in environments that maximize academic and social development, consistent with the goal of full inclusion.

3. States Parties shall enable persons with disabilities to learn life and social development skills to facilitate their full and equal participation in education

and as members of the community. To this end, States Parties shall take appropriate measures, including:

a. Facilitating the learning of Braille, alternative script, augmentative and alternative modes, means and formats of communication and orientation and mobility skills, and facilitating peer support and mentoring;

b. Facilitating the learning of sign language and the promotion of the linguistic identity of the deaf community;

c. Ensuring that the education of persons, and in particular children, who are blind, deaf or deafblind, is delivered in the most appropriate languages and modes and means of communication for the individual, and in environments which maximize academic and social development.

4. In order to help ensure the realization of this right, States Parties shall take appropriate measures to employ teachers, including teachers with disabilities, who are qualified in sign language and/or Braille, and to train professionals and staff who work at all levels of education. Such training shall incorporate disability awareness and the use of appropriate augmentative and alternative modes, means and formats of communication, educational techniques and materials to support persons with disabilities.

5. States Parties shall ensure that persons with disabilities are able to access general tertiary education, vocational training, adult education and lifelong learning without discrimination and on an equal basis with others. To this end, States Parties shall ensure that reasonable accommodation is provided to persons with disabilities.

Guidance

FRAMEWORK FOR THE ASSESSMENT OF CHILDREN IN NEED (assessment and care planning extracts)[1]

The process of assessing children in need

3.8 There is an expectation that **within one working day** of a referral being received or new information coming to or from within a social services department about an open case, there will be a decision about what response is required. A referral is defined as a request for services to be provided by the social services department. The response may include no action, but that is itself a decision and should be made promptly and recorded. The referrer should be informed of the decision and its rationale, as well as the parents or caregivers and the child, if appropriate.

3.9 A decision to gather more information constitutes an initial assessment. An initial assessment is defined as a brief assessment of each child referred to social services with a request for services to be provided. This should be undertaken **within a maximum of 7 working days** but could be very brief depending on the child's circumstances. It should address the dimensions of the Assessment Framework, determining whether the child is in need, the nature of any services required, from where and within what timescales, and whether a further, more detailed core assessment should be undertaken. An initial assessment is deemed to have commenced at the point of referral to the social services department or when new information on an open case indicates an initial assessment should be repeated. All staff responding to referrals and undertaking initial assessments should address the dimensions which constitute the Assessment Framework. There is more detailed discussion about the contribution of respective agencies in chapter 5.

3.10 Depending on the child's circumstances, an initial assessment may include some or all of the following:
- interviews with child and family members, as appropriate;
- involvement of other agencies in gathering and providing information, as appropriate;
- consultation with supervisor/manager;
- record of initial analysis;
- decisions on further action/no action;
- record of decisions/rationale with family/agencies;
- informing other agencies of the decisions;
- statement to the family of decisions made and, if a child is in need, the plan for providing support.

As part of any initial assessment, the child should be seen. This includes observation and talking with the child in an age appropriate manner. This is further discussed in paragraphs 3.41 to 3.43.

3.11 **A core assessment** is defined as an in-depth assessment which addresses the central or most important aspects of the needs of a child and the capacity of his or her parents or caregivers to respond appropriately to these needs within the wider family and community context. While this assessment is led by social services, it will invariably involve other agencies or independent professionals, who will either provide information they hold about the child or

---

1   © Crown Copyright 2000. Available from The Stationery Office or from the Department of Health: www.dh.gov.uk.

parents, contribute specialist knowledge or advice to social services or undertake specialist assessments. Specific assessments of the child and/or family members may have already been undertaken prior to referral to the social services department. The findings from these should inform this assessment. At the conclusion of this phase of assessment, there should be an analysis of the findings which will provide an understanding of the child's circumstances and inform planning, case objectives and the nature of service provision. The timescale for completion of the core assessment is a **maximum of 35 working days**. A core assessment is deemed to have commenced at the point the initial assessment ended, or a strategy discussion decided to initiate enquiries under s47, or new information obtained on an open case indicates a core assessment should be undertaken. Where specialist assessments have been commissioned by social services from other agencies or independent professionals, it is recognised that they will not necessarily be completed within the 35 working day period. Appropriate services should be provided whilst awaiting the completion of the specialist assessment.

3.12 The Department of Health has published an **Initial Assessment Record**, which has been developed for all staff to record salient information about a child's needs, the parents' capacity and the family's circumstances, to assist in determining the social services' response and whether a core assessment should be considered. This record is consistent with the **Core Assessment Record**. These have been developed to assist in assessing the child's developmental needs in an age appropriate manner for the following age bands: 0–2 years, 3–4 years, 5–9 years, 10–14 years and 15 and upwards. These age bands are the same as those used in **Looking After Children Assessment and Action Records** (Department of Health, 1995b). The initial and core assessment recording forms have been designed to assist in the analysis of a child and family's circumstances (Department of Health and Cleaver, 2000) and in the development and reviewing of a plan of action.

3.13 At the conclusion of either an initial or core assessment, the parent(s) and child, if appropriate, should be informed in writing, and/or in another more appropriate medium, of the decisions made and be offered the opportunity to record their views, disagreements and to ask for corrections to recorded information. Agencies and individuals involved in the assessment should also be informed of the decisions, with reasons for these made clear. This sharing of information is important to assist agencies' own practice in their work with the child and family. Local authorities are required by section 26 of the Children Act 1989 to establish complaints procedures, and children and parents should be provided with information about these. Parents who have a complaint about a particular agency's services should take it up with the agency concerned.

*****

Analysis, judgement and decision-making

4.1 The Guidance has emphasised that assessment is not an end in itself but a process which will lead to an improvement in the wellbeing or outcomes for a child or young person. The conclusion of an assessment should result in:

- an analysis of the needs of the child and the parenting capacity to respond appropriately to those needs within their family context;

- identification of whether and, if so, where intervention will be required to secure the wellbeing of the child or young person;
- a realistic plan of action (including services to be provided), detailing who has responsibility for action, a timetable and a process for review.

*****

Plans for Children in Need

4.32 The details of the plan are bench marks against which the progress of the family and the commitment of workers are measured, and therefore it is important that they should be realistic and not vague statements of good intent (Department of Health, 1995).

4.33 The analysis, judgement and decisions made will form the basis of a plan of work with a child in need and his or her family. The complexity or severity of the child's needs will determine the scope and detail of the plan. The different circumstances under which the assessment has been carried out will also determine the form in which it is recorded and the status of the plan:

- **Children in Need Plan** at the conclusion of a core assessment, which will involve the child and family members as appropriate and the contributions of all agencies. A format for the plan is contained in assessment records (Department of Health and Cleaver, 2000).
- **Child Protection Plan** as a decision of an inter-agency child protection conference, following enquiries and assessment under s47. The expectations of a child protection plan are outlined in paragraphs 5.81 to 5.84 of *Working Together to Safeguard Children* (1999).
- **Care Plan for a Child Looked After** as a result of an assessment that a child will need to be looked after by the local authority either in the short term or long term and placed in foster or residential care. The requirements for a care plan in these circumstances are laid out in Volume 3 of the Children Act 1989, Guidance and Regulations (paragraphs 2.59 to 2.62). A format for the care plan is an integral part of the Department of Health's Looking After Children materials (Department of Health, 1995).
- **Care Plans** for a child who is the subject of a care or supervision order or for whom the plan is adoption (see paragraphs 3.22 to 3.24).
- **Pathway Plan for a young person who is in care or leaving care** as outlined in the Government's intentions for young people living in and leaving care (Department of Health, 1999; Children (Leaving Care) Bill, 1999).

4.34 There are some general principles about plans for working with children and families, whatever the circumstances in which they have been drawn up. First that, wherever possible, they should be drawn up in agreement with the child/young person and key family members and their commitment to the plan should have been secured. There are two caveats which the professionals responsible for the plan need to bear in mind:

- objectives should be reasonable and timescales not too short or unachievable;
- plans should not be dependent on resources which are known to be scarce or unavailable.

Failure to address these issues can be damaging to families and jeopardise the overall aim of securing the child's wellbeing. Second, the plan must maintain a focus on the child, even though help may be provided to a number of family members as part of the plan. As Jones *et al* (1987) write 'It is never acceptable to sacrifice the interests of the child for the therapeutic benefit of the parents'.

SEN CODE OF PRACTICE 2001[2]

Writing the Statement

> Where an LEA, having made an assessment of a child, decide to make a statement, they shall serve a copy of a proposed statement and a written notice on the child's parent within two weeks of the date on which the assessment was completed.
>
> See Schedule 27, Education Act 1996 and the Education (Special Educational Needs) (England) (Consolidation) Regulations 2001

8:29 The notice must be in the form prescribed in Schedule 1 to the Regulations. The statement of special educational needs must follow the format and contain the information prescribed by the Regulations (see Schedule 2 to the Regulations):

Part 1 Introduction: The child's name and address and date of birth. The child's home language and religion. The names and address(es) of the child's parents.

Part 2 Special Educational Needs (learning difficulties): Details of each and every one of the child's special educational needs as identified by the LEA during statutory assessment and of the advice received and attached as appendices to the statement.

Part 3 Special Educational Provision: The special educational provision that the LEA consider necessary to meet the child's special educational needs.
a) The objectives that the special educational provision should aim to meet.
b) The special educational provision which the LEA consider appropriate to meet the needs set out in Part 2 and to meet the objectives.
c) The arrangements to be made for monitoring progress in meeting those objectives, particularly for setting short-term targets for the child's progress and for reviewing his or her progress on a regular basis.

Part 4 Placement: The type and name of school where the special educational provision set out in Part 3 is to be made or the LEA's arrangements for provision to be made otherwise than in school.

Part 5 Non-Educational Needs: All relevant non-educational needs of the child as agreed between the health services, social services or other agencies and the LEA.

Part 6 Non-Educational Provision: Details of relevant non-educational provision required to meet the non-educational needs of the child as agreed between the health services and/or social services and the LEA, including the agreed arrangements for its provision.

Signature and date

---

2   November 2001, Department for Education and Skills. Available from the Department of Education at www.education.gov.uk.

8:30 All the advice obtained and taken into consideration during the assessment process must be attached as appendices to the statement:
The advice appended to the statement **must** include:
A Parental evidence[3]
B Educational advice
C Medical advice
D Psychological advice
E Social services advice
F Any other advice, such as the views of the child, which the LEA or any other body from whom advice is sought consider desirable. In particular, where the child's parent is a serving member of the armed forces, advice from Service Children's Education (SCE).

8:31 LEAs should draft clear, unambiguous statements. Where diagnostic or technical terms are necessary or helpful, for example in referring to specific disabilities, their meaning should be explained in terms that parents and other non-professionals will readily understand. LEAs should take particular care to ensure that the text is placed in the correct part, so as to correspond with the form set out in Schedule 2 to the Education (Special Educational Needs) (England) Regulations 2001. Further detailed advice is provided in the SEN Toolkit.

Part 2: Special educational needs (learning difficulties)

8:32 Part 2 of the statement should describe **all** the child's learning difficulties identified during the statutory assessment. It should also include a description of the child's current functioning – what the child can and cannot do. The description in Part 2 should draw on and may refer to the professional advice attached in the appendices. Where the LEA adopt that advice in their description of the child's learning difficulties, they should say that they have done so. But merely stating that they are adopting the advice in the appendices is not sufficient. The advice received may contain conflicting opinions or opinions open to interpretation, which the LEA must resolve, giving reasons for the conclusions they have reached. All advice must be considered and appended to the statement. Part 2 should be set out in a fashion which can relate directly to the description of provision set out in Part 3 (b).

Part 3: Special educational provision

8:33 Once a child's special educational needs have been assessed and set out in full in part 2, the LEA must specify, in Part 3, the special educational provision to meet those needs. The key objective in specifying provision is to help the child to learn and develop.

8:34 Part 3 of the statement is divided into three sub-sections:
a) **the first sub-section** should set out the main objectives which the provision aims to meet. These objectives should directly relate to the needs set out in Part 2 and should be described in terms that will allow the LEA and the school to monitor and review the child's progress over time. They

---

3 Parental evidence will include parental representations presented to the LEA when considering the need for an assessment, and parental views and evidence submitted as part of the assessment and, when the statement is finalised, any parental representations made in response to the proposed statement.

should generally be of a longer-term nature than the more specific, short-term targets in the child's Individual Education Plan.

b) **the second sub-section** should specify all of the special educational provision the LEA consider appropriate for **all** the learning difficulties in Part 2, even where some of the provision will be made by direct intervention on the part of the authority, some will be made by the child's school from within its own resources, and some may be made by the health authority. It is the LEA that is responsible for arranging the provision in the statement, irrespective of who actually delivers it, unless the LEA is satisfied that the child's parents have themselves made suitable arrangements.

8:35 The Education (Special Educational Needs) (England) (Consolidation) Regulations 2001 say that a statement **must** specify:

(a) any appropriate facilities and equipment, staffing arrangements and curriculum

(b) any appropriate modifications to the application of the National Curriculum

(c) any appropriate exclusions from the application of the National Curriculum, in detail, and the provision which it is proposed to substitute for any such exclusions in order to maintain a balanced and broadly based curriculum; and

(d) where residential accommodation is appropriate, that fact.

8:36 A statement should specify clearly the provision necessary to meet the needs of the child. It should detail appropriate provision to meet each identified need. It will be helpful to the child's parents and teachers if the provision in this sub-section is set out in the same order as the description of needs in Part 2.

8:37 LEAs must make decisions about which actions and provision are appropriate for which pupils on an individual basis. This can only be done by a careful assessment of the pupils' difficulties and consideration of the educational setting in which they may be educated. Provision should normally be quantified (e.g. in terms of hours of provision, staffing arrangements) although there will be cases where some flexibility should be retained in order to meet the changing special educational needs of the child concerned. It will always be necessary for LEAs to monitor, with the school or other setting, the child's progress towards identified outcomes, however provision is described. LEAs must not, in any circumstances, have blanket policies not to quantify provision.

Index

Council for disabled children

CDC's vision is a society in which disabled children's life chances are assured, their needs are met, their aspirations supported and their rights respected.

The Council for Disabled Children (CDC) is the umbrella body for the disabled children's sector in England, with links to the other UK nations. We support a number of networks to bring together organisations and individuals with a focus on specific aspects of the disabled children's sector. Through our networks we reach over 4000 individuals working with or for disabled children, children with special educational needs (SEN) and their families.

We simply want disabled children and children with SEN to have full and happy childhoods; fulfil their potential; and be active within their community. And we want parents of disabled children to be parents first – living ordinary lives.

We are the only national network that brings together a diverse range of organisations from across the disabled children's sector to support the development and implementation of policy and practice. Our work impacts on over 770,000 disabled children and their families.

CDC is fully committed to the empowerment of disabled children and young people and their families. For this reason we are delighted to support *Disabled children: a legal handbook*. However, it should be noted that the views of the authors do not necessarily reflect those of CDC.